NOVA ALB

NOVA

BRITTON & REY'S
MAP
OF THE
State of California

Compiled from the U.S. Land & Coast Surveys, the
several Military, Scientific & Rail Road Explorations,
the State & County Boundary Surveys made under
the Order of the Surveyor General of California &
from Private Surveys.

BY GEORGE H. GODDARD, C.E.

Completed with Additions & Corrections up to the day of
publication from the U.S. Land Office & other reliable sources

SCALE OF STATUTE MILES.

LITH. J. BRITTON & REY, MONTGOMERY ST. COR. COMMERCIAL, S.F.

REFERENCES.
CAPITALS.
Small Towns & Ranchos.
Bars & other Mining Places
Stage & Wagon Roads
Emigrant & Mountain Trails
Canals & Main Ditches

Figures indicating Elevations from the level of the sea.

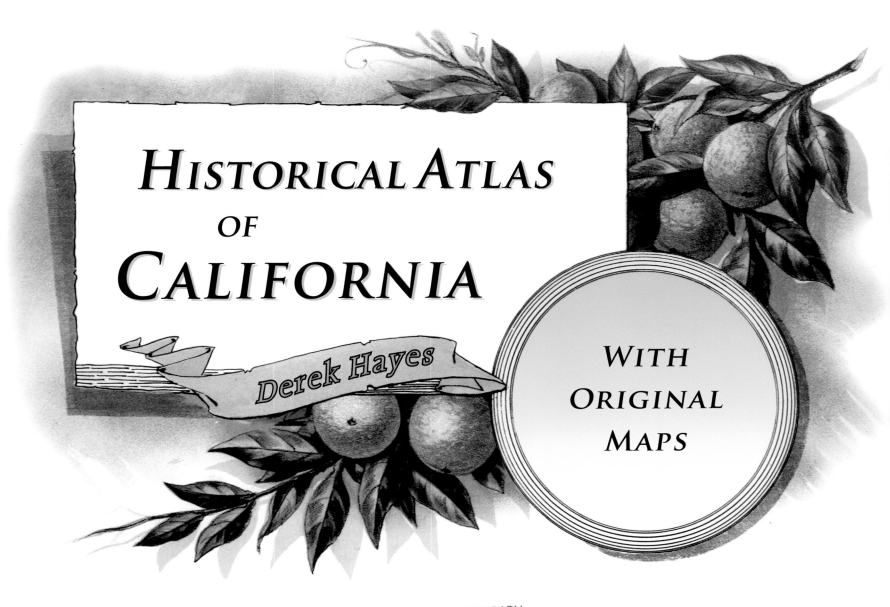

# HISTORICAL ATLAS
## OF
# CALIFORNIA

*Derek Hayes*

WITH
ORIGINAL
MAPS

中

UNIVERSITY OF CALIFORNIA PRESS

BERKELEY · LOS ANGELES · LONDON

University of California Press, one of the most distinguished university presses in the United States, enriches lives around the world by advancing scholarship in the humanities, social sciences, and natural sciences. Its activities are supported by the UC Press Foundation and by philanthropic contributions from individuals and institutions. For more information, visit www.ucpress.edu.

University of California Press
Berkeley and Los Angeles, California

University of California Press, Ltd.
London, England

Originated by Douglas & McIntyre Ltd.,
2323 Quebec Street, Suite 201, Vancouver, B.C., Canada V5T 4S7



Cataloging-in-Publication Data for this title is on file
with the Library of Congress.

ISBN 978-0-520-25258-5 (cloth : alk. paper)

Manufactured in China by C&C Offset Printing Co., Ltd.

15 14 13 12 11 10 09 08 07
10 9 8 7 6 5 4 3 2 1

Printed on acid-free paper

Design and layout: Derek Hayes
Editing and copyediting: Iva Cheung
Jacket design: Nicole Hayward

To contact the author:
www.derekhayes.ca / derek@derekhayes.ca

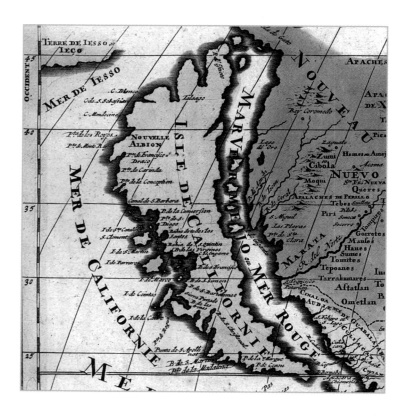

## Acknowledgments

A book of this nature could not have been written without the assistance of many people. Special thanks are due to Bill Warren, who helped in several different roles. Thanks are also due to Steven Davenport, San Francisco Maritime National Historic Park Library; Chris Cummings; Susan Snyder and Erica Nordmeier, Bancroft Library; Mike Farruggia, Farruggia Design; Julie Tashima, San Francisco Airport Museum and Archives; Peter Hiller and the estate of Jo Mora; Kathryn Santos and Ellen Halteman, California State Railroad Museum; David Wendell, Oregon State Archives; David Burkhart, author of *Earthquake Days*; Julie Sweetkind-Singer and Mattie Taorima, Stanford University Library; Joseph Bray, La Jolla; Bart Nadeau, Bay Area Electric Railway Association/Western Railway Museum Archives; Paul Trimble, author of *Sacramento Northern Railway*; Lynn Eichinger and John Soennichsen, Angel Island Association; Susan Ginoza Fukushima, Hirasaki National Resource Center, Japanese American National Museum; William Frank, Alan H. Jutzi, Mario Einaldi, and Bill Warren, Huntington Library; Glen Creason, Los Angeles Public Library; Colin Wood; Torbjörn Altren, National Library of Sweden; David Cobb, Harvard University Map Library; Dorothy Sloan; Scott Brown, Editor, *Fine Books & Collections*; Carl J. Barneyback; Patricia Gaspari-Bridges, Berta Harvey, John Delaney, Stephen Ferguson and AnnaLee Pauls, Princeton University Library; Steve Boulay; Ranger Kelly Elliott, Citrus State Historical Park, Riverside; Kelly Haigh, Young Research Library, UCLA; Douglas C. Sackman, University of Puget Sound and author of *Orange Empire*; Dean R. Ayer, Riverside Metropolitan Museum; Diane Siegel, Pasadena Museum of History; Floyd McDonald; Tracie Cobb, National Park Service, Cabrillo National Monument, San Diego; Claire Smith, Sunkist; Jeffrey Stanton, Venice; David Watson, Jane Kenealey, and Muriel Strickland, San Diego Historical Society; James Stack, University of Washington Library; and members of the California Map Society, including Bill Warren, Will Tefft, Warren Heckrotte, Patrick Pagni, Douglas Burrill, Glen McLaughlin, Phil Simon, and Tom Worth. Thanks also to Richard Walker, University of California, Berkeley, who read the final draft; Iva Cheung, my editor and copyeditor at Douglas & McIntyre; Randy Heyman, editor at University of California Press; and Scott McIntyre, publisher at Douglas & McIntyre.

MAP 1 (*half-title page*).
Acclaimed California artist Joseph Jacinto "Jo" Mora (1876–1947) produced a series of pictorial maps of the state, each meticulously illustrated with scenes from history far too numerous to list. The first was published in 1927 (see MAP 474, *page 249*), and this is a version created in 1945.

MAP 2 (*title page, left*).
George Henry Goddard's map of California was, at the time of its publication in 1857, easily the most accurate and complete map of the state. It was also beautifully executed, perhaps not surprising considering that Goddard was a man of many talents, not least of all as an artist. He was from England and came to California in 1850 at the age of thirty-three to seek his fortune—not working the goldfields but assisting those who did; he was a civil engineer and an architect, as well as a mapmaker. This version of his map is a wall map and was published by Britton and Rey, who were responsible for many of the early American maps of California.

The main title page design is modified from an 1887 map cartouche. The map is of the Placer County Citrus Colony, and the whole map is reproduced as MAP 266, *page 142*.

MAP 3 (*left*).
In the seventeenth and early eighteenth centuries California was often depicted as an island (see page 28). This is one version of the island myth, published by French mapmaker Alexis Hubert Jaillot in 1694.

The mission bells silhouetted on the contents page (*right*) are those of Mission San Gabriel in Los Angeles.

# Contents

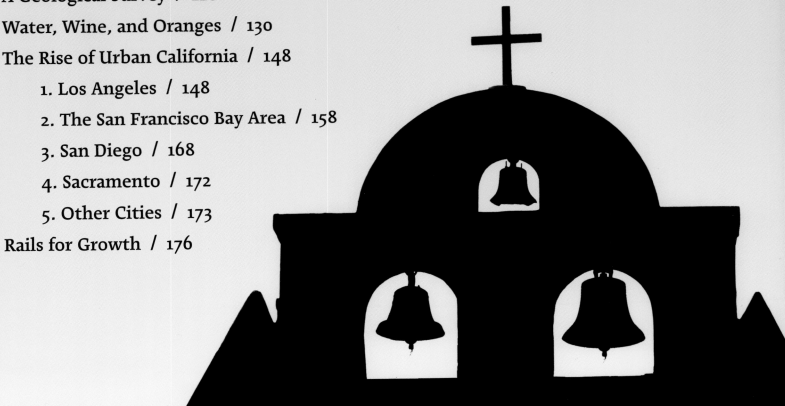

# A Visual California

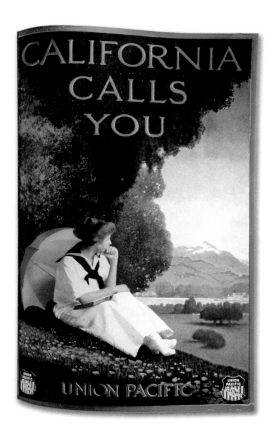

Many books have been written detailing and illustrating the history of California. Yet none have offered the unique geographical perspective that can be given to that history by contemporary maps. This book is an attempt to redress that imbalance.

Original maps drawn or published at a period in history can show what a promoter wanted his sponsors to believe, or what was known, or how the world, the continent, or the coast was perceived at that moment. They show explorations and discoveries, the finding of paths for the westward course of empire, the marketing of the state to everyone from eastern potential settlers to those who might stay elsewhere but eat California's agricultural bounty. California as some idyllic Eden is a recurring theme, used to sell oranges as well as land.

Here is California as the backside of America, as New Albion, or Quivira; here is English, Spanish, Mexican, Russian, and republican California before it was American. Here is the discovery of San Francisco Bay, the finding of gold, the hacking of a railbed across the wall of the Sierra Nevada, all with the maps drawn by soldiers, engineers, goldseekers, and railroad promoters. And when California became American, the battles, the division of the spoils, and the found-

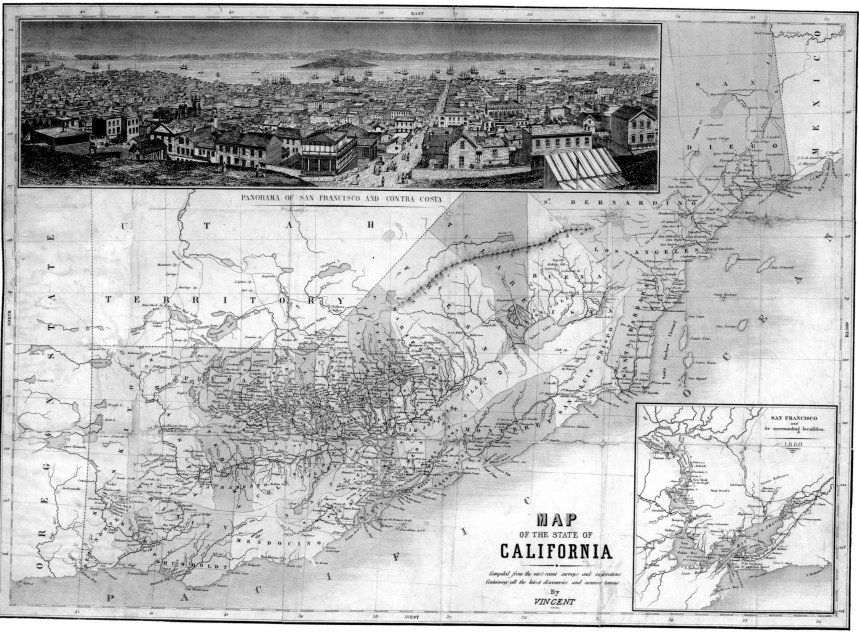

ing of cities are documented with maps. Legislators had to decide where to draw boundaries, even of their soon-to-be state of the Union itself, and where to establish a capital, and—eventually—bring law and order to a frontier society; each of these tasks required maps.

Geological maps were made to define the land's resources, navigational maps to guide the onslaught of shipping safely to harbor. Maps were made for railroads, for irrigation, to set aside parks to preserve the astonishing beauty of the land, to supply water to growing cities with aqueducts stretching into the Sierra, and to build and to inform about streetcar and interurban lines, roads, and in more modern times, freeways.

Maps defined the causes and course of the great fire that ravaged San Francisco in 1906, and then helped engineers and planners rebuild the city in ways that would, they hoped, avoid similar devastation in future. Then there are maps of the oil fields and power schemes, the building of bridges, the location of airports and the coming of air travel, and the defense of the West Coast in a world war, including maps documenting the deportation of thousands of Japanese Americans against their will and despite their protestations of loyalty.

As might be expected when a wide-ranging history is crammed into so few pages, the selection of maps illustrated is far from exhaustive. Nonetheless, an effort has been made to ensure that maps critical to California's history have been included, yet not to the exclusion of whimsical, pictorial, cartoon, or other amusing, interesting, informative, or artistic maps; MAP 5 (*right*) is a good example of the latter genre.

The map captions are an integral part of the accompanying text, which, although hopefully useful, are secondary to the maps themselves, for this atlas is essentially a visual history of California. Space being at a premium, explanations are concise so as to leave room for more maps. This book should be viewed as complementary to other California history texts, which may be consulted if more details are desired; an extensive bibliography of books consulted and recommended is included.

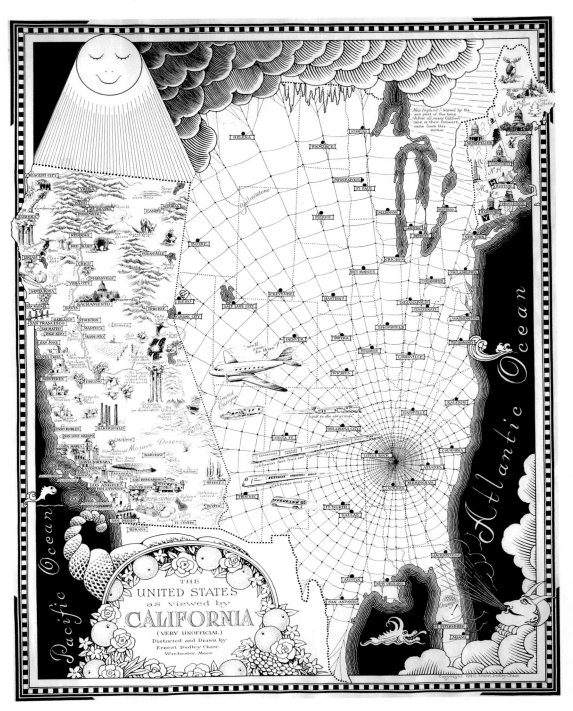

*Far left, top.*
*California Calls You*, a Union Pacific Railroad advertising brochure, published about 1910. The brochure encouraged both tourists and settlers to come to California—by Union Pacific, of course.

MAP 4 (*left*).
Quite different from many of the early maps of the state of California is this 1860 map with east at the top—generally, but only by convention, north is at the "top" (for a different view see MAP 473, *page 239*, which illustrates a modern so-called upside-down map of the state). The map is made all the more interesting by the inclusion of a panoramic view of San Francisco, which was the preeminent city in California—"a fit portal of an empire great and free"—until the rise of Los Angeles in the early decades of the twentieth century. At bottom right is an inset map of San Francisco Bay in more detail, including the all-important—and highly confusing—entrances to the Sacramento and San Joaquin rivers. The map was also different from most in that it was published in Paris, France; the discovery of gold a decade before had piqued a worldwide interest in California.

MAP 5 (*above*).
This delightful and amusing map shows *The United States as viewed by California (very unofficial), Distorted and Drawn by Ernest Dudley Chase*, a graphic artist from Massachusetts. It was created in 1940. Not surprisingly, California looms large on the map of America. Chase was an executive in the greeting card industry and drew maps like this as a hobby, one that grew into a small business, and he published a number of similar whimsical maps.

# THE FIRST CALIFORNIANS

The cornucopia that is California existed before the advent of the European and gave rise to a dense population of native peoples. The diversity of geography in turn led to the existence of many diverse groups, tribes, and languages. The entire West Coast, in fact, had the greatest cultural variation of anywhere in North America. MAP 6, *opposite,* shows the contrast in linguistic variation on the West Coast compared with the much larger area of homogeneity inland, where the living was harder. About sixty different languages were spoken in California, derived from over twenty language families, an interesting comparison with Mexico, where only two major languages were spoken.

Agriculture was not well developed in California, the natural bounty of the land being sufficient to support a substantial population as hunters and gatherers. Flour derived from acorns of the once numerous wild oaks allowed one of the benefits of agricultural practice without the requirement to sow or tend the crop.

The lack of development of agriculture-based civilizations similar in nature to those developed farther south by the Maya and the Mexica (Aztec)—and the consequent lack of interest in gold—is likely the main reason the Indians to the north little interested the Spanish interlopers for several centuries after the latter had annihilated the cultures of Mexico, Guatemala, and Peru. The Spanish were interested in cities of gold but did not want the work of finding it in the raw, and there were no such golden cities north of New Spain.

Ultimately, when in the eighteenth century Spain did decide to colonize Alta California, the seed of the wild oat was inadvertently carried north, creating the fuel for frequent wildfires that threatened the wild oaks and wiped out a food source.

It is still a matter of some speculation how long ago humans reached California. Certainly habitation existed 10,000 years ago, but it may be much older than that. Recently human footprints thought to be 40,000 years old were discovered at Puebla, near Mexico City. From a heartland in eastern Asia, humans migrated across what is now the Bering Strait and southward toward more livable climes. Long thought to have only taken place when the state of the continental ice sheet allowed both bridges across the sea and corridors through the land, coastal migration in small boats in a great North Pacific arc is now thought likely to have occurred, a movement independent of the contraction or expansion of the ice.

Estimates of the native population of California before the arrival of Europeans vary but is generally accepted to be in the range of 300,000 to 310,000 persons. The EuroAmerican onslaught reduced this number to a low point of only about 20,000 in 1900, the result of centuries of neglect, disease, and outright genocide. More than 100,000 native people died in 1833 from a malaria epidemic, and cholera, typhoid, and especially smallpox all took their toll. Although the new State of California passed a law in April 1850 for the protection of Indians, there continued to be many examples of EuroAmericans taking up arms to settle some perceived wrong and massacring Indians wholesale, acts that largely went unpunished. Nearly two hundred Indians were killed by so-called State Volunteers in Humboldt County in 1860. Two years later almost a hundred Inyo County Yuma and Mojave were drowned in an alkali lake as retaliation for raids on ranches and wagon trains.

Eighteen treaties with the federal government were negotiated in 1851 to set aside land for the Indians, but the treaties were never ratified by Congress (although they were incorporated in modified form into the 1928 California Indian Jurisdictional Act), and encroachment onto Indian territories became common. There was sporadic resistance by some groups fed up with their treatment. The Mariposa War erupted after the opening of the California Trail saw settlers and miners pouring into California, overwhelming the native populations; the last Indian War in the state, the Modoc War, ended in 1873 after the Modocs of Northern California were finally ousted from their stronghold in the Lava Beds.

Between 1848 and 1866 it was legal in some circumstances to kill Indians in California. Not until 1917 did the California Supreme

*Left.* A Miwok head-man, photographed in 1924 by the famous photographer of the Native West, Edward S. Curtis.

MAP 6 (*right, top*).

This map shows the distribution of native linguistic stocks. It was prepared in 1890 under the direction of famous explorer of the Colorado—and later director of the U.S. Bureau of Ethnology—John Wesley Powell. It illustrates the much denser variation in ethnic groups found on the West Coast, the result of a long period of easier living as compared with those tribes of the interior, which had far fewer resources to maintain life.

MAP 7 (*below*).

The original distribution of California's native peoples is shown in this modern map, from the California State Indian Museum.

MAP 8 (*right, bottom*).

The likelihood of random Asian migration to the west coast of North America was demonstrated by research done in the nineteenth century by Charles Brooks, who in 1876 published a map, of which this is part, showing the locations of documented shipwrecks of Japanese fishing boats (shown as small crosses), together with ocean currents (the lines of arrows). The cross at Cape Flattery, at the entrance to the Strait of Juan de Fuca, depicts the 1831 shipwreck of three Japanese fishermen who were rescued by traders from the Hudson's Bay Company and returned to Japan via London. Their fate on return was uncertain, for the Japanese government at that time did not want anyone "contaminated" with foreign ideas to return to the country, even mandating that fishing boats have a large rudder that would be certain to snap off in a storm. It seems possible, given the evidence presently available, that Oregon's "Kennewick Man" found his way to North America in this way.

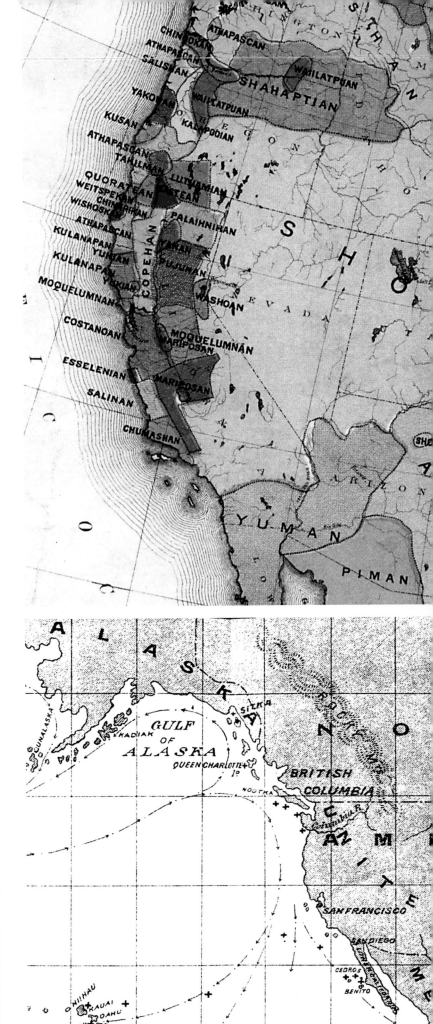

Court rule that Indians were even citizens; and not until 1924 did the U.S. Supreme Court rule that they were citizens of the United States.

It is possible, even likely, that the first non-native people to arrive in California were Chinese or perhaps Japanese, though if this is so, they made no lasting impression and left no record of their arrival, let alone maps. MAP 8 was published in 1876 and shows the distribution of shipwrecks of Asian peoples on the west coast of North America. Since the types of vessels used had not varied for centuries it seems likely that such a pattern would have persisted over a long period.

Ancestral Homelands of the Indigenous People

# NOTIONS OF A WESTERN SHORE

California is the West Coast. Yet there could be no west coast without a Pacific Ocean. Europeans first saw this ocean in 1513 and first sailed upon it 1520, yet long before this Martin Waldseemüller and Matthias Ringmann, academics and philosophers in Lorraine, imagined such an ocean and a separate American continent after hearing the ideas of Amerigo Vespucci. Vespucci had sailed to South America several times, although his later voyages are themselves in some doubt. Thus the construction of America, the Pacific Ocean, and the West Coast by Waldseemüller seems at best an inspiration that proved to be correct (MAPS 11 and 12, *opposite*).

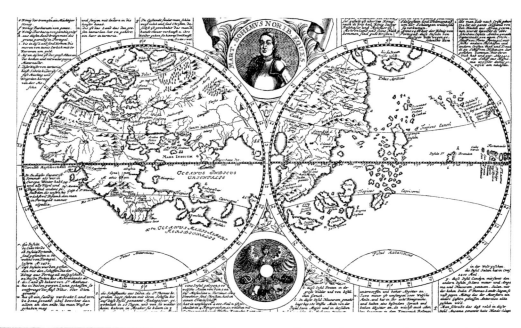

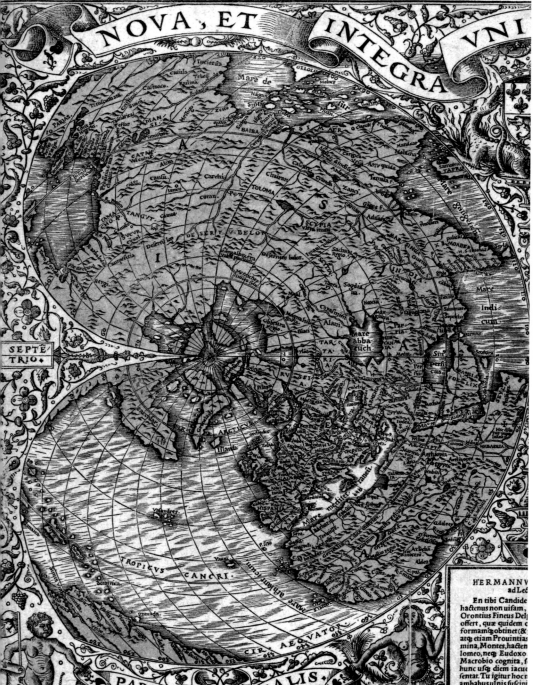

Following the westward voyages of Christopher Columbus and John Cabot at the end of the fifteenth century, the land encountered was considered to be simply an eastward extension of Asia. Several of the maps embodying this concept included islands in the ocean east of China, and the nebulous and uncertain location of these islands meant that when the Pacific Ocean was finally found, it was believed that these islands might then be close at hand, as the vast distances across the Pacific were not then appreciated (MAP 10, *left*).

MAP 9 (*above*).
Neither America nor California appear in this rendering of the world, a copy of a globe constructed in 1492 by German globe maker Martin Behaim as Christopher Columbus was en route to his discoveries. As such, it is the final depiction of the Old World. In the western sea, however, are many islands, including the largest, Cipangu (Japan). Cipangu and many of the islands were based on the accounts of Marco Polo, but additional other scattered smaller islands were the addition of a mapmaker's fancy.

MAP 10 (*left*).
French mapmaker Oronce Finé incorporated what he knew of the new continent into his 1531 map. North America is depicted as part of a continuous continent of Amero-Asia. The map is executed in a cordiform projection, which has the effect of splitting the east coast of North America off from the rest of the continent, but just above the divide on the left side Florida and the Gulf of Mexico are apparent. Farther up is a west coast complete with many offshore islands; these were the source of the myth of California as an island (see page 30).

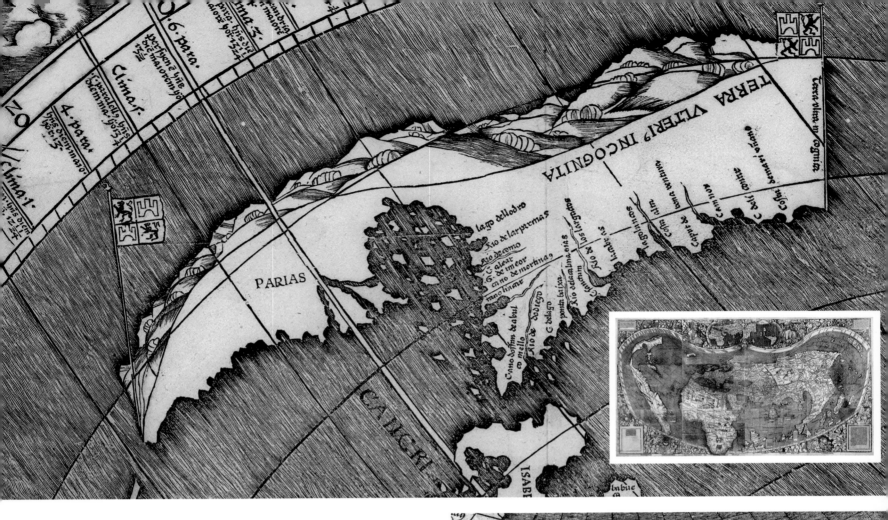

MAP 11 (*above and inset*) and MAP 12 (*right*).
Martin Waldseemüller and Matthias Ringmann's seminal world map of 1507 is shown in these three images. MAP 11 *inset* is the entire map, whereas MAP 11 is a detail of the main map, and MAP 12 a detail of the smaller map at top. Often referred to as "America's birth certificate," Waldseemüller's map was the first document of any kind to use the name America, after Amerigo Vespucci, albeit shown on the southern part of South America. The map was the first to embody Vespucci's idea that the Americas were continents separate from Asia. Many maps of the period showed America as an eastward extension of that continent, including that of Oronce Finé (MAP 10, *left*), drawn much later.

The west coast of North America is *Terra Vlteri' Incognita*, unknown land. At the flag on the main map is shown a passage through what is correctly the Isthmus of Panama, a hoped-for easy way around the continent that had got in the way of a westward passage to the Spice Islands and Cathay. Yet Waldseemüller hedges his bets on the inset map by showing North and South America joined at an isthmus.

Much has been made of the depiction of a west coast on this map, some six years before Vasco Núñez de Balboa crossed the isthmus and found a new ocean on the other side, and thirteen years before any European ship sailed upon it (Ferdinand Magellan in 1520) but there is no evidence whatever that Waldseemüller or Ringmann made anything but an educated guess at the new world topography, inspired as it turned out to be.

In the middle of the Pacific Ocean is *zipangri insula*, Cipangu, the island of Japan, and surrounding it are many smaller islands. Derived from the stories of Marco Polo, the existence of islands would later support the notion that California might itself be a collection of islands. By the late 1520s, as the Spanish established themselves at several ports on the Pacific coast, their interest turned northward, with the emerging idea that perhaps the East could be reached by following the coast around in a sweeping arc, or that it was not too far offshore to find outlying islands. The conquest of the gold-rich Inca empire to the south in 1532 for a while fueled the notion that similar civilizations might exist to the north, in California.

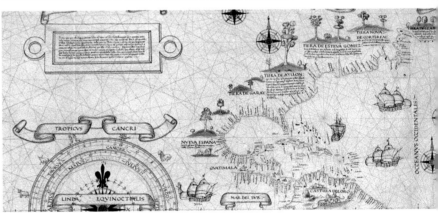

MAP 13 (*above*).
There was no west coast of North America on this world map by Spanish chief cartographer Diogo Ribiero in 1529. The map is thought to have been copied from the *Padrón general*, the official Spanish government map kept rigorously up-to-date with the latest discoveries. The west coast of Central America is shown, but it reaches no farther north than Guatemala.

# OF GOLD AND GALLEONS

In the aftermath of the conquest of Mexico the search for gold continued both to the south and to the north. Various factions pursued land and wealth, but none more than the still vastly ambitious original conqueror of the Mexica empire, Hernán Cortés.

But Cortés had a problem. The Spanish king was unwilling to see the rise of a powerful and challenging aristocracy in the New World such as he had had to deal with at home. He thus had granted the newfound lands sparingly and not all to one person. Cortés had to face the reality that the northern mainland of New Spain, called New Galicia, had been granted to his rival, the ruthless Nuño de Guzmán. Cortés therefore resolved to leapfrog over the claims of Guzmán and explore much farther to the north. If he could find the gold on the islands reputed to lie close offshore, so much the better, as his claim would then be non-contiguous with that of Guzmán and easier to protect from his rival's encroachment. Returning to Spain in 1529, Cortés secured a contract from the king giving him rights to discoveries he might make in the Pacific and islands to the west, but specifically excluding lands already granted to Guzmán. Cortés was granted "the concession of the twelfth part of all that [he] might discover in the said South Sea in perpetuity

for [his] heirs and successors." He was granted command and jurisdiction "in the first instance," though not in perpetuity, as he would have liked. Nevertheless the incentive must have been good enough, for Cortés now turned his attentions northward.

In 1532 Cortés sent one of his captains, Diego Hurtado de Mendoza, north. Hurtado reached the Rio Fuerte, which is about a third of the way up the Gulf of California's six-hundred-mile length. But Hurtado was dogged by both mutiny of his own men and attack by Indians, and only three of his men made it back to report to Cortés.

At this point information reached Mexico about the wealth of gold Francisco Pizarro found following his conquest of Peru. It

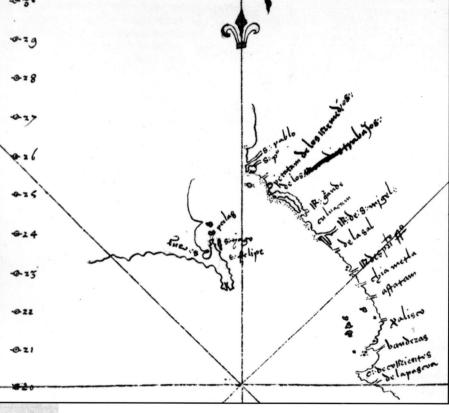

MAP 14 (*above*).
The first known map to show California—Baja California—is this sketch by Hernán Cortés. It was an attachment to an Act of Possession carried out on 3 May 1535 at La Paz, shown inside the bay on the eastern side of the peninsula. The offshore islands at the entrance to the Bahia de la Paz are shown; they are the present-day Isla Espiritu Santo and Isla la Partida.

MAP 15 (*left*).
Cortés's routes to and from the Bahia de la Paz, which Cortés named Santa Cruz, are shown on this map from a 1770 history of New Spain. The routes end within the bay more or less at the location of the modern city of La Paz, but Cortés's colony was actually at Bahia Pichilingue, about eight miles north on the eastern side of the bay. The name California is prominent but was likely added by the eighteenth-century engraver.

set off a gold rush first to Peru itself and then to the north, where a similar empire of gold was assumed to exist. In October 1533 Cortés dispatched two more ships. One discovered the offshore Isla Socorro, a prick in the ocean fabric three hundred miles south of the tip of Baja. Diego Becerra, commander of the second ship, was killed in a mutiny led by one of his pilots, Ortuno Jiménez (or Ximénes), who sailed the ship into the Bahía de la Paz, on the eastern side of Baja, landing at the small Bahía Pichilingue, just north of the modern city of La Paz. However tentatively, California had been found.

Misfortune seems to have dogged the early voyages; Jiménez and most of the men were killed by Indians, and the survivors who made it back to the mainland coast were captured by Cortés's rival Guzmán. One of the survivors did find his way back to Cortés with tales—also told to Guzmán—of pearls and gold. Cortés lost no time mounting another expedition in the hopes of forestalling Guzmán, but this time there would be no mistakes. He would lead it himself.

Such was Cortés's reputation that men flocked to his cause, and he soon had a fleet of three ships, more than 300 men including blacksmiths and carpenters, infantry, and cavalry with 130 horses. On 1 May 1535 Cortés sailed into Pichilingue with his first contingent of settlers. He carried out an Act of Possession for Spain two days later and named the country Santa Cruz. A week later he performed another ceremony establishing himself as governor under the terms of his 1529 contract. Cortés's reputation, however, could not save even this expedition from ultimate failure, for his three ships, sailing back for supplies, were hit by a storm, dispersed, and driven onto the shore. Cortés did, however, eventually get back to his settlers at Pichilingue and left a colony of thirty men headed by Francisco de Ulloa, with supplies for a year.

But other events intervened. Pizarro needed help to combat an Indian uprising in Peru, and Cortés diverted ships, men, and supplies to him. A new viceroy, Antonio de Mendoza, ordered the Baja colony removed, as the resources were not available to support it and the colony could not be self-sufficient agriculturally. Ulloa and his men explored the immediate vicinity of La Paz but found little of interest on the barren and hostile shore.

The search for gold then turned farther to the north. In 1536 the intrepid explorer Alvar Núñez Cabeza de Vaca arrived in Mexico City, one of three survivors from an expedition to Florida in 1528 that had been attacked by Indians on their arrival. Cabeza de Vaca had over the space of eight years floated on a raft to Galveston Island, Texas, and then, in an epic odyssey that included being enslaved by Indians, slowly made his way by land right across the Southwest, finally encountering Spanish traders in Sonora. In 1539 Mendoza sent Cabeza de Vaca's slave Estebán north with a Franciscan missionary, Marcos de Niza, to investigate Cabeza de Vaca's reports of cities, which in Mendoza's mind meant concentrations of riches. True to form, the pair brought back the news they knew was wanted, and the myth of the Seven Cities of Cibola was born (Map 18, *overleaf*, and Map 22, *page 16*).

The viceroy's reaction was to organize a large expedition to find and bring back the gold. Headed by Francisco Vázquez de Coronado, this expedition got under way early in 1540, not before Mendoza had issued an edict forbidding others to organize rival expeditions. However, the able Cortés had foreseen what was to happen and had launched his own venture six months earlier, well over a month before Mendoza issued his proclamation.

Cortés sent three ships north from Acapulco in July 1539 under his capable commander Francisco de Ulloa. Ulloa sailed up the Gulf of California to its end, visiting Pichilingue but otherwise hugging the mainland shore, looking for an approach to the cities of Cibola. As he neared the mouth of the Colorado River, the water

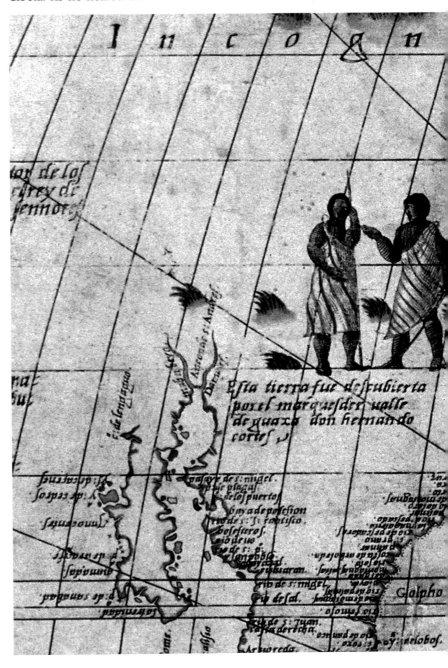

MAP 16.
This is part of the world map produced by the navigator Sebastian Cabot in 1544 and shows the knowledge gained from the voyage of Ulloa. Here most of the Baja peninsula is defined, as is the Gulf of California. The map showed that Ulloa considered that California was a peninsula rather than an island. Rivers representing the Colorado flow into the gulf at its northern end, although Ulloa did not sail up that river, so the European discovery of the Colorado is usually attributed to Hernando de Alarcón.

turned red from the sediment, and his report of this caused some mapmakers to depict the entire gulf in this color (MAP 17, *right*). In some maps the gulf is shown as the Vermilion Sea, or some variation of this name. On others it is the Sea of Cortés. Ulloa named the top of the gulf (only) Mar Bermejo.

No doubt disappointed at not having found any indications of golden cities, Ulloa traced the eastern coast of Baja south, describing it in disparaging terms: "high and bare, of wretched aspect without any verdure." Following his instructions from Cortés, when Ulloa reached the southern tip of the peninsula at Cabo San Lucas he turned north once more, this time along the outer Pacific coast. Here he encountered both calms and storms, finding out firsthand right away how difficult it would be to sail northward near to the coast. When he tried to land to find water his men were attacked by Indians. By the end of the year he had reached Isla Cedros about halfway up the peninsula. The Indians were aggressive, and his men again had difficulty landing to obtain water.

From this point on the going became really difficult, and attempts to continue north in February and March 1540 got essentially nowhere. In April, however, one of the ships did manage to sail north, perhaps as much as another two hundred miles. It is not known for sure because this part of Ulloa's narrative has been lost. On maps the coast is shown about another hundred miles north of Isla Cedros, but Ulloa's Cabo del Engano, Cape of Disappointment, is not clearly locatable. The maps (MAP 16 and MAP 17) suggest that Ulloa reached Punta Santo Tomas, about twenty miles south of the modern Mexican city of Ensenada and eighty miles south of today's international boundary.

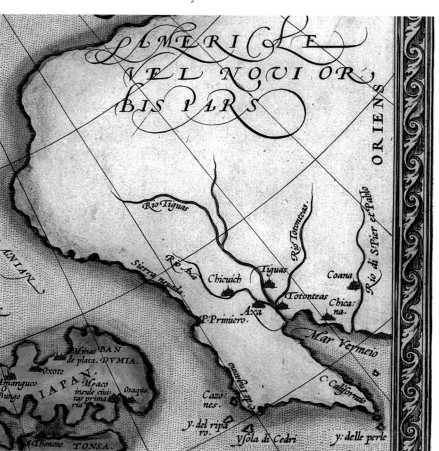

MAP 17 (*above*).
One of the first depictions of the Gulf of California was on this manuscript portolan map by the Genoese mapmaker Battista Agnese. The gulf is unnamed but colored red. The Pacific coast of the Baja peninsula is shown as far as Ulloa's Cabo del Engano (Cape of Disappointment), probably at about 30°N, where the coastline ends on this map and on MAP 16 on the previous page.

MAP 18 (*left*).
The Seven Cities of Cibola are shown on this map by Abraham Ortelius, published in 1570. The *Sierra nevada* named by Juan Rodríguez Cabrillo (see page 17) are shown on the coast.

MAP 19 (*right, top*).
This map was published in a 1770 history of New Spain and is a copy of a map said to have been made in 1541 by Domingo del Castillo, who was Alarcón's pilot and who may have also been with Ulloa. Here Alarcón's *Rio de buena Guia*, the Colorado, is clearly shown as it empties into the gulf. Much has been made of the fact that this map also carries the name *California* (on the lower part of the Baja peninsula) but this is likely simply an addition by the engraver in 1770. The reference in the caption to the *Marques de el Valle* is to Cortés, who was given the title Marquis of the Valley of the Oaxaca in recognition of his achievements conquering Mexico.

MAP 20 (*right, bottom*).
The prevalent concept of Pacific geography at this time is shown in this 1544 map. A very narrow North America has a Northwest Passage on its northern flank, and the coast is more or less continuous in a large sweeping arc to Cathay around a quite narrow Pacific Ocean.

MAP 21 (*far right, bottom*).
Another similar geographical concept of the Pacific, about 1565. The Seven Cities of Cibola are shown, and the large river discovered by Alarcón sweeps round to Asia, to which North America is connected. The Baja California peninsula is very prominent in this view.

Ulloa's two ships returned to Mexico in 1540 without having discovered any gold. Coronado had just left under Mendoza's orders to find the Seven Cities, and Hernando de Alarcón was dispatched on a support mission up the gulf. In August 1540 Alarcón reached the mouth of the Colorado, "a mighty river," he wrote, "with such a furious current that we could scarcely sail against it." With twenty men in two boats he ascended the river as far as the confluence of the Gila near Yuma and in the process became the first European to

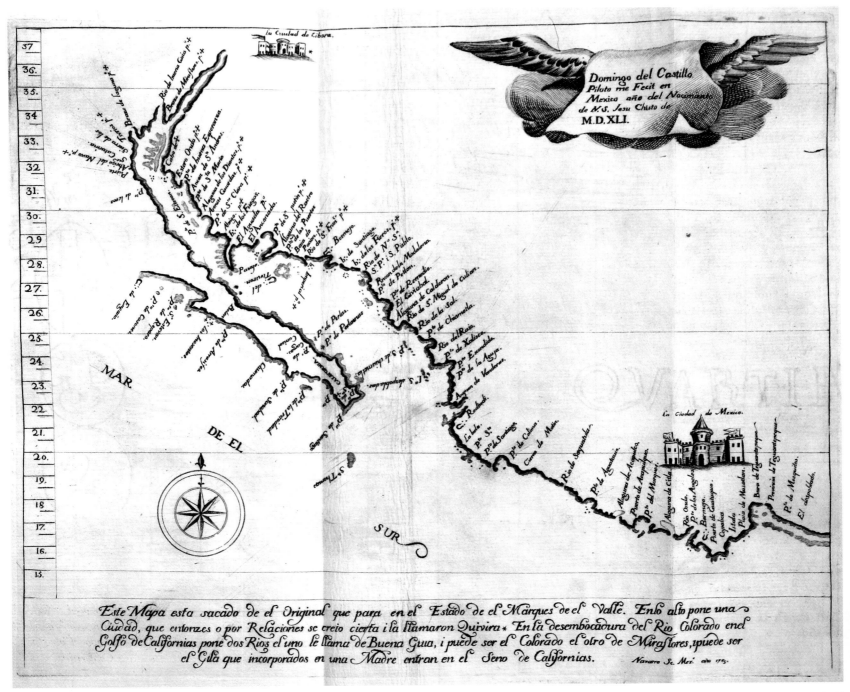

la Ciudad de Cibora.

Domingo del Castillo
Piloto me Fecit en
Mexico año del Nacimiento
de N.S. Jesu Chisto de
M.D.XLI.

MAR

DE EL

SUR

la Ciudad de Mexico.

Este Mapa esta sacado de el Original que para en el Estado de el Marques de el Valle. En lo alto pone una
Ciudad, que entonzes o por Relaciones se creio cierta i la llamaron Quivira * En la desembocadura del Rio Colorado en el
Golfo de Californias pone dos Rios el uno le llama de Buena Guia, i puede ser el Colorado el otro de Miraflores, i puede ser
el Gila que incorporados en una Madre entran en el Seno de Californias.

Navarro Sc. Mex. año 1769.

Zona temperata
Zona frigida
Indiæ Orientalis pars
Tropicus Estivus.
Baccalearum
EVROPA
Themistitan
Æquinoctialis
MARE
AT
LAN
TI
CVM
Barbaria
Getulia
Garama
res
AFRICA
Parias
PERV

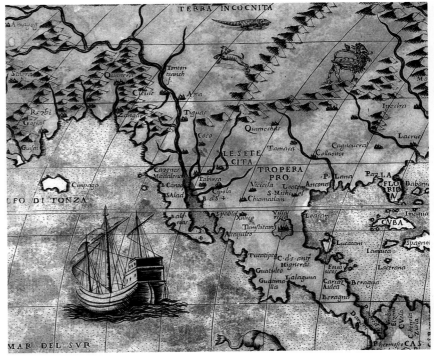

TERRA INCOCNITA

Quivira

Tiguat

LE SETE
CITA
TROPERA
PRO.

GOLFO DI TONZA

LA
FLO
RI
DA

CVBA

Spagnol

MAR DEL SVR

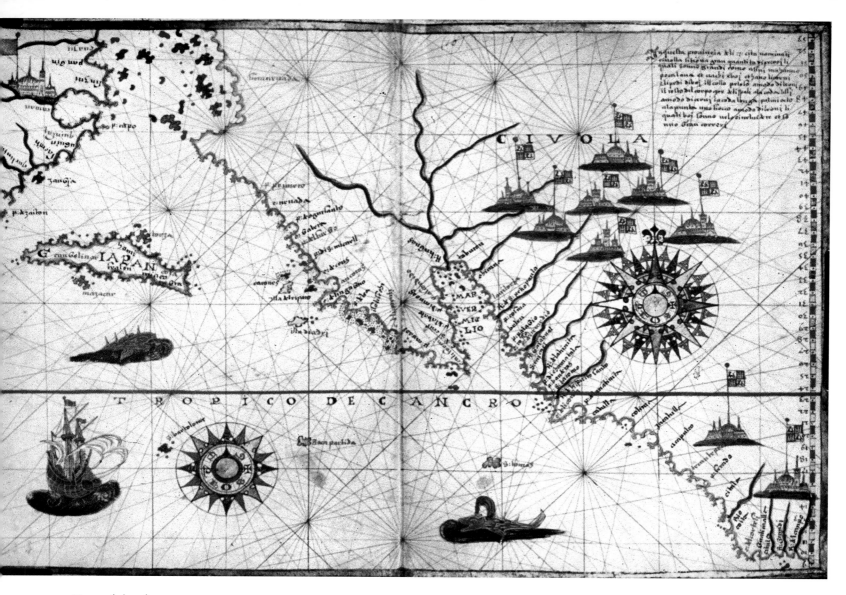

MAP 22 (above).

On no map were the mythical Seven Cities of Cibola, so much sought-after by the Spanish conquistadors, better shown than on this 1578 map by the Sicilian mapmaker Joan Martines. The California coast seems to reflect the Cabrillo expedition but clearly merges with fantasy to the north, and a huge island of Japan sits in the middle of the Pacific Ocean.

MAP 23 (left).

Although it only has two place names, this map, which was first published in 1601 in Antonio de Herrera y Tordesillas's *Historia General*, reflects knowledge from the Cabrillo expedition but not that of Sebastián Vizcaíno (see page 20), which was then about to set out. Bartolomé Ferrelo's track well off the coast (see page 18), coupled with his narrative, in which he said he was near to the coast, led to the depiction of a coast trending too much to the northwest.

MAP 24 (right).

Historian Henry Wagner called this "the sanest map of the northwest coast produced in the seventeenth century." It shows the discoveries of Cabrillo but not those of Vizcaíno and thus was out-of-date when it was published in 1630 by Dutch mapmaker Joannes de Laet. *C. Mendocino* was likely named in 1584 by Francisco de Gali, in a returning Manila galleon.

see what is now the State of California. Alarcón had Domingo del Castillo with him as his pilot, and the latter drew a map showing the Colorado at the head of the gulf (MAP 19, *page 15*).

Another expedition was soon organized by Mendoza to try to find Coronado and the approaches to the Seven Cities. This was the expedition of Francisco de Bolaños, which achieved little and about which not much is known. Bolaños did, however, name Cabo San Lucas, one of the few Spanish names of the period that has persisted. Later testimony by Bolaños's pilot, Juan Fernandez de Ladrillero, did demonstrate the Spanish perception of the geography of the Pacific at this time: the idea that the coast could be followed all the way round to Asia, and the idea that there was a Northwest Passage in temperate latitudes. Ladrillero thought it ran from the latitude of Vancouver Island to the Gulf of St. Lawrence.

In 1543, after a diversion required to put down an Indian uprising, Mendoza dispatched an expedition north led by one of the most able of the Spanish commanders, Juan Rodríguez Cabrillo, who had risen through the ranks from crossbow man to almirante (admiral). Cabrillo was instructed to find the entrance to the Northwest Passage (in the form of a large river; the two, though in reality mutually incompatible, were often mixed up), and perhaps to sail to China by following the coast north. The expedition was part of an overall plan that would also see others search westward across the Pacific for spice islands hoped to lie east of the Portuguese ones.

Cabrillo had two ships, both with lateen sails; these enabled the ships to sail closer to the wind than square-rigged ships.

Cabrillo left Navidad, a new port on the west coast of New Spain, in June 1542, and by the beginning of July had found the eastern shore of Baja California. Sailing then up the Pacific coast of Baja, he did not run into storms as Ulloa had done, and on 28 September found an excellent port that Cabrillo named San Miguel. It was today's San Diego, the bay renamed sixty years later by Sebastián Vizcaíno. Today Point Loma, at the entrance to San Diego Harbor, is the site of the Cabrillo National Monument, complete with an imposing statue of the explorer.

Leaving San Diego, Cabrillo is thought to have visited Catalina Island, then San Pedro, one day to be Los Angeles's harbor, before

going west along the Santa Barbara Channel. A storm would not allow him to double Point Conception, however, and so Cabrillo retreated to Cuyler Harbor on San Miguel Island, the northernmost of Southern California's Channel Islands, where he stayed for eight days waiting for the storm to abate.

Then, in a bold move, Cabrillo sailed north, and, after being driven back fifty miles, in three weeks reached a cape with tall pine trees he named Cabo de Pinos. It was Point Reyes, just north of San Francisco. Here the two ships had become separated, and so Cabrillo turned back to search for his other ship and coasted all the way back down the coast to Cuyler Harbor. On the way, Cabrillo found a large bay that looked promising as the mouth of a large river, which it was not; it was Monterey Bay. Here Cabrillo was forced to anchor quickly to avoid being blown onshore, finding to his surprise that he needed to tie 270 feet of ropes together to hold his anchor. This was because he had inadvertently found the submarine Monterey Canyon (MAP 469, *page 238*). South of Monterey Cabrillo saw snow-topped mountains, which he named the Sierra Nevada, one of the few Cabrillo names (though applied to different mountains) to survive.

Cabrillo intended to overwinter at San Miguel Island (although modern research suggests it may have been the adjacent Santa Rosa Island), but he died, perhaps from a previous injury. The expedition was taken over by the pilot, who was an excellent ocean navigator, Bartolomé Ferrelo (sometimes rendered as Ferrer or Ferrel). Under Ferrelo's command the ships once again sailed north. But he did not simply sail north. Deciding to make use of the winter

MAP 27 (*above*).
The route of the Manila galleon is shown very well on this 1684 map, which also depicts California as an island. The westward route is in about 20°N whereas the return route is at about 43°N, taking advantage of the westerly trade winds at that latitude. It was this route that interested the Spanish in searching for possible harbor refuges along the California coast.

MAP 28 (*left*).
One of the earliest maps to name California was this 1600 map of the Spanish domains by Gabriel Tatton, a Dutch mapmaker. The Gulf of California is *Mare Vermejo*.

southeasterly winds, he first tacked far out into the Pacific before turning north. Ferrelo reached about 42°N, the latitude of the modern northern boundary of the State of California, although he was about 170 miles off the coast. Here he decided the going was too rough and turned back. Ferrelo's reports, however, stated that he was "near to the land," and this claim resulted in maps showing a coastline trending distinctly northwest (for example, MAP 18, *page 14*, MAP 23 and MAP 24, *page 16*). The reason Ferrelo thought he was near to land was the presence of much floating driftwood, a characteristic of the Northwest Coast that would mislead many after him.

The Spanish long held the dream of accessing the Spice Islands from the west, to deny them from the Portuguese, who approached them from the opposite direction, by sailing east. The world had been divided between Portugal and Spain by the Treaty of Tordesillas following the voyage of Columbus to the west. The dividing line was in the middle of the Atlantic, but no one really knew where the division continued on the other side of the world, in the Pacific. In 1529 the king of Spain pawned any "right" he thought he had to the Spice Islands in return for a loan, but in any case by this time the Portuguese were in possession of the most important islands. The Spanish therefore decided to seek out the Philippines from the west, hoping that they might fall within the Spanish zone according to Tordesillas. Several expeditions were sent from New Spain, but although they could reach the Philippines by sailing near to the Equator, the prevailing winds would not let them return.

Not until 1565, that is. Late in 1564 four ships left Navidad under Miguel López de Legazpi carrying a Franciscan friar, Andrés de Urdaneta, who knew that a westerly wind existed north of about 40° and that this would be a route that could be used at certain times of the year. It seems that the voyage became a bit of a race, and one of Legazpi's captains, Alonso de Arellano, in his ship, the *San Lucas*, surged ahead, loaded up with spices, and sailed north to find Urdaneta's wind. He found it at about 43°N and, after twelve weeks and a turn southeastward (the winds turn northwesterly near the coast), made a landfall on Baja on 16 July 1565 at about 27°45´ N.

The Spanish were ecstatic. Legazpi established a permanent Spanish colony in the Philippines, with its capital at Manila, and from then on, a galleon loaded with gold and spices made an annual voyage from Manila to New Spain, the last leg of which was always southeast down the coast of North America, usually from a point south of Point Conception, but sometimes they made a landfall much higher on the coast of California.

This new trade route made it essential that harbors be found as possible places of refuge for the Manila galleon if it were in distress (as it often was) after it had crossed the vast Pacific Ocean. In addition, the appearance of the English in the Pacific in the form of Francis Drake and Thomas Cavendish (see page 22) heightened the apparent need for places of refuge for the galleon. Trying for exploration on a budget, the viceroy placed an experienced mariner, Sebastián Rodríguez Cermeño (or Cermenho) in command of the Manila galleon with orders to explore the California coast on its return. Cermeño left Manila in July 1595 in the galleon *San Augustín* and, likely deliberately steering somewhat to the north, made a landfall a little north of Eureka on 4 November.

From there he explored the coast southward as best he could given the lack of maneuverability of a galleon. He anchored at Drake's Bay, on the south side of Point Reyes, naming it Puerto y Bahía San Francisco (note that this is not today's San Francisco Bay; see MAP 77, *page 35*). He explored inland and built a smaller open boat to explore the inlets. But on 30 November a storm drove the galleon onshore and wrecked it. Cermeño and

MAP 29 (*above, top*).
Despite the Spanish voyages of discovery, still in a considerable realm of fantasy is this map by Cornelius de Jode, published in 1593. About the only reliable name is *Cabo Mendocino*, at the tip of the lower peninsula. *Quivira Regnu* is California, while *Anian* and *Bergi* are unknown northern lands approximating, purely accidentally, Alaska. There are at least four occurrences of *C. Blanco*, but, then, there are also sea monsters and unicorns. *El Streto de Anian* is at top left, and a Northwest Passage runs across the top of the map.

MAP 30 and MAP 31 (*left and below*). This is California and the west coast of North America shown in the first printed atlas to depict North America regionally. The atlas was published in 1597

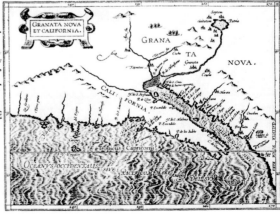

by Cornelius Wytfliet. *Cali: fornia* is named. Much of the geography is imaginary, and there is considerable similarity to the De Jode map above; undoubtedly some copying took place. The adjacent sheets of the West Coast have been positioned to join each other but are separate in the atlas.

Vizcaíno left Acapulco on 5 May 1602 with three ships and towing a longboat with which to survey inlets and bays. After an often difficult voyage north, battling contrary winds and storms, on 10 November Vizcaíno reached a port, which, he wrote, "must be the best to be found in all the South Sea," with good protected anchorage, water, and game. It was San Diego Bay, Cabrillo's San Miguel, now strangely forgotten or overlooked by the Spanish authorities, who gave Vizcaíno none of the information or maps from previous voyages. Exploration of the area led to his discovery of Mission Bay and the mouth of the San Diego River, shown as a circular inlet just north of the peninsula, Point Loma, on MAP 35, *far right, bottom.*

On 4 December Vizcaíno was tacking through off the coast just east of Point Conception; it being the saint's day of Santa Barbara, this saint's name was bestowed on the channel. Monterey Bay was reached and named after the viceroy, the Conde de Monterey, on 16 December. The map drawn, however, showed the bay as much snugger than it really was (MAP 35, *far right, bottom*). Vizcaíno wrote that it was "the best port that could be desired." Later this would cause problems when a bay fitting Vizcaíno's description could not be found (see page 38).

Scurvy was now beginning to take its toll, and so the sick were sent back to Acapulco on one of the ships. Two ships continued north. San Francisco Bay was missed, as it would also be on the return journey, as the ships were sailing too far offshore in order to round Point Reyes (also named by Vizcaíno). The expedition sent out specifically to locate harbors missed the finest harbor on the coast.

his men were forced to return to New Spain in the small boat. Cermeño insisted on continuing to survey the coast, but even in this small vessel he missed the entrance to (today's) San Francisco Bay.

Despite his considerable addition to the Spanish knowledge of the coast, Cermeño received nothing but condemnation for his efforts, as the loss of the galleon overrode all other considerations. The Spanish quickly came to the realization, however, that any exploration of the coast needed to be in a smaller, unladen ship sailing from New Spain.

In 1602 the viceroy appointed a merchant, Sebastián Vizcaíno, to command a new expedition to examine the California coast in detail, sound harbors, and make maps—and find pearls if he could. Vizcaíno had already been on a pearl-finding voyage to Baja in 1596, which had ended in near disaster—and without pearls—but which had given him both experience and the regard of the viceroy. Vizcaíno had also sailed on the Manila galleon and so knew of the problems that could arise; he had been aboard the galleon *Santa Ana* when it was captured by the English buccaneer Thomas Cavendish, who in 1587 had followed Francis Drake into the Pacific. Vizcaíno seems to have been the ideal choice for the exploration intended by the viceroy.

Overnight, the two ships became separated. Vizcaíno continued north to about 41°N, to Point St. George, just north of Crescent City. He had been instructed not to sail more than a hundred leagues beyond Cape Mendocino if the coast trended northwest, and thus potentially continued to China, and only explore farther if it trended north or northeast, which, it was thought, might mean that the Strait of Anian was nearby. In any case, the crew were becoming so incapacitated by scurvy that this question became academic, and a vote was taken to return to Acapulco as quickly as possible. Vizcaíno found the yellow mancanilla fruit on the coast of Mexico, and its antiseptic and antiscorbutic properties saved him and his men, though he failed to recognize their recovery as anything but a divine intervention.

The other ship, commanded by Martín de Aguilar, also continued north, reaching, it thought, the Klamath River in southern Oregon, though it is possible they found the Columbia. In any case, they reported finding the entrance to a large river, and this "entrada" of Aguilar appeared on many maps for more than a century as the mouth of the mythical River of the West, a large river—or even a strait—thought to flow right across the continent (MAP 49, *page 27*). Both Aguilar and his pilot, Antonio Flores, died in the cold of the northern shores, and the ship limped back to New Spain; only five men survived. Forty-two men had died on the three ships.

More than those of any Spanish explorer before him, Vizcaíno's place names survived. Vizcaíno himself went on to greater things, taking a pioneering Spanish embassy to Japan in 1611. Spanish exploration of the California coast, however, entered a hiatus that would last a century and a half, until Spain felt threatened by the encroachments of other nations enough to actually begin to colonize the land they had found.

MAP 32 (*left*).
Vizcaíno suffered obscurity for many years because of the Spanish official policy of secrecy. His map of the coast of Mexico and California as far north as Cape Mendocino, shown here, was not published by the Spanish government for exactly two hundred years, and only then because it was felt that Spanish claims to sovereignty on the coast were under threat from the publication in 1798 of the survey of Britain's George Vancouver, which included a detailed atlas of maps. Of particular note on this map is *P[uerto] bueno de s. Diego*, San Diego Bay, named after Vizcaíno's ship the *San Diego*. Finally here is a Spanish map on which many of the names bestowed lasted to modern times. The section of the map shown runs from Cedros Island, halfway up the Baja coast, at bottom right, to Cape Mendocino, at top left.

MAP 33 (*far right, top*), MAP 34 (*far right, center*),
MAP 35 (*far right, bottom*), and MAP 36 (*near right, bottom*).
Four detailed maps from the Vizcaíno voyage, probably drawn by a Barefoot Carmelite priest, Antonio de la Ascension, who was with Vizcaíno, and copied later by the pilot Enrico Martínez, the cosmographer of New Spain, who was not on the voyage.

MAP 33 is a cape labeled *Cabo Mendocino*, complete with distinctly easterly-trending coast immediately to its north. This was the most northerly of the Ascension maps, but it is, however, not clear which headland it depicts. Historian Henry Wagner believed it represented Humboldt Bay north to Trinidad, but it bears little resemblance to that coast. It may instead be Point St. George, at today's Crescent City, which seems to be the farthest north that Vizcaíno reached.

MAP 35 shows Monterey Bay (at bottom) to *ensenada grande*, the large bay at the center of which is the unnoticed Golden Gate, the entrance to San Francisco Bay. MAP 34 overlaps MAP 35 and runs from *ensenada grande* to Drake's Bay and Point Reyes (*Punta de los rejes*, named by Vizcaíno). The river is probably the Russian River.

MAP 36 shows San Diego Bay with the Coronado peninsula, the Point Loma peninsula, and Mission Bay to the north of the latter.

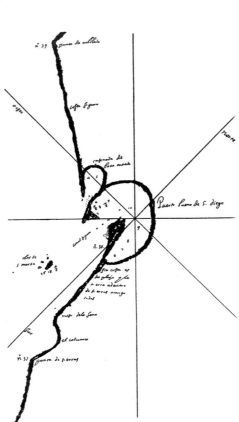

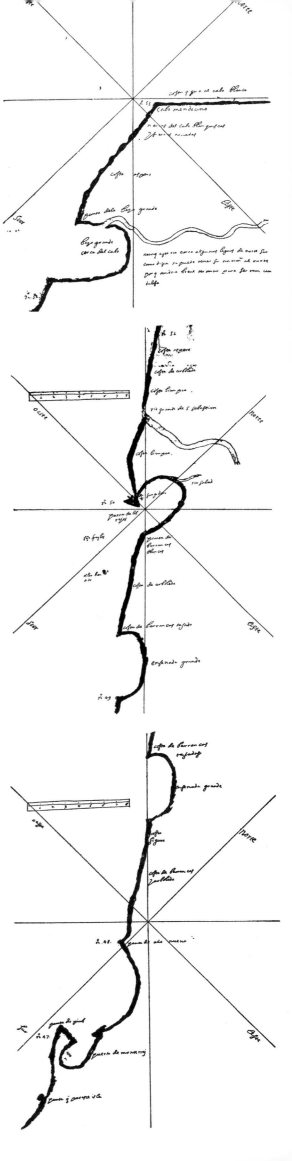

# THE FIRST NEW ENGLAND

What better name could an English adventurer of empire bestow on a land of sanctuary from the storms of the Pacific and the pursuit of the Spanish? New England, ten thousand miles from the old one, was the name given to California by that most famous of all the English Elizabethan buccaneers, Sir Francis Drake. In its Latin form it was Nova Albion, and it was to be displayed on the map of the world as such for two hundred and fifty years hence.

The Spanish comfort in the Pacific Ocean was rudely interrupted in 1579 by the appearance of Francis Drake, an English freebooter who had already made a fortune when he captured a Spanish mule train crossing the Isthmus of Panama in 1572–73. Now, on a likely quasi-commercial venture, and certainly with investors and at least the tacit backing of Queen Elizabeth, he had sailed from England late in 1577 and made his way into the Pacific through the Strait of Magellan, becoming the first Englishman to navigate that strait. For the better part of a year Drake then harassed Spanish shipping and ports along the coasts of South and Central America, burning ships and towns and making off with treasure. Finally he captured a galleon sailing from Callao, Peru, to Panama, loaded with silver, gold, and jewels. So much was captured that it took three days to transfer the treasure to Drake's ship, the *Golden Hind*. Then, laden down with booty, Drake decided it was time to get back to England.

How best to do this? If he reversed his course back through the Strait of Magellan, he knew that the Spanish would be lying in wait for him. What about the Northwest Passage, shown across the northern part of North America on maps that Drake certainly had with him, such as MAP 44, *page 24*, drawn by his kinsman, Humfray Gylbert? In a bold move intended to outflank the Spanish, Drake sailed north to search for the western entrance to the passage, the Strait of Anian. The best evidence shows that Drake reached about 48°N before giving up his search for a passage because of cold conditions in the North Pacific, but various speculations have placed his northernmost point much farther, even in Alaska.

However far north he reached, Drake's ship was by now leaking badly, and he needed to find a place to careen and repair it. He turned back and searched the coast for

MAP 37 (*above*).
This portrait of Sir Francis Drake, by Dutch engraver Crispin van de Passe, was published in 1598 and shows the buccaneer as an honored founder of empires. The portrait is complete with a map of the world that copies, more or less, the geography of the Hondius map below.

MAP 38 (*below*).
A decade after Drake's exploits in California a world map was published by the Dutch mapmaker Jodocus Hondius. This is the identical map in the 1595 edition. Drake's track along the coast of California and Nova Albion seems to suddenly peter out, as though erased, reaching only about 42°N. This is the cartographic manifestation of the controversy about how far north Drake sailed and to some confirms the idea that there was a conspiracy in England on Drake's return to conceal the true route from Spanish spies, perhaps to give them the notion that a Northwest Passage had indeed been found for England. This is the map on which Drake's New Albion Port (MAP 40, *right, center*) is an inset.

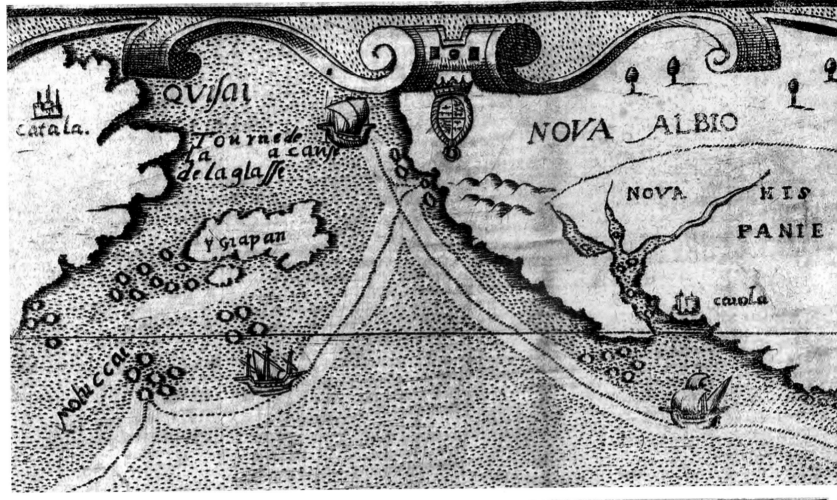

**MAP 39** (*above*).

The other major map of the Drake circumnavigation was a French one, drawn by Nicola van Sype about 1581. Here the question of how far north Drake sailed is depicted by the disappearance of his track behind a conveniently located ship, never to reemerge. Four islands are shown off the coast of *Nova Albio*—which itself now stretches across the continent—with Drake's track clearly touching one of them. These islands have been interpreted as Washington's Olympic Peninsula, Vancouver Island, the Queen Charlottes, and Prince of Wales Island in Alaska, which would place New Albion far north of California. However, the same four islands were also shown on a 1564 world map by Abraham Ortelius and thus predate Drake's visit.

**MAP 40** (*right*).

One of the insets in the 1589 and 1595 Hondius world maps (MAP 38, *left*) is this little map of *Portus Novæ Albionis* where Drake careened his ship, also shown. The cove's location has been the subject of endless debate, but most evidence still points to Drake's Bay at Point Reyes.

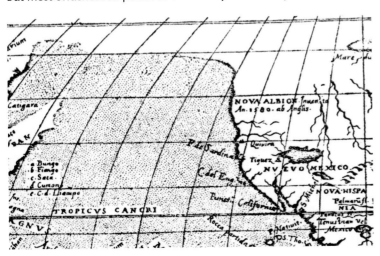

**MAP 41** (*left*).

The English chronicler Richard Hakluyt published this 1587 map drawn by Peter Martyr, which showed Drake's *Nova Albion* as having been discovered by the English in 1580. He was a year out. The coast continues north and then trends west toward Asia.

**MAP 42** (*right*).

*Pº. Sir Francico draco* is shown on this map of California (as an island) drawn by Dutch mapmaker Joan Vinckeboons about 1650. The whole map is shown as MAP 58, *page 30*.

MAP 43 (*above*).
Another of the famous English chroniclers and boosters for England was Samuel Purchas. This is the title page to his 1625 book *Purchas His Pilgrimes*, a book on English exploration and empire. The map shows the explorations of Englishmen, including Sir Francis Drake, whose name appears against his ship off the coast of California. *Nova Albion* is also shown. The Pacific appears as it was typically shown on maps at this time: far too narrow. A large island of Japan is also seen, with the name of John Saris, the first English East India trader to visit the country.

*Above right* is an engraving of Drake's ship, the *Golden Hind*, from the margins of the Ortelius map (MAP 38, *page 22*). Drake left Britain in the *Pelican* but renamed his ship in honor of his patron, Sir Christopher Hatton, who had a golden doe, or hind, on his coat of arms.

MAP 44 (*right*).
This woodcut map shows very clearly why Drake was interested in what the English called the "backside of America": the western entrance to the Northwest Passage is shown just north of *Si: Nevada*—the Sierra Nevada, named by Cabrillo in 1542. The information was copied by one of Drake's fellow adventurers, Sir Humfray Gylbert, from Abraham Ortelius's world map of 1564. The map was published in 1576, the year before Drake set sail on his epic circumnavigation. Gylbert was one of the leading advocates of exploration to find the Northwest Passage.

a suitable location—one sheltered but also invisible to any Spanish ships that might come looking for him. Many places have been proposed as the location for Drake's repairs on the West Coast, tantalizingly shown as Portus Novæ Albionis on a map (MAP 40, *page 23*). These include Bodega Bay, a small bay somewhere within San Francisco Bay; Whale Cove, Oregon; and even Boundary Bay, south of Vancouver, in British Columbia. Nevertheless, most evidence points to Drake's Bay, in the lee of Point Reyes, the same bay that Cermeño would name Puerto de San Francisco sixteen years later.

An account of the voyage, stated to have been written by Drake but which was more likely written by Francis Fletcher, Drake's chaplain, was published in 1628, entitled *The World Encompassed.* It stated that "in 38 deg. 30 min we fell in with a convenient and fit harborough [harbor] and June 17 came to anchor therein: where we continued till the 23. day of July following." The cold that had forced their return south continued: "During all whiche time, notwithstanding it was the height of Summer, and so neere the Sunne, yet we were continually visited with nipping colds." There is some evidence, from narrower tree rings, meaning slower growth, that this period was colder in this region than at other times.

Drake and his men encountered Miwok Indians who lived in the area, and somehow a ceremony took place in which Drake was "crowned" by the Miwok chief. This was

taken by the Englishmen to mean that "right and title in the whole land" had been given to them, and Drake renamed what he now considered to be English soil. "This country our generall named Albion," Fletcher writes, so "that it might have some affinity, even in name also, with our owne country," the name derived from the Latin form of the word England and for the "white bancks and cliffes" along the shore,

MAP 45 (*right*).
The first map to show the presence of Drake on the west coast of North America was this strangely proportioned map drawn by the merchant and Northwest Passage promoter Michael Lok. At the top of a hugely misshapen California are the words *Anglorum 1580*, the English, 1580, the year once more wrong by a year. To the east, past the *Sierra Nevada*, stretches a sea passage, in this case the so-called Sea of Verrazano "found" in 1524 by that explorer when he looked over the sand dunes of the offshore islands of the Carolina and thought he saw a sea reaching all the way to China.

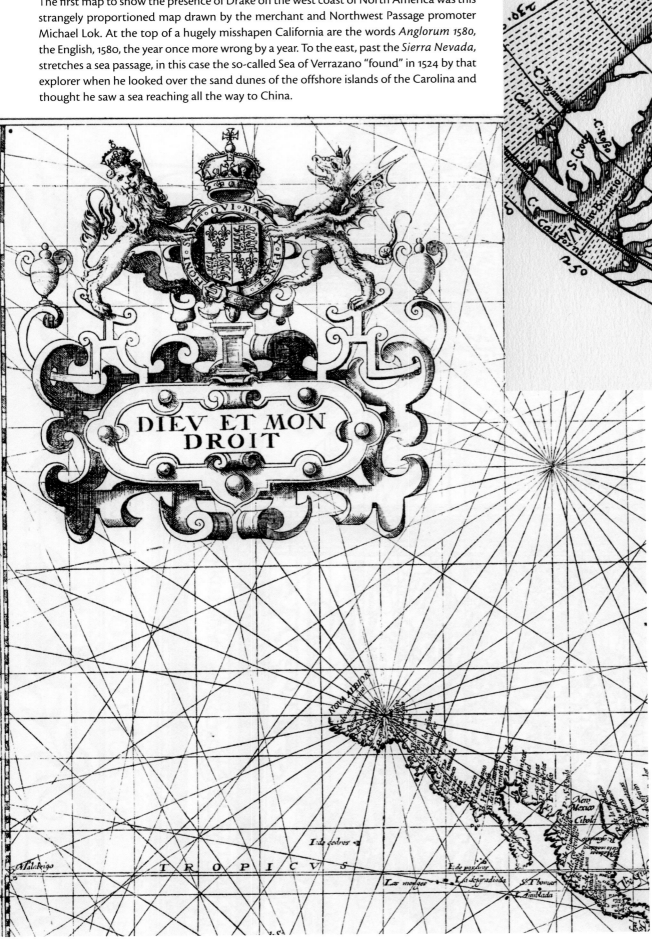

MAP 46 (*left*).
The imprimatur of the English royal coat of arms is firmly and unequivocally stamped on the unknown lands of the Northwest in this map published by chronicler Richard Hakluyt in the 1599 edition of his *Principall Navigations*. The detail of the California coast is from English sources—Drake—with parts from Spanish sources. Whatever the source, it is all *Nova Albion* here.

which reminded them of the chalk cliffs of southern England. For two centuries maps would depict Nova or New Albion rather than California. To bolster the idea that sovereignty could be given by the Miwoks, *The World Encompassed* is careful to state that "the Spaniards never had any dealing, or so much as set a foote in this country."

When Drake and his men explored inland they noted that it was "farre different from the shoare, a goodly country, and fruitfull soyle, stored with many blessings fit for the use of man." This description—which certainly sounds like California—contributes to the evidence that the location of Drake's harbor was at Drake's Bay, for as soon as one leaves Point Reyes the land rises and is indeed different from the coast lands of the point.

The debate about where Drake went will likely never end unless more evidence is uncovered. In 1647 Robert Dudley published the first English sea atlas, *Dell'Arcano del Mare* ("the secrets of the sea"), a massive undertaking that took twelve years to engrave. The map of the West Coast from that atlas (MAP 47, *right*) is of special interest, because Dudley was the son of one of Drake's financial backers, and it is presumed he thus had an inside knowledge of what really happened. At the northern end of the coastline shown on this map is a peninsula, which has been interpreted as Cape Flattery, at the entrance

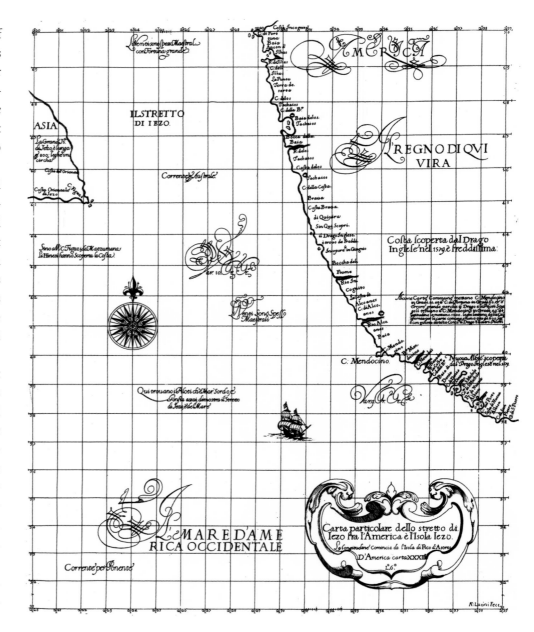

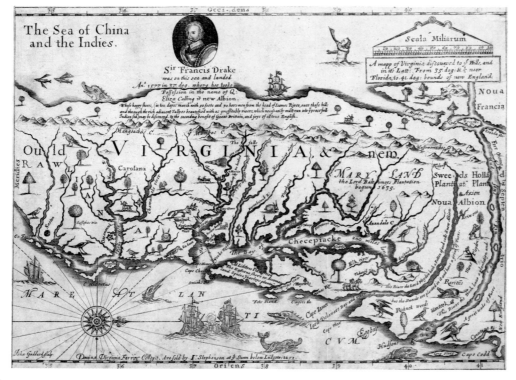

MAP 47 (*above*).
Robert Dudley's 1647 map of the West Coast, from his monumental atlas. The copper engraved maps, for the first time in an English sea atlas, used Mercator's projection, a useful projection for mariners because straight lines drawn on the map are great circle routes on the globe.

MAP 48 (*left*).
California and Virginia on a map, with nothing in between! Until the late eighteenth century it was not known how wide the continent of North America was. This was due principally to the lack of a means of accurately measuring longitude but also to the optimism of explorers. This map of Virginia, drawn for the Virginia Company in 1651, manifested the expectation that the South Sea—the Pacific—was but a few days' march from the headwaters of the coastal Atlantic rivers. Here the visit to—and sovereignty over—California is emphatically stated, complete with Drake's portrait. Now the date is two years too early.

to the Strait of Juan de Fuca. If this is correct, then the map shows the entire coast south in some detail, which suggests that Drake explored it southward while looking for a harbor in which to careen his ship. Yet Asia remains just offshore on the same map, hardly an accurate representation of reality.

Drake's sojourn on the California coast was short, and it can be argued quite reasonably that he had little effect on subsequent history. But this is not quite true, for the English used his visit as a diplomatic bargaining chip even once it became clear that British sovereignty was unenforceable. And as the maps on these pages attest, New Albion adorned maps, especially but not exclusively British maps, for a long time.

MAP 49 (*right, top*).
Drake is all over this state-of-the-art British map of 1768. Published by eminent commercial mapmaker Thomas Jefferys, *New Albion* looms large, with the appellation *So named by Sr. Francis Drake to whom the Country was surrendred by the King in 1578*, one year before Drake's visit. Mapmakers certainly had difficulty getting the dates of Drake's exploits right. The "King" refers to the Miwok chief who supposedly "crowned" Drake. On the coast, below a reference to Cabrillo's *Sierra de Navadas in 1542*—the date correct—is an indentation marked *Port S<sup>r</sup>. Francis Drake 1578 not S<sup>t</sup>. Francisco*. Note also the *Opening discover'd by Martin d'Aguilar in 1603*; Aguilar was with Vizcaíno that year (see pages 20–21). Jefferys magically connects this to the mythical *River of the West*. Baja is *Kalifornia*.

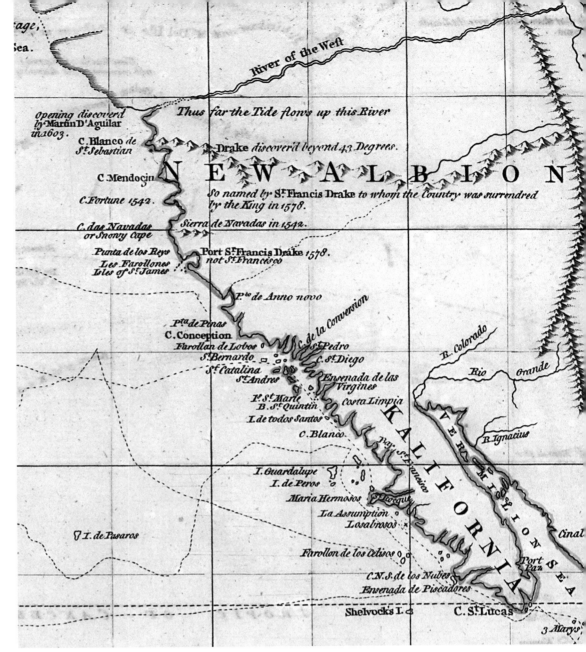

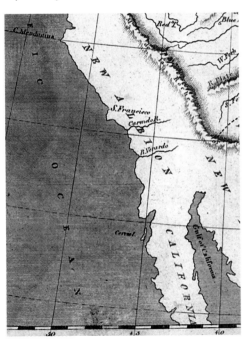

MAP 50 (*left*).
Not much but *New Albion* is shown on this map published by Philadelphia mapmaker Samuel Lewis in 1804. The mountains are the Rockies, not the Sierra Nevada, and are shown far too close to the Pacific. *S. Francisco* seems to still refer to Cermeño's location from 1595, as no San Francisco Bay is shown.

MAP 51 (*right*).
New Albion it might have been, but not everyone got it right. Here, in a 1794 map by Philadelphia mapmaker Jedediah Morse, the land that would be California is depicted as *New Albania*. The *Chanel of St. Barbara* is correct, and perhaps *C. Mendocino*, but the date of Drake's encounter with California is off by a year. The ship's track at top is that of James Cook in 1778. Cook asserted Britain's claim to the West Coast based on its "discovery" by Drake.

# ON THE RIGHT HAND OF THE INDIES

MAP 52 (above).
This little engraving of the Western Hemisphere with California very clearly an island is from the title page of a geography book published by the French mapmaker Nicolas de Fer in 1717, well after California had been shown *not* to be an island.

MAP 53 (above).
This portion of a map of North America, drawn in 1542 by Alonzo de Santa Cruz, shows the first manifestation of California as an island: Baja California with a cut-off channel. This seems to illustrate the view of California for a number of years following its discovery by Cortés. The inscription, in Spanish, at the tip of Baja reads "the island which the Marques del Valle [Cortés] discovered." To the north another inscription states that it is "the land that Don Antonio de Mendoza [the viceroy] sent [explorers] to discover."

MAP 54 (right).
What appears to be the first publication of California as an island in its second incarnation was on this map, from the title page of Antonio de Herrera's *Description de las Indias Occidentales* in the 1622 edition. The map was drawn by Father Antonio de la Ascensión, who had been with Vizcaíno in 1602 (see page 21) and who seems to have been the originator of the idea—for the second time around—that California was an island.

California got its name, it seems, from fantasy fiction. A fifteenth-century book by one Garcia Ordoñez de Montevaldo, called *Las Sergas del muy esforzado caballero Esplandian*—"the exploits of the very powerful cavalier Esplandian"—contains the first reference to the name. "Know that to the right hand of the Indies," Montevaldo writes, "was an island called California, very near to the region of Terrestrial Paradise, which was populated by black women, without there being any men among them, that almost like the Amazons was their style of living." The island of Amazons was ruled by the beautiful Queen Calafia. Here was the germ of the idea that California—wherever it might be—was an island.

In addition, from the earliest times Europeans had the notion that the seas of the Orient were full of islands, a concept derived from the probably equally fictional writings of Marco Polo. Early maps show islands in the sea west of the landmass that had prevented Columbus from sailing to the Indies (MAP 10, *page 10*). It was an easy leap, then, when Hernán Cortés found Baja California in 1535, known to be surrounded by seas on three sides, to assume that this too, must be one of these islands, perhaps even that fabled island of California. Was it not at the right hand of the Indies—the distance across the Pacific then believed to be short? Cortés himself believed that he had found an island when he drew his map (MAP 14, *page 12*), although he was restrained enough to only draw what he actually knew. There are a few maps extant that show this initial concept of California as an island, and the maps drawn in 1542 by Alonzo de Santa Cruz (MAP 53, *left*) is one of them. The map was drawn after Francisco de Ulloa had determined that California was not an island, in 1539 (see page 13), but Santa Cruz was a trendsetter; he was the first of many, many mapmakers not to let what was known stand in the way of what he thought.

Indeed, for much of the second half of the sixteenth century, Lower California was thought to be just what it is, a peninsula. Then came the voyage of Sebastián Vizcaíno.

One of the members of this expedition was Father Antonio de la Ascension, who wrote a long account of the voyage to which he added his own conclusions. Drawing principally on the fact that he had not seen any large rivers, he decided that the reason was that they were all relatively short, such as would be the case if the coast were in fact an island rather than a continental littoral. "I hold it to be very certain and proven," he wrote, "that the whole Kingdom of California discovered on this voyage, is the largest island known or which has been discovered up to the present day, and that it is separated from the provinces of New Mexico by the Mediterranean Sea of California." Of course, the reason Ascension had seen no great rivers was that both of the principal rivers that drain California—the Sacramento and the San Joaquin—empty into San Francisco Bay, an opening that was missed by the Vizcaíno expedition as it was by many others.

The reasoning seemed, to many seventeenth-century minds, compelling, coming as it did from one who had been there. And so California embarked on a voyage of over a century as an island once more.

The first to perpetrate this island myth after Ascension appears to be the London mapmaker Henry Briggs, who in 1625 published a magnificent map of North America to illustrate the discoveries of the Arctic explorer Thomas Button (MAP 55, *right*). This was followed by a map from another English Arctic explorer who clearly had studied Briggs's map, Luke Foxe. In the corner of his map, published in 1635, is the tip of California, the island (MAP 56, *overleaf*).

The depiction of California as an island began to take on a life of its own as mapmakers copied the work of others. In the second half of the seventeenth century there were more than a hundred maps produced that show the island. Some of the more interesting are shown on the following pages.

MAP 55 (*right*).
The western half of Henry Briggs's famous 1625 map *The North part of America*. It was the first published view of California as an island after that of Antonio de la Ascension, the instigator of the second coming of the island concept.

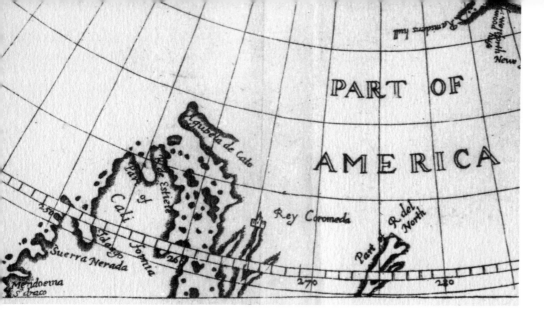

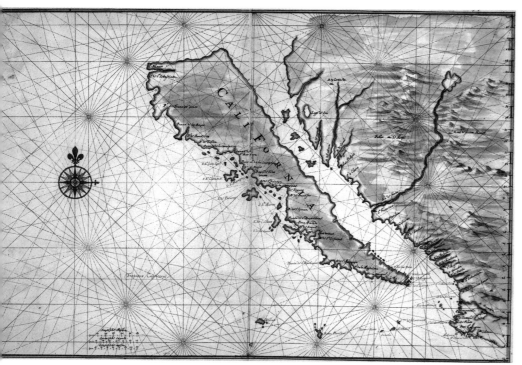

MAP 56 (*left, top*).
This is the bottom left corner of the map published by Arctic explorer Luke Foxe in 1635. The map illustrated his Arctic voyage of 1631. It shows *Part of California*, complete with Cabrillo's *Suerra Nevada* on the coast of the island.

MAP 57 (*left, center*).
One of the first printed maps to depict the island of California separately as an atlas plate was this map of *Californie Isle*, originally published by French mapmaker Nicolas Sanson in 1657. This edition was published about 1683. Two bays have now appeared on the north coast of the island.

MAP 58 (*left, bottom*).
One of the most finely drawn maps of the island of California was this one, by Dutch cartographer Joan Vinckeboons. The date of this manuscript map is uncertain, but it is likely about 1650.

MAP 59 (*above*).
Another Dutch mapmaker, Jan Jansson, published a beautiful map of North America in 1670 showing *Insula California* still in the style of Henry Briggs.

MAP 60 (*above*).
This map by Nicolas Sanson, published in 1650, follows the island style of Briggs. Sanson added northern bays a few years later (MAP 57, *left, center*). This map became a new and much copied model.

MAP 61 (*left*).
Not everybody embraced the island concept. This simple map of California appeared in 1683 in *Nouvelle Description de la Louisiane*, the book by Louis Hennepin about his explorations of the upper Mississippi River.

MAP 62 (*right, top*).
This superbly illustrated map was produced by the Venetian Franciscan Vincenzo Coronelli in 1696 and was modeled after Sanson. Here a range of mountains has appeared along the east coast of the island.

MAP 63 (*right, bottom*).
Almost an island, a precarious California hangs by a tiny bridge of land, attached to the rest of the continent. This map was in a later edition of Louis Hennepin's book, published in 1697. Perhaps Hennepin's mapmaker was losing faith in the attachment of California to the mainland? Note *N. Albion*, the only name marked along the Pacific coast.

Map 64 (*above*).
The Sanson morphology, with north coastal bays, is apparent on this 1685 map by English mapmaker Philip Lea.

Map 65 (*below*).
Another English mapmaker, Herman Moll, published this map in 1719; he did not accept that the island concept had been discredited.

Map 66 (*above*).
Joducus Hondius did not depict California as an island in 1640 when this map was published.

Map 67 (*right*).
This different morphology of the island of California was published in 1717 by Nicolas de Fer in a geography book and atlas entitled *L'Amerique, Merionale et Septentrionale* (America South and North).

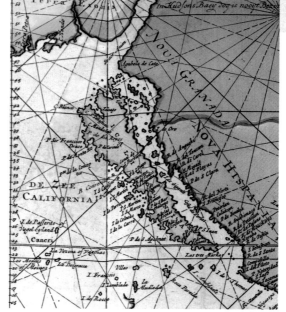

Map 68 (*left*).
This rather spectacular map of the island of California was published by Dutch mapmaker Gerard van Keulen in 1728, well after he would have been aware of the report and maps of Eusebio Kino proving that California was a peninsula. The map was in theory an update of an earlier edition, and likely Van Keulen did not want to change it.

But myths are myths, and sooner or later reality will intrude. Father Eusebio Kino, a wide-ranging Jesuit missionary, reached the confluence of the Colorado and the Gila rivers and realized that he was north of the Gulf of California. Further explorations in 1701 and 1702 led him down the Colorado to the head of the gulf, from where he could see that there was land north of the gulf rather than water. He therefore correctly concluded that Baja California was a peninsula, not an island. His report included a map of the northern end of the Gulf of California, which was quite accurate (Map 69, *right, top*) and which was widely reprinted in several languages.

Myths, however, can be stubborn. Quite a few mapmakers continued to depict California as an island despite their knowledge of the Kino expedition. In 1746 another Jesuit, Fernando Consag, traveled to the head of the Gulf of California in a canoe, again proving that it terminated and that Baja California was a peninsula.

Finally, in 1747, the king of Spain, Ferdinand VI, issued no less than a royal decree that "California is not an island." Woe betide any Spanish mapmaker, at least, who dare depict California as an island after that! The knowledge that California was part of the mainland was to facilitate the colonization of Alta California that was soon to follow.

Map 69 (*right, top*).
This is the 1705 French edition of the pivotal Kino map that negated the myth that California was an island. It shows the land connection across the head of the Sea [Gulf] of California.

Map 70 (*right*).
Five maps in one present the cartographic history of California to 1757. This is from a French encyclopedia published in 1770. It shows, as numbered on the maps: I. A 1604 Florentine-drawn map, copied from a Spanish one, showing California as a peninsula. The asterisk in mid-peninsula indicated where the sea was supposed to flood at high tide, thus transforming the southern part of the peninsula into an island—a nice compromise, if without evidence; II. California as an island by Nicolas Sanson, 1657; III. Guillaume De L'Isle's 1700 map showing California as a peninsula (De L'Isle stated he could not determine whether California was an island based on the evidence available to him); IV. Kino's map; V. Fernando Consag's map of 1767, first published in 1757, showing California as a peninsula, after the final resolution of the question.

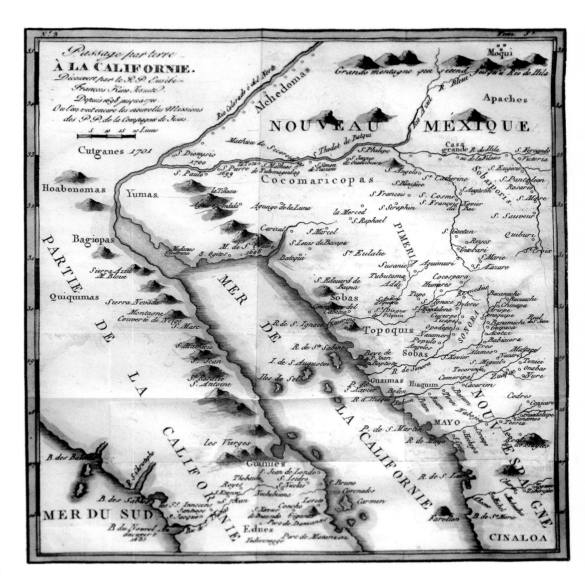

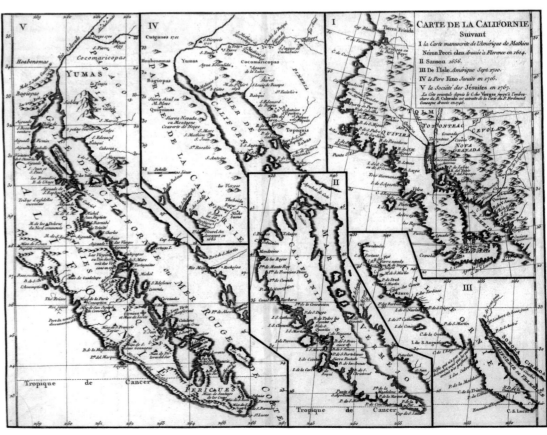

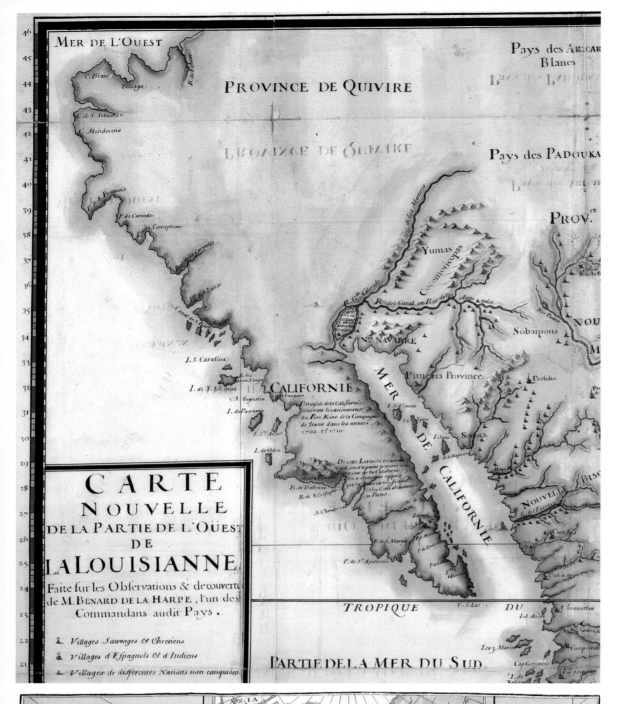

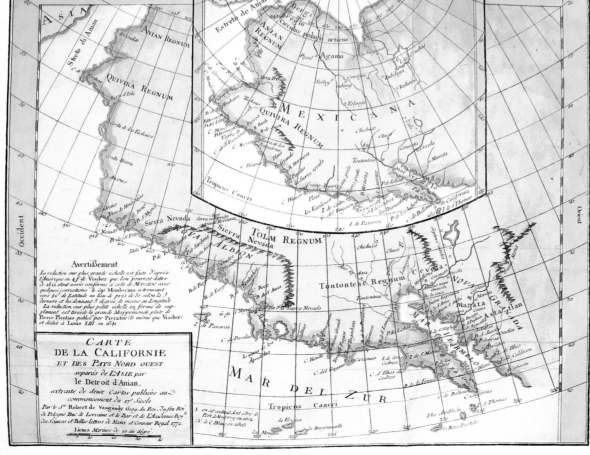

MAP 71 (left, top).
The maps on this page illustrate the still poor geographical knowledge of California in the years before the decision by the Spanish to colonize Alta California.

This artistic map, which was drawn about 1724, is the western half of a map found in the journal of the explorer of the Red River (a west bank tributary of the Mississippi), Jean-Baptiste Bénard, Sieur de La Harpe, and now in the Library of Congress. It was drawn by Jean de Beaurain to illustrate the journal. California is a rather blank looking *Province de Quivire*, *Californie* is Baja, and a *Mer de L'Ouest* terminates California to the north.

MAP 72 (left, bottom).
This 1772 map by French geographer Robert de Vaugondy well illustrates the fact that mapmakers often did not know what was the correct form for their maps. Here the inset map shows a different coastal outline from that on the main map; Vaugondy was presumably hedging his bets. But no one seemed to mind the obvious contradictions.

MAP 73 (below).
A large *Terre de Iesso* (Land of Jesso) stretches across the North Pacific in this 1702 woodcut map. *California* peeks out from the right-hand margin, terminated on its northern coast by *Detroit Anian*, the Strait of Anian, the supposed western entrance to the Northwest Passage.

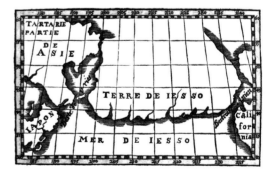

MAP 74 (below, bottom).
More fantastic geography of the West Coast, this time by French mapmaker Philippe Buache. The map was first published in 1752.

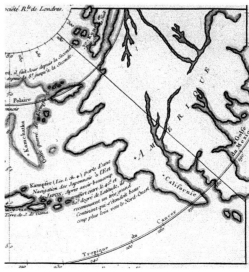

## Map 75 (right).

So little was known of the Northwest Coast in the first half of the eighteenth century that the novelist Jonathan Swift used it as the location for his 1726 book *Gulliver's Travels.* Here he placed his Brobdingnag, the land of giants. What better place to locate a fictitious land than beyond the pale of exploration? Here is *New Albion, C. Mendocino, P^{to}. S^{r}. Fran^{s}. Drake,* and *P. Monterey,* but no California; Swift was British.

## Map 76 (far right).

French encyclopedist Denis Diderot put this map in his 1755 edition, part of one of the most fantastic maps of the North Pacific ever published. Here a vast *Mer L'Ouest* (Sea of the West) penetrates far inland just at the northern coast of California—though not the northern coast we might think of today. *Port S^{t}. Francois* is Cermeño's Puerto y Bahia de San Francisco at Point Reyes, found in 1595 and also shown on Map 77.

## Map 77 (below).

This map represents the cumulative knowledge from Spanish exploration up to 1769, on the eve of the move to colonize Alta California. At bottom right is *[Cabo] S^{n}. Lucas,* at the tip of Baja, and at top left is *C^{o}. Mendosinos.* Of special note near *P^{ta}. [Punta] de los Reyes* is *P^{to}. [Puerto] de S^{n}. Fran[cis]co,* the bay found and named by Sebastián Rodríguez Cermeño in December 1595 (see page 19); the name was soon to be usurped by a larger bay a few miles to the south, which would be discovered by the Spanish in 1769.

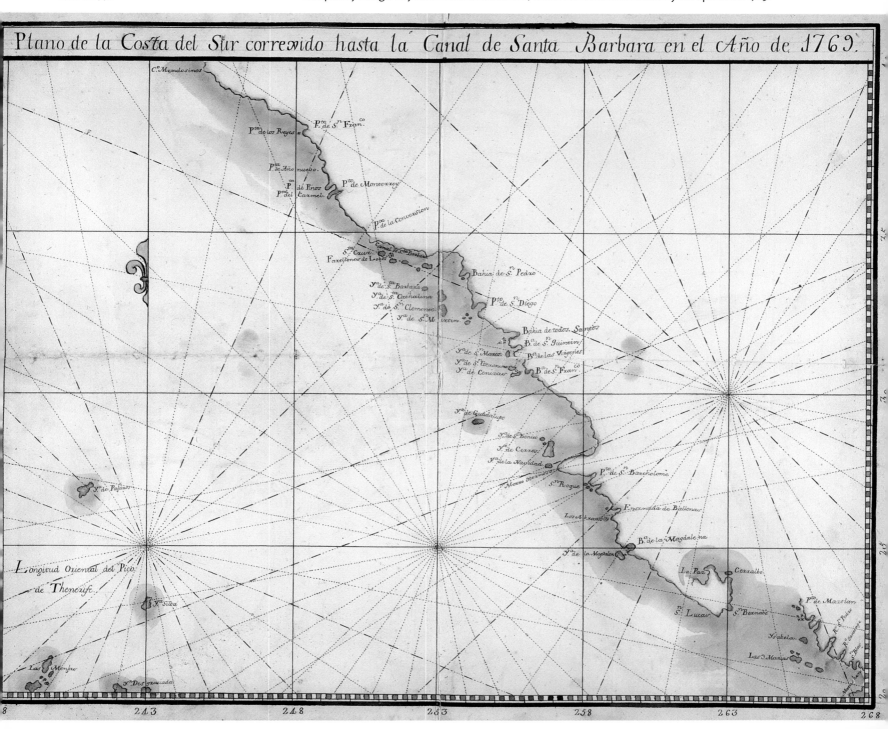

# SPAIN ✝ MOVES NORTH

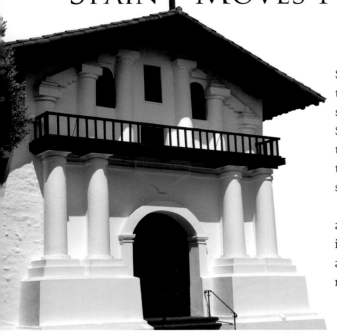

Spain made little effort to continue to explore Alta California after the 1602 voyage of Sebastián Vizcaíno; the Manila galleon continued its annual cruise down the southern coast often seeing but keeping well away from the coast. Father Eusebio Kino had established missions in Sonora and today's Arizona, and it was from a northern mission that he had made his explorations north and west that showed that Baja was not an island (see page 33). Beginning in 1697 the Jesuits were allowed to establish missions in Lower California, and by 1767 there was a string of fourteen missions in Baja.

Spain's apparent disregard for its lands to the north was shaken about this time by the activities of other nations. In 1760 Britain had finally wrested New France from the French, and it was believed that the Spanish dominions in North America might be the next to receive the attentions of the British. In fact, nothing was further from the truth, but the perception was nonetheless there. It was added to when knowledge of the voyage of Commodore John Byron

*Above.* Mission San Francisco de Asís, today better known by its popular name Mission Dolores, was founded in San Francisco on 9 October 1776. Its second name derived from a nearby lake, the *Laguna de los Dolores* (Lake of the Sorrows), now drained. The mission just escaped the 1906 fire following the great earthquake of that year and has now been restored and is still active.

MAP 78 (*below*).
The first separate map of San Francisco Bay, drawn by Father Juan Crespi in 1772. Crespi had been with the expedition of Gaspar de Portolá in 1769 (see next page) when the bay was discovered. This map, of which there are several versions, was drawn for his diary of the expedition of Pedro Fages to the East Bay in 1772, when the rivers entering the bay from the northeast had been found and the Golden Gate—*La Boca*—seen. Although a little strangely portrayed and not to scale—it was a sketch map, not a survey—most of the major features of the bay are depicted.

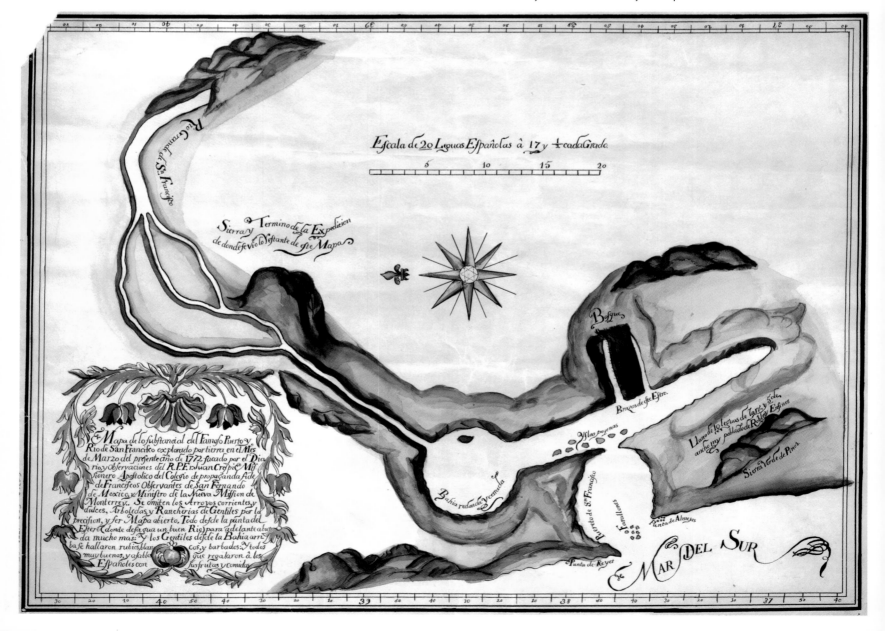

(grandfather of the poet) filtered through to the authorities in Spain. In HMS *Dolphin,* Byron had been dispatched to the Pacific by the British government in 1764, instructed to search the coast north of 38°N, Drake's supposed landing place, to find the Strait of Anian. In 1765 Byron had taken possession of the Falkland Islands, which the Spanish considered their own, but once in the Pacific Byron had disregarded his instructions and not sailed north at all. But his voyage added to Spanish disquiet. Not only did the Spanish have the British to worry about, but also Vitus Bering and Aleksei Chirikov had discovered the Northwest Coast for Russia in 1741, sailing from Kamchatka. Now there were disturbing stories that Russian fur traders were moving south toward California. These accounts were untrue, but at the time nobody knew for sure.

A new king of Spain, Carlos III, decided in 1767 to expel the Jesuits from the Spanish dominions in retaliation for supposed political intrigues at a high level. In so doing he was following what many other European countries were doing. In New Spain and Baja the job fell to *Visitador* (inspector general) José de Gálvez, who had been sent to New Spain in 1765. Gálvez recruited a veteran army commander, Gaspar de Portolá, to carry out the expulsion of the Jesuits from Baja and enlisted a replacement religious order, the Franciscans, led by Father Junípero Serra, to take over the missions. Despite Portolá's best efforts, the expulsion was still accompanied by the execution of hundreds of Indians loyal to their Jesuit guardians.

With the Jesuits shipped out, Gálvez, Portolá, and Serra together with the viceroy, Carlos Francisco de Croix, were already planning to establish missions to the north of Baja, and in January 1768 their plans were confirmed by a royal order to expand the Spanish frontier to the north, occupy Monterey Bay, and begin colonizing Alta California as a bulwark against the supposed foreign incursions.

To ensure success, Gálvez decided to send men by land and by sea. Cognizant of the significance of their effort the campaign was named the Sacred Expedition. Two land parties marched north from Baja in 1769. The plan was to rendezvous with three ships in the bay Vizcaíno had named San Diego. The ascetic Serra

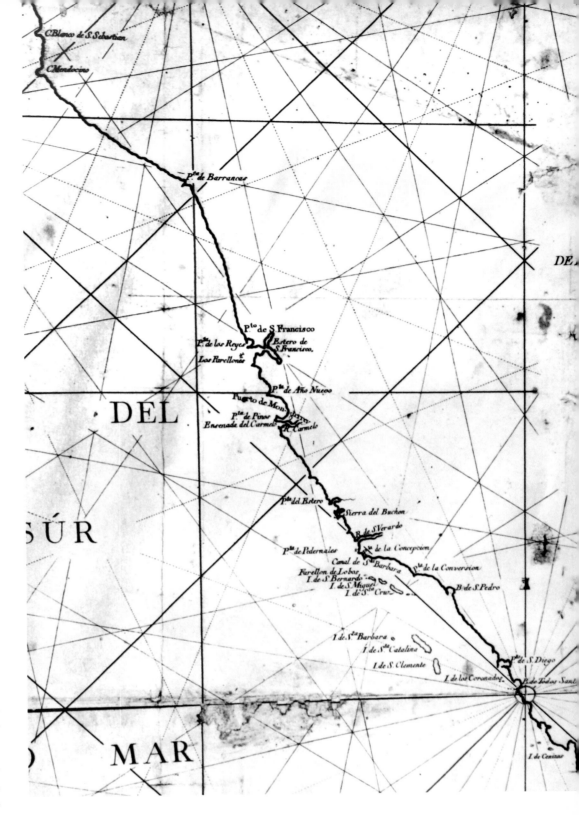

MAP 79.

With the 1769 Portolá expedition was Miguel Costansó, an army engineer. He was with the group of soldiers who first found San Francisco Bay that year. The original manuscript map, dated 30 October 1770, was part of Costansó's diary. It was, unusually for the Spanish authorities, allowed to be printed, engraved by royal geographer Tomás López in Madrid in 1771. It still bears the 1770 date but has an important update—the *Estero* [bay] *de S. Francisco.* It is unclear why the feature was not on the manuscript map, given its obvious significance, but it is likely because the entrance to the bay had not yet been found, and would not until Juan de Ayala sailed into the bay in 1775. The position of the entrance on Costansó's map is but a guess. This map, then, is the first map to show San Francisco Bay, but only part is from observation. *Puerto de Mon-terrey* is indicated, site of the presidio and mission founded in June 1770. At bottom right is $P^{to}$. *de S. Diego.* The map was not widely available outside Spain despite being printed; few copies were made, and the map is today quite rare. In 1790 the British geographer Alexander Dalrymple obtained the map and copied it, publishing his *Chart of California by Miguel Costansó.* By that time other maps of the coast had been produced, and the existence of San Francisco Bay had been known to the world for some time.

insisted on walking; most rode horses, but the expedition quickly ran into problems. By the time they all met at San Diego at the beginning of July 1769, one ship had vanished, and on the other two ships most of the sailors were ill with scurvy. Half of the men of the expedition had died.

Portolá, however, proved to be a resourceful leader. He sent one ship back for supplies and more men while he marched north with the fittest men he could muster. Serra stayed in San Diego to found, on 16 July 1769, the first of the Alta California missions, San Diego de Alcalá. Another Franciscan, Juan Crespi, went north with Portolá.

At the beginning of October Portolá reached Monterey Bay but was unsure if he had reached the right place because what he saw hardly matched Vizcaíno's description (see page 20). He therefore searched farther north, thinking he might find the real Monterey Bay, or failing that, Cermeño's Bahia de San Francisco. On 1 November an advance party led by Sergeant José Ortega came to the crest of a hill and saw before them a large expanse of water. It would later be given—and would take over—the name of Cermeño's bay. The new bay would prove to be far more useful to the Spanish than Monterey Bay ever could have been.

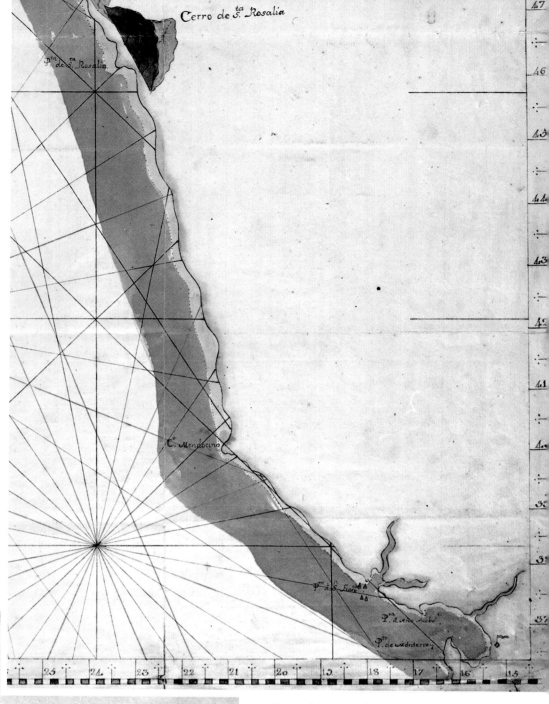

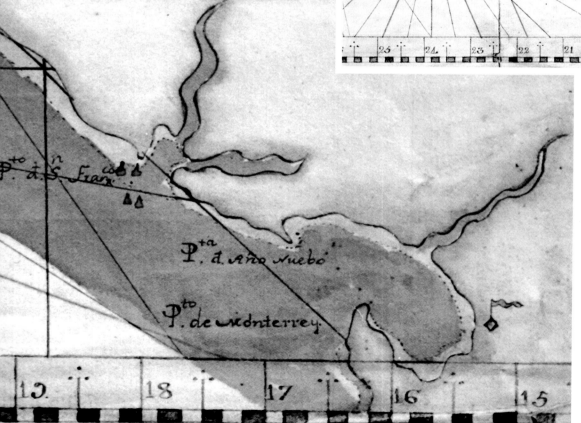

Map 80 (*above, and enlarged detail left*). On this map, San Francisco Bay is not so well drawn as on Costansó's or Crespi's maps on the previous pages, and Monterey Bay is drawn to be more as it was imagined to be before 1769, due to Vizcaíno's 1602 description—a harbor snug from the winds of the Pacific. The position of the presidio established at Monterey is shown by the little flag. Despite its relative crudity, this is an important map in that it is the first to show the West Coast north of Cape Mendocino from exploration. The map was only discovered about twenty years ago, and in a most unlikely place: the U.S. National Archives. No one knows how it got to be in that august repository, but it may have been acquired for boundary negotiations around 1846. The map is the only cartographic record of the voyage of Juan Pérez in 1774; he sailed as far north as the Queen Charlotte Islands. The map was drawn by Pérez's pilot, José de Cañizares.

After returning to San Diego, Portolá realized that the bay he had reached in October was indeed Monterey Bay, and because he had a royal order to occupy it, he returned there and established a settlement in June 1770. A mission was founded there, and this became Serra's headquarters for the string of California missions he and other Franciscans would establish in the years to come.

In 1772 Lieutenant Pedro Fages explored from Monterey north along the eastern shore of San Francisco Bay. Finally the entrance to the bay was found—by looking outward. The Sacramento and the San Joaquin rivers were discovered, and Fages explored far enough east for him to realize the existence of the Central Valley. With Fages was Father Juan Crespi, who drew the first separate map of the bay (MAP 78, *page 36*); it was also the first map of the complete bay drawn from observation.

The Spanish efforts to investigate farther north came to fruition in 1774 when a new viceroy, Antonio María de Bucareli y Ursua, dispatched a single ship, the *Santiago,* under an experienced captain, Juan Pérez. He reached the northern tip of the Queen Charlotte Islands, thus vastly expanding Spain's knowledge of the coast. His pilot, José de Cañizares, drew MAP 80 (*left*), which was the first map to depict the entire northern Californian coast from exploration.

In 1773 Juan Bautista de Anza, a veteran soldier posted at Tubac, one of the northernmost presidios of New Spain, was ordered to establish a more extensive military presence for Spain in California. Anza, sometimes called "the last conquistador" for his role, left Tubac in January 1774 and marched north with thirty men to confirm that there was a viable land link between Mexico and California, a project that he had originally suggested. With Anza was Father Francisco Garcés, already an experienced explorer of the Southwest and destined to explore further in the interior of California. Despite Garcés's experience, Anza and his men became lost in the desert, and it was two months before they struggled in to San Gabriel Mission, which had been founded three years earlier where Los Angeles now stands. Anza later headed north as far as Monterey before returning to Tubac.

Anza's success was encouraging to viceroy Bucareli, who planned a more extensive expedition the following year. In addition, Pérez's voyage had convinced Bucareli that another voyage far to the north might be productive despite the fact that Pérez had found no encroaching Russians. The effect of the Russian bogeyman on the minds of the Spanish authorities at this time should not be underestimated. Gálvez, back in Spain, was in 1775 made minister of Indies, and thus took over control of Spain's efforts to colonize its frontiers; he had at one point earlier gone temporarily insane and reported seeing Russians himself.

A maritime expedition was organized with—initially—three ships, the *Santiago,* now to be commanded by Bruno Hezeta, not Pérez, the thirty-foot-long *Sonora,* and the *San Carlos.* Due to the insanity of the commander of the *San Carlos* soon after sailing, Lieutenant Juan de Ayala from the *Sonora* took over command of the *San Carlos,* and his original second-in-command, Juan Francisco de la Bodega y Quadra, took over the diminutive *Sonora.* While the *San Carlos* was to take supplies to Monterey, the *Santiago* and the *Sonora* were to sail

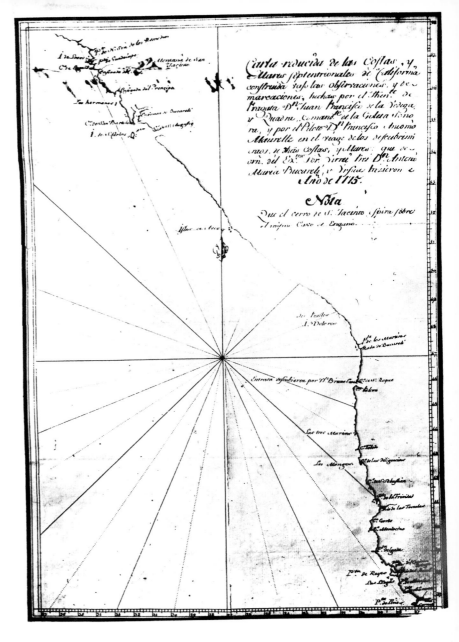

MAP 81 (*above*).
The West Coast is better defined in California and in Alaska than it is in between in this map drawn by Juan Francisco de la Bodega y Quadra of his epic voyage north in the thirty-foot-long *Sonora* in 1775. This resulted from the necessity of sailing offshore in order to make any progress northward. The entire West Coast would be better defined three years hence, when Britain's James Cook sailed in these waters on his third voyage, sent to find—or disprove the existence of—a Northwest Passage.

north to search for Russians and a Northwest Passage. Hezeta became the first to explore much of the coast of Washington and Oregon, while Bodega y Quadra distinguished himself by sailing far up into the Gulf of Alaska in appalling weather. Bodega y Quadra's map is shown here (MAP 81, *above*), and Pedro Font's map (MAP 88, *page 43*) also depicts the *Sonora* off the coast of San Francisco.

Ayala, meanwhile, anchored in Monterey Bay and sent a smaller boat under the command of his pilot, José de Cañizares, north along the coast specifically to find the entrance to San Francisco Bay, which was now, thanks to the Fages expedition, known to exist. Cañizares found the entrance and on 5 August 1775 became the first to sail through the Golden Gate. The following day the *San Carlos* also sailed into the bay.

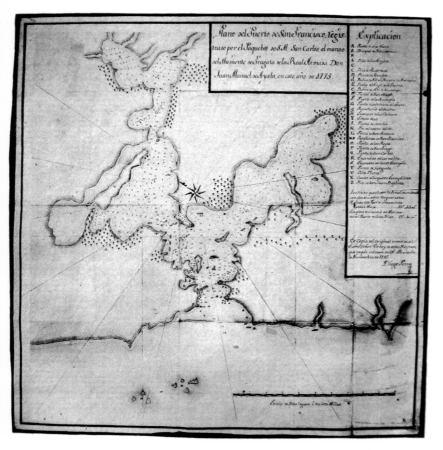

A survey of the bay was made using the longboat (Map 82, *left*), and the following year Ayala returned with Cañizares, his pilot, who did the actual surveying, to carry out a more extensive charting of this extensive and valuable bay (Map 83, *below*).

Also in 1776, Anza returned to Alta California. With him was the Franciscan Pedro Font, who kept a detailed diary and drew a number of maps of the expedition (see page 43). Also with Anza initially was Francisco Garcés, but he left the expedition at the Colorado River and struck out on his own to find souls to convert. He made an extensive traverse of southern California, reached the San Joaquin Valley, and then went back to the Colorado, ascending it to the Grand Canyon (Map 87, *page 42,* and Map 98, *page 46*).

Anza had with him 240 people, including, significantly, settlers, and 29 women. There were at the beginning of the trek 695 horses and mules and 355 head of cattle, the numbers of which diminished due to deaths, loss, and trade as the expedition proceeded. This time Anza continued north to Monterey and then to San Francisco, where he arrived on 27 March 1776 (Map 86, *page 42*). Here he found "favorable conditions for establishing the presidio contemplated" and selected a

**Map 82** (*above*).
This is Juan de Ayala's original map of San Francisco Bay, drawn in 1775. It was surveyed and drawn by José de Cañizares, Ayala's pilot. All the other maps of the bay shown here were the result of another, more detailed survey carried out the following year.

**Map 83** (*right*).
This was the map of San Francisco Bay that resulted from Ayala and Cañizares's second survey, carried out in 1776. Now the mission and presidio (though their positions have been erroneously switched) are shown at *V* and *X*; they were established in 1776.

*Q* are *Bosques de buenas maderas* (groves of good timber, always a significant feature for maritime nations in the days of wooden ships). *G* is San Rafael Bay and the northern part of San Francisco Bay itself; *H* is San Pablo Bay; *J* is Southampton Bay, Benicia; *K* is Suisun Bay, with Grizzly Bay unmarked as the next bay toward the top of the map. *N* is *gran Río sin acabar de descubrir su fin*, a large river with no end in sight, likely the Sacramento or if not, the combined channel of that river and the San Joaquin. *O* are places where the survey crew met friendly Indians and traded with them. *L* are low islands in fresh water. *B* is Point Reyes and *A* Bodega Head; *f* is *Ysla de Santa María de los Angeles*—today Angel Island.

This version of Cañizares's map was engraved and printed in Mexico City in 1781 and intended for publication in a book that seems to have been suppressed by the Spanish authorities, as no book containing this map was ever published. This kind of censorship was not unusual at the time, as Spain was still trying, not very successfully, to keep news of its discoveries from other European powers, especially Britain.

Z Punta del Angel de la Guarda.
a Punta de año nuebo.
b Rio de la Salud.
c Punta de Almejas.
d Tarallones de S. Frãcisco.
e Quantioso Canal a la entrada entrada del Puerto 58 brazas.
f Ysla de Santa Maria de los Angeles.
g Ysla de Alcatrazes.

A Punta Recalada
B Punta de Reyes.
C Puta de Santiago.
D Punta de San Carlos.
E Ensenada del Camelita.
F Ensenada del S.to Evangelio
G Bahia de N.S.ª del Rosario la Marinera.
H Gran Bahia Redonda ò de N.S.ª de Guadalupe.
Y Estero.
J Puerto de la Asunta.
K Punta de los Evangelistas.
L Yslas Razas entre agua dulse
M Agua dulse entre tulares.
N gran Rio sin acabar de descubrir su fin.
O Rancherias de Indios Amigos Comerciantes en Tabaco, y Pescado.
P. unta de San Antonio.
Q. Bosques de buenas Maderas
R. emate del Estero y fin reconocido de Agua Salada à Cañizares.
S Punta de Concha.
T Entrada del Estero.
V Nueva Mision de S. Fran.co fudada en 4 de Oct.e d.1776
X R.l Presidio establecido en 17 de Sep.re de 1776.
1 Punta de San Jose ò Cantil Blanco.

**PLAN DEL GRAN PUERTO DE SAN** Francisco descubierto, y demarcado por el Alferez graduado de Fragata de la Real Armada, D.n Jose de Cañizares primer Piloto del Departamento de San Blas, Situado en la Costa Occidental de la California al Norte de la Linea, en el Mar Asiatico en Latitud Norte 37g. 44. minutos, y gravido por Manuel Villavicencio Añ. de 1781.

Escala de nueve leguas Francesas.
1 2 3 4 5 6 7 8 9

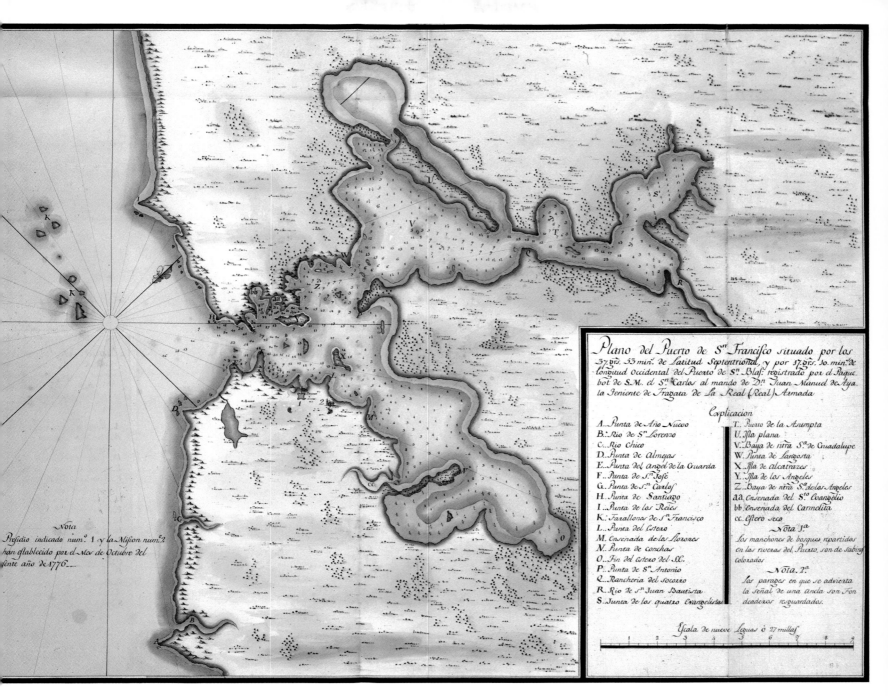

*Plano del Puerto de Sⁿ Francisco situado por los 37 grs. 53 min. de Latitud Septentrional, y por 17 grs. 10 min. de longitud occidental del Puerto de Sⁿ Blas: rejistrado por el Paquebot de S.M. el Sⁿ Carlos al mando de Dⁿ Juan Manuel de Aya la Teniente de Fragata de La Real (Real) Armada*

**Explicacion**

A.. Punta de Año Nuevo
B.. Rio de Sⁿ Lorenzo
C.. Rio Chico
D.. Punta de Almejas
E.. Punta del Angel de la Guarda
F.. Punta de Sⁿ José
G.. Punta de Sⁿ Carlos
H.. Punta de Santiago
I.. Punta de los Reies
K.. Farallones de Sⁿ Francisco
L.. Punta del Estero
M.. Ensenada de los Llorones
N.. Punta de conchas
O.. Fin del Estero del S.C.
P.. Punta de Sⁿ Antonio
Q.. Rancheria del socorro
R.. Rio de Sⁿ Juan Bautista
S.. Junta de los quatro Evangelistas

T.. Puerto de la Asumpta
U.. Isla plana
V.. Baya de nrᵃ Srᵃ de Guadalupe
W.. Punta de Langosta
X.. Isla de alcatrazes
Y.. Isla de los Angeles
Z.. Baya de nrᵃ Srᵃ de los Angeles
aa.. Ensenada del Sⁿ Evangelio
bb.. Ensenada del Carmelita
cc.. Estero seco

*Nota 1ª*
Los manchones de bosques repartidos en las riveras del Puerto, son de Sabino colorados

*Nota 2ª*
los parages en que se advierta la señal de una ancla son Fondeaderos resguardados.

*Escala de nueve Leguas ó 27 millas*

*Nota*
Presidio indicado num. 1 y la Mision num 2 han establecido por el Mes de Octubre del sente año de 1776.

---

site overlooking the Golden Gate, now the square in front of the National Park Service visitor center, as the site for the presidio, or fort. Anza also determined the site for the mission, on a stream a little to the south.

Anza soon went back to New Spain, leaving Lieutenant José Moraga in charge of the settlers. Moraga formally established the presidio on 17 September 1779, and the mission was opened on 9 October by Serra's deputy, Francisco Palóu.

Map 84 (*above*).
A presentation version of the 1775 map made by José de Cañizares of San Francisco, drawn the following year. The presidio (*1*) and Mission San Francisco de Asís (Mission Dolores) have been added, correctly, unlike the 1781 engraving of the 1776 resurvey (Map 83, *left, bottom*). Mare Island is shown as an island, and the shape of Grizzly Bay is closer to reality than in the resurvey, but Southampton Bay is shown too large. The Napa-Sonoma marshes are shown as a large circular bay.

Map 85 (*right*).
This map is the result of a reexamination of the seaward part of San Francisco Bay by Josef Camacho, pilot of the Alaska expedition of Ignacio de Arteaga, carried out on the way back to New Spain in 1779. The presidio and mission are shown, as is the *Laguna de los Dolores*, the Lake of Sorrows, from which the stream of the same name flowed to the bay; the remnant of this today is the Mission Creek Marina. The stream quickly gave the Mission San Francisco de Asís its popular name of Mission Dolores.

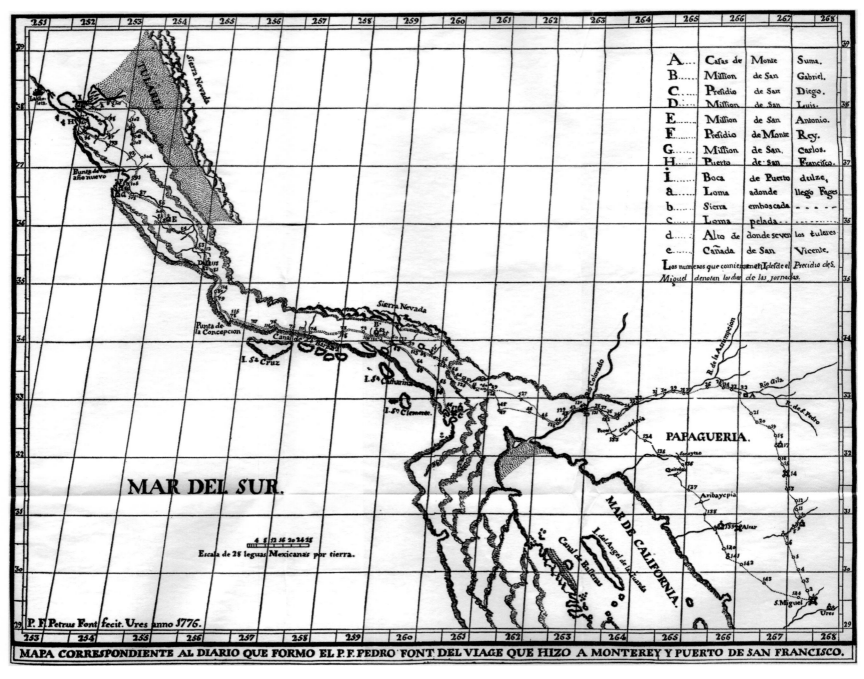

A ...... Casas de Monte Suma.
B ...... Mission de San Gabriel.
C ...... Presidio de San Diego.
D ...... Mission de San Luis.
E ...... Mission de San Antonio.
F ...... Presidio de Monte Rey.
G ...... Mission de San Carlos.
H ...... Puerto de San Francisco.
I ...... Boca de Puerto dulze.
a ...... Loma adonde llego Fages.
b ...... Sierra emboscada - - - - -
c ...... Loma pelada - - - -
d ...... Alto de donde seven los tulares.
e ...... Cañada de San Vicente.

Los numeros que comienzan en Iglesde el Presidio de S. Miguel denotan los dias de las jornadas.

Sierra Nevada

TULARE

Sierra Nevada

Punta de año nuevo

Punta de la Concepcion

Canal de Sta. Barbara

I. Sa Cruz

I. Sa Catharina

I. So Clemente.

R. de la Assumpcion

Rio Gila

Rio de S. Pedro

Rio Colorado

PAPAGUERIA.

Aribaypia

Altar

MAR DEL SUR.

Escala de 25 leguas Mexicanas por tierra.

MAR DE CALIFORNIA.

I. del Angel de la Guarda

Canal de Ballenas

S. Miguel

Ures

P. F. Petrus Font fecit. Ures anno 1776.

MAPA CORRESPONDIENTE AL DIARIO QUE FORMO EL P. F. PEDRO FONT DEL VIAGE QUE HIZO A MONTEREY Y PUERTO DE SAN FRANCISCO.

Baguioba

Yutas

Nuevo Mexico

Pajuche Colorado

Mochi

R. S. Felipe

Nochi

Zuñi

Tzobaji

Tanaya

Yabipai

Punta de la Concepcion

Canal de Sta Barbara

I. de Sta. Cruz

Apacheria

MAR DEL SUR

I. de Sta. Catalina

I. de So Clemente

Tegua

Coco

Pinto Gila Rio. Gila

Maricopa

Yumas Cajuenches Cucapa

Papagueria

Pimeriaalta

Carta Geographica de la Costa y parte de la Peninsula de la California Naciones que comprehende hasta el nuevo Mexico, y viage q' hizieron Fr. Fran.co Garces y Fr. Pedro Font al Rio Colorado S. Gabriel y Moqui el Año de 1777.

Manuel Villavic. lo A. 1781.

MAP 86 (above).

Juan Bautista de Anza's march to Monterey and San Francisco in 1775–76 is shown on this map from the diary of Pedro Font, a Franciscan who accompanied him. The presidio at Tubac, where the expedition assembled, is at *14*, otherwise unnamed. San Miguel, from which Font's march began, was a villa and presidio farther south. This map appears to be the first to name and place the *Sierra Nevada* in the position of the mountain range of today.

MAP 87 (left).

This rare map shows the route of the Franciscan Francisco Garcés in 1776. Garcés was with Anza on both his expeditions into California, but on the second, in 1776, he left the main party in February to search the interior for Indians to convert. He reached the San Joaquin Valley, then turned east to the Colorado River, becoming the first European to see the Grand Canyon since the Coronado expedition in 1540. Pedro Font, referred to in the cartouche, was also with Anza but continued with him north to San Francisco Bay. The map was engraved in 1781.

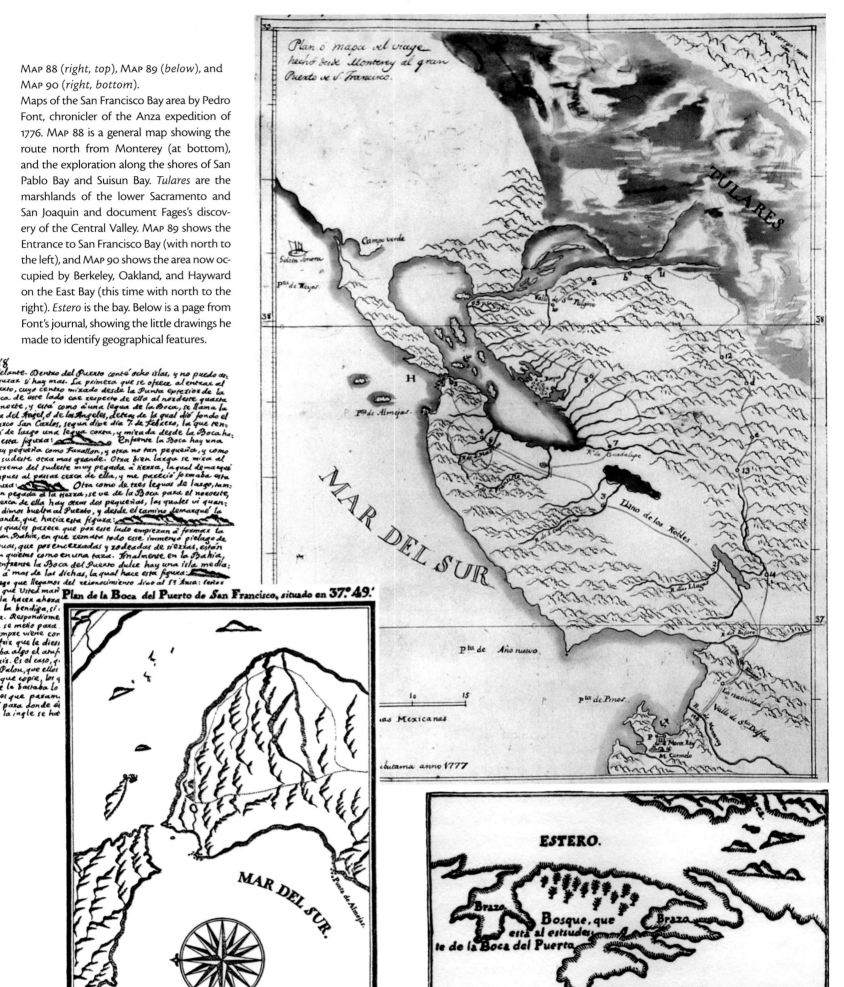

Map 88 (*right, top*), Map 89 (*below*), and Map 90 (*right, bottom*).

Maps of the San Francisco Bay area by Pedro Font, chronicler of the Anza expedition of 1776. Map 88 is a general map showing the route north from Monterey (at bottom), and the exploration along the shores of San Pablo Bay and Suisun Bay. *Tulares* are the marshlands of the lower Sacramento and San Joaquin and document Fages's discovery of the Central Valley. Map 89 shows the Entrance to San Francisco Bay (with north to the left), and Map 90 shows the area now occupied by Berkeley, Oakland, and Hayward on the East Bay (this time with north to the right). *Estero* is the bay. Below is a page from Font's journal, showing the little drawings he made to identify geographical features.

# MISSION DOLORES

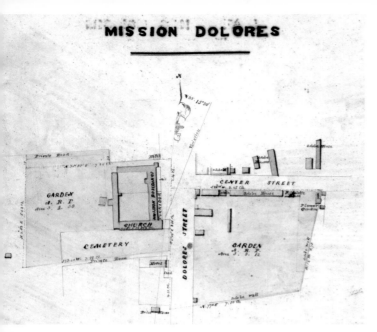

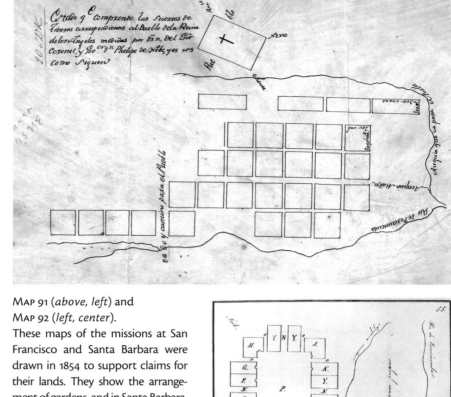

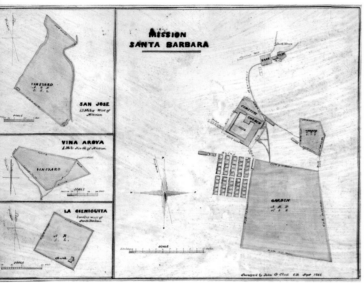

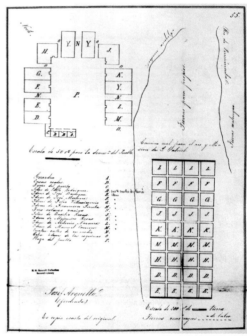

MAP 91 (*above, left*) and
MAP 92 (*left, center*).
These maps of the missions at San Francisco and Santa Barbara were drawn in 1854 to support claims for their lands. They show the arrangement of gardens, and in Santa Barbara, the Indian housing (then in ruins) and the irrigation systems with two storage tanks (shown in blue). There were ultimately eighteen Franciscan missions established in California.

MAP 94 (*above, right*) and
MAP 95 (*right*).
Two maps of the 1781 pueblo at Los Angeles. MAP 94 shows the central plaza and the farmlands but not the house lots. MAP 95, which is two maps on one sheet, shows the plaza on a scale about ten times larger than the agricultural lands; ownership is shown on both. The house lots are also mapped. Both maps show the river and irrigation ditches, plus the location of the *camino real*, the main road that ran from the pueblo to the mission at San Gabriel.

MAP 93 (*below*).
The pueblo of San José and its surrounding pueblo lands, here termed public lands. The map is from an 1847 land claim filed by the pueblo following the American annexation of California.

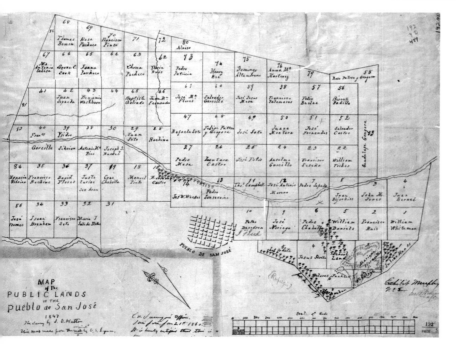

The Spanish had a long time ago developed a system for the colonization of its frontier lands, which was brought into play in California. Missions were to be established to convert the native peoples—forcibly if necessary—into Christian laborers, tending the fields and learning crafts. Eventually, in theory at least, they were to be free colonists but this was not really achieved in practice, and the mission system has come under heavy fire for its poor treatment of the Indians, culminating in a movement to prevent Junípero Serra from being declared a Catholic saint. Nonetheless, despite the system's faults and despite many abuses, the intention seems to have been honorable. During Spanish tenure in California, eighteen missions were built and at their peak they controlled about 20,000 Indians.

The second part of the colonization system was the presidio, a fort intended to provide a refuge and stronghold from which the will of Spain could be enforced. California had four such presidios: San Diego, San Francisco, Monterey, and Santa Barbara.

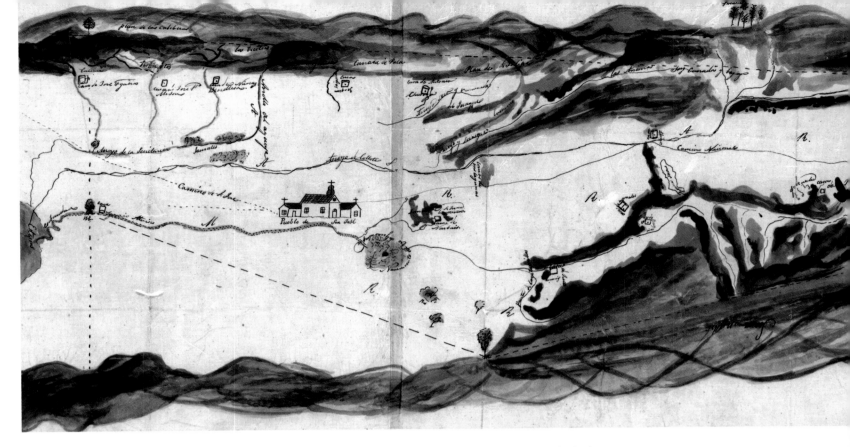

The presidios were supposed to be self-sufficient, though they never were in practice. To supply them with food, civil townships were to be established, populated with farmers and surrounded by their fields. Only two were created in California. In 1777 a new military governor, Felipe de Neve, collected fourteen families from the Monterey and San Francisco presidios and settled them at the southern end of San Francisco Bay at a place they named *San José de Guadalupe.* This was the first pueblo, today the city of San José. In 1781 a similar pueblo was created about nine miles southwest of the San Gabriel Mission, and twelve poor families from Sinaloa settled there. The pueblo was named *El Pueblo de Nuestra Señora la Reyna (or Reina) de los Angeles del Río de Porciúncula,* soon shortened, first to Angeles, then to Los Angeles. Another pueblo, the *Villa de Branciforte,* was founded in 1797 at Santa Cruz. Intended as a sort of retirement residence for soldiers, the pueblo never materialized because no soldier wanted to stay in California any longer than he had to.

In 1780 two unusual missions that incorporated features of the presidio and the pueblo were established on the California bank of the Colorado River near today's Yuma. Unfortunately for the Spanish, the Yuma Indians were able to retaliate for any mistreatment, and in 1781 both missions were destroyed, and a military detachment passing through was annihilated. With the soldiers, and also killed, was the great explorer Francisco Garcés. This incident, called the Yuma Massacre, was the worst disaster to befall the Spanish in all the years they occupied California. It effectively closed the overland route that Anza had blazed from New Spain to California, which could now only be supplied by sea. The difficulty ushered in a period of neglect, but Spanish power was on the wane from the closing years of the eighteenth century in any case. First Spain and then Mexico would neglect Upper California to the extent that both would ultimately lose it to a country not even in existence when colonization began in 1769—the United States.

MAP 96 (*above*) and MAP 97 (*below*).
These two crude land claim maps (*diseños*) with a folk art charm date from the 1840s and show the pueblo and mission at San José. On MAP 96 San Francisco Bay is at left, and on MAP 97 it is at bottom. MAP 96 shows the road south, here labeled the *Camino Nationale.*

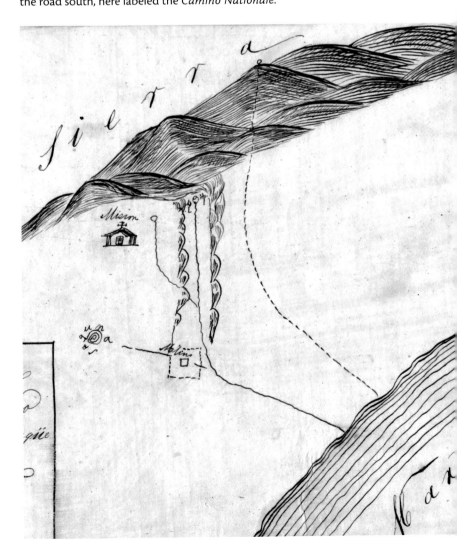

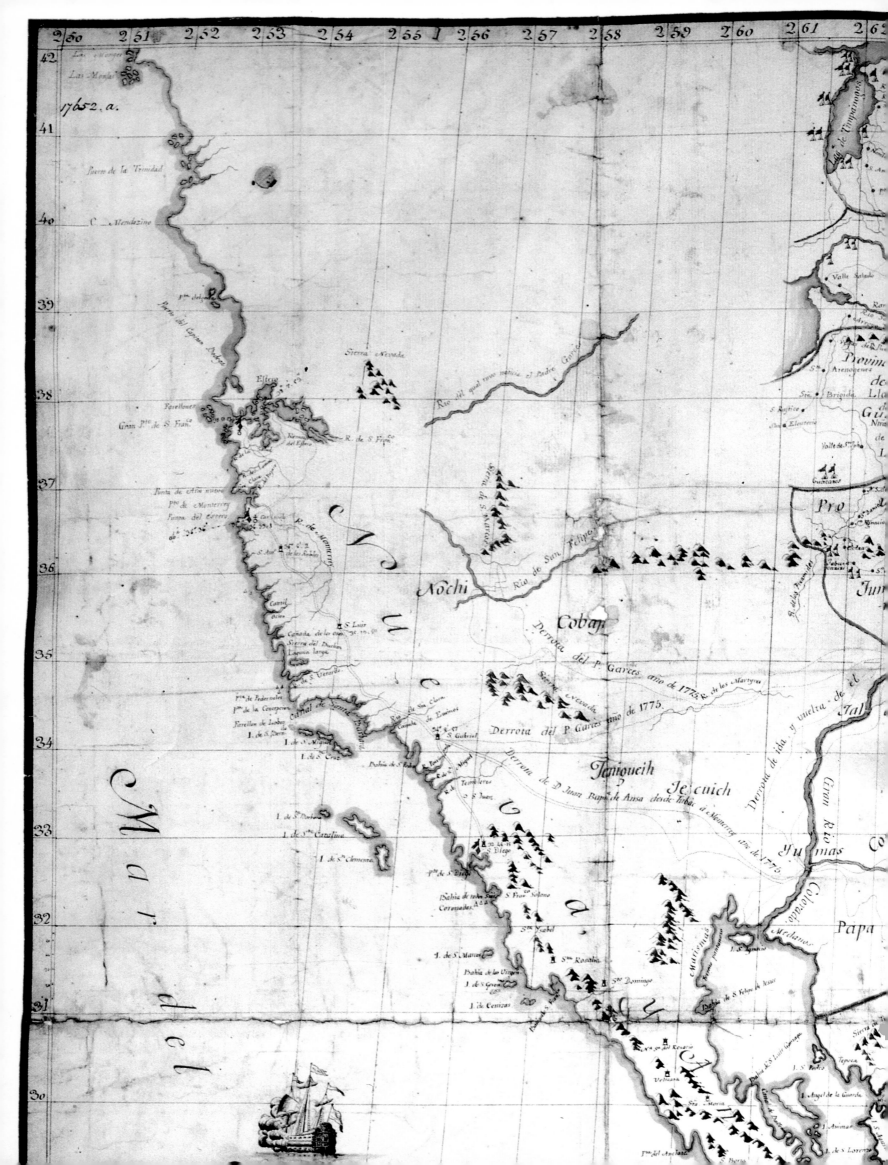

MAP 98 (left).

This superb summary map of the West was drawn in 1782 by Manuel Agustin Mascaro. The routes of Juan Bautista de Anza are shown, together with those of Father Francisco Garcés, whose 1775 wanderings in search of Indian converts to his faith led him to crisscross the Southwest. San Francisco Bay is well drawn, and much of the detail of the coast is correct. The missions established by 1782 are shown in both Alta (*Nueva*) and Baja (*Antigua*) California. Little detail was available to Mascaro regarding the regions north of San Francisco, which were at the time ignored by the Spanish. The idea that a river must flow to the Pacific from the large lake found in 1776 by the Franciscan Silvestre Véléz de Escalante (who saw Utah Lake and heard of the Great Salt Lake from the Indians and combined them on his maps) is indicated by the northernmost river shown, with no beginning or end. The other such river is the *Río de San Felipe*, the San Joaquin, found by Garcés in his travels in May 1776.

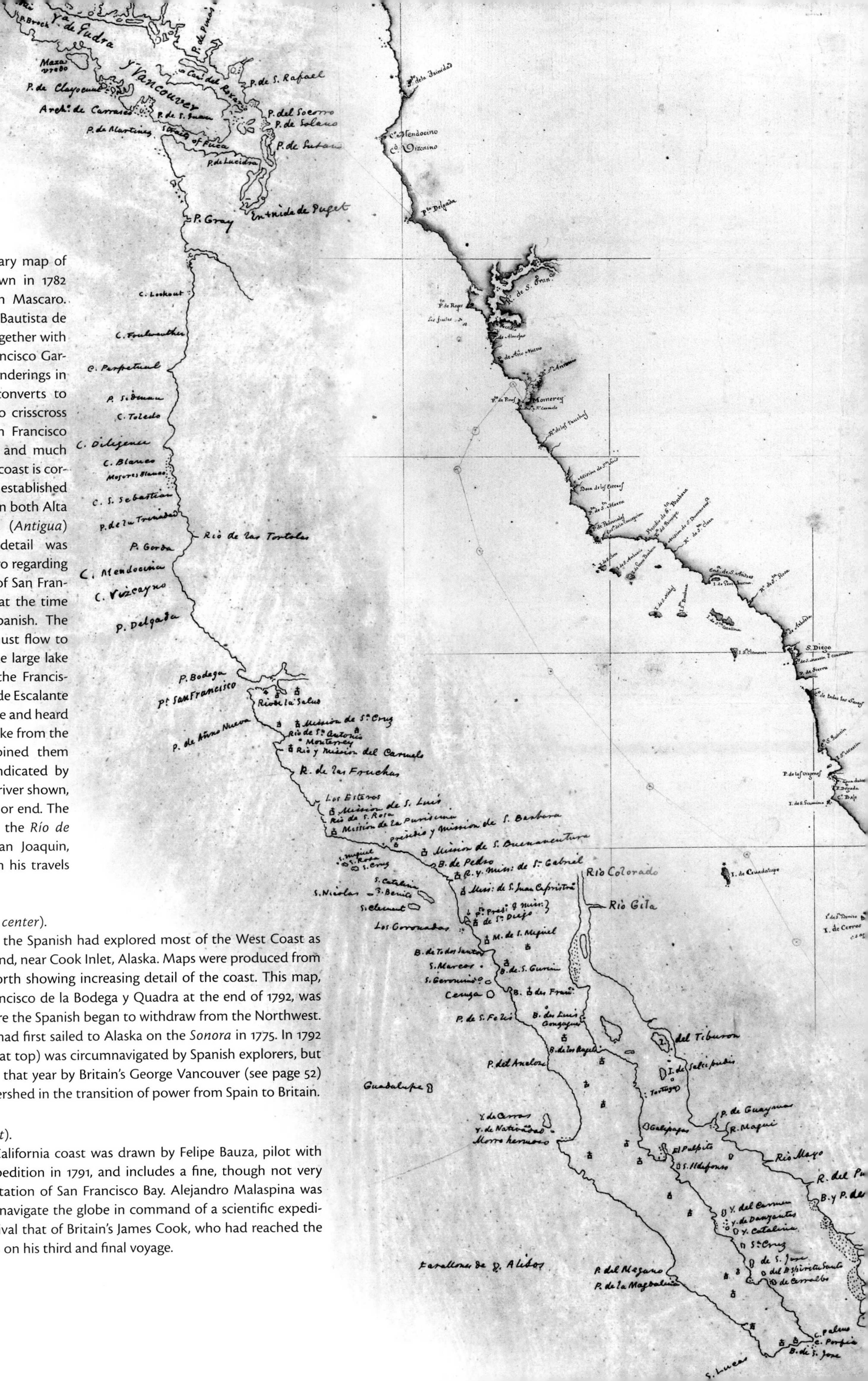

MAP 99 (this page, center).

By the end of 1792 the Spanish had explored most of the West Coast as far as Unalaska Island, near Cook Inlet, Alaska. Maps were produced from various voyages north showing increasing detail of the coast. This map, drawn by Juan Francisco de la Bodega y Quadra at the end of 1792, was the final map before the Spanish began to withdraw from the Northwest. Bodega y Quadra had first sailed to Alaska on the *Sonora* in 1775. In 1792 Vancouver Island (at top) was circumnavigated by Spanish explorers, but this was also done that year by Britain's George Vancouver (see page 52) and marked a watershed in the transition of power from Spain to Britain.

MAP 100 (top, right).

This map of the California coast was drawn by Felipe Bauza, pilot with the Malaspina expedition in 1791, and includes a fine, though not very accurate, representation of San Francisco Bay. Alejandro Malaspina was ordered to circumnavigate the globe in command of a scientific expedition designed to rival that of Britain's James Cook, who had reached the West Coast in 1778 on his third and final voyage.

Plano
del Puerto de S. Diego situado en la Lat.
N. de 32°. 40' Long. 12° al O. de S. Blas descubierto por Sebastian Vizcayno el
año de 1603

Varacion 8°. N.E.

MAP 101 (above).
This 1779 map of San Diego shows the position of the *Presidio* and the *Mision de S. Diego*. The latter was on the banks of the San Diego River about eight miles from its mouth. The bay with islands is Mission Bay. *P*<sup>ta</sup>*. de la Loma* (Point Loma) is shown, with another fortification at its tip.

MAP 102 (right).
The Spanish belatedly realized that their claim to sovereignty of the west coast of North America was being eroded by the explorations of other nations, especially Britain. George Vancouver's account of his 1792–94 survey of the Northwest Coast was published in 1798 and was the final straw for the Spanish. In 1802 Spain reversed its policy of secrecy and published the *Relación del Viage Hecho por Las Goletas Sutil y Mexicana*, ostensibly a record of a single voyage to the Northwest in 1792, but which contained the accounts and maps of Spanish explorers since Vizcaíno two centuries earlier. This map depicts Monterey Bay and shows *Mision de S. Carlos* near the bottom (in its final position); *Mision de S[an]ta Cruz* at top; and the *Presidio de Monte-Rey* at the southern end of the bay. MAP 104 (far right, top) is also from the *Relación*.

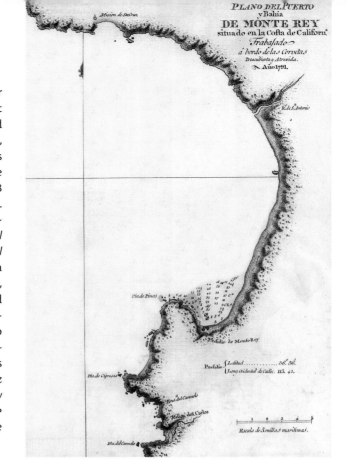

PLANO DEL PUERTO
y Bahía
DE MONTE REY
situado en la Costa de Californ.ᵃ
Trabajado
á bordo de las Corvetas,
Descubierta y Atrevida.
Año 1791.

**Map 103** (*left, bottom*).

This map published in 1787 in Mexico City seems to be the first to show a division of Baja and Alta California. The line, drawn just south of San Diego in approximately the position that the international boundary would occupy after 1848, was then a religious boundary, between the Dominicans in *Antigua California* (they had taken over the Baja missions from the Franciscans in 1772) and the Franciscans in *Nueva California*. The location of all missions is shown, including the two ill-fated ones on the Colorado. The map was published in Francisco Palóu's biography of his mentor Junípero Serra, which may be the reason its publication was permitted.

**Map 104** (*right, top*).

This map from the 1802 *Relación* can be viewed as the final Spanish map of the California coast. See also **Map 102** (*left*).

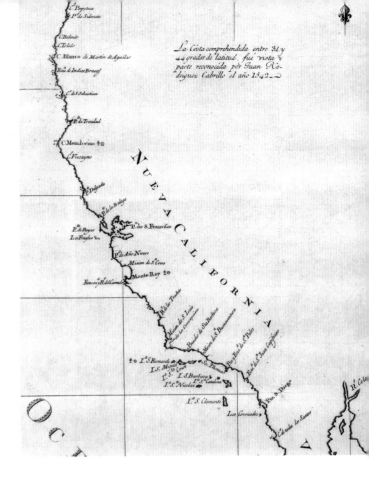

**Map 105** (*below*) and **Map 106** (*below, bottom*).

The American claim to the West Coast was for long indefinite, stemming from the 1803 purchase of Louisiana from the French. However, no one knew precisely what had been bought. **Map 105** shows an 1814 American map of Missouri Territory (which is what the rest of Louisiana was called after the creation of the much smaller state of Louisiana, shown at bottom right, in 1812) reaching the Pacific Ocean with boundaries at Puget Sound in the north and just north of *F S Francisco* (Fort San Francisco) to the south, carefully excluding *Port Francis Drake* from Spanish territory. A later edition of the same map (**Map 106**), also dated 1814 but likely actually published about 1819, has straightened the boundary line to reflect, in the north, an Anglo-American convention of 1818 (following the War of 1812), which agreed on a boundary of 49°N as far west as the Rocky Mountains, with the Oregon Country beyond a region of joint occupancy. In the south the boundary line reflects the 1819 Transcontinental Treaty between the United States and Spain, which established the northern boundary of Spanish territory at 42°N, a compromise between the American demand for 43° and the Spanish counter of 41°. It was this line that eventually became the northern boundary of the state of California.

**Map 107** (*right, bottom*).

The Transcontinental Treaty of 1819 defined the boundary between the United States and Spain in the West and in the process defined what would later become a number of state boundaries of the United States, including the California-Oregon boundary at 42°N. The United States was able to negotiate such a boundary, which was considerably in its favor, by threatening to go to war over Florida, which the treaty also recognized as American. Spain by this time had neither the resources nor the will to fight with the United States and was about to lose Mexico to revolution. The treaty was officially called the Treaty of Amity, Settlement, and Limits Between the United States of America and His Catholic Majesty, and is also known as the Adams-Onís Treaty after its principal negotiators, John Quincy Adams and the Spanish minister to the United States, Luís de Onís.

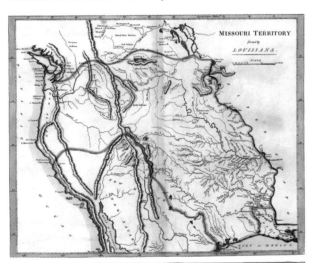

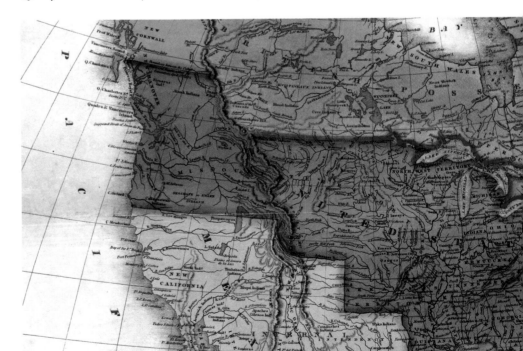

# COASTAL SURVEYS

Although the Spanish were the first to explore the coasts of California, it was not long before rival powers came looking. The first of these was of course England's Francis Drake in 1579, causing the Spanish for the first time but not the last to worry about their claims to the Northwest Coast. Drake was soon followed by Thomas Cavendish, but both were more interested in Spanish gold than Spanish claims to land.

The first to come calling into California waters arrived all but two hundred years after Drake. Britain's most famous navigator, James Cook, however, saw no more than a glimpse of California before he turned north in ferocious weather to seek a harbor, which he did not find until he reached Nootka Sound, on the west coast of Vancouver Island, after which he continued north to seek a Northwest Passage. Cook did, however, for the first time properly define

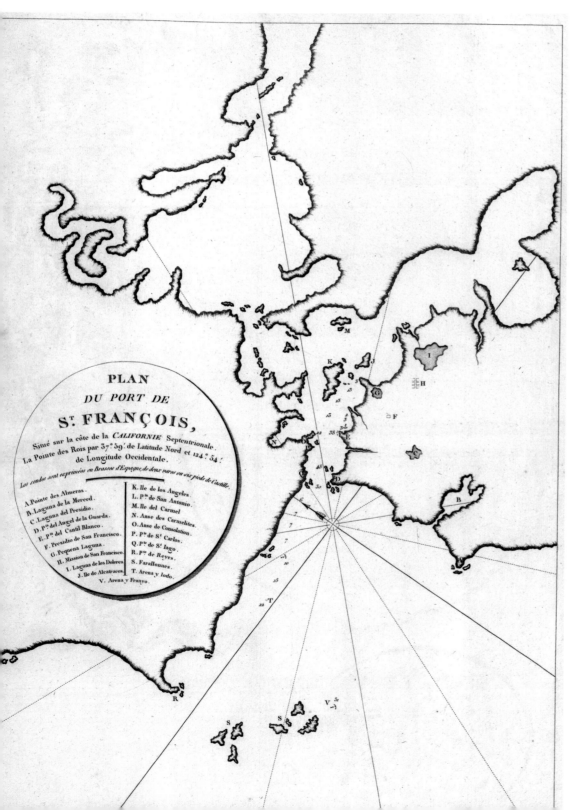

for the world (the Spanish having kept their calculations secret) *where* the west coast of North America as a whole *was*, since he was skilled in astronomical observation and carried with him some of the very first chronometers, allowing longitude for the first time to be calculated accurately and while at sea. No longer would the width of the continent be in doubt (see MAP 48, *page 26*).

It was a French rival to Cook who next arrived in California. Jean-François Galaup, Comte de La Pérouse, was dispatched by his government in 1785 to attempt a scientific circumnavigation in the same vein as Cook's to recoup some of the lost glory for his country. His busy schedule only allowed three months to survey the entire West Coast, but he made things easier by first going to Alaska and then following the coast south. In this way he avoided fighting the winds and currents that made sailing north so difficult.

La Pérouse was the first foreign visitor to inspect a Spanish mission in California when he visited the Mission San Carlos Borromeo in Carmel, leaving us a valuable first-hand record from a presumably unbiased source. La Pérouse was anything but impressed; he felt the church's treatment of the Indians closely resembled the slave plantations he had seen in the Caribbean.

**Map 108** (*left, top*).
James Cook charged one of his long-time officers, Henry Roberts, with the task of creating a new map of the world containing all of his new discoveries. Those of his third voyage included the first survey of the Alaska coast to a point north of the Bering Strait. This is the California portion of this map. Cook arrived on the coast just north of Cape Mendocino and thus did not add much new to the map. The entire California coast, however, south almost to San Diego is unequivocally labeled *New Albion*, Britain's claim to the hitherto Spanish domains.

**Map 109** (*left, bottom*).
French explorer La Pérouse's map of his *Port de St. François*—San Francisco—published in 1797, eleven years after his expedition had surveyed the bay.

**Map 110** (*right*).
This is the original manuscript map, now in French archives, of the La Pérouse visit to the West Coast in 1786. It was drawn by Joseph Dagelet and Gérault-Sébastien Bernizet, two of La Pérouse's officers, and shows the coast as far south as Monterey, together with the track of La Pérouse's ships into Monterey. The whole coast is labeled *Californie Septentrionale*—North California.

**Map 111** (*below*).
The published 1797 version of La Pérouse's map of Monterey, showing the presidio and the mission.

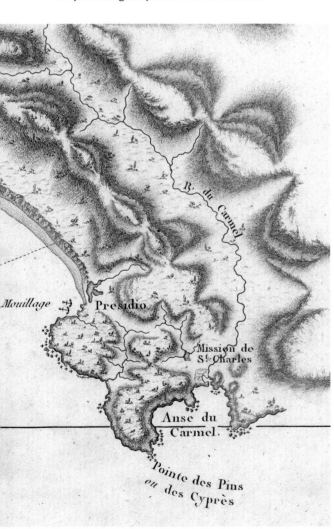

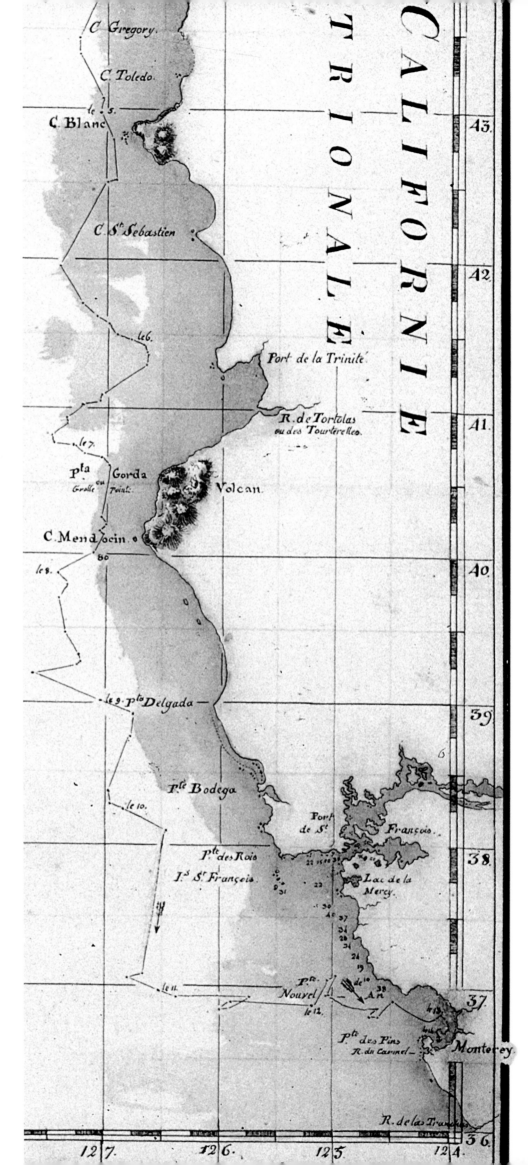

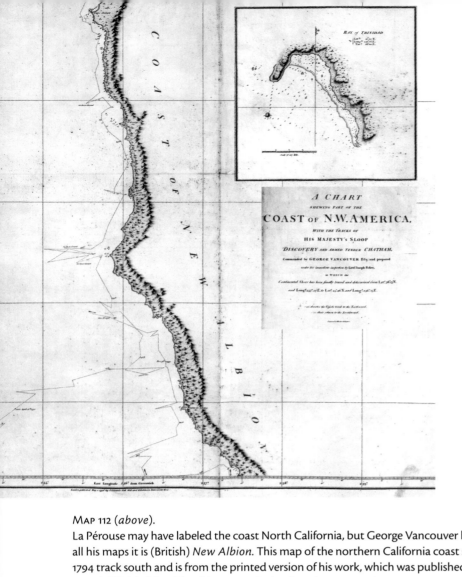

La Pérouse never made it round the world; he was wrecked on a South Pacific reef. His maps lived on, however, because he had taken the precaution of leaving them with the British authorities in Botany Bay, Australia. Because of the French Revolution, and the fact that La Pérouse was an aristocrat, his work was not published until 1797, by which time much of it was out of date.

By that time, Britain had sent George Vancouver to carry out his monumental survey of the Northwest Coast. Vancouver arrived in 1792, and spent the next three years surveying and mapping every detail of the coast as far north as Cook Inlet in Alaska, disproving once and for all the idea that a Northwest Passage might be lurking at the end of some northern inlet.

MAP 113 (*below*).
This is from a French edition of George Vancouver's atlas, published, unchanged, in 1828. It shows the Southern California coast from Point Arguello to San Diego.

MAP 114 (*below, bottom inset*).
Vancouver's map of San Diego Bay from the 1828 French edition. The presidio is marked but not named, and the mission is off the map.

MAP 115 (*below, upper inset*).
Vancouver's map of Monterey Bay, again from the 1828 French edition of his atlas.

MAP 112 (*above*).
La Pérouse may have labeled the coast North California, but George Vancouver had other ideas: on all his maps it is (British) *New Albion*. This map of the northern California coast shows Vancouver's 1794 track south and is from the printed version of his work, which was published in an atlas in 1798. Inset is Trinidad Bay. The title cartouche has here been moved.

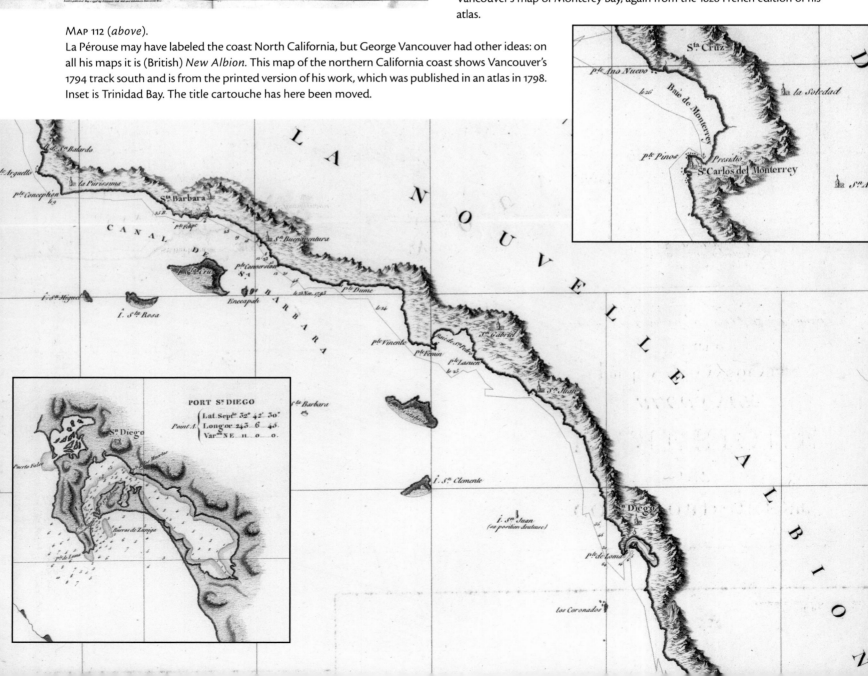

Vancouver finally visited California several times between 1792 and 1794, the latter while on his way back to Cape Horn and England, and was allowed to visit some of the missions and the presidios. Like La Pérouse, he penned some valuable observations about California life at the end of the eighteenth century. And he was even more scathing than his French predecessor. "If we except its natural pastures, the flocks of sheep, and herds of cattle, there is not an object [in California] to indicate the most remote connection with any European or other civilized nation," he wrote. This seems to have been the beginning of a long disdain for the value of the West Coast by Britain, which allowed the United States government to negotiate such an advantageous boundary in 1846 (the forty-ninth parallel except for Vancouver Island) and have Britain stand by and not interfere when the United States took over California so relatively easily in 1846–48. Britain was the premier world naval power at the time and could, with the motivation, easily have laid claim to much more of the coast.

Neither was Vancouver enamored of the mission system, but largely because he thought it not to be working very well. At the San Francisco mission, the Indians' "truly worthy and benevolent pastors," he wrote, "whose object has been to allure them from their life of indolence and raise them in a spirit of emulous industry," failed, according to Vancouver, because their Indian charges were "deaf to the important lessons and insensible of the promised advantages," and thus they "still remained in the most abject state of uncivilization."

Britain and Spain had come to an agreement—forced on Spain by a threat of war—that Spain would relinquish her exclusive claims to the coast farther north. This was the Nootka Convention, of which there were three, in 1790, 1793, and 1794. But the Northwest Coast was not viewed with much

MAP 116 (right, top).
George Vancouver's original manuscript chart of the coast of California, deposited with the hydrographer of the navy at the end of his voyage. The tracks of his voyage northward in 1792 are distinguished from those of his southward track in 1794, as he was returning home via Cape Horn following his three-season survey of the Northwest. The map was drawn by Lieutenant Joseph Baker, Vancouver's first officer. Again there is no doubt about the British claim; the *Coast of New Albion* is written to span the entire coast.

MAP 117 (right).
Vancouver's map of the entrance to San Francisco Bay. The Spanish presidio is shown, as are soundings through the Golden Gate. This is a French edition of the map, printed in 1828.

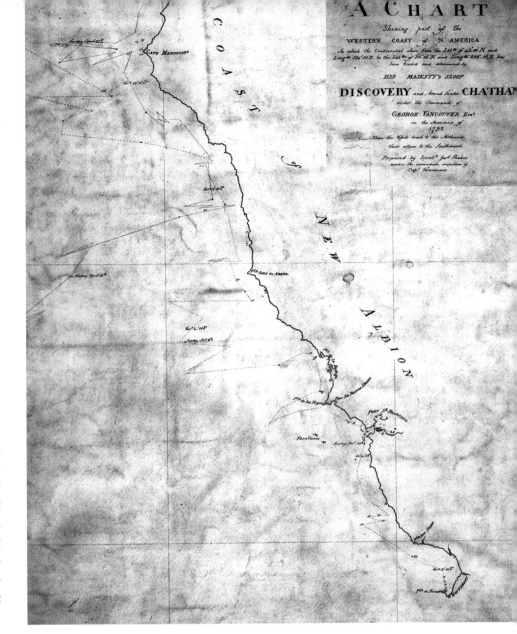

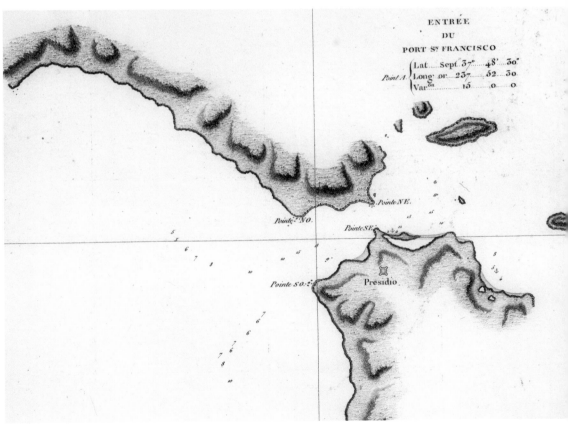

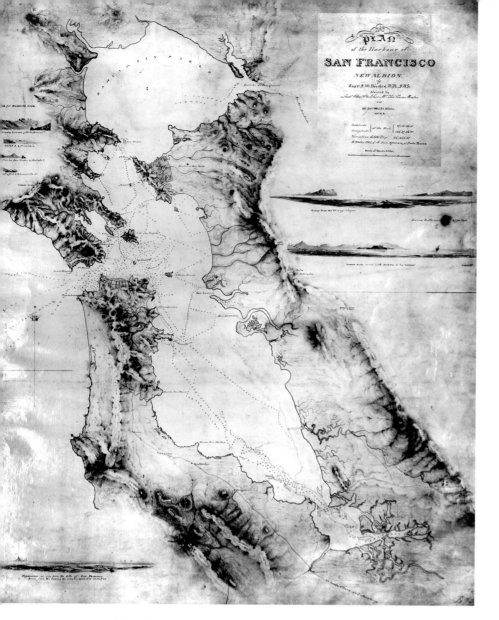

MAP 118 (*above*).
The original manuscript version of part of Frederick William Beechey's map of San Francisco Bay, surveyed in 1827. The names of Alcatraz and Yerba Buena islands are reversed from those on Ayala's map, and it is Beechey's names that have stuck.

MAP 119 (*below, left*) and MAP 120 (*below, right*).
Two maps from the visit to California of Eugène Duflot de Mofras in 1841. MAP 119 is the harbor at San Pedro (Los Angeles), and MAP 120 is Santa Barbara. Another map by Duflot de Mofras is that of the coast around Fort Ross, MAP 138, *pages 64–65*. He was a trade attaché with the French legation in Mexico City and was trying to acquaint himself with trading opportunities in California. Most of the individuals who came to California in the years prior to the American annexation were enterprising traders looking to expand their horizons. The most important to California history was a Swiss entrepreneur named John A. Sutter (see page 79).

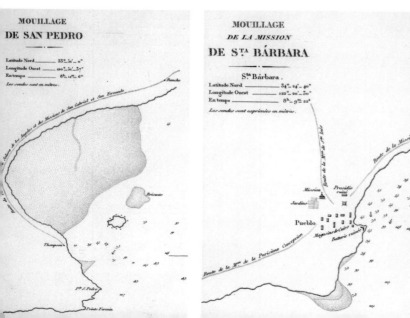

interest by Britain, and few ships visited the coast despite this agreement. The northern coast was left to a few British and, increasingly, American fur traders, and the Spanish abandoned it almost entirely. California, in the Spanish mind, withdrew southward, and even that remnant would suffer the neglect of a declining empire.

The Russians visited California in 1806 prior to establishing their own settlement in 1813 (see page 64). The next British visitor was Frederick William Beechey, who arrived in the Pacific with HMS *Blossom* in 1826 to be available to assist Arctic explorers Edward Parry and John Franklin should they emerge from Bering Strait. In 1827 Beechey produced the first reliable map of the whole of San Francisco Bay, and it was his map that would be hastily reprinted for the use of the ships bringing gold miners to the port in 1849. In his survey, however, Beechey made a few mistakes, the most notable of which being the reversing of the names of Alcatraz and Yerba Buena islands, given to them by Ayala in 1775.

Beechey was again sent to the Pacific in 1835 with HMS *Sulphur* and HMS *Starling,* under Henry Kellett. Beechey became ill and left the expedition at Valparaiso, and his second-in-command, Edward Belcher, took over command at Panama. The ships visited San Francisco in 1837. One of his midshipmen, eighteen-year-old Francis Guillemard Simpkinson, was left on board ship while others explored upriver in boats. Simpkinson wrote about Mexican California, finding that "San Francisco [Bay] affords so little novelty that in a very short time one gets quite tired of it"; he found the people "lazy and indolent in the extreme." Another interesting observation was that "though San Francisco is such a magnificent harbour in point of extent, there are still several disadvantages connected with it. So great is the distance of the watering place from the usual anchorage (that of Yerba Buena) that vessels are obliged to anchor in the watering harbour (called Sausalito) previous to their leaving . . . the Bay of Sausalito is as good if not better anchorage than that of Yerba Buena, and I think it is a pity that the settlers have not established themselves there instead of at the latter place. The other disadvantage in San Francisco is the immense extent of the harbour. In this respect it more resembles an inland sea or a sound . . . there is room for a heavy sea to get up within the confines of it."

Other visitors came to California, but they were remarkably few. Most viewed California as a sleepy backwater, difficult to get to and not worth the trouble. The most notable arrival was the United States Exploring Expedition in 1841. Under Charles Wilkes, this was a scientific circumnavigation with several ships. On the West Coast, Wilkes realized that Puget Sound was the only good harbor north of San Francisco Bay, and it was his report that encouraged the American negotiators in 1846 to press for an international boundary far enough north to include it. It was not until after California had become American territory that same year

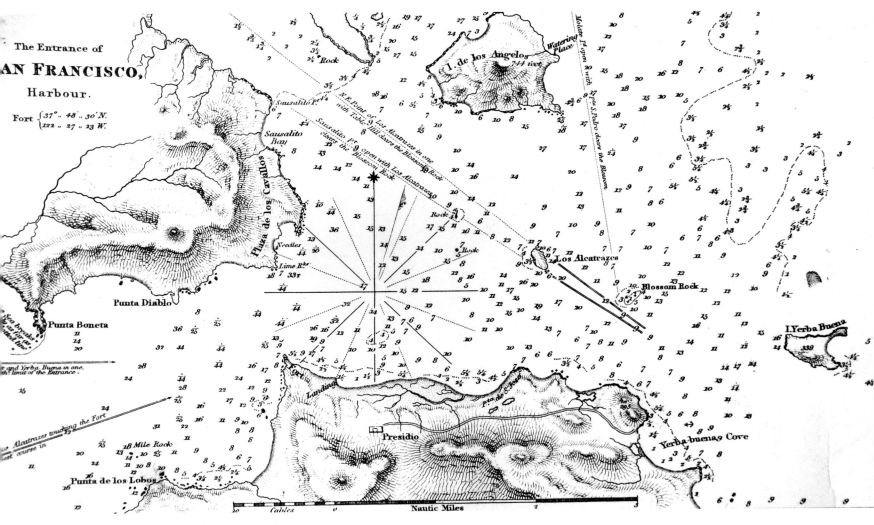

The Fort in one with Yerba Buena Isl.ᵈ leads over the Bar in 4 fᵐˢ No ship should cross it further North on account of the rolling swell.

**The Entrance of SAN FRANCISCO, Harbour.**

Fort { 37° „ 48 „ 30' N. / 122 „ 27 „ 23 W. }

and gold was discovered two years later that interest in California exploded, and visitors, many of whom would become settlers, poured in.

MAP 121 (above).
Beechey's detailed map of the entrance to San Francisco Bay, surveyed in 1827. The *Presidio* and *Yerba buena Cove* are shown. *Above* is a sailing sketch designed to assist mariners in finding the entrance, which was difficult to see from the sea. Beechey's maps were not superseded until after the gold rush. This map was published in 1833 and was part of a British Admiralty hydrographic chart, for a century or more considered the most reliable of maritime charts all over the world.

MAP 122 (right).
Another chart made by French traders, this one showing the important entrance to San Francisco Bay, was drawn in 1843 by Abel Aubert Dupetit-Thouars.

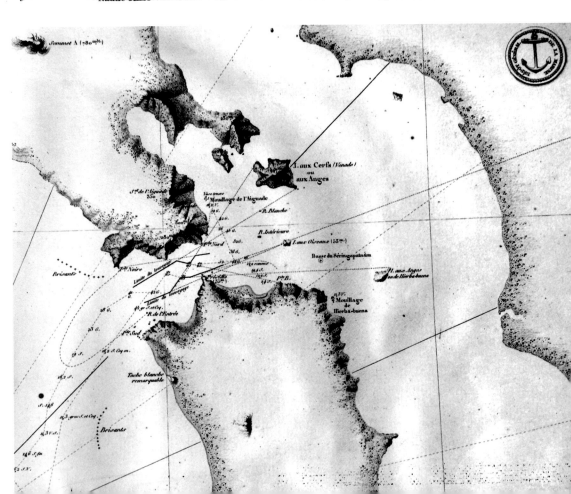

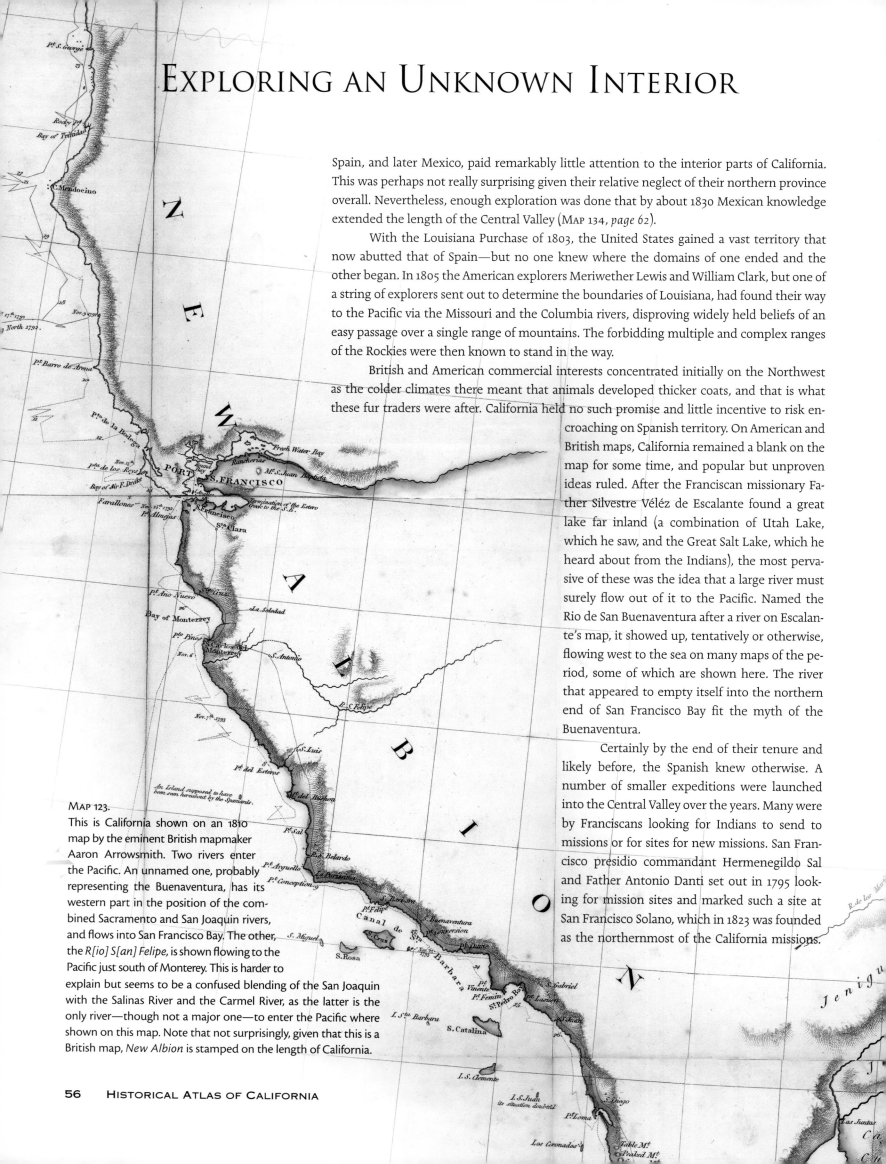

# EXPLORING AN UNKNOWN INTERIOR

Spain, and later Mexico, paid remarkably little attention to the interior parts of California. This was perhaps not really surprising given their relative neglect of their northern province overall. Nevertheless, enough exploration was done that by about 1830 Mexican knowledge extended the length of the Central Valley (MAP 134, *page 62*).

With the Louisiana Purchase of 1803, the United States gained a vast territory that now abutted that of Spain—but no one knew where the domains of one ended and the other began. In 1805 the American explorers Meriwether Lewis and William Clark, but one of a string of explorers sent out to determine the boundaries of Louisiana, had found their way to the Pacific via the Missouri and the Columbia rivers, disproving widely held beliefs of an easy passage over a single range of mountains. The forbidding multiple and complex ranges of the Rockies were then known to stand in the way.

British and American commercial interests concentrated initially on the Northwest as the colder climates there meant that animals developed thicker coats, and that is what these fur traders were after. California held no such promise and little incentive to risk encroaching on Spanish territory. On American and British maps, California remained a blank on the map for some time, and popular but unproven ideas ruled. After the Franciscan missionary Father Silvestre Véléz de Escalante found a great lake far inland (a combination of Utah Lake, which he saw, and the Great Salt Lake, which he heard about from the Indians), the most pervasive of these was the idea that a large river must surely flow out of it to the Pacific. Named the Rio de San Buenaventura after a river on Escalante's map, it showed up, tentatively or otherwise, flowing west to the sea on many maps of the period, some of which are shown here. The river that appeared to empty itself into the northern end of San Francisco Bay fit the myth of the Buenaventura.

Certainly by the end of their tenure and likely before, the Spanish knew otherwise. A number of smaller expeditions were launched into the Central Valley over the years. Many were by Franciscans looking for Indians to send to missions or for sites for new missions. San Francisco presidio commandant Hermenegildo Sal and Father Antonio Danti set out in 1795 looking for mission sites and marked such a site at San Francisco Solano, which in 1823 was founded as the northernmost of the California missions.

MAP 123.
This is California shown on an 1810 map by the eminent British mapmaker Aaron Arrowsmith. Two rivers enter the Pacific. An unnamed one, probably representing the Buenaventura, has its western part in the position of the combined Sacramento and San Joaquin rivers, and flows into San Francisco Bay. The other, the R[io] S[an] Felipe, is shown flowing to the Pacific just south of Monterey. This is harder to explain but seems to be a confused blending of the San Joaquin with the Salinas River and the Carmel River, as the latter is the only river—though not a major one—to enter the Pacific where shown on this map. Note that not surprisingly, given that this is a British map, *New Albion* is stamped on the length of California.

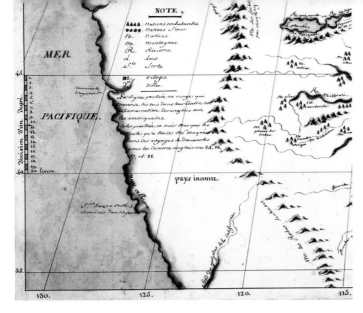

MAP 124 (*above*).
Even the Spanish surveyor general of Louisiana, Antoine Soulard, did not know anything about the country west of the Rockies, which he placed on his 1795 map far too near the Pacific. California is part of *pays inconu*, unknown country.

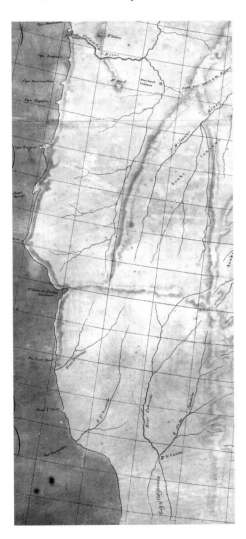

MAP 125 (*left*).
This is part of the copy made by Nicholas King in 1803 as a composite of the maps of William Clark, of Lewis and Clark fame. He demonstrates the profound lack of knowledge—or was it interest—in the lands to the south of the Columbia River, (at top), where Lewis and Clark reached the Pacific. This was due in no small part to the fact that California was still firmly established in American minds as Spanish territory, not to be encroached upon (as the explorer Zebulon Pike had found farther to the east) without raising Spanish ire.

MAP 126 (*right*).
Upper California might as well have been the far side of the moon according to this French map, drawn by a New Orleans merchant, James Pitot, in 1802. *Californie* is located on Baja, but otherwise the West Coast is almost unrecognizable. To be fair, the map was of the whole of the southern part of North America and was principally drawn to show the course of the Mississippi: California was clearly on the fringes of Pitot's knowledge.

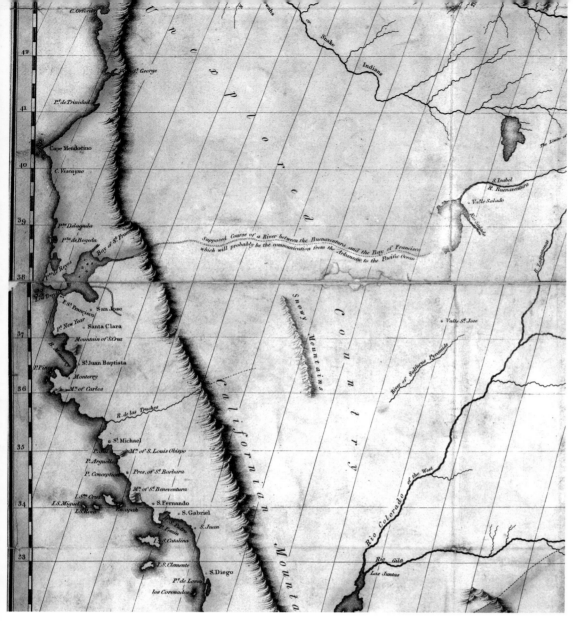

Father Juan Martín left Mission San Miguel Arcángel in 1804 and reached Tulare Lake. He was searching for Tulare Indians to send to missions. Father José María de Zalvidea similarly found Buena Vista Lake farther south when he explored from Mission Santa Barbara in 1806.

The most extensively traveled explorer of California at this time was Gabriel Moraga, an army officer and son of José Moraga, the founder of the San Francisco presidio, in 1776. The junior Moraga, accompanied by Father Pedro Muñoz, explored from Mission San Juan Bautista in 1806 looking for possible mission sites. They crossed the San Joaquin River and traversed the Central Valley from the Mokelumne River in the north to the end of the valley in the south, finding Tejon Pass and continuing to the San Fernando Mission.

In 1808 Moraga made another foray into the Central Valley, this time going north, exploring the rivers flowing into the valley from the Sierra Nevada and reaching a point on the Sacramento River about 15 miles north of Colusa.

After again exploring in the Central Valley for mission sites, two years later

MAP 127 (*above*).
The West shown on an 1816 map by Philadelphia mapmaker John Melish. A range of mountains, presumably the Sierra Nevada, is shown as the California Mountains. *A Supposed Course of a River between the Buenaventura and the Bay of Francisco* is depicted. A *Rio de las Truches* flows *through* the mountains to the Pacific well south of Monterey, and what appears to be a somewhat misplaced San Joaquin River, though unnamed, flows into the east side of San Francisco Bay. Most of the missions are marked, but there is a great deal of *Unexplored Country*.

MAP 128 (*left*).
Part of an 1814 map of Missouri Territory, shown complete as MAP 105, *page 49*. Despite a lack of details, both the coastal mountains and the Sierra Nevada are indicated, with the suggestion of a valley between. The latter range could, however, have been a mapmaker's doodlings for a Rocky Mountain chain of only approximate location.

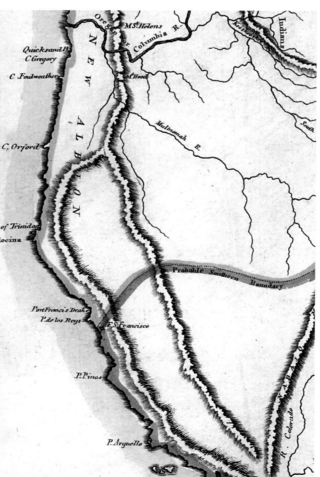

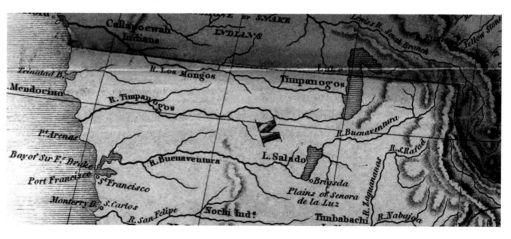

Moraga was again sent north, finally for a different purpose: to investigate reports of Russian incursions. He visited the Russian settlements at Bodega Bay, where a Russian fur trading post was established in 1811, and Fort Ross, built in 1812, a number of times over the next few years (see page 66).

The first recorded navigation of the Sacramento River was achieved in 1811 by Father Ramón Abella, on a search for mission sites by water.

There followed an extended period in which the Spanish, and later the Mexicans, forayed into the interior to find Indian runaways from the missions or attack them for their resistance. A major roundup of runaways took place in 1815 by detachments of soldiers under Juan Ortega and José Dolores Pico who searched the southern end of the San Joaquin Valley. Although military in nature these expeditions did gather geographical knowledge.

Indian resistance became stronger after the ouster of the Spanish by the independent Mexicans. But the Mexican authorities seemed equally determined to

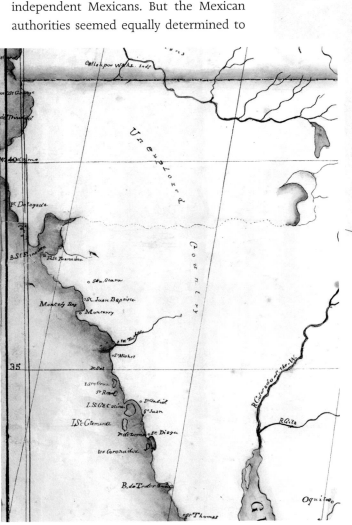

Map 129 (far left, bottom, center).
A full-fledged R. Buenaventura is shown flowing from a large L. Salado (Great Salt Lake) to the Pacific at San Francisco Bay in this part of an 1826 American map.

Map 130 (above).
British mapmaker James Wyld goes one step better in this 1823 map. No fewer than three major rivers flow more or less directly from the interior to the Pacific. Here the R. de Sta. Buenaventura has been displaced south and flows to the sea south of Monterey, while the R. Timpanogos now flows into San Francisco Bay. Lake Timpanogos was an early name for the Great Salt Lake. Farthest south, the R. de St. Felippe flows from the Snowy Mountains to the sea just north of Point Arguello, likely confused with the real Santa Maria River. Overall, this map is a creative mix of fact and fiction.

Map 131 (left).
Much less creative is this 1821 map showing California with a great deal of blank space and Unexplored Country. A hint of a cross-basin river remains.

## CARTA ESFERICA

DE LOS

### TERRITORIOS DE LA ALTA Y BAJA

## CALIFORNIAS

Y

### ESTADO DE SONORA

Construida por las mejores noticias y observaciones
propias del Teniente de Navio D. Jose M. Narvaes

AÑO DE
1823

#### ESPLICACION

- ◉ CIUDAD
- ◎ VILLA
- ○ Pueblo
- ☉ Mision
- ◉ Presidio
- ⌂ Hacienda
- △ Rancheria
- ℞ Real de Minas
- ◌ Ojo de agua

## Map 132 (*left*).

This map is in many ways the final Spanish map of California, having been created in 1823 just as Spanish rule ended. Yet it incorporates surprisingly little of the Spanish knowledge of the interior gained over many years by many explorers. It shows mission districts and a fair amount of coastal detail but beyond the thirty-mile or so coastal zone there is little detail. The Sierra Nevada are shown in two sections, thus clearly giving expression to the idea that there might be a valley between them, and there are none of the rivers flowing directly from the interior to the sea shown on the maps of American and British mapmakers during this period. The map was drawn by José María Narváez, an experienced naval chartmaker and veteran of several major expeditions to the Northwest, after delivering the emissary of the new Mexican government to Monterey in 1822. Eight years later Narváez produced another map incorporating much more up-to-date knowledge (Map 134, *next page*).

## Map 133 (*below right*).

This 1827 French map, a composite of several sheets, uses up the "blank" space in the middle of California and the West with explanatory texts about *Nouvelle Californie* (New California) and Mexico. It was one cartographic device to disguise a lack of knowledge on a commercial map. The map shows a river flowing into the northern end of San Francisco Bay, however, significantly now labeled *R[io] S[an] Sacramento ou Climpanos Navigable à plus 50 lieues*—navigable to 50 leagues. This appears to be the first appearance of a named Sacramento River on a European or American map.

punish Indians for their perceived misdeeds, the main one of which was simply running away from the missions.

In 1824 a force commanded by Pablo de la Portilla marched to Buena Vista Lake to round up escapees from several coastal missions, and the following year Pico led another force into the San Joaquin Valley. Another punitive expedition took place in 1828 under Sebastiáan Rodriguez, this time mainly to look for stolen horses, which the Indians had taken a fancy to eating instead of their staple acorn. In 1829 no fewer than three expeditions took place against Estanislao, a runaway mission Indian who had gathered together the escapees to form an effective resistance. The Indians were finally defeated by a large force under Mariano Vallejo—destined later to be a significant person in California history—along the Stanislaus and Tuluomne rivers.

In the 1830s the Indians took to attacking the missions, ranchos, and towns, often to obtain horses, which, as well as becoming a diet item, had allowed them to become expert riders and a highly mobile attack force, precisely the opposite of what the Spanish and Mexican mission system had tried to achieve.

The myth of the Buenaventura was finally disproven to European and American mapmakers by the travels of a so-called mountain man searching for new sources of furs. This was the legendary Jedediah Strong Smith, fur trader and explorer of vast areas of the West. As well as blazing trails to California, Smith explored extensively within what is now the state. In 1826–27 Smith explored southward down the Colorado and then struck out across the Mojave Desert. Then he went north, finding the San Joaquin River—and lots

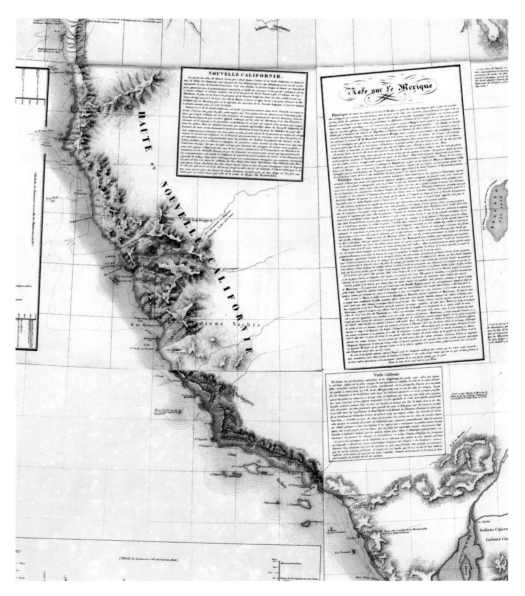

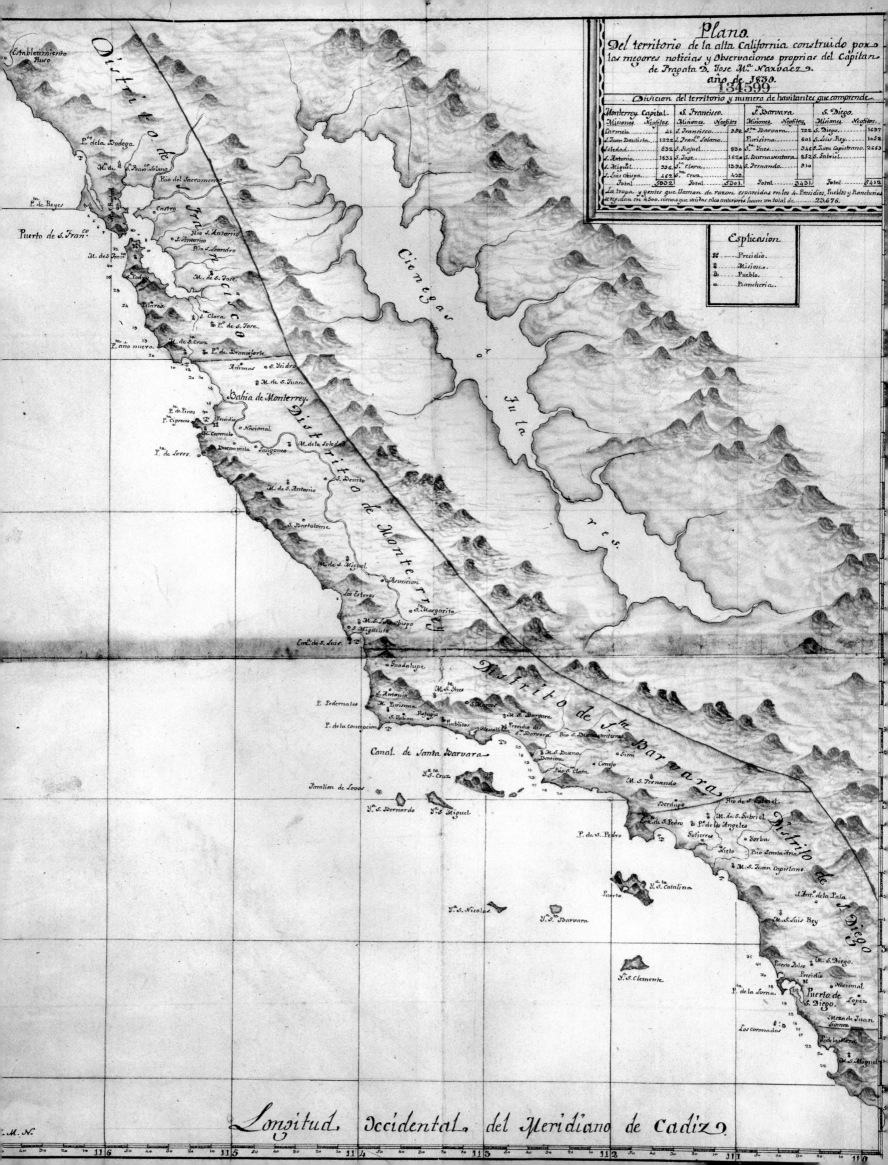

of beaver, his trading interest—and after one failed attempt to cross the Sierra Nevada going east due to heavy snow, he took two other men and crossed Ebbetts Pass, and then traversed the entire Great Basin in an epic thirty-two days, reaching the Great Salt Lake. Ten days later he set out again, repeating his route, crossing the Mojave Desert; this time he was attacked by Indians. The Mexican governor had him arrested as a spy, but he escaped, took a ship to San Francisco, then traveled up the Sacramento and north yet more to the Umpqua River in Oregon, where fourteen of his men were killed by Indians. Smith and only two others escaped north to Fort Vancouver.

Smith's original maps have been lost, but the information they contained was passed on to mapmaker David Burr, whose map of the United States in 1839 incorporated Smith's routes (Map 135, *right*). Smith finally disproved the myth of the Buenaventura and added much to the knowledge of the geography of the West.

Map 134 (*left*).
This important map of California was drawn by José María Narváez in 1830 as an improvement to his 1823 map (Map 132, *page 60*), with added information. For the first time the Central Valley is definitively shown between the coastal ranges and the Sierra Nevada. There are no rivers here flowing from the interior directly to the Pacific. A large area of *Cienagas*, marshland, is depicted covering the entire northeast side of the Central Valley. The *Establecimiento Ruso*, the Russian Establishment, Fort Ross (see next page), is shown on the coast at top left. Missions, presidios, and other habitations are also depicted. The table at top right gives population figures, with a total of 23,676 for all of California.

Map 135 (*right, top*).
Official cartographer of the House of Representatives, David Burr, published a map of the United States in 1839, which in the West incorporated the lost maps of Jedediah Smith, whose routes are marked on the map. In many cases, Smith's exact routes are not known, and Burr's map (and Brué's, on this page) is all that we have left to go on. *Inconstant R.* marks Smith's route, twice traveled, across the Mojave Desert. *J. S. Smith's Route across the Sandy Plain in 1827* shows Smith's epic trek across the Great Basin via the Humboldt Valley and Carson Sink with only two other men. His route north to Fort Vancouver is also marked by a dashed line but not annotated. The Sacramento is named the *Buenaventura*, flowing from the north, not the east. Also shown is the *Russian Establishment* on the coast; this is Fort Ross.

Map 136 (*right*).
Also published in 1839 and also showing the routes of Jedediah Smith is this map by French mapmaker A.H. Brué. Here the Central Valley is more clearly depicted. A year later Brué issued another edition of this map, revised to show the Buenaventura ending at a sink in the desert. This was the Carson Sink in Nevada, and the river was the Humboldt (see Map 158, *page 75*).

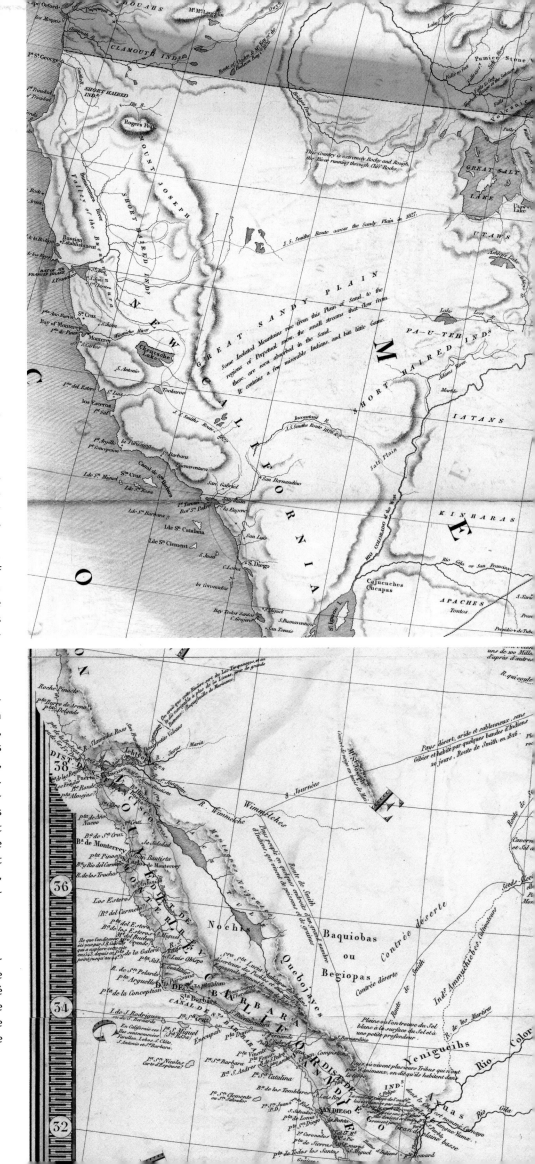

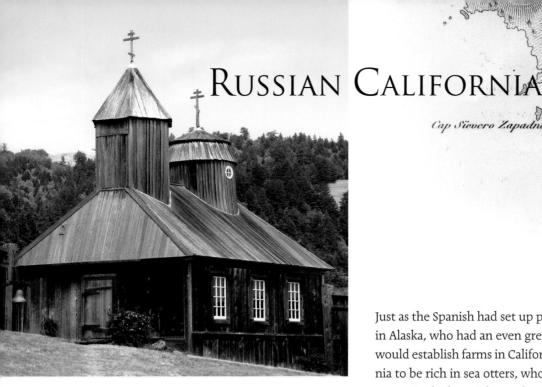

# RUSSIAN CALIFORNIA

*Cap Sievero Zapadnoi*

FORT ROSS

*Cap Louro Vospiotchnoi*

*Above.* The restored chapel at Fort Ross. The original was destroyed in the 1906 earthquake.

MAP 137 (*below*).
Part of a large map of the Pacific Ocean drawn by Grigorii Shelikov, one of the founders of the Russian American Company. The map was printed in 1787 and demonstrates that at that time the Russians had as good an idea of the geography of the coast of California as did the Spanish.

Just as the Spanish had set up pueblos to supply the presidios with food, the Russians in Alaska, who had an even greater problem with food supply, had the idea that they would establish farms in California to supply them with food. They also found California to be rich in sea otters, whose warm and valuable fur they coveted.

In the late eighteenth century Russian fur traders had advanced eastward from Siberia. A base was established on Kodiak Island in 1784, and in 1799 the Russian American Company was chartered to exploit the lands discovered and claimed for Russia by Vitus Bering and Aleksei Chirikov in 1741. After the Russians were almost wiped out by Tlingit in 1802, Novo Archangel'sk (Sitka) was founded the following year. The company was mainly a fur trading enterprise and was always on the lookout for new fur regions to exploit. In 1803 Alexandr Baranov, the company manager, organized a joint venture with Boston captain Joseph O'Cain, who ranged as far south as Baja gathering sea otter furs, was profitable, and encouraged the Russians to consider the waters to the south. In 1806 Aleut hunters under Jonathan Winship, in an American ship in the employ of the Russian American Company, discovered Humboldt Bay in Northern California while searching for sea otters. The bay, however, would not be entered again until 1850.

The Russian posts were always short of food, and in 1806 Nicholai Resanov, one of the founders of the Russian American Company, who was in Alaska on a tour of inspection, sailed to San Francisco to try to obtain wheat and other foodstuffs for the Alaskan posts. The Spanish had a prohibition on trade with the Russians, but Resanov, by skilled diplomacy—not least of which was offering to marry the port commandant's daughter—managed to buy food. On his return to Alaska, Resanov and Baranov hatched a plan to establish a settlement on the coast north of San Francisco, which Resanov had noted the Spanish did not occupy, to be used for the dual purpose of growing food to supply the Alaska posts and gathering furs.

Baranov's assistant Ivan Kuskov was sent to California several times to reconnoiter the coast to find a suitable site for a settlement. In 1809 he built temporary structures at Bodega Bay (MAP 139) while Aleut fur hunters gathered about two thousand furs. In March 1812 he returned with twenty-five Russians, many of them craftsmen, and eighty Aleuts. Bodega Bay was not considered secure enough from possible Spanish attack, and so Kuskov purchased land farther up the coast of Sonoma from the local Kashaya Indians—not the Spanish—paying for it with blankets, clothes, tools, and beads. On a convenient coastal terrace the Russians constructed a stockaded fort with the same sort of architecture as was used in their settlements in Alaska—distinctly Russian in style. The site was dedicated at the end of August as *Rossiia*—Russia. It quickly became known to others as Fort Ross (MAP 141, *overleaf*). Outlying farms were also established to take advantage of agriculturally advantageous sites.

The Spanish were outraged, especially when Aleut hunters started gliding around San Francisco Bay hunting sea otters, but could do little. When Spain ordered the commandant at the San Francisco presidio to remove the Russians in 1819, he refused, saying he lacked the military strength. New missions at San Rafael and Solano were founded in 1817 and 1823 with the idea that they might act as a buffer against more Russian encroachment.

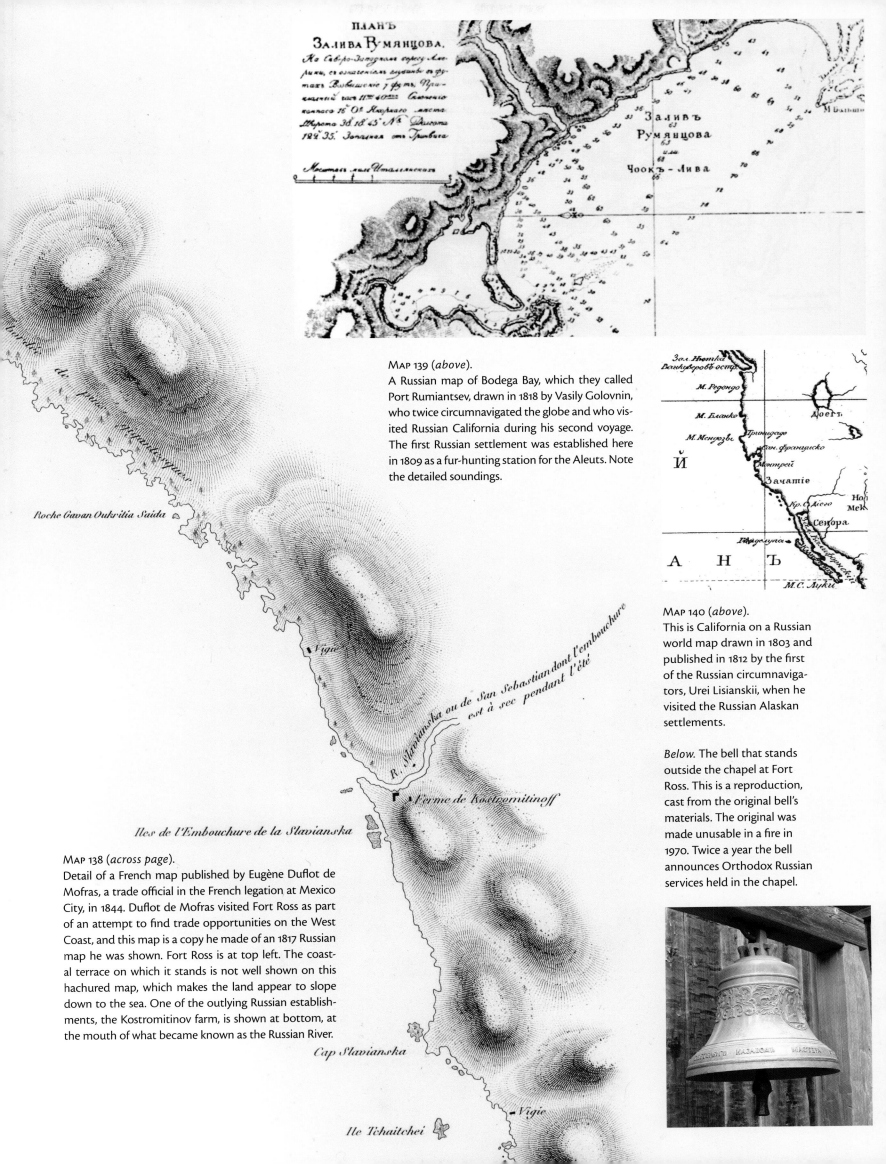

ПЛАНЪ
ЗАЛИВА РУМЯНЦОВА.

Залив Румянцова

Чоок — Лива

М. Большой

МАP 139 (*above*).
A Russian map of Bodega Bay, which they called Port Rumiantsev, drawn in 1818 by Vasily Golovnin, who twice circumnavigated the globe and who visited Russian California during his second voyage. The first Russian settlement was established here in 1809 as a fur-hunting station for the Aleuts. Note the detailed soundings.

МАP 140 (*above*).
This is California on a Russian world map drawn in 1803 and published in 1812 by the first of the Russian circumnavigators, Urei Lisianskii, when he visited the Russian Alaskan settlements.

*Below.* The bell that stands outside the chapel at Fort Ross. This is a reproduction, cast from the original bell's materials. The original was made unusable in a fire in 1970. Twice a year the bell announces Orthodox Russian services held in the chapel.

*Roche Gavan Oukritia Saida*

*Vigie*

*R. Slavianska ou de San Sebastian dont l'embouchure est à sec pendant l'été*

*Ferme de Kostromitinoff*

*Iles de l'Embouchure de la Slavianska*

МАP 138 (*across page*).
Detail of a French map published by Eugène Duflot de Mofras, a trade official in the French legation at Mexico City, in 1844. Duflot de Mofras visited Fort Ross as part of an attempt to find trade opportunities on the West Coast, and this map is a copy he made of an 1817 Russian map he was shown. Fort Ross is at top left. The coastal terrace on which it stands is not well shown on this hachured map, which makes the land appear to slope down to the sea. One of the outlying Russian establishments, the Kostromitinov farm, is shown at bottom, at the mouth of what became known as the Russian River.

*Cap Slavianska*

*Vigie*

*Ile Tchaitchei*

The walls of Fort Ross today, from within the stockade. This is the northeast corner blockhouse, top left in the plan of the fort (*A*) in Map 141 (*right*).

Map 141 (*right*).
An 1817 plan of the fort and its environs. Fort Ross is *A*, with blockhouses shown as circles at top left and bottom right. Other polygons show the gardens, some with habitations, principally along the stream flowing into Fort Ross Cove. The serrated-type lines represent cliffs, the edges of the relatively flat coastal terrace. There appears to be a representation of a windmill at top left. Just south of the fort is a collection of tiny rectangles, fourteen Aleut *yurts*, made of planks. On the west side of the stream where it enters the cove is the fort's ship, the brig *Rumiantsev*.

Map 142 (*left*).
A Russian map of part of the northern California coast, 1817. Fort Ross is at the top, Bodega Bay is in the center, and Tomales Point, at the entrance to Tomales Bay, is at bottom. The map was drawn by Ivan Kislakovskii, a navigator with Leontii Andrianovich Gagemeister (or Hagemeister), who was another of the Russian circumnavigators who arrived on the West Coast in 1817 during an 1816–19 circumnavigation. The Russian American Company was experimenting at this time with supplying their settlements in Alaska and California by ship rather than the arduous overland trip across Siberia. The Duflot de Mofras map (Map 138, *previous page*), is a copy of detail of this map.

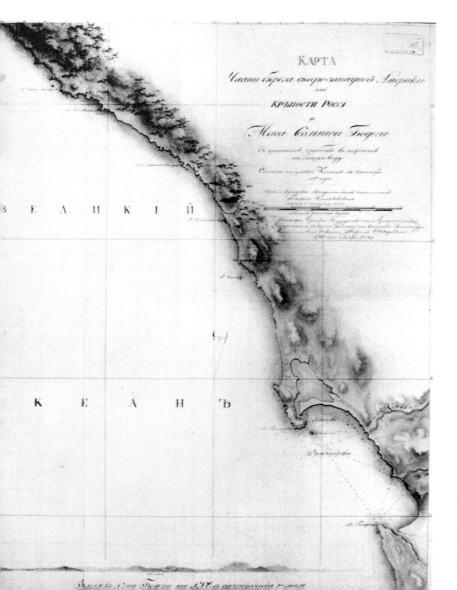

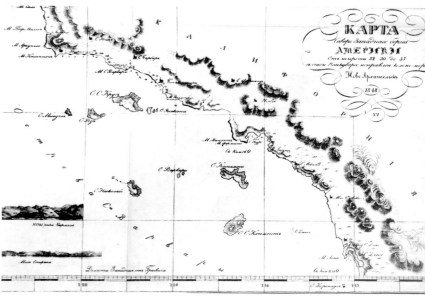

Map 143 (*left, bottom*), and Map 144 (*right*).

Maps by Mikhail Dimitrievich Tebenkov, a Russian naval officer who from 1845 to 1850 was manager of the Russian American Company. Tebenkov had organized surveying expeditions and collected all the geographic and hydrographic information he could find, including the maps of George Vancouver, when in 1852 he put it all together and published an *Atlas of the Northwest Coasts of America*, which contained these maps.

Map 143 is the southern California coast from Point Arguello to San Diego; and Map 144 is the coast between Fort Ross, shown at top, and Monterey Bay, together with a detailed inset map of the entrance to San Francisco Bay.

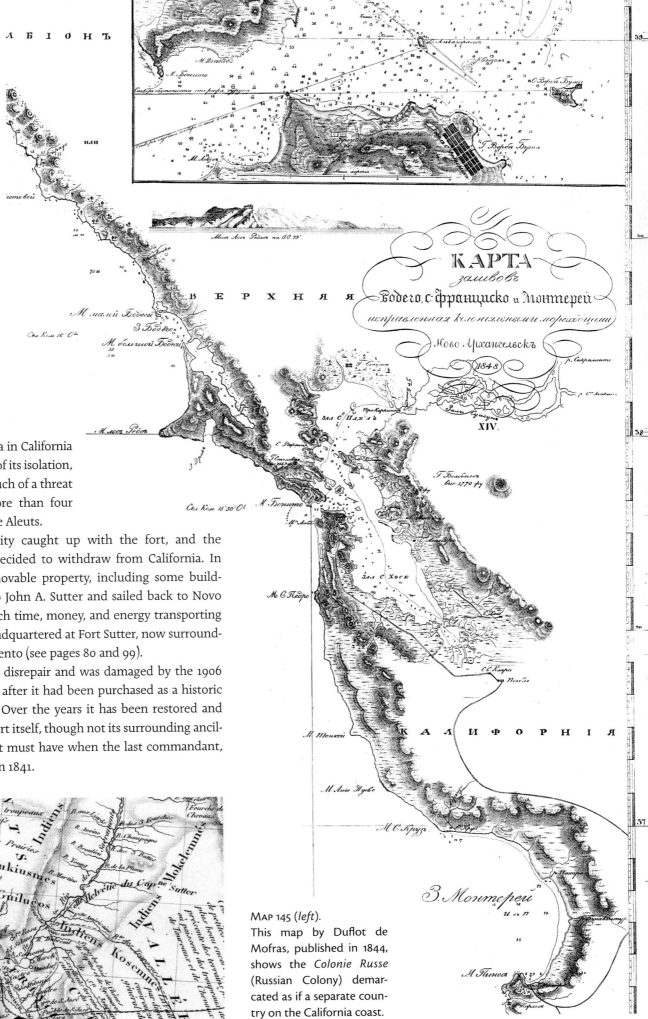

But the little bit of Russia in California never really flourished because of its isolation, and the Russians were never much of a threat because there were never more than four hundred Russians, including the Aleuts.

Eventually, unprofitability caught up with the fort, and the Russian American Company decided to withdraw from California. In 1841 they sold most of the movable property, including some buildings, a schooner, and cattle, to John A. Sutter and sailed back to Novo Archangel'sk. Sutter spent much time, money, and energy transporting his purchases to his rancho, headquartered at Fort Sutter, now surrounded by the urban area of Sacramento (see pages 80 and 99).

Fort Ross fell into some disrepair and was damaged by the 1906 earthquake, less than a month after it had been purchased as a historic site by the State of California. Over the years it has been restored and reconstructed, and today the fort itself, though not its surrounding ancillary buildings, looks much as it must have when the last commandant, Alexandr Rotchev, moved out in 1841.

Map 145 (*left*).

This map by Duflot de Mofras, published in 1844, shows the *Colonie Russe* (Russian Colony) demarcated as if a separate country on the California coast.

# MEXICAN CALIFORNIA

The Mexican Revolution went on for many years, but by 1821 a new government was firmly established in Mexico City, and by the following year Alta California had a new—Mexican—governor. The Mexicans were to prove not much more interested in their northern province than had been their predecessors.

The new Mexican constitution, however, endorsed the equality of all people regardless of race, and there was thus an immediate call for the secularization of the missions. The mission system in fact intended for this to happen eventually, as the missions achieved their goals of converting Indians into colonists, but the Mexican takeover accelerated a process that might otherwise have taken a century. The California missions were secularized in 1834; the missions were closed and their Indian populations essentially abandoned. In the process some of the missions' often considerable land holdings became available to others.

In 1824 the Mexican government passed a Law of Colonization, which was to encourage the settlement of frontier regions—such as California—by the granting of land both to Mexicans and to foreigners. In this way it hoped to build a bulwark against encroachment by other nations. The law was clarified four years later with a regulation giving the frontier governors the authority to grant land in this way. However, no land was to be granted in regions were there was a mission system, and it was not until 1833 that José Figueroa was sent to assume the governorship with orders to end the mission system. A year later Figueroa secularized the missions; land could then officially be granted under the law of 1824. (A small number of grants of public land had been made by the territorial legislature before 1834, but the vast majority occurred after that date.)

Mexican land grants had a considerable impact on the landscape of California, lasting through to today. The alignment of many boundaries and streets owe their origin to the shape of a Mexican grant. Grants also tended to concentrate large holdings of land—the ranchos—in relatively few hands and encouraged the growth of large farms and ranch properties in many parts of the state. The method of granting ranchos, however, has left a legacy of confusion of land titles in many areas, due to the somewhat haphazard method used. Since there was no official surveyor, it was up to each applicant to provide his own map of the area requested. Naturally enough, some were better at this task than others; some employed a person with surveying skills, while many just sat on a piece of high ground and drew a plan as best they could. The result was a range of sketch maps, called *diseños,* a few of which are illustrated here. Each accompanied the usually only verbal request for a land grant, or *concedo.* It was a recipe for an attractive variety of maps but a later legal mess.

In fact, many of the *diseños* have survived because they were presented as evidence of previous ownership after the annexation of California by the United States (see page 82) and used to adjudicate overlapping claims.

MAP 146 (*below, left*).
Rancho San Bernardino was originally an Indian rancheria. In 1819 the Mission San Gabriel appropriated it and built an *estancia* (sometimes incorrectly referred to as an *asistencia*), a ranch outpost. In 1834 the rancho was closed down when the missions were secularized, and several people made applications to be granted the land. The land was granted in 1839 to Antonio Maria Lugo, who was to establish a colony with eighteen persons, but this was not successful. However, in 1842 the land was again granted to Lugo and other members of his family. The grant was a large part of the San Bernardino Valley, an area of 59 square miles. In 1851 Lugo sold the rancho to Mormons, who built a settlement, Fort San Bernardino. The City of San Bernardino was incorporated in 1854.

MAP 147 (*right, top*).
Certainly one of the most charming of the *diseños* is this one depicting Rancho San Joaquin ó Rosa Morada, 7,424 acres granted to Cruz Cervantes in 1836. It is in the upper Santa Clara Valley just east of Hollister. The two highest peaks shown are likely San Joaquin Peak and Santa Ana Mountain. *Arroyo de S[an] Felipe* is Pacheco Creek. No house is shown, but there is a *Corral de borregos* in the center, a sheepfold. The lack of a house was to lead to problems for Cervantes when he tried to prove his claim to the land before the Board of Land Commissioners in 1852, as one of the terms of the grant was that he build a house. However, no one else had preempted the land, and after a Supreme Court decision in 1856 Cervantes retained his title.

MAP 148 (*right, bottom*).
Rancho Providencia, just over 4,000 acres in the San Fernando Valley, granted to Vicente de la Ossa in 1843. At the time no one was living in this area; now it forms the southwestern part of the City of Burbank. Confusingly, the mountains both to the north and to the south are labeled *Sierra Lindero;* those to the north (top) are the Verdugo Mountains and those to the south the Santa Monica Mountains. The Los Angeles River runs across the middle of the map and right through the grant. Across the northern part is the *Camino real de San Fernando a los Angeles,* now San Fernando Road and closely followed by part of Interstate 5. Ossa sold his rancho in 1849 to David Alexander for a sum for which one would now be lucky to buy a few square feet: $1,500.

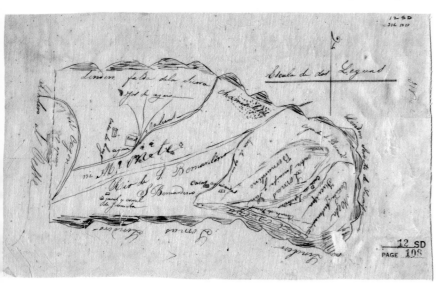

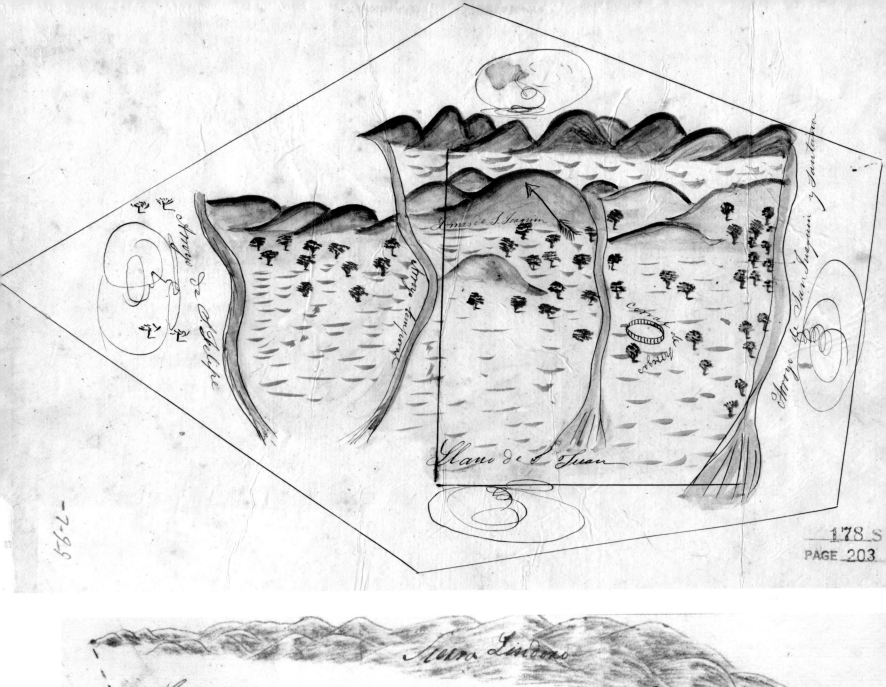

Arroyo de S. Felipe

Ymando S. Joaquin

Arroyo de San Joaquin y Santana

corral de coballas

Llano de S. Juan

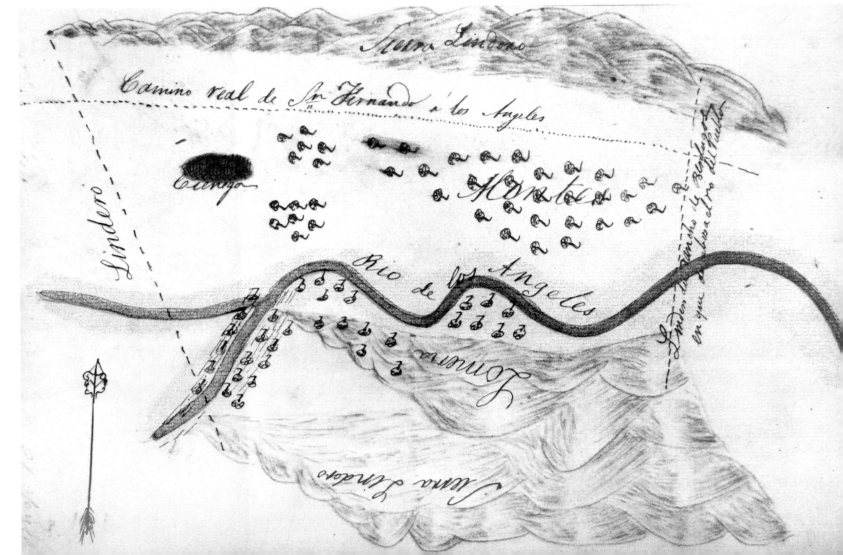

Sierra Lindero

Camino real de Sn Fernando á los Angeles

Cienga

Monte

Lindero

Rio de los Angeles

Loma

Lindero del Rancho y Respaldo en que se divisa otro del Pueblo

Loma Lindero

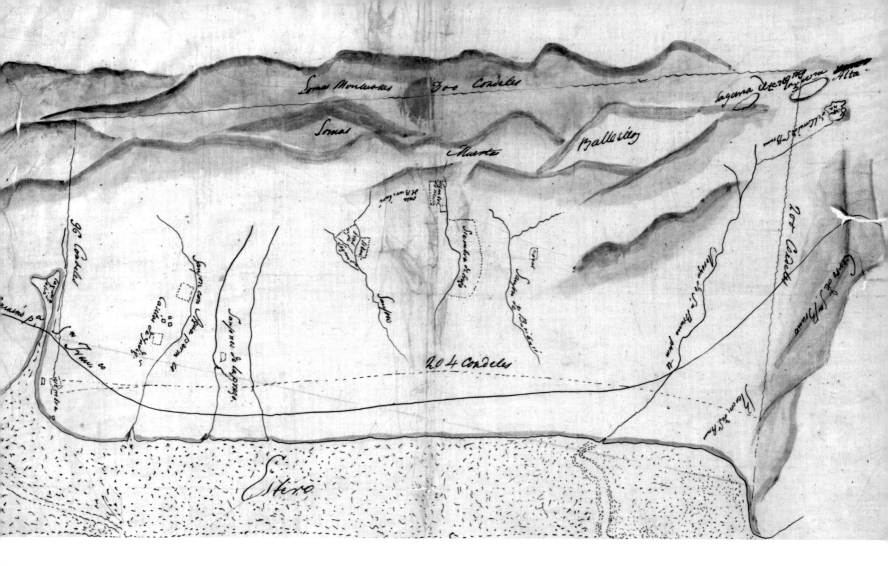

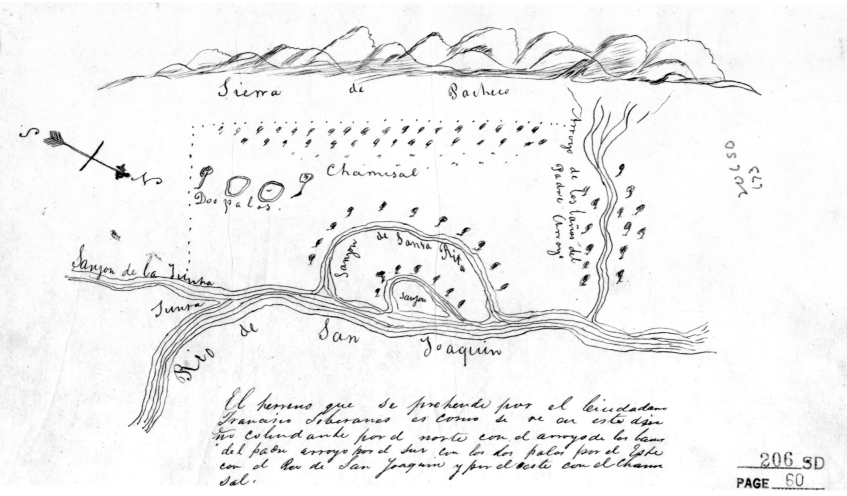

El terreno que se pretende por el ciudadano Francisco Soberanes es como se ve en este diseño colindante por el norte con el arroyo de las lomas del padre arroyo por el sur con los dos palos por el Este con el Rio de San Joaquin y por el oeste con el chamisal.

MAP 149 (*left, top*).
Rancho Buri-Buri, in San Mateo County, with San Francisco Bay at bottom; the map is oriented with north to the right, where San Bruno Mountain is depicted. The rancho, which covered 14,600 acres, included what is now San Francisco International Airport (see also MAP 417, *page 216*).

MAP 150 (*left, bottom*).
The *diseño* of the Rancho de Sanjon de Santa Rita, dating from the mid-1840s. This huge rancho, covering about 76 square miles, was in what is now central Merced County, straddling the San Joaquin River, shown at center. The mountains at top (southwest) are part of the Diablo Range. *Chamisal* is a burned area.

MAP 151 (*above*).
The *diseño* of Rancho San Miguelito de Trinidad is one of the most colorful and artistic of these maps. Drawn in 1841 or 1842, it was used by Lieutenant José Rafael Gonzalez, a veteran of the Mexican war for independence, to petition Governor Alvarado for 22,135 acres in what is now southern Monterey County between the San Antonio River (off the bottom of the map) and the Santa Lucia Mountains, shown at top. The river immediately below the mountains is the Nacimiento (*4*), and that flowing in a reversed "S" across the center of the rancho lands (*20*) is Stony Creek. The rancho itself is the building at center. Gonzalez lived in Monterey and continued to do so after he was granted San Miguelito. In 1846 the American consul Thomas O. Larkin reported that Gonzalez was "of landed property and cattle . . . of some note and influence." But the possession of land did not guarantee continued wealth. Gonzalez's son Mauricio took over the rancho and borrowed money against it. In 1864, the lender foreclosed, and the younger Gonzalez lost all his lands. In 1877 he was reported to be "driving an express wagon" for a living.

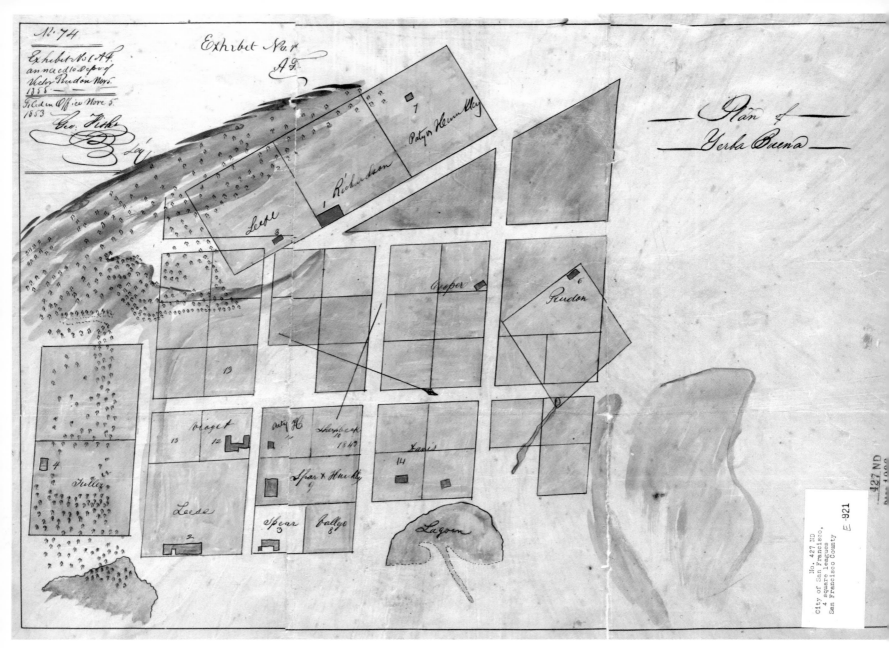

MAP 152 (*above*).

The first map of San Francisco based on a proper survey was this one surveyed by Jean Jacques Vioget in 1839, when the settlement was still known as Yerba Buena. An Englishman, William Richardson, settled here in 1835, setting himself up as a trader for visiting ships. From 1836 town lots were sold, and by 1839 it was thought necessary to create an official street plan. Vioget, a Swiss engineer, was on hand and was given the job. He began with what is now Montgomery Street, then at the waterfront, and surveyed three blocks westward and four from north to south. Note the names of Richardson and Vioget on lots, and also that of another pioneer, Jacob Leese.

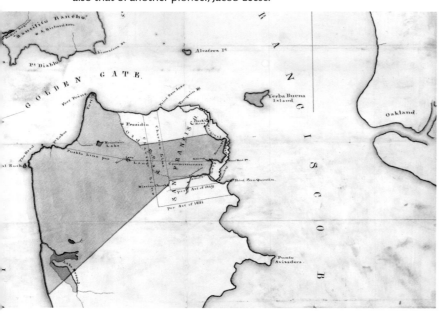

MAP 153 (*left*).

Yerba Buena was part of the pueblo of San Francisco created in 1834 and whose town council, elected in December that year, took office in January 1835. Pueblo lands were created by the Mexican governor, José Figueroa, in San Francisco, San Diego, and Santa Barbara, all locations where the presence of a presidio had attracted a population. The grants of land were set at four square leagues, about 30,000 acres, but the precise boundaries and sizes of the grants were later the source of much contention and litigation; San Francisco received much less than San Diego (MAP 155, *right*) and had to fight the claims of others to get it. This map, based on one dated about 1843, is one of several submitted to the Board of Land Commissioners by other claimants for lands now in the City of San Francisco. This claim (the area colored red) was by José Limatour. After many years of legal wrangling, the city was finally granted a patent for 17,754 acres in 1884. This map also shows the *Charter Line as per Act of 1849*, the boundaries of the City of San Francisco as originally constituted under American tenure, and *Charter Line as per Act of 1851*, the city boundary as expanded a little later. The waterfront lands reclaimed are also well illustrated on this map (see page 160).

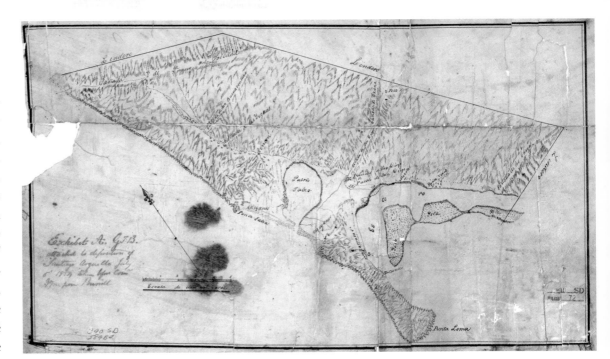

Settlements that had grown up around the presidios of San Francisco, Santa Barbara, San Diego, Monterey, and Sonoma were granted pueblo status in 1834 (though some, like San Francisco, seemed never to receive official documentation, an oversight that would lead to endless problems later). The pueblo organization allowed the election of an *ayuntamiento* (town council) and an *alcalde* (magistrate/mayor) to govern local affairs and provided for the granting of pueblo lands, a surrounding area that was, as with the Spanish-established pueblos at San José and Los Angeles, intended to make the pueblo self-sufficient. The pueblo had three types of land tenure: the *propios,* proprietorships, for houses or stores; *suertes,* rented land for agriculture; and *ejidos,* common pasture lands.

The pueblo lands sometimes conflicted with other actual or supposed land grants, and, like the ranchos, were the subject of litigation after the American takeover. San Francisco, for instance, did not get its pueblo lands finally confirmed until 1884. San Diego, which had better maps than most, did not receive its patent until 1874, so convoluted were the machinations of conflicting claimants. Ownership of the pueblo lands played a significant role in the subsequent development of the cities.

MAP 154 (*right, top*).
This map of the pueblo lands of San Diego is from the city's claim in 1854, the deposition of Santiago Argüello, the subprefect at San Diego in 1845. The map represents the original assumed extent of the pueblo lands granted in 1834. The map was drawn in 1845. Notably it includes both the North Island–Coronado peninsula, and Point Loma, both of which were later excluded.

MAP 155 (*right*).
Dated 1858, this map shows the pueblo lands of San Diego as they were finally confirmed by the U.S. Board of Land Commissioners in January 1856 and reaffirmed by the U.S. District Court in June 1857. The size of the original pueblo land grant, 48,566 acres or almost 76 square miles, was reduced by 1,233 acres in 1874 to exclude the federal military reservation on Point Loma.

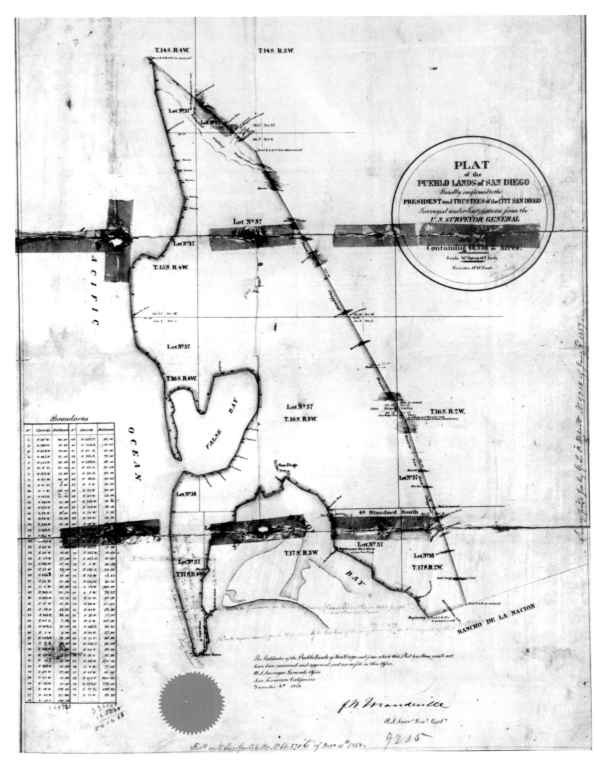

# WEST TO CALIFORNIA

American interest in the West can be said to have begun with the Louisiana Purchase in 1803 and the subsequent expedition of Meriwether Lewis and William Clark to the Pacific.

Robert Stuart of John Jacob Astor's American Fur Company first found the all-important South Pass across the Continental Divide in 1813, on a return journey from the Columbia. The rediscovery of the pass in 1824 by Jedediah Smith led to its becoming much more widely known. Because of its gradual slopes, South Pass later became the principal route for emigrant wagons heading for both Oregon and California.

The California Trail was the same route as the Oregon Trail until it split from the Snake River at Fort Hall, built in 1834, near today's Pocatello, Idaho. It then headed south to connect with the Humboldt Valley across the Great Basin. The Humboldt route, which would one day be followed by the first transcontinental railroad, was discovered by a British explorer of the Hudson's Bay Company, Peter Skene Ogden, in 1828–29, on the fifth of a wide-ranging set of explorations that covered the entire Northwest (Map 158, *right*). Ogden's interest, as was that of most of the early explorers, was finding new sources of furs.

*Above.*
A replica of an 1846 ox-drawn emigrant wagon stands at Sutter's Fort. The wagon is about ten feet long, very narrow, and has no seat, no springs, and no brakes. Yet at the beginning of its journey a wagon such as this would have been loaded with two thousand pounds of supplies. Note the oxen yoke leaning against the rear wheel.

Map 156 (*right*).
This may be the first map to show South Pass, the important key to crossing the Continental Divide by wagon discovered by Robert Stuart in 1813. This 1816 map by John Melish shows *Southern Pass,* but in the wrong location, suggesting that it may have been Melish's best attempt to locate the pass from only verbal information. The Yellowstone River flows into the Missouri, whereas the Sweetwater, in the correct location of South Pass, flows into the North Platte. Yet the pass is shown on Stuart's correct route along the Snake River, here *South Fork of Lewiss R.*

Map 157 (*below*).
This map correctly shows the location of South Pass, round the southern end of *Wind River Mts.,* but curiously does not name it. This is even stranger given that the map appeared in an 1836 book, *Astoria,* by Washington Irving, commissioned by John Jacob Astor to document the achievements of his Astorians. This widely distributed and immensely popular book was responsible for a growing interest in Oregon and California.

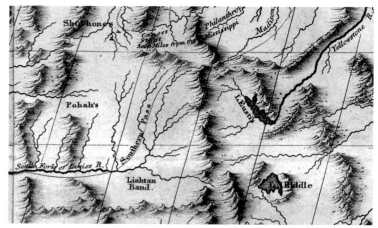

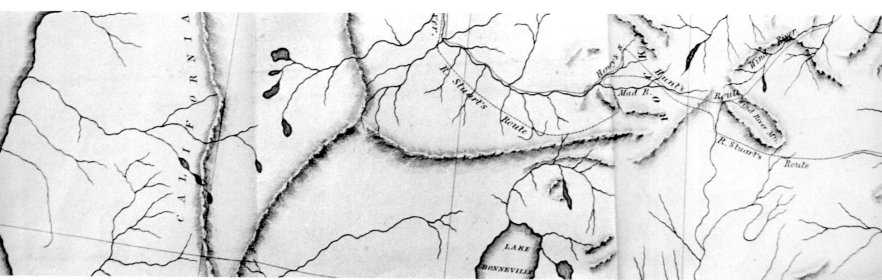

In 1831, Captain Benjamin Louis Eulalie de Bonneville took leave from the U.S. Army and began a western exploration that would last several years. In 1833 Bonneville sent one of his men, Joseph Reddeford Walker, to find that old myth the Buenaventura River and follow it to the Pacific. Walker found the Humboldt and followed it and then, having run out of river, looked for a route across the Sierra Nevada. It is thought that the route he took included the Yosemite Valley. In November 1833 he reached the Pacific. However, Walker knew that the route he had taken was not suitable for emigrants and so searched to the south for an easier path across the mountains. He found it from the southern San Joaquin Valley, a low and easy pass known today as Walker Pass; it was to become another major emigrant route.

The visit in 1841 of the United States Exploring Expedition to Oregon and California, and the glowing reviews that its leader, Charles Wilkes, wrote about the West, further served to publicize the virtues of western emigration. The first wagon train reached Oregon in 1842. Two years later, the first wagon train entered California. The Stephens-Townsend-Murphy party followed a trail they found from Humboldt Lake up the Truckee River and across the Donner Pass—the same route that would prove disastrous for the party after which it is named, and the same pass followed by the Central Pacific Railroad in 1869. The pioneers of 1844 were guided to this route by Caleb Greenwood with the assistance of Northern Paiute Indians led by Chief Truckee. Getting the first wagons through involved an incredible effort hauling wagons up precipitous rock

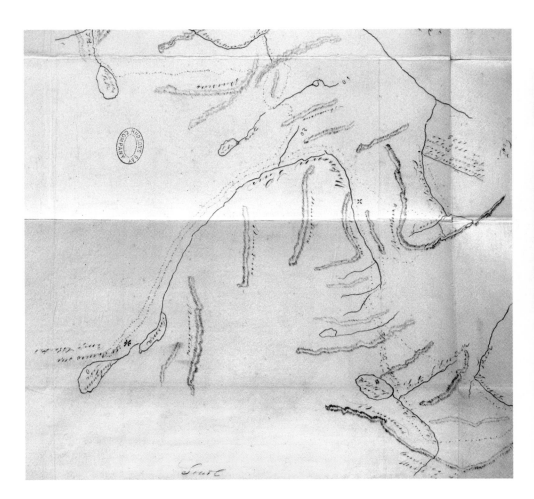

MAP 158 (*right, top*).
Oriented here with north more or less at the top, this is Peter Skene Ogden's map from his fifth expedition, in 1828–29. It shows his exploration of what would become the California Trail across the Great Basin of Utah and Nevada along the valley of the Humboldt River (here toward bottom left), ending at Humboldt Lake in Carson Sink. At that location is the notation (upside down) *280 Indians seen Camp attacked.* The *Great Salt Lake* is at bottom right. Despite some relative positions being portrayed inaccurately, Ogden's travels, and his map, were an important early trailblazer of the overland route to California.

MAP 159 (*right*).
Benjamin de Bonneville's *Map of the Territory West of the Rocky Mountains* reflects his travels and those of Joseph Reddeford Walker in 1832–35. The map was published in 1837. The Humboldt River is shown as *Mary or Ogden's River.* The Great Salt Lake is *Lake Bonneville.* The Sierra Nevada are shown as a continuous range south from Oregon, but, surprisingly, the important pass that Walker found— today Walker Pass—is not shown.

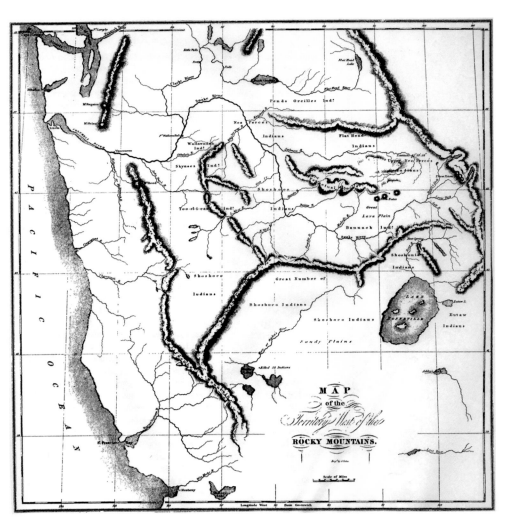

St George

Rocky P.

Head Waters of the ma...

Rio Sacramento

P.ta Barro de Arena.

Rio de las Plumas

Rio de las American...

Nueva Helvetia

R. de los Cosumnes

R. de los Mokelumnes

R. del Calaveras

Stanislaus R.

Rio de los Merced.

Rio San Joaquin

P.ta de los Reyes

S. Francisco

Monte Rey

Rio San Buenaventura

Pyramid Lake

Great Boiling Spr.

Mud Lake

SIERRA NEVADA OF CALIFORNIA

Lake Fork

S. Luis Obispo

La Purissima

S. Ynes

P.ta Concepcion

S. Barbara

S. Buenaventura

S. Fernando

S. Gabriel

Pueblo del los Angeles

Mohahve R.

O C E A N

5000 feet, surrounded by lofty mountains, contents almost unknown, but believed to be filled with rivers and lakes which have no communication with the sea, deserts and oases which have never been explored, and savage tribes, which no traveller has seen or described. See Fremont's Report, pages 275-6.

36

35

34

76

117

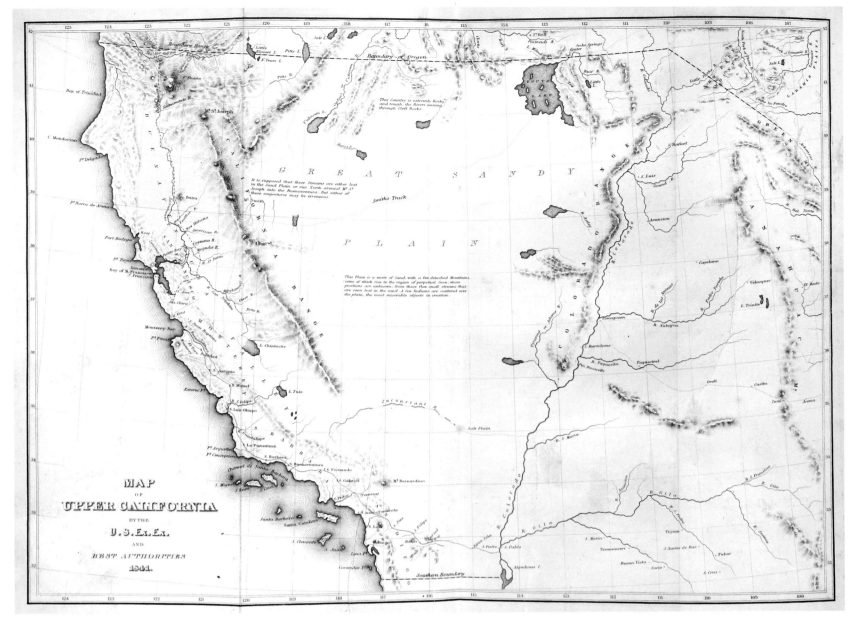

slopes. The Donner route was the last critical link in the California Trail, and other Americans soon followed, despite the fact that California was still in Mexican hands.

Another important figure in the finding of routes to California was John Charles Frémont, destined to play a role in California's history in other ways. An officer in the Army Corps of Topographical Engineers, "the Pathfinder," as he was known, mapped the Oregon Trail in 1842 with his surveyor-cartographer Charles Preuss. In 1843–44, instructed to connect Wilkes's surveys with his own, Frémont came down the eastern flank of the Sierra Nevada from the north, traversing the western edge of the Great Basin, to make sure, once more, that there was no Buenaventura River. Then, in a monthlong march through deep snow, he crossed the Sierra over Truckee Pass, then into the valley of the American River, reaching Sutter's Fort at today's Sacramento. His route is shown on MAP 160 (left).

Frémont stayed at Sutter's Fort until March 1844, when he traveled south down the San Joaquin Valley and crossed the Sierra again at Tehachapi Pass, which he mistook for Walker Pass. The following year he would be back to play a different role (see page 83).

MAP 160 (left).
Frémont's route in 1843–44 is shown in this detailed map published in his 1845 report. Just the topography around his route south from the Columbia River is shown; Frémont was not one for speculation. Sutter's Fort is at *Nueva Helvetia* on the *Rio de los Americanos.* The half-shown unnamed lake at center is Lake Tahoe.

MAP 161 (above).
This is the map of Upper California from the report of Charles Wilkes's United States Exploring Expedition, which was on the West Coast in 1841. The Sacramento River and its tributaries, which Wilkes surveyed, are shown in some detail, but the route across the Great Basin is still simply *[Jedediah] Smith's Track.*

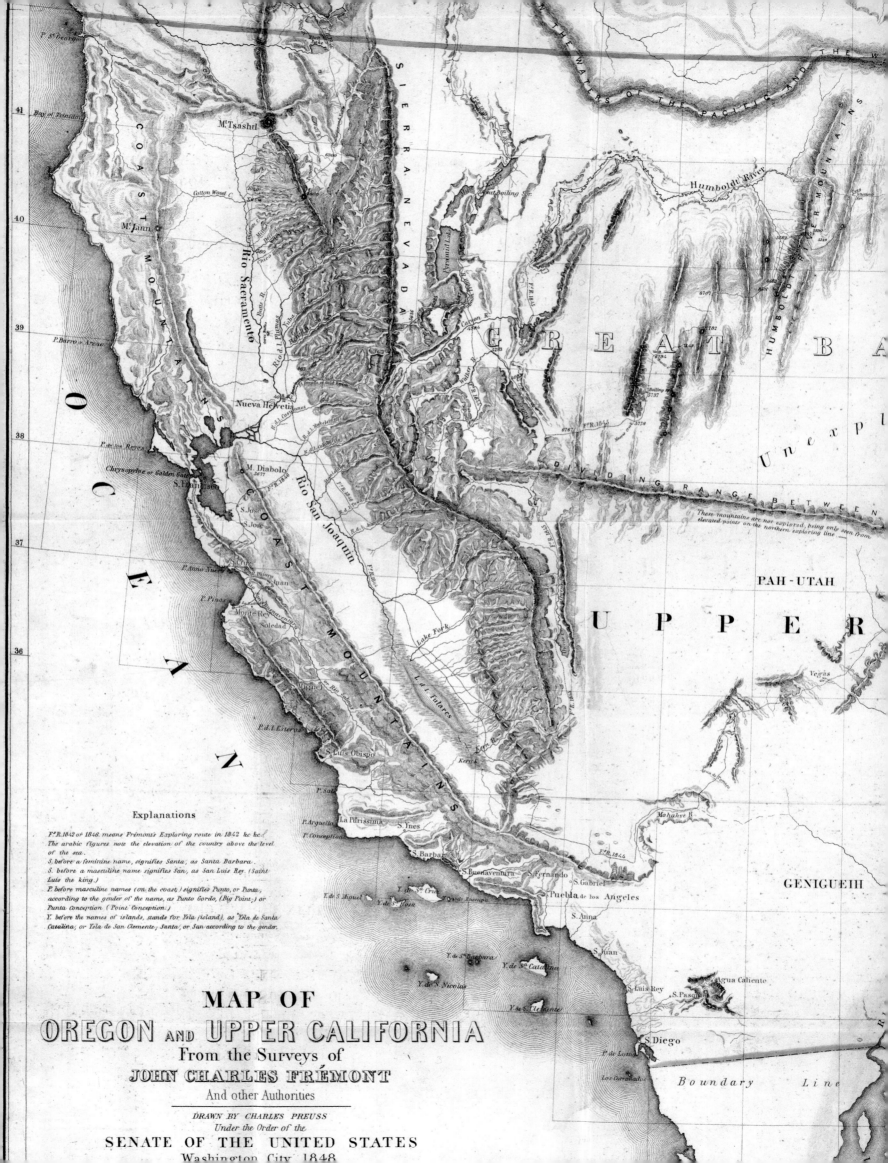

# MAP OF
## OREGON and UPPER CALIFORNIA
### From the Surveys of
#### JOHN CHARLES FRÉMONT
And other Authorities

*DRAWN BY CHARLES PREUSS*
Under the Order of the
## SENATE OF THE UNITED STATES
Washington City 1848

**Explanations**

F.ᵗ R.1842 or 1846. means Frémont's Exploring route in 1842 &c &c.
The arabic figures note the elevation of the country above the level
of the sea.
S. before a feminine name, signifies Santa, as Santa Barbara.
S. before a masculine name signifies San, as San Luis Rey. (Saint
Luis the king.)
P. before masculine names (on the coast,) signifies Punto, or Punta,
according to the gender of the name, as Punto Gordo, (Big Point,) or
Punta Conception (Point Conception.)
Y. before the names of islands, stands for Ysla (island), as Ysla de Santa
Catalina; or Ysla de San Clemente; Santa, or San according to the gender.

**Map 162** *(left)*.

Frémont's final map of California and the West, published in 1848, just in time to be of use to the wave of emigrants that would begin to flood into California seeking gold. That Frémont's maps were useful there can be no doubt. To facilitate migration west, Congress ordered the printing of ten thousand copies of his detailed map of the Oregon Trail. This 1848 map incorporates all his previous surveys and combines them with all other reliable geographical knowledge then available. The result was the most accurate and comprehensive map of the West to date.

**Map 163** *(below)*.

This is the westernmost sheet of a four-sheet map of the Oregon and California trails, published by T.H. Jefferson in 1849. It is now an extremely rare map, with only five copies extant. Unlike the other major map guide for emigrants (Map 164, *overleaf*), this map's author had actually traveled the route espoused on his map. Jefferson published this map himself to take advantage of the large market that had suddenly presented itself with the discovery of gold in California. Much of the map reflects his own experiences, although information from Frémont and others is also incorporated. With the map came a pamphlet entitled *Brief Practical Advice to the Emigrant or Traveller*. In it Jefferson offered advice on party size, wagons, animals, provisions, arms and ammunition, and other useful articles, including goods in demand by Indians that could be used for trade. Women, he advised, should discard side saddles, wear "hunting frocks, loose pantaloons, men's hats and shoes," and ride the same as men. Jefferson's map was the first to show the route taken by the ill-fated Donner party, including the Hastings Cutoff, a shortcut recommended by Lansford Hastings that caused the Donners much of the delay that caught them in the Sierra snows. The Donners were only three days behind Jefferson in 1846.

During the Mexican War, Army surveyors of the Corps of Topographical Engineers mapped a southern route to California from Santa Fe. Map 171, *page 83,* shows the California part of the survey William Hemsley Emory carried out in 1846 as he accompanied Stephen Kearny's little army west. The route, however, would prove to be of more interest to railroads than to gold seekers because of the arid conditions and hostile Indians.

Maps and guides were hastily published in 1849 to guide gold seekers to the Californian Eldorado (Map 163, *below,* and Map 164, *overleaf*). Some advocated shortcuts such as that of Lansford Warren Hastings, south of the Great Salt Lake—a route shorter, indeed, but perilous in the extreme, for water was very hard to find. One party, that of the Donners, had taken the Hastings Cutoff in 1846 and delayed themselves so much that they became stuck in the snows of the Sierra pass that is now named after them, famously resorting to cannibalism to survive.

The first "civilization" many of the wagon trains found was at Sutter's Fort, now in Sacramento, the headquarters of the rancho of John Augustus Sutter, a French-speaking German immigrant of Swiss parents who had been granted the land in 1841 and who developed a considerable agricultural empire in the Sacramento Valley. Sutter, who had arrived in California in 1839, was arguably the most successful of the foreign rancho owners, and it was on his land in 1848 that the gold was found that would change California forever (see page 88).

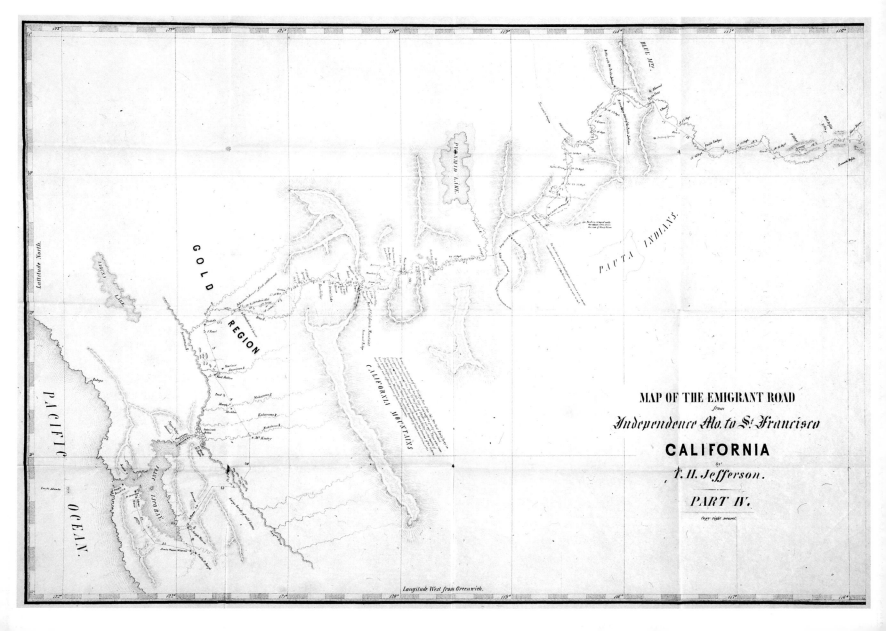

MAP OF THE EMIGRANT ROAD
*from*
*Independence Mo. to S! Francisco*
**CALIFORNIA**
*by*
*T. H. Jefferson.*

*PART IV.*

*Copy right secured.*

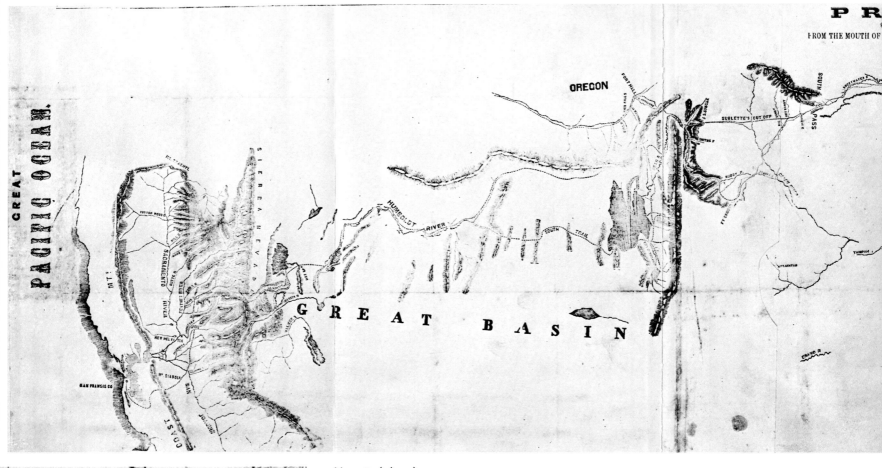

OREGON

PACIFIC OCEAN.

GREAT

G R E A T   B A S I N

Nueva Helvetia

MAP 164 (above).

Joseph E. Ware's *Map of the Route to California,* published in 1849. Ware, like Jefferson, published his map with a guide, to take advantage of gold seekers traveling to California. He, however, had not traveled the route himself, and so the map is entirely a compendium of the work of others, particularly that of Frémont. Nonetheless, it was fairly reliable, though Ware in his guide dangerously romanticized the valley of the Humboldt as full of grass and timber. Ware himself attempted to reach California but became ill and died on the way after being abandoned by his companions. Ware's guide drew on information about outfitting wagons from Lansford Hastings, but his map does not show all of the Hastings Cutoff, the route south of the Great Salt Lake, although part, from the lake west, is depicted and labeled *South Trail.*

MAP 166 (below, right).

In 1848 Sutter had this plan of his fort published in a magazine for German immigrants as part of a "marketing plan" to bring more settlers to his lands. He also included text extolling the virtues of California. Sutter was soon overwhelmed by numbers, but of gold seekers rather than German immigrants. The rooms around the walls accommodated many functions, including a granary; a cooper's shop; a bakery; a torch and lantern room; a carpentry shop; and living quarters. Sutter's own house was at center. Outside the main walls to the south (toward the bottom) are not structures but corrals. To the north was a slough, for water and protection. *Below* is a view of the interior of the restored Sutter's Fort as it is today.

MAP 165 (above).

This enlarged portion of Frémont's 1848 map shows the end point of the California Trail: Sutter's Fort on the American River near its junction with the Sacramento in John Sutter's *Nueva Helvetia*—New Switzerland. The fort is today surrounded by the urban area of Sacramento, a block from the Capital City Freeway, Interstate 80.

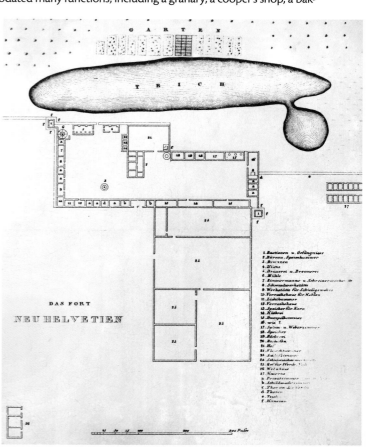

DAS FORT
NEUHELVETIEN

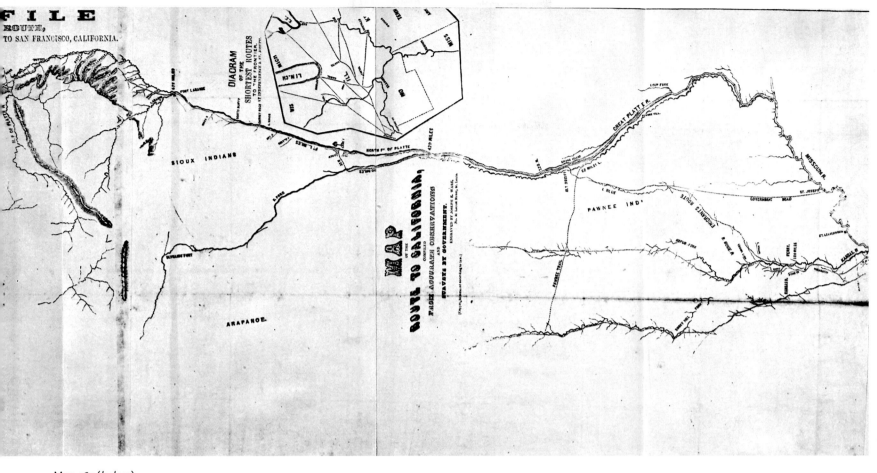

Map 167 (*below*).
Sutter was granted a rancho he called Nueva Helvetia, New Switzerland, in 1841, and this was the *diseño* (see page 68) used to claim it after the American annexation. At left (west) is the *Rio Sacramento,* with the *Rio de los Americanos* (American River) flowing into it across the map. Sutter's *Establecimenta,* popularly known as Sutter's Fort, is shown, today in the middle of the City of Sacramento.

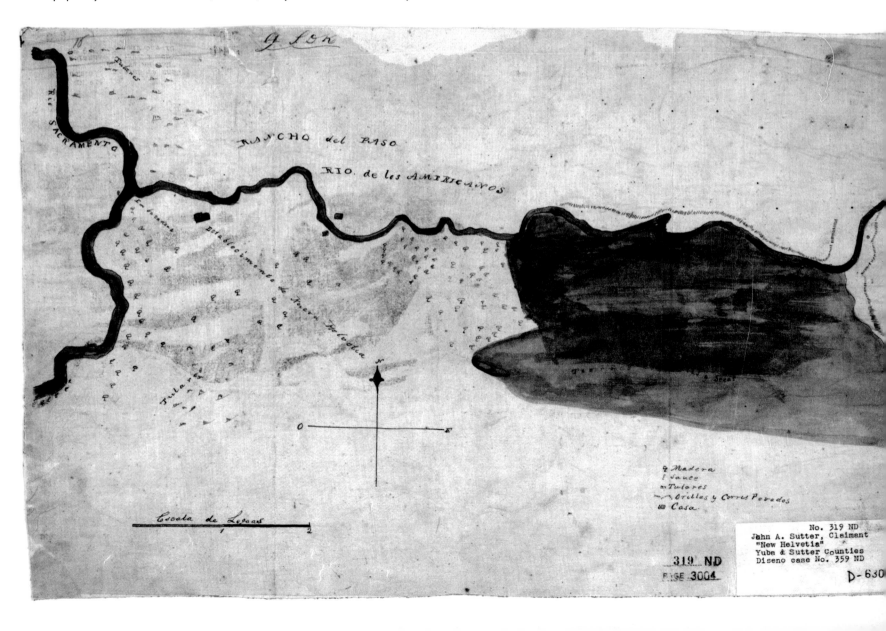

# AMERICAN CALIFORNIA

The Mexicans surrendered California to the United States not once, but three times. The first was in 1842, the second in 1847, and the third in 1848. For many years, few doubted that Mexico was heading in the direction of losing California, such was the benign neglect of its northern province, although it was not clear, even to the United States, whether another power—Britain—might have designs to the south of its territories.

The first surrender of California was the result of a misunderstanding. Commodore Thomas ap Catesby Jones, patrolling in South American waters with the American fleet, developed the idea—apparently from reading the newspaper—that the United States and Mexico were at war over Texas. He sailed two ships to Monterey where, on 18 October 1842, he demanded and received the surrender of California from the (recently retired) governor Juan Bautista Alvarado. It took the intervention of an American merchant, Thomas Oliver Larkin, to persuade Catesby Jones that in fact no war had been declared, and the red-faced commodore was forced to apologize—and give the country back!

Although this surrender was quickly reversed, it was a signal to the world of the United States' intentions, and events soon unfolded that led to a permanent annexation. The United States and Mexico were moving toward war over Texas, which had declared its independence in 1836 but never had it ratified by Mexico. Thus was the situation in March 1845 when a new, overtly expansionist president, James Polk, took office. Oregon was brought into the American fold in June with the signing of a treaty that seemed to indicate the end of any British intentions farther south, though the threat still lurked in many minds.

The Pacific Fleet, now under Commodore John Drake Sloat, was ordered north to patrol between Mexico and Hawaii, with instructions to seize the critical port of San Francisco Bay if he should hear that war had begun. A dispatch was sent to Thomas Larkin in Monterey appointing him a "confidential agent" of the American government. He was instructed to "conciliate" any signs of unrest among the *Californios* and urge their support of annexation. At the same time, Larkin was to assure them that if California seized its independence, the United States would

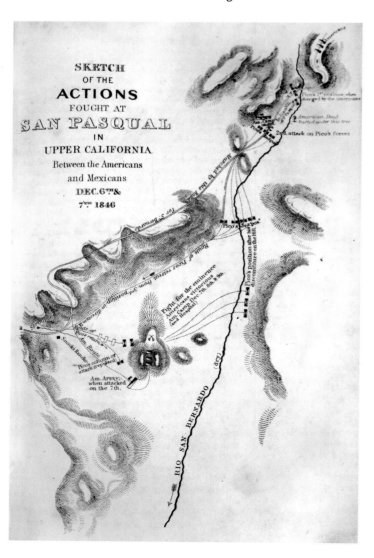

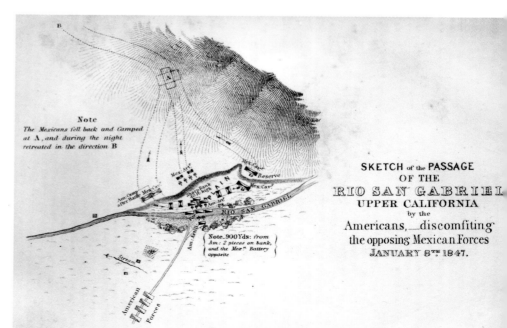

"render her all the kind offices in our power as a Sister Republic," and spread word that if *Californios* wished to "unite their destiny with ours," they would be received as brethren. Larkin wasted no time in ensuring that this message got out, discussing it with such powerful people as the influential one-time California military chief General Mariano Guadalupe Vallejo, now in charge of the army garrison at Sonoma.

On 28 December 1845 Texas was admitted to the Union, an act that Mexico had sworn would mean war.

John Charles Frémont, who had met with Polk in May, had been dispatched west on another of his grand tours of exploration, in reality to be available should he be required. Frémont, however, was not content to sit on the sidelines watching and had quickly grown restless, behaving as if he were trying to provoke the war sooner rather than later. In March 1846 Frémont with about sixty men occupied Gavilán or Hawk's Peak (now Fremont Peak) near Monterey, threatening the town. It was an act of sheer bravado, and he soon thought the better of it. Commandante José Castro gathered some two hundred volunteers and marched out to confront Frémont, who, after three days, gave up the show and departed, retreating temporarily into Northern California.

Larkin sent a message to Sloat asking him to send a warship to ensure the safety of American citizens. The *Portsmouth,* under John B. Montgomery, anchored in Monterey Bay on 21 April 1846. Montgomery began distributing, as he had been ordered to by Sloat, copies of the American and Texas constitutions, translated into Spanish.

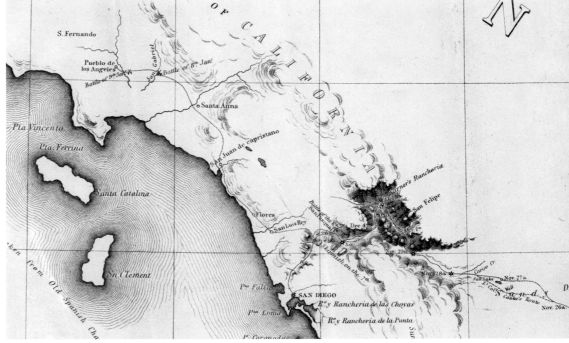

Map 169 (*left*) and Map 172 (*right*).
The battles for Los Angeles, 8 and 9 January 1847 at the San Gabriel River (Map 169) and La Mesa, also known as the Battle of Los Angeles (Map 172). These plans, recording the movements during these battles, and also Map 168 and Map 170, were drawn by topographical engineer William Hemsley Emory, one of Kearny's officers, and were later published in a report.

Map 170 (*right, top*).
This is Sonoma, location of the Bear Flag Revolt and proclamation of the California Republic on 14 June 1846. The republic lasted until American annexation on 9 July. The map was published in 1919, but apart from a few houses and the two railroads, not much had changed. The central plaza is the square with a single building at the north end of the north-south road at left center.

Map 171 (*right, center*).
Emory's general map shows the progress of Kearny's little army across the Southwest, and its western part shows the locations of the battles at San Pasqual, Rio Gabriel, and Los Angeles.

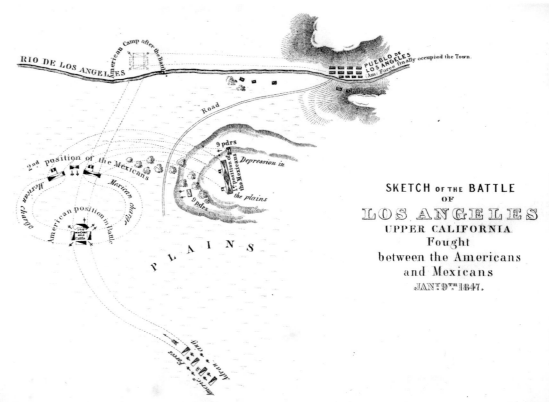

SKETCH of the BATTLE
OF
LOS ANGELES
UPPER CALIFORNIA
Fought
between the Americans
and Mexicans
JAN 9TH 1847.

### VIEW OF SAN FRANCISCO, FORMERLY YERBA BUENA, IN 1846-7
#### BEFORE THE DISCOVERY OF GOLD

WE THE UNDERSIGNED HEREBY CERTIFY THAT THIS PICTURE IS A FAITHFUL AND ACCURATE REPRESENTATION OF SAN FRANCISCO AS IT REALLY APPEARED IN MARCH 1847

*J. D. Stevenson*
COMMANDING 1ST REGT. OF N.Y. VOLS. IN THE WAR WITH MEXICO.

*Gen. M. G. Vallejo*

*George Hyde*
FIRST ALCALDE DIST. OF SAN FRANCISCO 1846-7

Just at this time Archibald Gillespie, a young naval lieutenant on a special secret mission from the president also arrived in Monterey, briefed Larkin, and then chased after Frémont with other secret instructions. It has never been satisfactorily explained what precisely was in the secret messages, as Gillespie memorized them and then destroyed them, and one assumes that any such information was conveniently forgotten after California became American. Nonetheless, by the time the first military engagements of the Mexican War began in Texas, at the end of April, the United States was relatively well organized in California. War was officially declared on 13 May.

Reports that the expulsion of foreign settlers was now expected whipped up discontent and agitation, and a Mexican cavalry detail gathering horses was attacked. Then thirty-three settlers seized Sonoma on 14 June and forced the surrender of Vallejo and his garrison, thus hoping to hinder Mexican attempts to form an army to expel them. Though not very coordinated, the attack coalesced into the so-called Bear Flag Revolt—named after the flag the settlers raised—largely, it seems, through the exhortations of one man, William B. Ide, a carpenter from Massachusetts. He was immediately rewarded with the presidency of the new republic, but it did not last long, for on 23 June Frémont took over the command of the group, adding his sixty men, and on 9 July the republic was annexed by the United States.

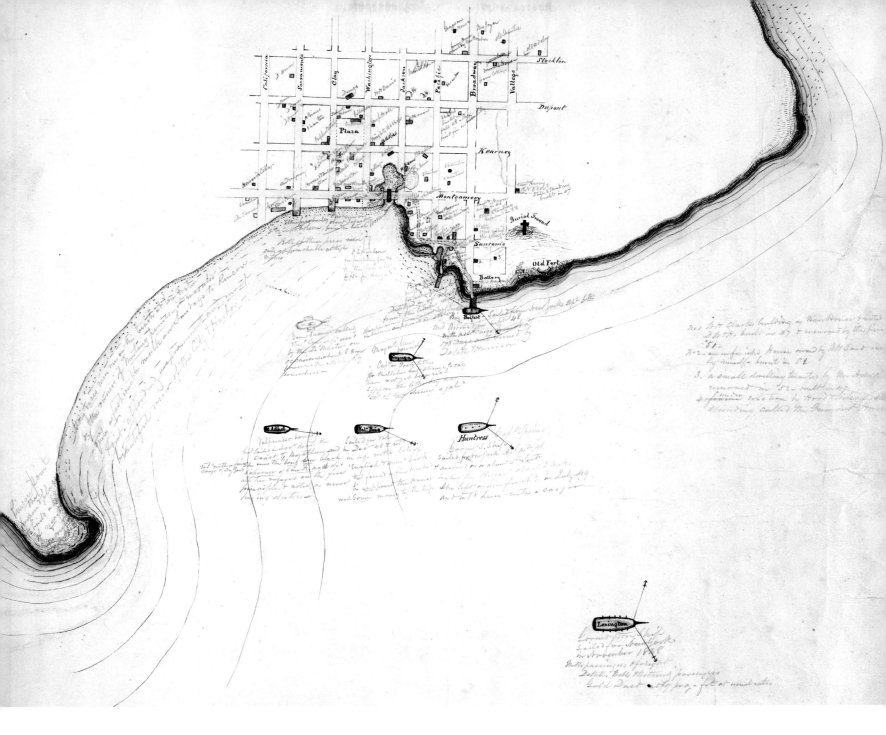

**Map 173** (*left, top*).
A combination view and map showing San Francisco as it was in March 1847. Yerba Buena was officially renamed on 30 January 1847 by proclamation of *alcalde* Washington Bartlett. Although drawn later, the print has the signatures of residents at the time authenticating it, including that of Mariano Vallejo. The American warship *Portsmouth* sits at anchor in Yerba Buena Cove. Montgomery Street was named after its captain, John B. Montgomery. This part of the street is now seven blocks from the bay.

**Map 174** (*left, bottom*).
Yerba Buena is shown on this detail of an American military reference map drawn in 1847.

**Map 175** (*above*).
This is San Francisco in September 1848. The street pattern can be compared to that in **Map 173**. This map was drawn by Augustus Harrison, master of the brig *Belfast*, shown at a newly built dock called Clark's Wharf. The ship was the first to dock in San Francisco rather than anchor in the cove. Harrison has made copious pencil notes as to the destinations of the ships in the cove, some added a few months later.

Commodore Sloat, anchored in Monterey Bay, had dallied, not wanting to commit once again the sins of his unfortunate predecessor Catesby Jones, but, after long discussions with Thomas Larkin, on 7 July he loaded 225 sailors and marines into boats and sent them to seize Monterey. He read to the citizens a proclamation he had written designed to alleviate their fears. "I declare to the inhabitants of California," he read, "that although I come in arms with a powerful force, I do not come among them as an enemy to California; on the contrary, I come as their best friend, as henceforth California will be a portion of the United States, and its peaceful inhabitants will enjoy the same rights and privileges as the citizens of any other portion of that territory."

The *Portsmouth* sailed into San Francisco Bay and on 9 July seventy sailors were landed, led by Lieutenant Charles Warren Revere, who read the proclamation at Yerba Buena and raised the Stars and Stripes. Later that day the ceremony was repeated at Sonoma, and the twenty-five-day-old California Republic came to an end.

Sloat, however, had been working on the assumption that Frémont had been acting on orders from above when he barricaded himself at Hawk's Peak and later took over command of the Bear Flaggers, orders, perhaps, carried by Gillespie. But, on 19 July, he finally met Frémont and was informed that the explorer had acted by himself. Sloat had done the right thing, as it happened, but for the wrong reason.

At this point Sloat's replacement as commodore arrived. He was Commodore Robert Field Stockton, and he was as aggressive as Sloat had been passive. And he liked Frémont. Stockton soon hatched a plan in tandem with Frémont to move their men south to confront the Mexican forces, led by José Castro, who had moved to join his by now straggling soldiers with those of the governor, Pío Pico, in Los Angeles. But both knew they did not have the strength to resist the Americans now marching toward them, and they fled to Mexico. On 17 August Stockton—now referring to himself as the "Commander-in-Chief and Governor of the Territory of California"—issued a new proclamation announcing that California was now part of the United States.

And that might have been that, if it were not for a counter revolt of *Californios* who had initially welcomed the Americans. Mainly through arrogance and insensitivity, Stockton lost control of Los Angeles and San Diego, though the latter was regained a few days later. Archibald Gillespie, left in charge at Los Angeles, proved to be an imperious and arbitrary ruler, totally unsuited for the situation he faced.

In the meantime, an army led by Brigadier General Stephen Watts Kearny had marched to Santa Fe, and New Mexico had been annexed with hardly a shot being fired. Kearny was on his way to California, via the southern Gila Valley route, when he learned that it was already in American hands. He therefore dispatched the majority of his army to assist the war in Mexico, while he continued west with only about a hundred men. He could have used more, for at the village of San Pasqual, just north of San Diego, on 6 December 1846, Kearny bungled an attack on a smaller force of *Californios* (Map 168, *page 82*). Twenty-two of his men were killed.

As soon as Stockton and Kearny met, they began bickering about who was in charge in California. The lack of clarity was due to out-of-date orders that both men held, a function of the long

MAP 176.
The City of Benicia, located at a strategic point on the Carquinez Strait, the way from San Francisco Bay to both the Sacramento and San Joaquin rivers, is shown on a grand but at the time hypothetical plan drawn in 1851. The land was purchased by Robert Semple and Thomas Larkin from Mariano Vallejo in 1847 for $100 and the promise to name the city after his wife. But Vallejo's wife's first name was Francesca, and this was considered to be too close to the name of the rival city of San Francisco. So Benicia, her second name, was used instead. The city was briefly the state capital in 1853, and the photograph (*left*) shows the capitol building as it is today.

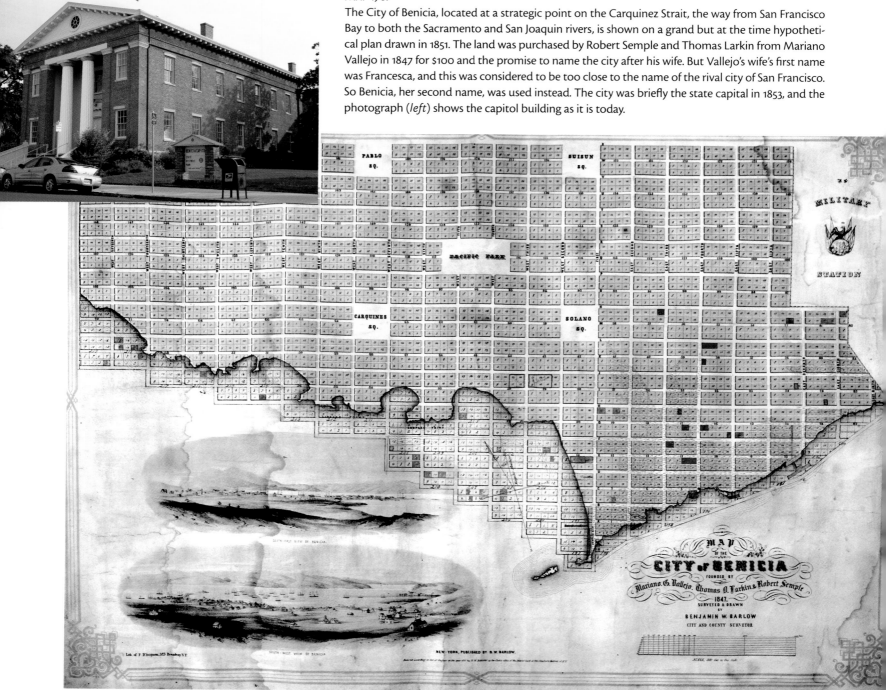

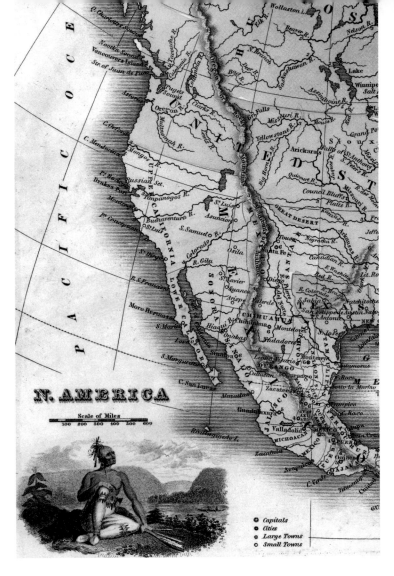

MAP 177 (*above*).

The continental situation in 1842 is shown on this map. Mexican Alta California extends to 42°N, and the current states of Oregon and Washington and the Canadian province of British Columbia form the Oregon Country, a region by treaty of "joint occupancy" by the United States and Britain—that is, it was open to the nationals of both countries until its status could be agreed upon.

MAP 178 (*right*).

This map was rushed into print in 1848 to show the western situation at the end of the Mexican War. The boundary between British and American territory is now drawn at 49°N (except for Vancouver Island), and the United States controls all of Upper California and New Mexico. *Upper or New California* was California for two years, until statehood in 1850 (see page 102). MAP 194, *page 102*, shows the original map used to negotiate the treaty.

distances and poor communication with Washington, and the fact that Stockton was Navy while Kearny was Army. Nevertheless, both cooperated enough to retake Los Angeles. The Mexicans were engaged at the San Gabriel River on 8 January 1847 (MAP 169, *page 82*) and the following day on the plain of La Mesa, a battle often referred to as the Battle of Los Angeles (MAP 172, *page 83*). On 10 January Los Angeles was occupied.

Frémont was approaching Los Angeles from the north with four hundred men when he encountered a Mexican force under José María Flores, whom he induced to sign a document surrendering California to the United States. This was the Treaty of Cahuenga, and this time the Mexican surrender of California would stick.

The debacle between Kearny and Stockton continued, with Frémont, though an Army man, taking Stockton's side. Stockton's replacement, Colonel Richard Barnes Mason, immediately accepted Kearny's command, assuming the military governorship when Kearny left in June 1847. Frémont was ordered to accompany Kearny east and was arrested and court-martialed for mutiny. President Polk intervened to save Frémont, now even more a national hero, but, outraged, Frémont resigned from the Army.

To the south, an American force under General Winfield Scott invaded Mexico in March 1847. After a long campaign and many battles Mexico City fell on 13 September, thus ensuring that California would remain American, as would most of the Southwest; Mexico lost half of its territory. By the Treaty of Guadalupe Hidalgo, signed on 2 February 1848, Mexico surrendered California once more. At the time Upper California seemed of little value to Mexico, which had, after all, neglected the province, yet, the month before this final treaty was signed, and before it had even been ratified by Congress, gold was found along the banks of the Rio de los Americanos, henceforth to be the American River.

# THE GOLD RUSH

At the time of the American annexation of California in 1846 there were about 14,000 people of EuroAmerican origin in California. By 1853 there were 300,000. A new land opened up to settlement, but the impetus for immediate and explosive growth was gold.

Rarely was a new land jump-started the way California was. Suddenly the country arose from its Mexican pastoral lethargy and entered a new American world of bustling commerce and purpose. Nowhere was this more apparent than in San Francisco, transformed in a twinkling of an auriferous eye from a sleepy village to a busy if rough and ready Pacific entrepot with a harbor packed with ships.

The gold that started it all was found on John Augustus Sutter's land on the American River. Sutter had survived the dangerous transition from Mexican frontier agent to American settler and retained possession of his considerable empire in the Sacramento

Valley. But Sutter was in debt. He had purchased—and still not fully paid for—Fort Ross from the Russians. So he was looking for ways to benefit from the new circumstances of California and was poised, he hoped, to profit from the hordes of wagons that would be sure now to flock west. In 1847 Sutter was looking for a suitable place to build a water-powered sawmill to produce planking he could sell in San Francisco. With James Marshall, a millwright, a sawmill was built forty miles above the fort on the South Fork of the American River at a place later named Coloma. Marshall was to operate the mill while Sutter was to keep it supplied.

On Sunday afternoon, 23 January 1848, Marshall was inspecting the tailrace of the mill when his "eye was caught with the glimpse of something shining in the bottom of the ditch." It was, of course, gold, and the course of California's history changed overnight. Within six weeks others had found gold in a hundred nearby locations. Sutter knew a large gold find was to bring him problems, but he was unable to contain news of the discovery even until he could register title to some of the land. By the middle of March, San Francisco's newspaper *The Californian* was announcing that "gold has been found in every part of the country." So many people would soon flock to "the diggings" that *The Californian,* and its rival *Star,* would soon be out of business because there were not enough subscribers. Fully three quarters of San Francisco's population had "gone to the mines."

The exodus spelled trouble for all employers. Sutter's Fort was almost deserted, and Sutter could not find enough men to harvest his wheat. Military governor Colonel Richard Mason found his soldiers deserting at every turn. In July Mason toured the gold areas with a detail of his men, only to have almost all of them desert when

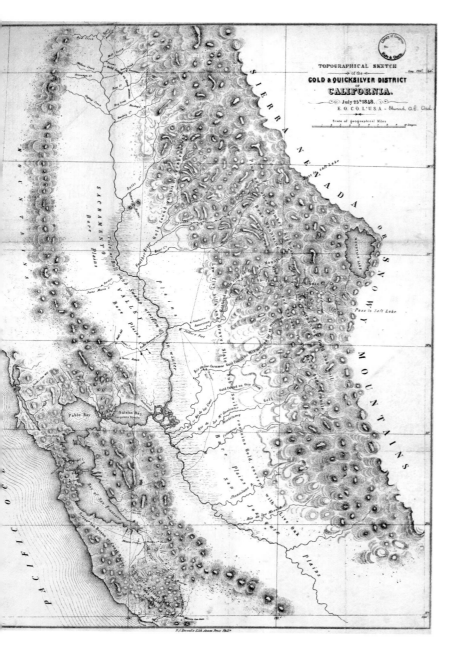

MAP 179 (*left*).
One of the first maps of the gold region, dated only six months after Marshall's discovery, was produced by Army Lieutenant Edward Otho Cresap Ord, based at Monterey. The site of the original gold find is at *Uppermine Mill,* on the South Fork of the American River, hard to see among the heavily hachured representation of relief. San Francisco is still Yerba Buena. Ord, who would go on to become a war hero during the Civil War, surveyed Los Angeles in 1849 in preparation for it becoming a city the following year (see MAP 282, *page 149). Top left* is a scene from an 1849 Currier and Ives print.

MAP 180 (*right*).
Published by entrepreneur and late American consul at Monterey, Thomas O. Larkin, this map was copied from one surveyed by John Bidwell, who was Sutter's right-hand man at his fort. The map is only of the Sacramento Valley, and despite its title, it does not cover the areas where the majority of the gold workings were, higher in the Sierra. But it was a good map, and good maps were at a premium in the early days of the gold rush. Bidwell surveyed the Sacramento Valley in connection with pending land claims that were to go before the courts in the next few years as settlers attempted to prove their ownership of ranchos from Mexican grants, which were to be respected if proven. MAP 190, *page 97* is also a Bidwell map.

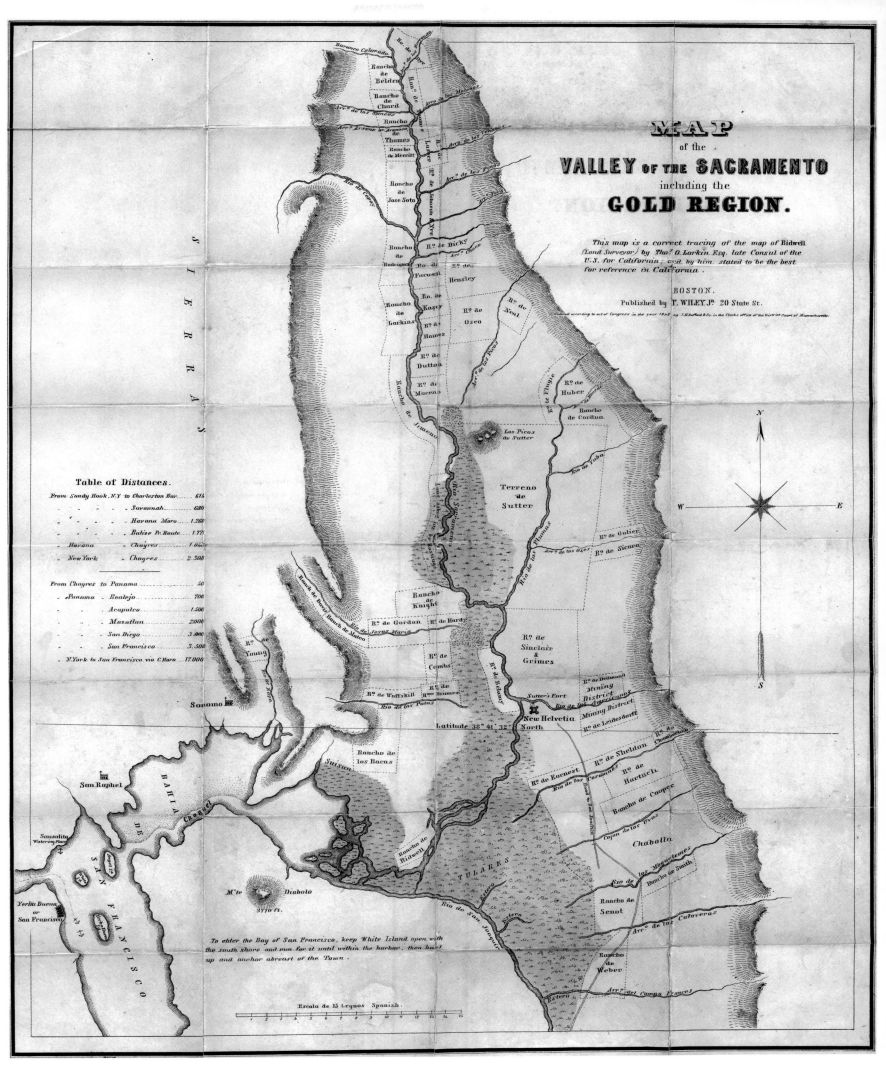

# MAP
## of the
# VALLEY OF THE SACRAMENTO
### including the
# GOLD REGION.

This map is a correct tracing of the map of Bidwell (Land Surveyor) by Thos. O. Larkin Esq. late Consul of the U.S. for California; and by him stated to be the best for reference in California.

BOSTON.
Published by T. WILEY Jr. 20 State St.
Entered according to act of Congress in the year 1848 by J.H.Bufford & Co. in the Clerks office of the District Court of Massachusetts.

### Table of Distances.

From Sandy Hook, N.Y to Charleston Bar ... 614
" " " Savannah ... 680
" " " Havana Moro ... 1.260
" " " Balize Pt. Route ... 1.771
Havana " Chagres ... 1.050
New York " Chagres ... 2.308

From Chagres to Panama ... 50
Panama " Realejo ... 700
" " Acapulco ... 1.500
" " Mazatlan ... 2000
" " San Diego ... 3.000
" " San Francisco ... 3.500
N.York to San Francisco via C.Horn ... 17.000

Latitude 38° 41' 32"

To enter the Bay of San Francisco, keep White Island open with the south shore and run for it until within the harbor, then haul up and anchor abreast of the Town.

Escala de 15 Leguas Spanish.

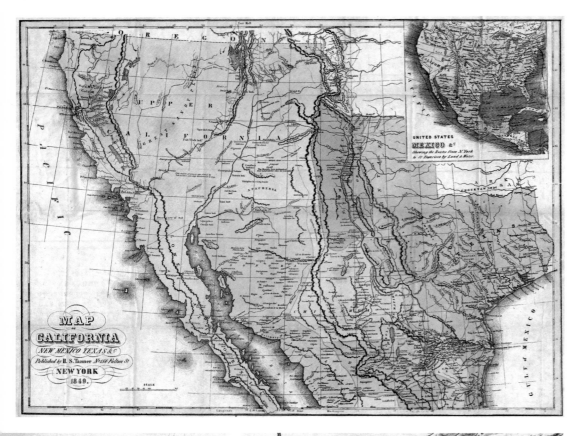

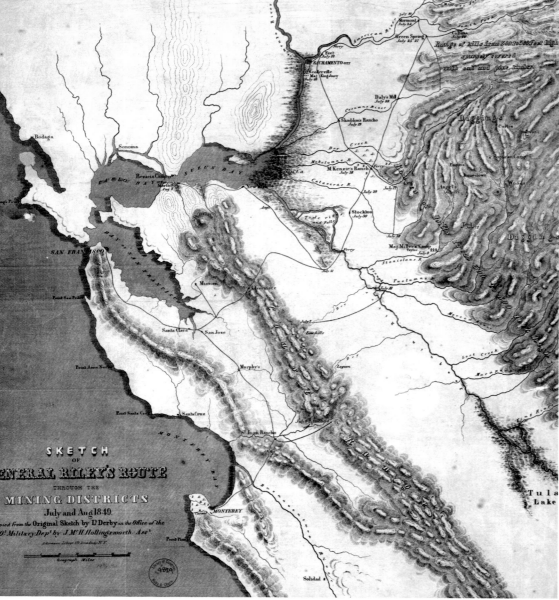

they got there. Only the officers could be relied upon, one of whom was a young Lieutenant William Tecumseh Sherman. Desertion was to become a big problem for the Army; as Mason wrote in a report to the War Department, "the struggle between right and six dollars a month and wrong at $75 a day is rather a severe one." In the eighteen months between July 1848 and the end of 1849 the Army of Northern California lost 716 men to desertion, well over half its original number.

Mason's report (which included MAP 179, *page 88*), written in August, acknowledged that he did not have enough men to control the gold diggers or even to levy any sort of fee or tax. He did, however, recommend the establishment of a mint so that the gold would stay within the United States. After another visit to the gold workings in September, Mason, Sherman, and William Warner, another officer (author of the map of Sacramento on page 99), formed a partnership to run a store at Coloma and within two months had trebled their investment.

MAP 181 (*left, top*).
As soon as gold fever hit the East Coast, commercial mapmakers began hastily turning out maps to inform the public where the gold was and how one could reach it. Many were vastly overstated, either through ignorance or the desire to sell maps. This 1849 general map from Henry Tanner shows much of the Central Valley in yellow, with the words *Gold M.* and *Gold Regions* liberally applied. California is *Upper California*, the entire area gained from Mexico.

MAP 182 (*left*).
A map of the tour of inspection of the gold regions carried out by Brigadier General Bennett, military governor of California, in 1849. *Columa* (Coloma) is at top right. The marshy areas along the rivers are indicated with shading.

MAP 183 (*right*).
This superb broadsheet was published in 1849, finding a ready market among those contemplating the journey to riches. The merits and dangers of various routes are outlined: the sea-land-sea route across the Isthmus of Panama; the all-sea voyage around Cape Horn; and *Another Route*, to Vera Cruz, overland to Mazatlan, and then by sea or overland north to California. Parties of forty or fifty are recommended to prevent attack by bandits.

# MAP OF THE GOLD REGIONS OF CALIFORNIA.
## Showing the Routes via Chagres and Panama, Cape Horn, &c.

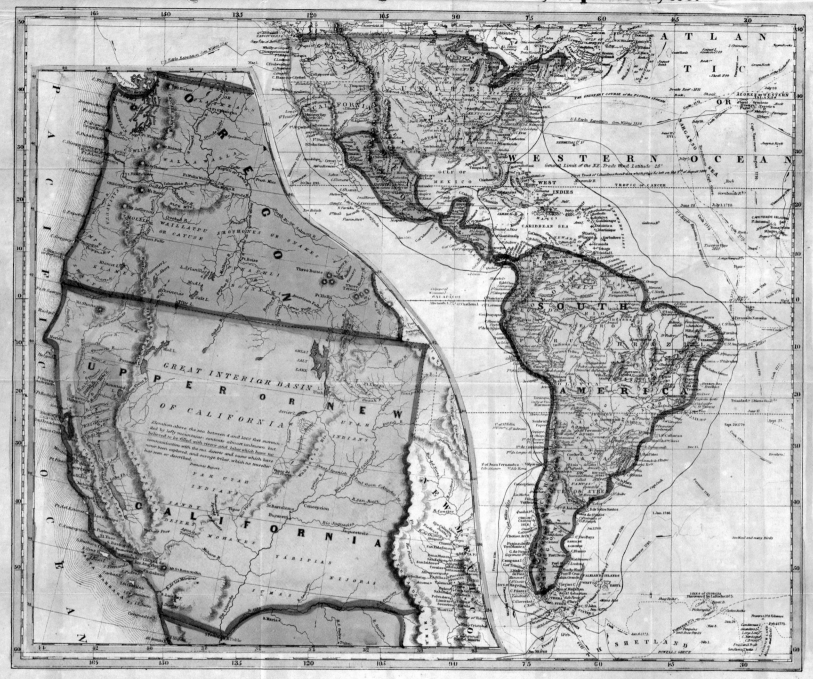

# IMPORTANT DIRECTIONS
## TO PERSONS EMIGRATING TO CALIFORNIA.

### ROUTE via CHAGRES and PANAMA.

For the information of those going to California either as Adventurers or Permanent Settlers, it is important that they have access to all information obtainable, for want of which, the necessary precautions are neglected, which may result in much suffering and disappointment.

On account of the great saving of time and distance, this route is chosen by many, and to such it is important to know something of the difficulties connected with it. No *isolated* individual ought to think of engaging in this enterprise, for there will be many circumstances where a friend will be found of essential benefit. It would be well if parties of ten or more should unite who would be devoted to, and who could place in each other that confidence which the love of Gold could not destroy. Probably, those who pay their passage *and are found* to Chagres, will not find all the accommodations on shipboard to realize their expectations, both from the crowded state of the ship and the *fare*, and it would be well for all to take an extra supply of stores. The Town called CHAGRES is only a small village of one story houses or rather huts, situated at the mouth of the river of that name, which empties into the Atlantic Ocean, and has a small but secure harbour. The place has a very unsightly appearance, being situated in the midst of a swamp, and the continual rains prevailing there would render the streets almost impassable were it not for logs of wood laid along the centre, for the accommodation of pedestrians.

The *Climate* at this point is very unhealthy—the thermometer ranging from 78 to 86 most of the year—which, with its continual rains, produces bilious remittant and congestive fevers, consequently a short stay is most desirable. The population is about 500. Owing to the great amount of travellers across the Isthmus, no dependance can be placed upon obtaining a proper amount of provisions at Chagres for the journey. Hams, biscuits, sausages and preserved meats are the most desirable to carry. The journey to Panama is made by taking small canoes (or a steamboat which has now gone there) to the town of Cruces or Gorgona, a distance of about 33 miles, and from there to Panama, about 24 miles by land. The river part of the route formerly cost from one to four doubloons (16 dollars each) but when the steamboat is there the expense will probably be less. The swamps, stagnant waters, reptiles, &c. in the vicinity of the river, render walking across next to impossible. Gorgona, the first landing place, is a small village, situated on a small plain on the banks of the river. Cruces,

the other landing is a few miles further up, from both of which places are roads leading to Panama, about the same distance, and which unite about nine miles from that city. This 24 miles of land route is usually performed on horses or mules, with another mule to carry baggage, and a Muleteer to act as guide. Owing to rains and the face of the country, the progress is slow, as the road is merely a bridle path, and the journey occupies 10 to 12 hours before reaching the city of Panama.

Not over 100 to 150 lbs. of baggage can be carried without much extra charge. PANAMA, (in 1848) contained about 7000 inhabitants, but accommodations for travellers are poor, there being only one hotel in the place, and board from two to four dollars per day. The climate however is much more healthy than at Chagres, but it is dangerous to camp out, or live in tents as it will soon prove fatal to the unacclimated. One who knows says, "avoid the sun, keep within doors during the day, refrain from eating fruits, even when ripe, with the exception of oranges, which may be eaten moderately. Do not touch the oysters, wear flannel next the skin by day and night, avoid spirituous liquors, and it is needless to say, be off the first opportunity." The distance from Panama to San Francisco is about 3400 miles.

### ROUTE BY CAPE HORN.

This Route is the most acceptable as far as cost and facilities are concerned, but loss of time balances the difference in the price of passage, &c., which varies from one hundred to three hundred dollars, according to accommodations.

The distance from New York to San Francisco, via Cape Horn is about 18,000 miles, and will occupy nearly five months in making the passage. Notwithstanding this appears to be a long voyage, yet it is, (in the present amount of travel across the Isthmus, and the probable want of vessels from Panama to San Francisco) the surest route.

### ANOTHER ROUTE,

Which is said to be "the cheapest, quickest, and safest," is, to take passage in a vessel to Vera Cruz; thence overland to Mazatlan via Guadalajara, Tepic and San Blas; thence either by vessel, or by mule or horse travel by land up the coast. To prevent danger of being attacked by robbers through Mexico, persons should go in parties of 40 to 50, or more. The cost of this route varies from 150 to 300 dollars, and may be accomplished in 60 days.

# DESCRIPTION OF CALIFORNIA,
## OR THE NEW GOLD REGION.

The Gold mines of California were known to have existed in the 16th century, for as early as 1578, about the time Sir Francis Drake made a voyage to the coast, the Jesuits were in possession of certain tracts which they knew to be of more than ordinary value, and employed means to depreciate the country, by erroneous reports to the Spanish government. The government however, appointed Don Joseph Galves commander of a fleet to explore this region, who made favorable reports of the country and its mines. The intelligence, however, did not appear to command the attention of the Spanish Court, and its existence was allowed to pass from age to age apparently unnoticed—reserved till this late day, it would seem, for discovery by a Yankee mechanic, while building a saw mill! Already the active and enterprising, with which our country happily abounds, are in full chase to obtain the earliest advantages this new field offers.

The geographical position of SAN FRANCISCO is one of the most desirable in point of commerce, in this or any other continent, and no doubt is destined to be one of the greatest disbursing depots in the world.

There is an island about three miles opposite, of about two miles length, between which and the town a good anchorage is afforded for vessels. The Bay of San Francisco has been celebrated, from the time of its first discovery, as one of the finest in the world, and is justly entitled to that character, even under the seaman's view of a mere harbor. But when all the accessory advantages which belong to it—fertile and picturesque dependent country, mildness and salubrity of climate, connection with the great interior valley of the Sacramento and San Joaquin, its vast resources for ship-timber, grain and cattle—when these advantages are taken into the account, with its geographical position on the line of communication with Asia, it rises into importance far above that of a mere harbor, and deserves a particular notice in any account of maritime California. Its latitudinal position is that of Lisbon; its climate is that of southern Italy; settlements upon it for more than half a century attest its healthfulness; bold shores and mountains give it grandeur; the extent and fertility of its dependent country give it great resources for agriculture, commerce, and population. The Bay is separated from the sea by low mountain ranges, and is connected with it by a strait about one mile broad in the narrowest part, and five miles long from the sea to the bay. It is about 70 miles long and has a coast lining of about 275 miles.

It is divided by straits and projecting points into three separate bays, of which the northern two are called San Pablo and Suisoon bays. These two are connected by a strait called Carquines, about one mile wide and eight or ten fathoms deep. The Suisoon is connected with an expansion of the river formed by the junction of the Sacramento and San Joaquin rivers, and there commences its connexion with the noble valleys of these rivers. The GOLD REGION of California is in the Sacramento and its tributaries, and covers an extent of territory variously estimated from two to six hundred miles in length, north and south, and some sixty east and west. The valley of the Sacramento is probably the most fertile on the Pacific, and GOLD, as well as the various productions of the earth, can be at all times obtained with the use of the plough, harrow and spade in the hands of an industrious man.

The climate of the country has no winter in the valley, but the rainy season and the dry, and is remarkably healthy. The rainy season begins in November and continues to the middle of February or the beginning of March; the rest of the year is without rain, but the streams from the Sierra Nevada afford all the facilities for irrigation in the heats of July and August. The whole valley abounds with wild cattle, horses, elks, deer, antelopes, grizzly bears, partridges, water fowl, salmon, &c. &c. All the products of the United States, from apples to oranges, from potatoes to sugar cane, may be produced in the valley of the Sacramento and San Joaquin rivers.

The places where Gold is found in the greatest abundance at present are on the Sacramento, Feather and Yerba rivers and the American Fork, north and south branches, the Cosamer, also in many dry ravines, and indeed on the tops of high hills.

According to the reports of analyzers, it is of a superior quality and fineness—and the assays of the U. S. Mint at Philadelphia, prove it to be nearly, if not quite, as pure as American coin. Much of it has already been sent or brought here, which proves conclusively that the region of California is possessed of vast mines of Gold and other metals, which will doubtless enrich this country, and be the means of populating that portion of it, to a degree not heretofore anticipated. Such is California—the richest, most picturesque and beautiful region, for its extent, upon the face of the earth. Such is the El Dorado of the Gold mines; and such is the great acquisition of the late war with Mexico.

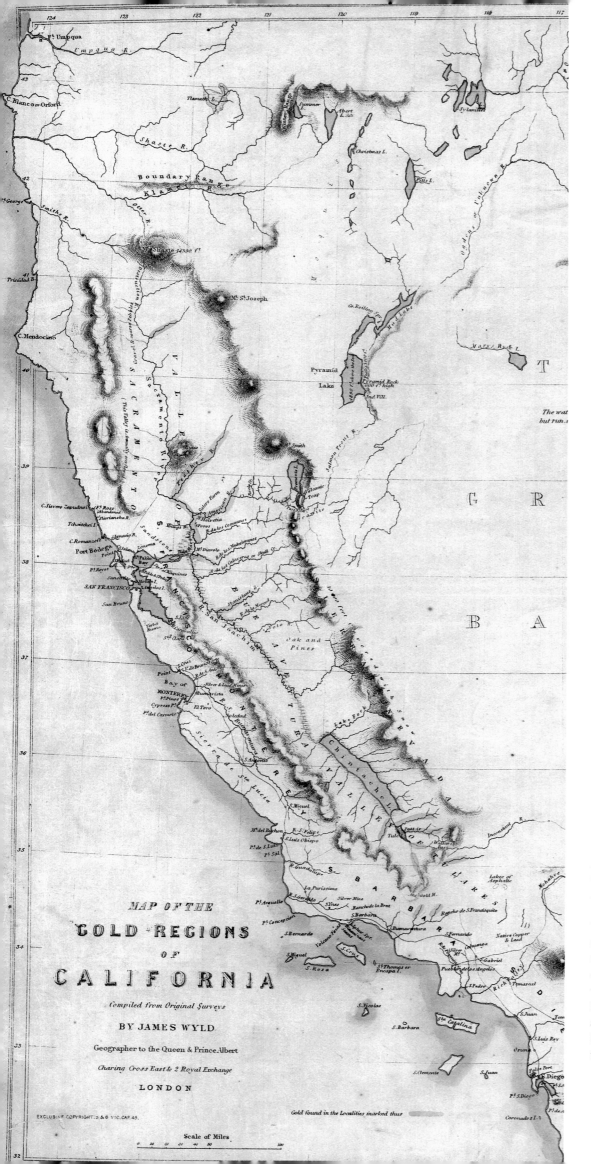

MAP OF THE

GOLD-REGIONS

OF

CALIFORNIA

*Compiled from Original Surveys*

BY JAMES WYLD

*Geographer to the Queen & Prince Albert*

*Charing Cross East & 2 Royal Exchange*

LONDON

Gold found in the Localities marked thus

Scale of Miles

The Navy also had a problem with desertion. Thomas ap Catesby Jones, back in charge of the Pacific Squadron between 1848 and 1850 despite his earlier over-exuberance, felt the only way he could deal with it was by "much cruising." By November 1848 Catesby Jones was offering $500 to $2,000 in silver dollars as a reward for the return of deserters, to little effect.

Soon reports of the gold find began to appear in eastern newspapers. The first was on 19 August, an item in the *New York Herald*, a rewrite of something published in the *California Star* in April. At the end of July Catesby Jones dispatched one of his young officers, Edward "Ned" Beale, to carry the news of the gold discovery to Washington. Beale made the trip in record time, crossing Mexico,

MAP 184 (*left*).
British commercial mapmaker James Wyld published this map in 1849 once information about the gold discoveries reached London. The gold areas are indicated by gold color.

MAP 185 (*right*).
One of the many ships to sail from the eastern seaboard for California in 1849 was the *Apollo*. Moses Yale Beach, a merchant and publisher of the *New York Sun*, purchased the ship and filled it with merchandise that could be sold in San Francisco at a bloated profit. He also had passenger accommodation installed, and his son, Joseph P. Beach, who went along as ship's agent, kept a journal of the voyage and drew a map showing the ship's position each day. The track taken is typical of the ships plying this route. Beach's journal included illustrations such as that of the marlinspike bird (or Red-tailed Tropic-bird, or Bo'sun-bird) shown here. The *Apollo* sailed from New York on 17 January 1849 and reached San Francisco eight months later. Eight days later, after Beach found it impossible to find a crew willing to take her back to New York, the ship was hauled up onto the mud flats, her rigging removed and her structure covered over. For eighteen months she served as a warehouse and store, as shown in the contemporary engraving. It was one of 148 ships that were converted in this way. Then, on the night of 3–4 May 1851 the ship was destroyed by fire, along with a number of other ship-warehouses nearby. The site was quickly filled in, and the waterfront retreated. In 1925 the remains of the ship were discovered during excavations for a new Federal Reserve Bank, and artifacts were collected and displayed by the bank, which in 1980 donated the collection to the San Francisco National Maritime Museum.

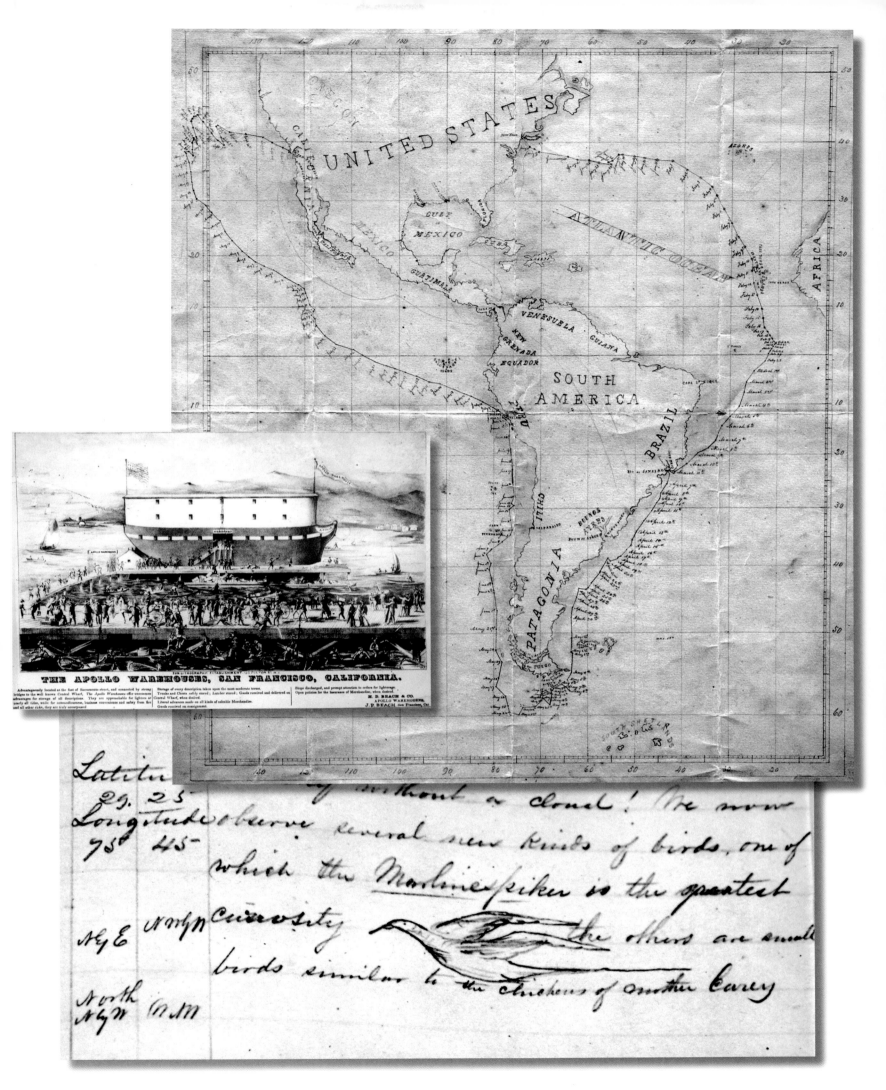

THE APOLLO WAREHOUSES, SAN FRANCISCO, CALIFORNIA.

MAP OF THE
**UNITED STATES**
THE BRITISH PROVINCES
*MEXICO &c.*
Showing the Routes of the U.S. Mail
Steam Packets to California,
and a Plan of the GOLD REGION.

PUBLISHED BY J.H. COLTON,
*86 CEDAR ST. NEW YORK.*
1849.

MAP 186 (*above*).
Commercial mapmaker J.H. Colton's 1849 map outlined quite comprehensively the various routes from the Eastern Seaboard to California. Wagon trails are shown from Independence, Missouri, the beginning of the Oregon and California trails, and also shown is another trail via Bent's Fort, on the Arkansas River. Surprisingly, the Oregon Trail–California Trail connection just north of Great Salt Lake is not indicated, although this was the most popular overland route. A southern overland route is shown across northern Mexico. Combination sea and land routes are shown from the East Coast and from the Mississippi to the Isthmus of Panama and to Vera Cruz, with the coastal sea routes on the Pacific coast. Finally, partly shown with the inset map of South America, the all-sea route round Cape Horn is marked. A detailed inset map of the gold regions of California is also included, making this just the sort of map that a would-be Argonaut would want to buy and consult. Colton, of course, was just giving his market what it was demanding.

finding an American warship at Vera Cruz, which took him to Mobile, and finishing his journey by stagecoach, arriving in Washington on 14 September. It had taken him only forty-seven days. Here was proof positive of the immense gold discovery. In December, Lieutenant Lucien Loesser arrived in Washington. He had been dispatched by Mason to travel by sea and across the Isthmus of Panama at about the same time as Beale had left California, and carried with him 230 ounces of raw gold in what was characterized as a "tea caddy." This really set the Eastern Seaboard alight with gold fever. On 5 December, as if official confirmation were needed, President Polk mentioned the gold discovery in an address to Congress.

Ships were chartered, overland journeys planned, maps and globes pored over. A month after Beale arrived in Washington the first ship, the *California,* sailed from New York, bound for Panama, the first of many to ply that route. Within months, ships set sail around the Horn, and St. Louis assumed new importance as a staging post for

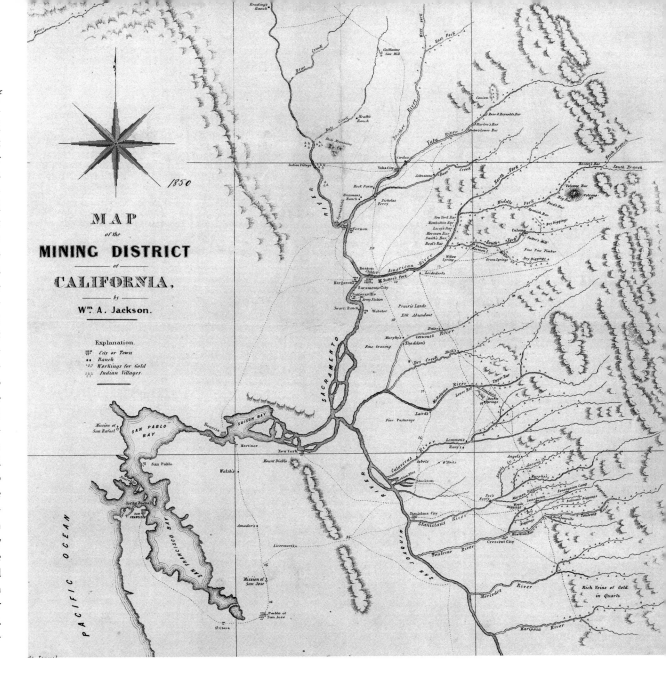

**Map 187** (*right*).

William Jackson's 1850 *Map of the Mining District of California* was one of the most detailed maps of the mines published. Not only does is show *Workings for Gold*, but also, unusually at this time, *Indian Villages*. The construction project that started it all, *Sutter's Mill* at *Culoma* (Coloma) is shown on the South Fork of the American River. The names of some of the sandbars being worked for gold on the American River betray the origins of the miners: *New York Bar*, *Manhattan Bar*, and *Mormon Bar*. The first shipload of American emigrants to reach California had arrived at San Francisco at the end of July 1846 and were mainly Mormons led by Samuel Brannan. Brannan soon abandoned any godly purpose when he found out about the gold discoveries. It was Brannan who in March 1848 famously strode through the streets of San Francisco announcing "Gold! Gold on the American River!"—but only after he had bought up all the prospecting supplies he could find. *Brannans Ranch* is shown on this map on the Yuba River just north of the Sacramento. Note the many named settlements that no longer exist.

the West. The stream of fortune seekers, self-styled Argonauts later dubbed "California Forty-niners," swelled and poured west. Some 70,000 made it to California in 1849 alone. More came by sea than overland. Reliable figures are hard to come by, but estimates for 1849 are 40,000 by sea and 23,000 overland. The winter of 1848–49 was wet on the plains, and swollen rivers prevented westward emigration for a while. In 1850 some 45,000 streamed across the Sierra, and a larger number arrived in San Francisco by ship. Between 1848 and 1851 36,000 of those arriving by sea had chosen to cross the Isthmus of Panama and take ship again at West Coast Mexican ports.

And then there were the inventions, some of which found form in published cartoons of the day, reflecting the general frustration at how long it took to get to California. One cartoonist proposed—and drew—"The Grand Patent India-Rubber Air Line Railway to California," a rubber band stretched coast to coast. Rufus Porter, who went on to found the magazine *Scientific American,* came up with a steam-powered balloon he called an "aerial locomotive," but, perhaps not surprisingly, found no investors.

By 1853, it seemed all the easy placer gold had been found, and miners resorted to hydraulic mining, the washing out of old gold-bearing gravel deposits using a high-powered jet of water contrived by a careful damming and channeling of water from higher up. This method, which was disastrous environmentally, required more capital and a longer-term investment than most gold seekers could manage, and the men became employees of larger concerns. Some hard rock blasting was also used to mine gold.

John Augustus Sutter was, as he had predicted, ruined by the gold rush. First all his workers had left, and then squatters moved onto his land and stole his crops. His real estate developments came to naught, though those of his son flourished (see Map 194, *page 99*), and the elder Sutter's legacy is essentially the City of Sacramento (Map 195, *page 99*), despite its initiation by his son.

The California Gold Rush was all but over by 1855, and gold seekers who had not found their fortunes drifted away or settled down to more mundane but sustainable activities. The gold rush brought California to the attention of the world and assured its prosperity from the very beginning. California was quickly admitted as a state of the Union (see page 102) and within twenty years would be connected to the East with a transcontinental railroad (see page 116).

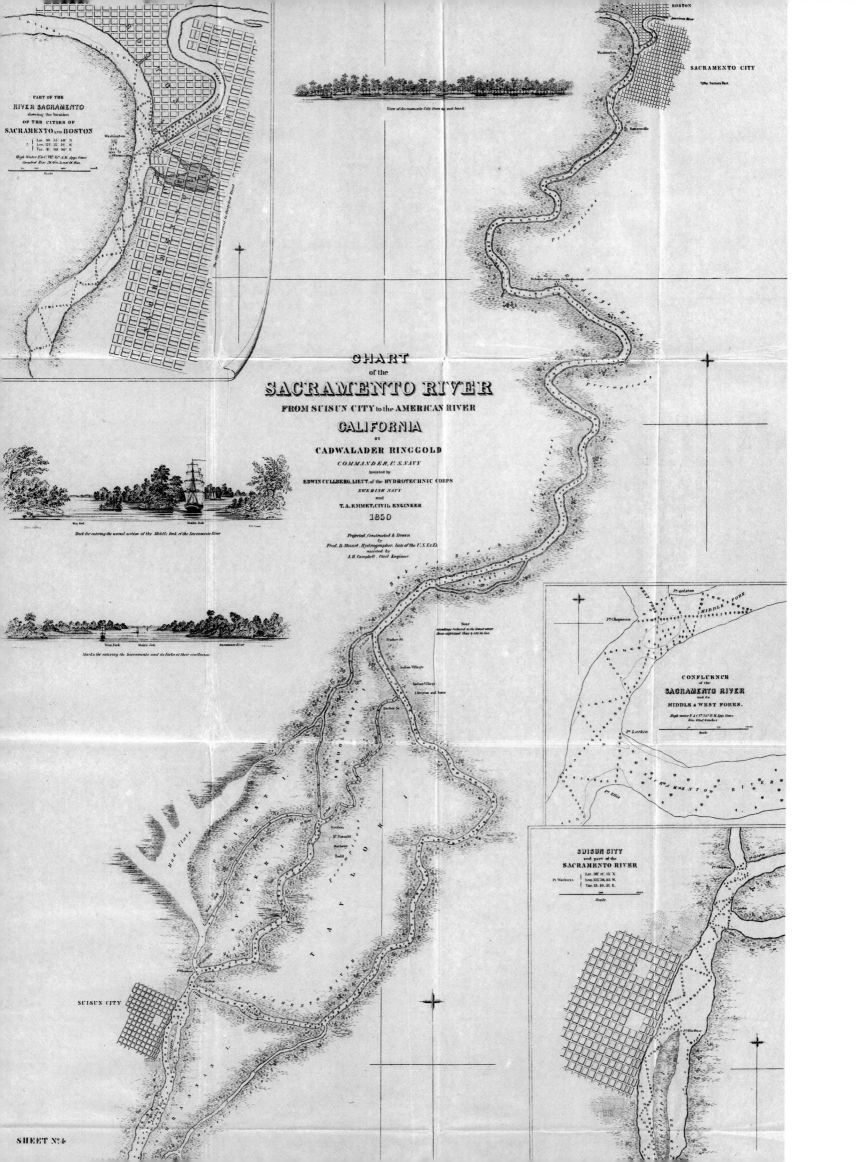

PART OF THE
RIVER SACRAMENTO
shewing the location
OF THE CITIES OF
SACRAMENTO AND BOSTON

CHART
of the
SACRAMENTO RIVER
FROM SUISUN CITY to the AMERICAN RIVER
CALIFORNIA
BY
CADWALADER RINGGOLD
COMMANDER, U.S.NAVY
Assisted by
EDWIN CULLBERG, LIEUT. of the HYDROTECHNIC CORPS
SWEDISH NAVY
and
T. A. EMMET, CIVIL ENGINEER
1850

Projected, Constructed & Drawn
by
Fred. D. Stuart, Hydrographer, late of the U.S. Ex.Ex.
assisted by
A.H. Campbell, Civil Engineer

View of Sacramento City from the west bank

Mark for entering the second section of the Middle Fork of the Sacramento River

Marks for entering the Sacramento and its forks at their confluence

CONFLUENCE
of the
SACRAMENTO RIVER
and its
MIDDLE & WEST FORKS.

SUISUN CITY
and part of the
SACRAMENTO RIVER

SUISUN CITY

BOSTON

SACRAMENTO CITY

SHEET N.° 4

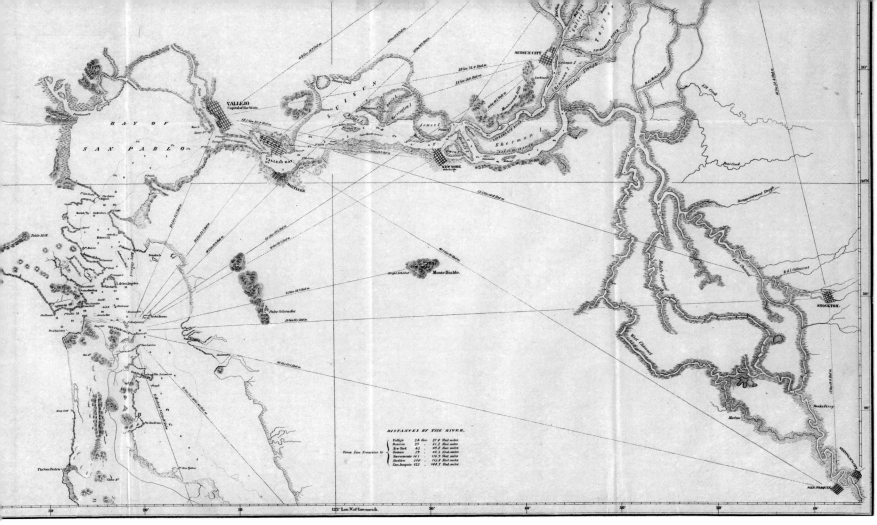

Map 188 (*left*) and Map 189 (*above*).

Cadwalader Ringgold had been the commander of one of the ships in Charles Wilkes's United States Exploring Expedition, which had visited California in 1841, and Ringgold had been in charge of a surveying expedition of San Francisco Bay and the Sacramento River. He was the natural choice for a survey commissioned in 1849 by a group of San Francisco merchants who realized that an up-to-date chart of the shifting sandbars of Suisun Bay and the Sacramento River, the main highway to the goldfields, was essential, together with the placement of buoys to mark the dangerous shoals. Also required was an up-to-date survey of San Francisco Bay. At this time promoters of various city sites engaged in nefarious tactics to promote their site over others. Even Thomas Larkin is known to have offered Ringgold money to display the name of his city, Benicia, more prominently on the chart. Ringgold, a traditional Navy man, refused. Others were promoting *New York of the Pacific* (founded in 1839 and renamed Pittsburg in 1911). After work was completed on the Sacramento River and San Francisco Bay some attention was paid to the sea approaches to the harbor, and another chart was produced for this. The whole survey was completed in June 1850. The survey was to a very high standard and gave the merchants of San Francisco exactly what they wanted. *A Series of Charts with Sailing Directions* was published in Washington and went through five editions before being superseded by the charts of the U.S. Coast Survey (see page 106).

Map 190 (*right*).

One of John Bidwell's excellent maps of the Sacramento Valley, covering the same area as Map 180, *page 89*, which was a copy and modification by Thomas Larkin. Originally the map was prepared for Mexican governor Manuel Micheltorena in 1844 to show land grants. Bidwell prepared about forty *diseños* for individual ranchos. This map also shows the extent of marshlands quite clearly.

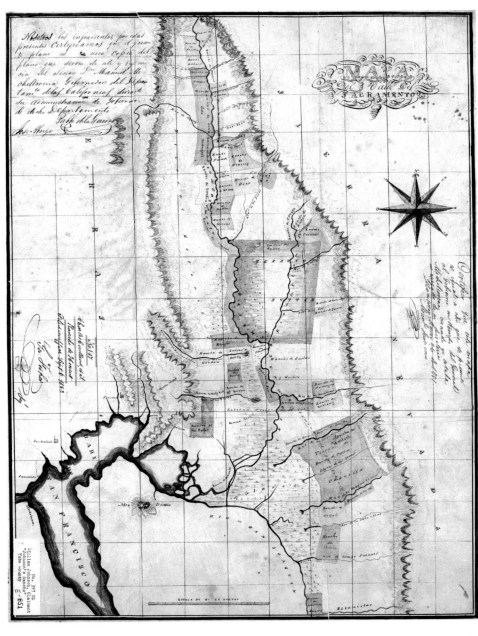

DRAWN DEC. 20TH 1849 BY G.V. COOPER.

LITH. OF WM. ENDICOTT & C° N. YORK.

A  Hensley, Redding & C°
B  Peoples Market
C  T. McDowell & C°
D  S. Taylor
E  Round tent (S. Weeks)
F  Montgomery & Narbour (Lion Store)
G  Myrick, Nelson & C°
H  The Gem
I  Deperker Brothers
J  Machanikians
K  Oregon Bowling Saloon
L  Colton Boxie & C°

# SACRAMENTO CITY C.ª

## FROM THE FOOT OF J. STREET,

### SHOWING I. J. & K. STs WITH THE SIERRA NEVADA IN THE DISTANCE.

NEW YORK PUBLISHED BY STRINGER & TOWNSEND 222 BROADWAY.

Entered according to Act of Congress in the year 1850, by A. Brainard in the Clerks Office of the District Court of the Southern Dist. N.Y.

M  R.M Camp & C°
N  Robert M. Folger
O  Barne Hotel
P  Van Dorais Hotel
Q  Gondola
R  H.E. Robinson & C° (Post Office)
S  Empire
T  Mansion House (lately S.Brannan Store)
U  United States Hotel
V  J.B Starr & C°
W  Jackson's Hotel
X  Locust & C° Express Office

DRAWN FROM NATURE by
GEO. W. CASILEAR &
HENRY BAINBRIDGE

Entered according to Act of Congress in the year 1850 by Casilear & Bainbridge
in the Clerks Office of the District Court of the Southern District of
New York.

LITH. OF SARONY, NEW YORK.

# VIEW OF SACRAMENTO CITY.

## AS IT APPEARED DURING THE GREAT INUNDATION IN JANUARY 1850.

The City is situated on a Plain on the east Bank of the Sacramento River about 145 miles from San Francisco. The rise of the River during the flood occasioned by heavy rains and the melting of Snow from the Mountains was about 20 feet. The small Island covered with tents at the head of J. St on the left is called by the Indians Sa'ann a Knoll of ground made by the Indians and the only dry spot visible for miles during the flood. In the distance at the head of J. St will be seen Sutters Fort about 2½ miles from the Levee. In the extreme distance will be seen the Sierra Nevada Mountains or the Gold Region where tops are mostly covered with Snow the year round and present a most striking and beautiful appearance when viewed from the City. The City Hotel, the large Frame building facing on the Levee or River on the left of J. St. was built during the summer 1849 at a Cost of $75,000. The Sutter Hotel the large frame building facing the Levee on the extreme right was built during the fall of 1849 Cost $ 30,000.

We cheerfully concur in recommending the above Picture as being a true and accurate Drawing of the City of Sacramento as it appeared during the flood of January 1850.

Capt L.A. Sutter

I.F. Thomas  Alcalde of Sacramento City.

J.S. Cabe  Editor of the "Placer Times" Sacramento City.

Robert Gordon  "Firm of Priest Lee, N°7 Sacramento City.

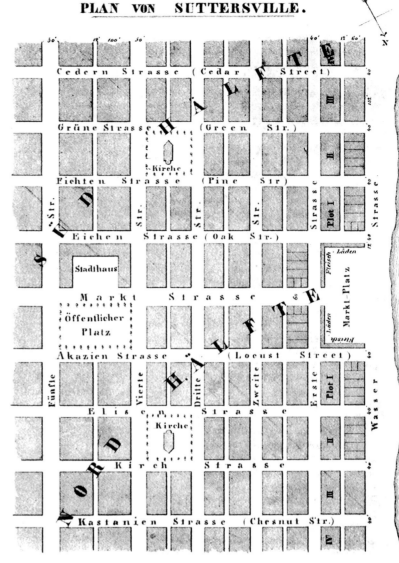

Map 191 (*left, top*), Map 192 (*left, bottom*),
Map 193 (*right*), and Map 194 (*below*).

Sacramento grew up on the lands around Sutter's Fort. In 1846 Sutter began laying out a townsite, to which he expected to be able to direct the many settlers soon to come his way. The site he first selected was on the banks of the Sacramento River about five miles from the fort, which he intended to name Montezuma. By the following year he seems to have changed his mind and decided on a site three miles from the fort, likely because of flooding over the winter. Here a town was laid out (Map 193) complete with a location for city hall (*Stadthaus*), a public plaza (*Öffentlicher Platz*), and market square (*Markt-Platz*). Construction of houses and businesses began, and the town soon became known as Suttersville (sometimes Sutterville). Map 193 was drawn up in German for the same reason as for Map 166, *page 80*: to market California to potential German or Swiss emigrants. North is at bottom on this map.

In the late fall of 1848, gold having been discovered, Sutter had gone to Coloma to set up a store and was snowed in. While he was absent, speculators, the chief among whom seems to have been the erstwhile Mormon Samuel Brannan, convinced Sutter's son (who had joined his father in California in 1848) that Suttersville would never prosper, due to flooding, but another site three miles to the north, which they called Sacramento, would be much better. Better, that is, for Brannan and his cronies, for although this was still Sutter land, they received choice lots for next to nothing. The elder Sutter was furious at his son's apparent duplicity, but the deed was done. The new townsite quickly grew, competing with and soon eclipsing Suttersville in number of houses and businesses (Map 191). In 1849 a grandiose survey was carried out and almost a thousand lots platted out, on paper at least (Map 194). This map is a copy of the original survey done by an Army surveyor earning some extra money doing private surveys—William Warner. During the winter of 1849–50 the new townsite was flooded out; the new site was worse than the old (Map 192). Suttersville residents and businessmen attracted people from Sacramento and tried hard to protect their investments, agreeing to give half their lands to a trio of San Francisco merchants if they would build a wharf and a bridge from the levee to high ground, about twenty feet. Despite all these efforts and a number of improvements, by 1853 Sacramento was growing faster than Suttersville, which rapidly went into decline. Today the Sacramento plan (Map 194) encompasses all of downtown Sacramento out to Route 500 on the south and Interstate 80 on the east, and includes the original townsite by the river, restored from 1966 on and preserved as a State Historic Park. The site of Suttersville has been overtaken by urban Sacramento and is that part of the riverbank close to Sacramento Zoo; one remaining piece of evidence of its existence is a road name: Sutterville Road.

*Below.*
The California State Capitol in Sacramento. It was built between 1861 and 1874.

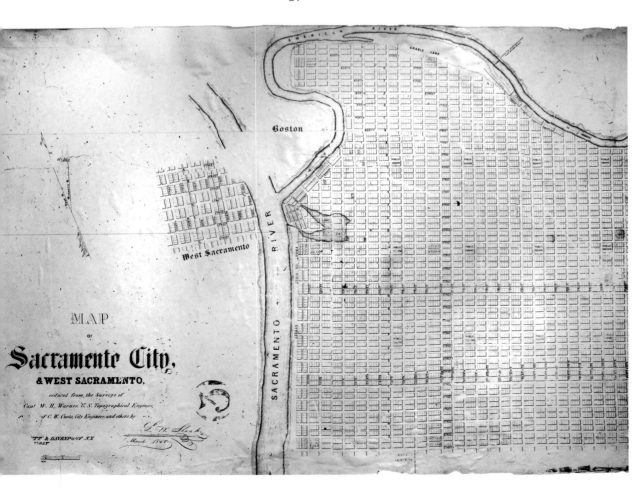

MAP 195 (*left*).

San Francisco surveyor William M. Eddy, later surveyor general of California (see MAP 203, *page 105*) published this map in 1849, although the survey was carried out in 1848. In May 1848 San Francisco's population was about nine hundred, with two hundred buildings and only two hotels and twelve stores. The street system shown here was thus only sparsely filled with actual buildings. The street plan has been extended out into Yerba Buena Cove. Eventually all this area, and more besides, was filled in. At center is a long wharf (marked *Wharf Street*) which was just that: Long Wharf, the first and longest of the wharves. It was not begun until July 1849 despite being shown on this 1848 survey. It would connect with the Embarcadero, a perimeter wharf at the edge of the shallow water that, later, when the cove was filled in, would become the waterfront street.

MAP 196 (*below*).

This map is another valuable historical record of San Francisco, this time as it was in 1852. The original shoreline is shown, and the land created or in the process of creation by landfill is shaded. As indicated in the key, the *Lately planket Streets* are shown bolder than the others. Long Wharf, shown on the Eddy map above, is here extended farther and named *Central Wharf*. An engraving of an unnamed building, said to have been a bank, fills a space in the bottom right corner. The marshy land extending inland from Mission Bay is shaded.

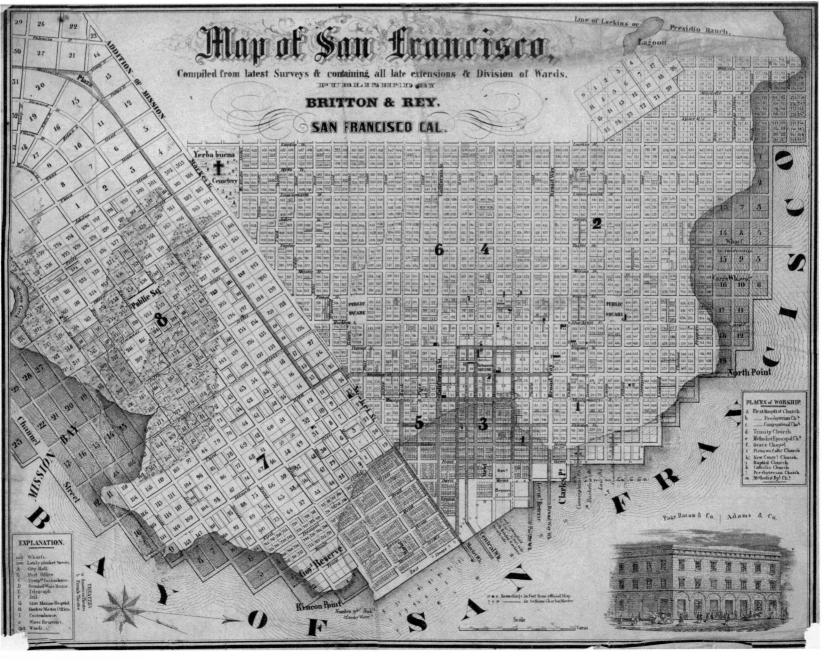

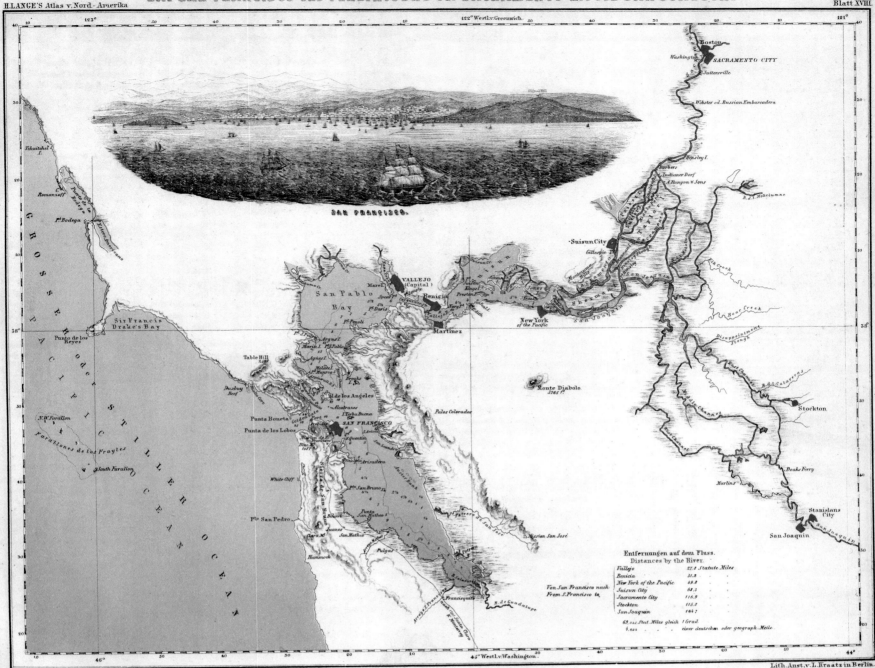

BAI SAN FRANCISCO UND VEREINIGUNG DES SACRAMENTO MIT DEM SAN JOAQUIN.

Blatt XVIII

H.LANGE'S Atlas v. Nord-Amerika

Braunschweig, Verlag v. George Westermann.

Lith.Anst.v.L.Kraatz in Berlin.

**Entfernungen auf dem Fluss.**
**Distances by the River.**

| | |
|---|---|
| Vallejo | 27,4 Statute Miles |
| Benicia | 31,2 |
| New York of the Pacific | 49,3 |
| Suisun City | 64,3 |
| Sacramento City | 116,9 |
| Stockton | 115,2 |
| San Joaquin | 144,7 |

Von San Francisco nach
From S. Francisco to

69,046 Stat. Miles gleich 1 Grad.
9,405          einer deutschen oder geograph. Meile.

MAP 197 (*above*).

This elegant German map of the San Francisco Bay region and the Central Valley from Sacramento to Stockton was published in 1854 in an atlas of North America. An engraved view of San Francisco is prominent. The marshlands of the delta are shaded.

MAP 198 (*right*).

One of the first acts of the new state legislature in 1850 was to grant San Francisco a charter as a city. The original boundaries from the 1850 charter are shown on this map as the red line. The boundaries as extended in a charter amendment the following year are shown in green. This map was created in 1854 when the city was attempting to prove its right to pueblo lands beyond these boundaries.

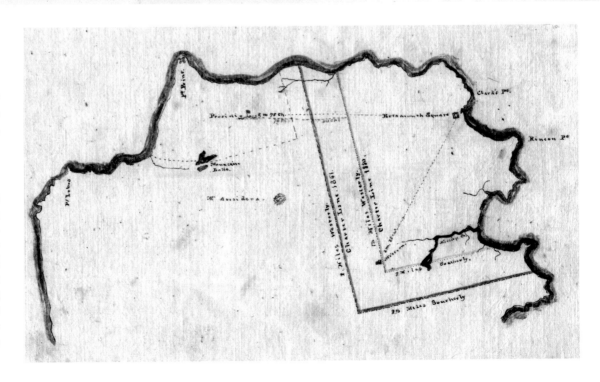

# THE STATE OF CALIFORNIA

The normal criterion for admission to statehood was a population of at least 40,000. Because of the discovery of gold, California had clearly exceeded this requirement by 1848, and the continuing insurge of people necessitated more than military government.

As with all potential states at this time, the thorny question of whether to allow slavery had first to be decided. California's gold miners did not want slavery allowed, but this mattered not to the Southern states, who were more concerned about being outnumbered by non-slave states in the Senate. In the end the matter was resolved at the federal level by what is known as the Compromise of 1850: a set of five bills that admitted California as a free state; banned the slave trade in the District of Columbia; created Utah and New Mexico territories without prohibition of slavery, the matter to be decided at a later date; required U.S. citizens to assist in the return of runaway slaves (the Fugitive Slave Act); and compelled Texas to give up its claims to western lands, to avoid the possibility that they might become part of a slave state, which Texas was.

On 9 September 1850, Congress passed *An Act for the Admission of the State of California into the Union.*

Whereas the people of California have presented a constitution and asked for admission into the Union, which constitution was submitted to Congress by the President of the United States, by message dated February thirteenth, eighteen hundred and fifty, and which, on due examination, is found to be republican in its form of government:

*Be it enacted by the Senate and House of Representatives of the United States of America in Congress assembled,* That the State of California shall be one, and is hereby declared to be one, of the United States of America, and admitted into the Union on an equal footing with the original States in all respects whatever.

A new president, Millard Fillmore—Taylor died in July 1850—signed the bill for the admission of California the same day.

It had not been clear precisely what territory would comprise the new state. Presidents Polk and Taylor had supported a very large state, one which encompassed essentially all of what had been the Mexican province of Alta California (MAP 199, *below,* and MAP 178, *page 87*). When a convention had been called at Monterey by military governor Bennett Riley for September 1849, delegates had only been summoned from places as far east as the Sierra. This geographical definition of California was soon questioned, and a committee, which included John Sutter, was appointed to determine

*Above.* The Great Seal of the State of California. Eureka—I've found it!—derives from gold rush days. This example was found on a state building in San Francisco.

MAP 199 (*left*).
This was the actual map used for the negotiation of the Treaty of Guadalupe Hidalgo, signed on 2 February 1848, which formally annexed Mexican territory, including all of *Alta California,* to the United States. It was this area (with one minor difference), here colored brown-orange (and difficult due to color change over time to distinguish from the lighter yellow used to color the continued Mexican province of Sonora), that President James Polk recommended as the initial area for a state of California. The minor difference was that Polk included all territory north of the Suanca branch of the Gila River rather than the middle branch shown here. The boundary is also shown on MAP 178, *page 87,* which was effectively a commercially produced version of this map.

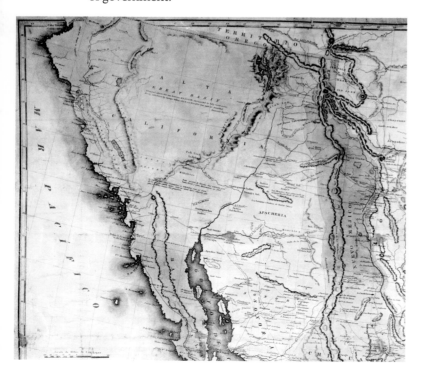

MAP 200 (*above*).

This interesting German map shows the boundaries of a proposed Mormon state of Deseret, encompassing a vast tract of the original Mexican province of Upper California; as well are shown the corresponding boundaries of California. California is shown with an eastern boundary along the crest of the Sierra Nevada, as this was at first thought of as the boundary by Bennett Riley and supported by some delegates at the Monterey Convention. But this map shows Deseret taking in most of what is now Southern California, although carefully just excluding the *Pueblo de los Angeles* (and not very accurately portraying the new international boundary agreed upon with Mexico in 1848). The yellow boundary lines may look roughly drawn in, yet it is known that there is more than one copy of this map, with identical boundaries, so clearly it was not just one person's doodlings. There were significant numbers of Mormons in California. The first shipload of American emigrants to California, who arrived in San Francisco Bay on 31 July 1846, had been 130 men, 60 women, and 40 children, mainly Mormons led by Samuel Brannan, who gave up his leadership role in favor of making money from the gold rush. The Monterey Convention rejected boundaries for a state of California similar to this proposal for Deseret; one of the reasons was that the Mormons living in the Great Salt Lake area were not represented at the convention.

suitable boundaries for a new state. They considered the original boundaries of Upper California but quickly concluded that these encompassed far too large an area to reasonably be a single state. There was poor communication across the Sierra; the Mormons of Great Salt Lake were not represented at the convention, had not been consulted, and had "religious peculiarities" that suggested to the committee that they desired isolation and no direct political connection with coastal Californians.

The boundary committee felt that it was important to set reasonable boundaries for the state right from the beginning to prevent the possible later dismemberment of the territory as remote regions became populated and demanded their own government. There was even the possibility that Southern factions might contrive to carve new states out of California's territory to create slave-holding states to maintain a balance in the Senate. The notion that California might lose some of its

sea coast weighed heavily on the minds of some delegates. The committee therefore proposed an eastern boundary for the new state at 116°w, south to the boundary with Mexico, an area that would have encompassed two thirds of today's Nevada (the eastern boundary of which is at almost 114°w).

This was not accepted at the convention, and delegates put forward various proposals of their own. There was no disagreement about the southern boundary, to be the international boundary; or the northern boundary, to be at 42°N. Dissension was entirely over the location of the eastern boundary. Some thought it should be the boundary between New Mexico and Upper California shown on Frémont's 1848 map (about 107°w) while others wanted the northern part to be anywhere from on the 120°w line of longitude to 115°w, and extending south to 38° or 39°N before paralleling the crest of the Sierra southeasterly either to the international boundary (thus including the southwestern corner of what is now Arizona) or to the Colorado River.

Most delegates agreed that whatever the decision, it should not delay the entry of California into the Union, and thus although the final vote for the California as we see it today was for a "thin" state, it was agreed that should Congress require a larger state as a condition of admission this would be accepted. But Congress was satisfied to let the decision of the local delegates stand.

Surprisingly, too, given the tenure of the times (and the assertions of several historians), there was no evidence of any attempt to arrive at state boundaries for sectional reasons, to create a large state so that it could be later subdivided into several smaller ones—some of which might be slave-holding.

### Map 201 (left, top).
Even when the Mormons had lost any part of California as part of their proposed state of Deseret, there was still the hope that they would retain vast tracts of the western lands, most of the remainder of Upper California that had been gained from Mexico by the 1848 treaty. This 1850 map shows the state of Deseret forming the entire eastern boundary of California.

### Map 202 (left).
The first—or certainly one of the first—maps to show California as a state was this one, rushed into print in 1850 by commercial mapmaker Samuel Augustus Mitchell. The base map was created five years earlier, and the new boundaries were added to the older map, thus speeding up the production process.

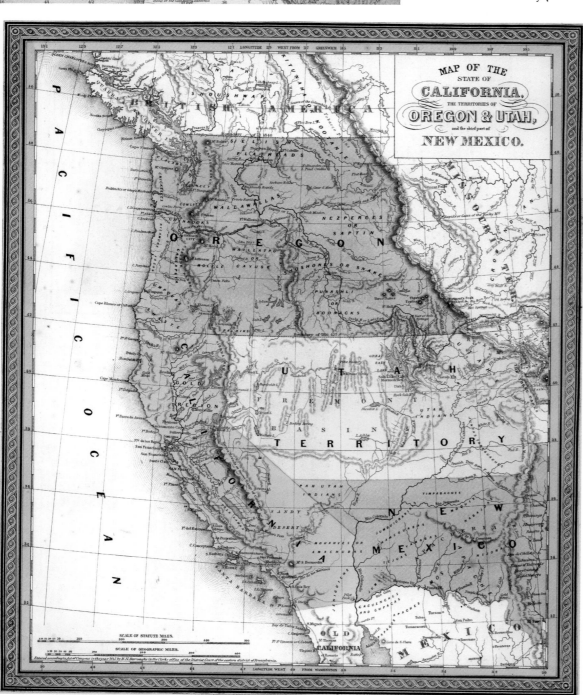

MAP 203.
William Eddy, one-time surveyor of San Francisco (see MAP 195, *page 100*), went on to become the official state surveyor of California, and in this capacity he compiled the first "official" map of the state of California in 1853. By the time it was published the following year, poor Eddy had died.

California came into being with twenty-seven counties, having effectively operated as a state for a year before it was officially one. The state now has fifty-eight. The location of smaller counties on this map reflects the distribution of population, which was concentrated around the gold regions.

# THE UNITED STATES COAST SURVEY

The United States Coast Survey was created in 1807 as the Survey of the Coast, having originally been suggested by Thomas Jefferson. It was charged with charting the coastline of the United States to make it safe for shipping. The acquisition of Florida and Texas dramatically increased the coast to be mapped, and when the United States acquired Oregon and California it was immediately clear that resources were required on the Pacific to chart this newly American coast. Urgency was emphasized by the discovery of gold; suddenly hundreds of American and foreign ships were sailing for San Francisco Bay.

Initial mapping of some areas such as San Francisco Bay itself was surveyed on a private basis, such as that by Cadwalader Ringgold in 1850, financed by a group of San Francisco merchants (see page 97). In October 1848 the superintendent of the Coast Survey, Alexander Dallas Bache, ordered a survey vessel, the *Ewing*, under Lieutenant William P. MacArthur, to the Pacific, but it did not sail until January 1849, arriving in San Francisco in August. Then, however, it suffered the same fate as many vessels in the bay at this time. The crew deserted, and a replacement crew could not be found, for the gold fields were luring away all available manpower.

Enough personnel were mustered in the spring of 1850, and the *Ewing* began its survey work south from the mouth of the Columbia River, quickly amassing enough hydrographic data to produce a three-sheet reconnaissance chart covering the coast from the Columbia to Mexico. These reconnaissance charts, so-called because they were less detailed than a chart of an individual bay or harbor

but fixed all the main navigation points along the coast, were published in several editions in the 1850s, beginning in 1851, complete with views of the coast from the sea to aid recognition of locations (MAP 208, *page 109*). They were surveyed using triangulation, which allows an accurate survey to be projected from the actual measurement of the position of two points on the coast and the length of a baseline using carefully measured angles to calculate the position of a further point. The process was repeated down the coast until checked and corrected by the measurement of the position of another point. The triangles thus drawn are shown on the maps reproduced here.

In 1850, land-based surveys were also begun, headed initially by George Davidson of the U.S. Coast Survey. The following year naval Lieutenant James Alden headed another survey party to collect hydrographic data. Both Davidson and Alden's names can be seen on a number of the maps.

MAP 204 (*below*) and MAP 205 (*right*).
From a progress report of the United States Coast Survey in 1855 come these charts, one showing the triangulation of San Pedro and the Santa Barbara Channel and the other San Francisco Bay, Point Reyes, and vicinity. For maps in such a technical report they are surprisingly rather beautiful, although they give some idea of the complexity involved in the connection of the various positions with the survey triangles. Note that although the survey is of the coast, the triangulation is from the land, it being difficult to fix a position at sea with any accuracy and impossible to mark it if fixed. The early survey of the relatively few harbors that could be used by shipping was the early priority of the U.S. Coast Survey: for economic use and also, like the Spanish galleons of previous centuries, as places of refuge on an often wild coast.

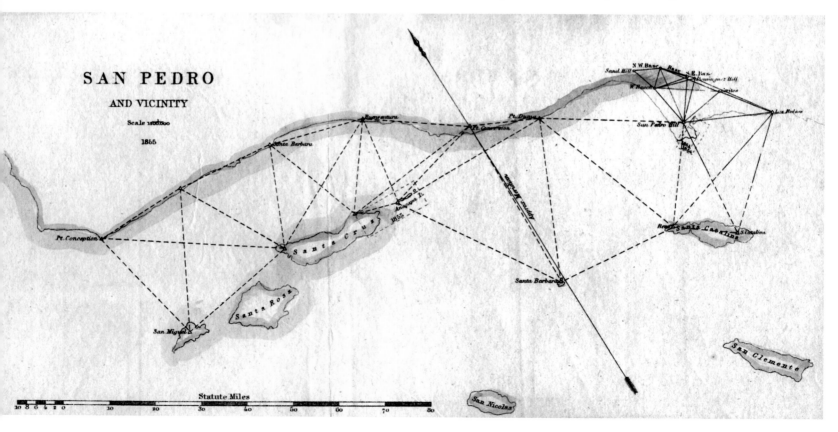

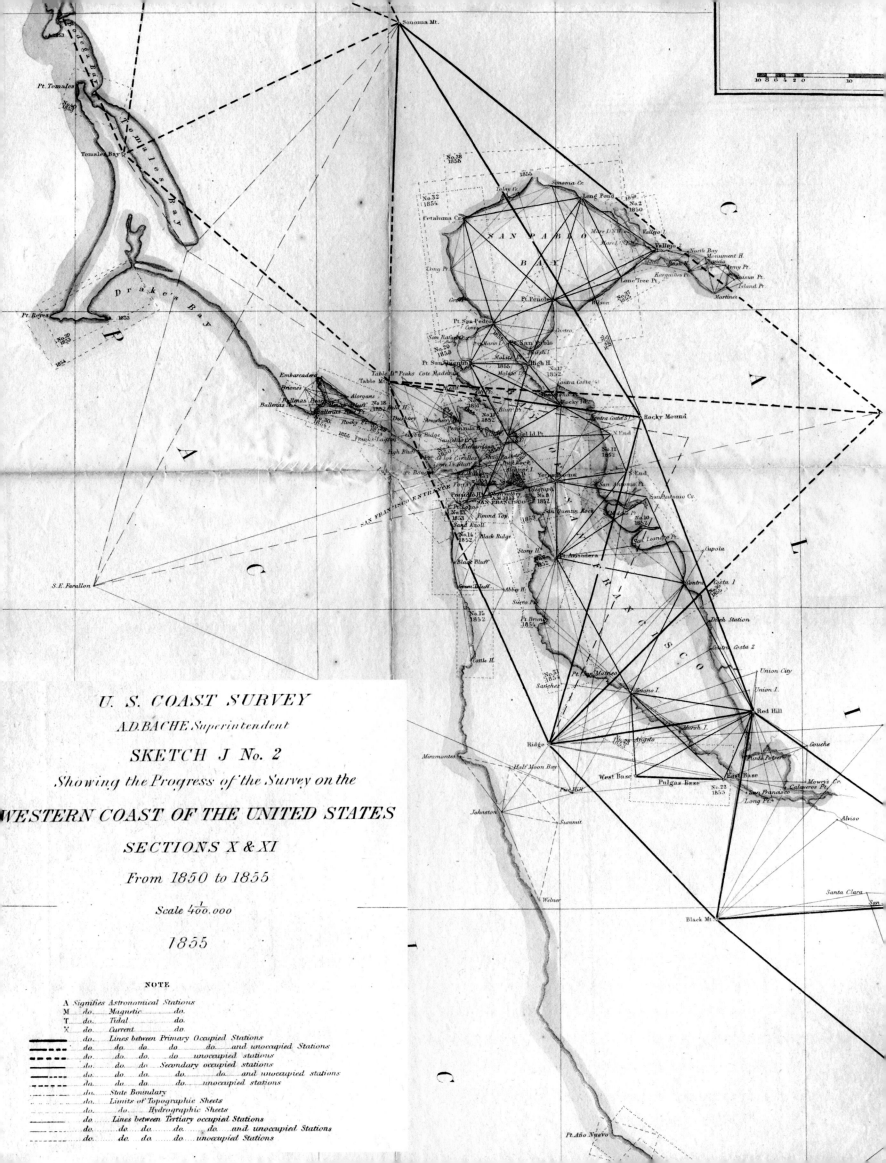

U. S. COAST SURVEY

A.D.BACHE Superintendent

SKETCH J No. 2

Showing the Progress of the Survey on the

WESTERN COAST OF THE UNITED STATES

SECTIONS X & XI

From 1850 to 1855

Scale 1/400.000

1855

NOTE

A Signifies Astronomical Stations
M   do.   Magnetic   do.
T   do.   Tidal   do.
X   do.   Current   do.
    do.   Lines between Primary Occupied Stations
    do.   do.   do.   do.   and unoccupied Stations
    do.   do.   do.   do.   unoccupied stations
    do.   do.   do.   Secondary occupied stations
    do.   do.   do.   do.   and unoccupied stations
    do.   do.   do.   do.   unoccupied stations
    do.   State Boundary
    do.   Limits of Topographic Sheets
    do.   do.   Hydrographic Sheets
    do.   Lines between Tertiary occupied Stations
    do.   do.   do.   do.   do.   and unoccupied Stations
    do.   do.   do.   do.   unoccupied Stations

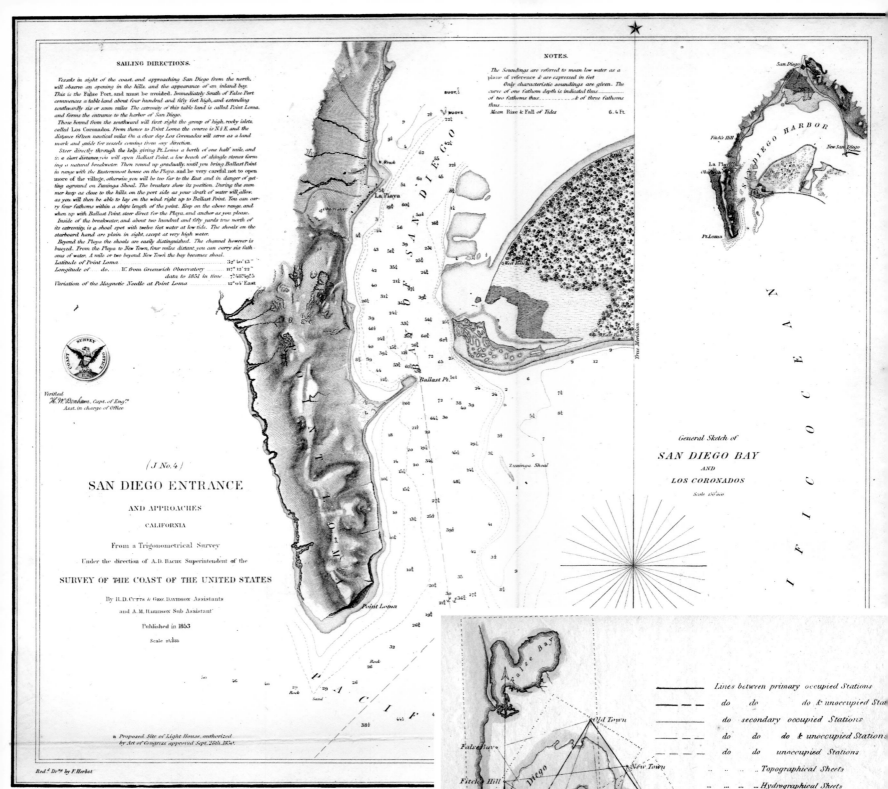

**Map 206** (*above*).

The first United States Coast Survey of San Diego Bay concentrated on the critical entrance at Point Loma, and this was the first chart published by the Survey. Relief is shown by finely engraved hachure lines. Depths are indicated with soundings in feet but, confusingly, with depth contours in fathoms (1 fathom = 6 feet) for one, two, and three fathoms. *The Proposed Site of Light House authorized by Act of Congress approved Sept. 28th 1850* is indicated at the highest point of Point Loma.

**Map 207** (*right*).

From the 1855 progress report comes this nicely colored chart of the triangulation of the whole of San Diego Bay. The *Initial Pt.* is where the international boundary meets the ocean. Note that two of the triangulation points are at San Diego's *Old Town* and *New Town* (see page 168).

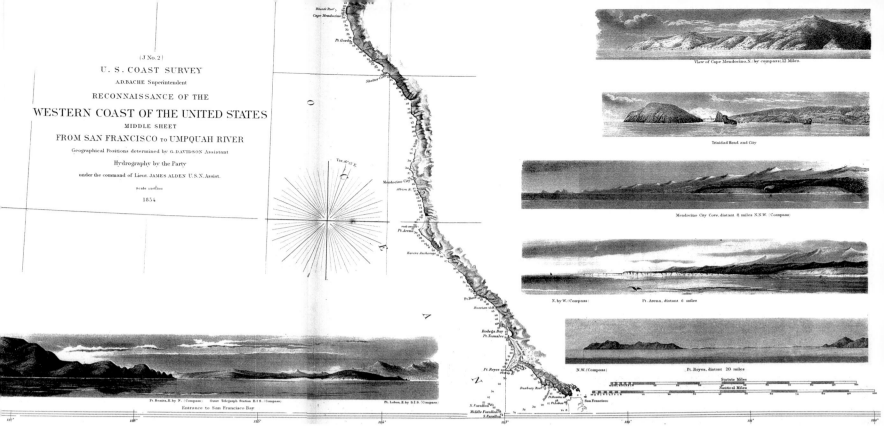

George Davidson and his survey crew spent a good deal of 1851 at San Diego. Here they constructed an observatory to exactly determine latitude and longitude, since this was at one end of the survey. One of the earliest charts produced was the one of the important entrance to San Diego Bay (Map 206, *left, top*). By 1852 the Survey was able to report that it had completed preliminary triangulation and measurement of the topography of the bay in "all that portion required for commerce."

Consideration was also given to the location of sites for lighthouses. Congress in 1852 authorized the first of eight lighthouses for the Pacific coast, to be illuminated using a new French invention, the Fresnel lens. One of the first lights to be constructed was at Point Loma at the entrance to San Diego Bay, completed in 1854 by a contractor on the highest point of land, at 422 feet. It was first lit the following year and for years was the highest lighthouse in the United States. But the location proved to be a mistake because the frequent coastal fogs obscured the light far too often. A replacement lighthouse was erected at the tip of Point Loma in 1891 at a height of 30 feet. The old lighthouse became part of the Cabrillo National Monument in 1913.

As a result of the efforts of the U.S. Coast Survey, which in 1878 became the U.S. Coast and Geodetic Survey, the California coast slowly became safer for mariners, and the charts in use today are the descendants of these early charts, corrected as much for changing coastal features as the correction of errors in the original survey, which was remarkably accurate for its time.

Map 208 (*above*).
The coast north of San Francisco, shown at bottom, is covered on this middle sheet of three reconnaissance survey sheets of the Pacific coast. It is dated 1854.

Map 209 (*right*).
Triangulation of Monterey Bay, from the 1855 U.S.C.S. progress report.

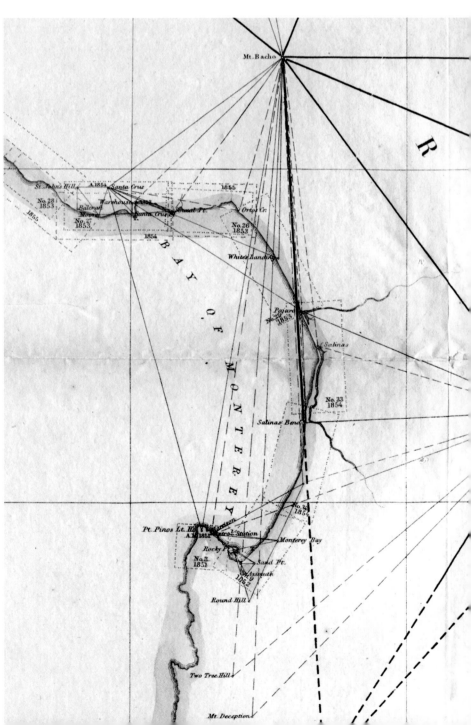

# SEARCHING FOR A RAILROAD PATH

The enormity of such a project as building a railroad clear across the country always meant that government would be involved. And for the federal government to be involved necessitated agreement as to a route. But there were so many factional interests that it was impossible to get agreement until after the Civil War had begun. Not only were there disagreements based on a line to the North or South, with the possible spread or otherwise of slavery that that might represent, but also at a more local level there was rivalry between many cities that felt their future prosperity at stake if the railroad did not pass through or terminate in their city.

It was, therefore, a compromise in itself, forced on both sides when they realized their choice would not prevail, when Congress on 2 March 1853 authorized the Army Topographical Corps to survey a number of possible routes to the West and recommend the best one based—in theory—on purely technical and non-factional reasons. Even this did not work, for certain of the Army men, notably Colonel John James Abert, the Corps's commander, and William Emory, who had already surveyed a southern route during the Mexican War (see MAP 171, *page 83*), were accused of having a southern bias. Emory's brother-in-law owned shares in the paper town of New

San Diego (see page 168), which depended for their value on the construction of a southern railroad. So when Emory and Abert recommended a southern route—likely truly the best route—no one believed that their recommendations were impartial.

The surveys were carried out under the general direction of the Secretary for War, since the railroad was seen first as a strategic necessity. But the Secretary for War was none other than Jefferson Davis, later a senator from Mississippi, and afterward the first and only president of the Confederate States of America. He was, therefore, hardly an unbiased overseer.

Of the routes surveyed that ended in California, the northernmost was the survey begun between the 38th and 39th parallels by Lieutenant John W. Gunnison, but he only got as far west as Sevier Lake in Utah before being killed by Paiute Indians. The survey was continued by Lieutenant E.G. Beckwith along the 41st parallel because Gunnison had determined that the 38th parallel route was infeasible due to costs of tunnels and bridges. The route at these middle latitudes had been favored by Thomas Hart Benton, Frémont's booster and father-in-law and, until 1851, Missouri senator, who had at first wanted Frémont to lead the survey. Beckwith discovered two passes into the northern Sacramento Valley—one from the Madeline Plains, which was his recommended route, and another from Honey Lake (MAP 211, *right, top,* and MAP 214, *overleaf, right*).

The survey of the 35th parallel route (MAP 212, *right, bottom*) was detailed to Lieutenant Amiel Weeks Whipple. His line of

MAP 210 (*below*).
This 1853 map published before the Pacific Railroad Survey got under way shows some of the railroad routes into California and the Northwest that could be considered. Two dashed lines indicate the *Direct Line . . .* between St. Louis and San Francisco and Walker Pass, a possible route through the Sierra.

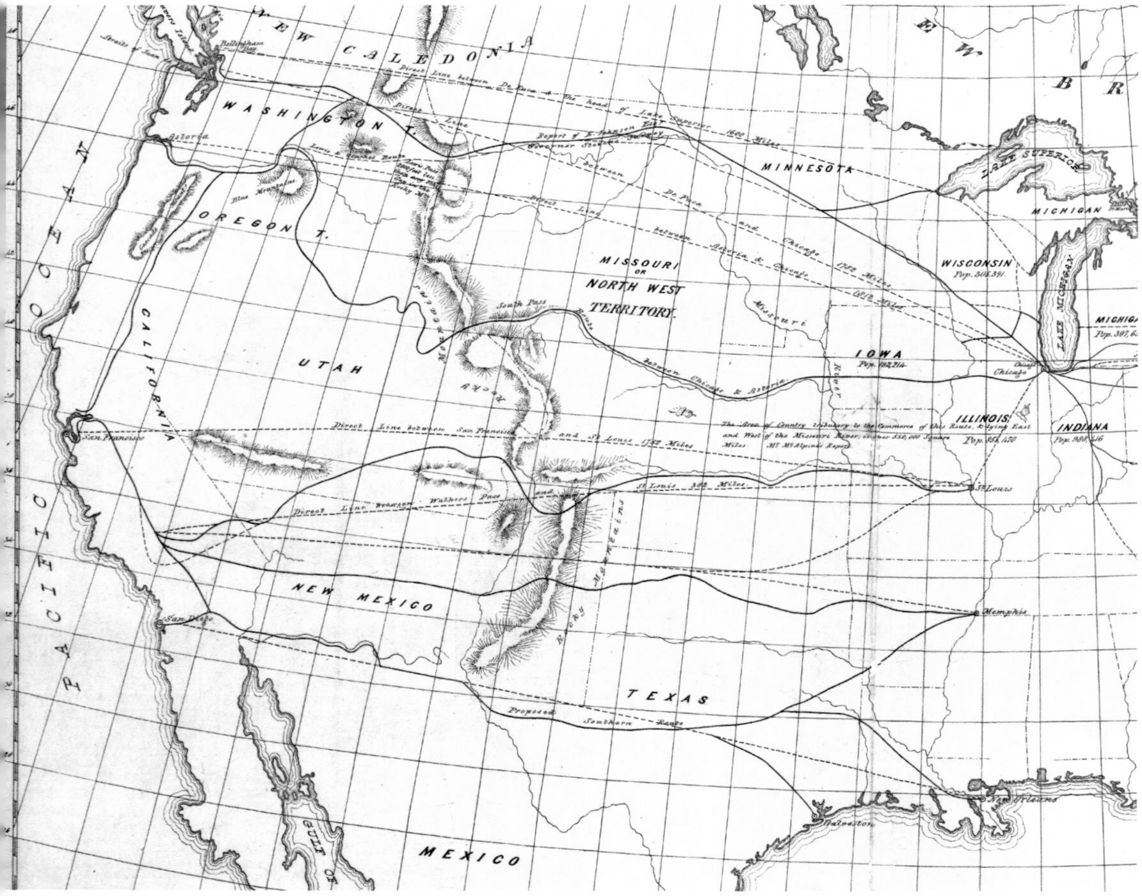

MAP 213 (*overleaf, left*).
Lieutenant Robert S. Williamson's map of the southern Sierra Nevada, showing the passes he found and surveyed. They include *Walker's Pass* at top right; *Tay-ee-chay-pah Pass* (Tehachapi Pass); and *Arroyo de los Uvas,* just south of which is Tejon Pass (not marked on this map). Both are today the route of Interstate 5. The map is an accurate and detailed rendering of a topographically complex area.

MAP 214 (*overleaf, right*).
This is E.G. Beckwith's map of part of his survey of the 41st parallel, with the *Proposed Railroad Line* route from the southern end of the Great Salt Lake. In California the line passes from *Madelin [Madeline] Plains* to the valley of the *Pitt [Pit] River* following the approximate route of today's Highway 139, and then follows the Pit until it joins the *Sacramento River* (today it flows into the artificial Shasta Lake) at the northern end of the Sacramento Valley.

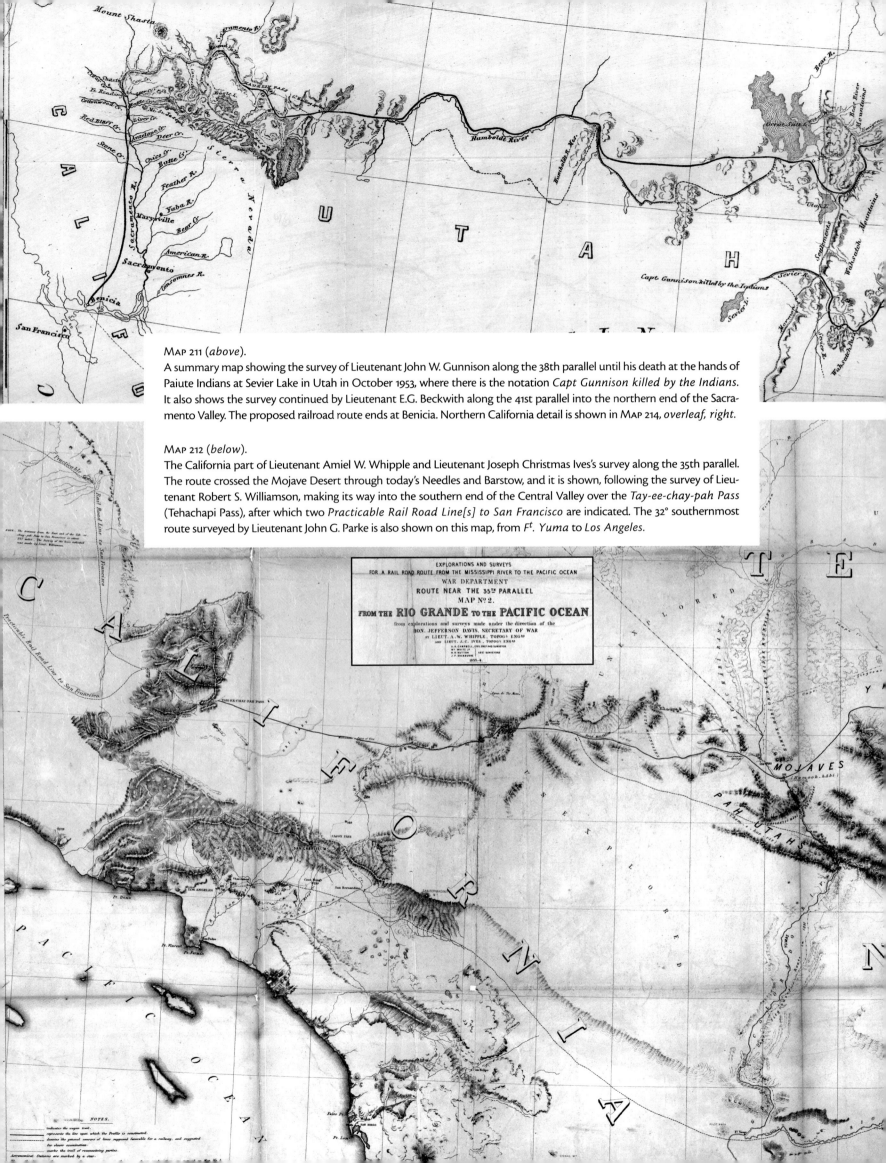

**Map 211** (*above*).

A summary map showing the survey of Lieutenant John W. Gunnison along the 38th parallel until his death at the hands of Paiute Indians at Sevier Lake in Utah in October 1953, where there is the notation *Capt Gunnison killed by the Indians*. It also shows the survey continued by Lieutenant E.G. Beckwith along the 41st parallel into the northern end of the Sacramento Valley. The proposed railroad route ends at Benicia. Northern California detail is shown in Map 214, *overleaf, right*.

**Map 212** (*below*).

The California part of Lieutenant Amiel W. Whipple and Lieutenant Joseph Christmas Ives's survey along the 35th parallel. The route crossed the Mojave Desert through today's Needles and Barstow, and it is shown, following the survey of Lieutenant Robert S. Williamson, making its way into the southern end of the Central Valley over the *Tay-ee-chay-pah Pass* (Tehachapi Pass), after which two *Practicable Rail Road Line[s] to San Francisco* are indicated. The 32° southernmost route surveyed by Lieutenant John G. Parke is also shown on this map, from *F$^t$. Yuma to Los Angeles*.

EXPLORATIONS AND SURVEYS
FOR A RAIL ROAD ROUTE FROM THE MISSISSIPPI RIVER TO THE PACIFIC OCEAN
WAR DEPARTMENT
ROUTE NEAR THE 35$^{th}$ PARALLEL
MAP N$^o$ 2.
FROM THE RIO GRANDE TO THE PACIFIC OCEAN
from explorations and surveys made under the direction of the
HON. JEFFERSON DAVIS, SECRETARY OF WAR
BY LIEUT. A.W. WHIPPLE, TOPOG$^l$ ENG$^{rs}$
AND LIEUT. J.C. IVES, TOPOG$^l$ ENG$^{rs}$
1853-4.

FOR A RAIL ROAD ROUTE FROM THE MISSISSIPPI RIVER TO THE PACIFIC OCEAN.
WAR DEPARTMENT.

ROUTES IN CALIFORNIA TO CONNECT WITH THE ROUTES NEAR THE 32ND AND 35TH PARALLELS.

# MAP OF PASSES
## IN THE SIERRA NEVADA
### FROM WALKER'S PASS TO THE COAST RANGE:

from Explorations and Surveys made under the direction of the
#### HON. JEFFERSON DAVIS SECRETARY OF WAR
by Lieut. R. S. Williamson Topl. Engr assisted by Lieut. J. C. Parke Topl. Engr
and Mr. Isaac Williams Smith, Civ. Engr.

1853

Scale of Miles

Scale 1:240,000

TULARE VALLEY

The Park

Post Creek

Depot Camp

Kern River

Po-sung-co-lu

Buenavista Lake

Kern Lake

Arroyo de los Alisos

Posé Creek

Arroyo San Ammelio

TE-ON

Tejon

Arroyo de los Uvas

THE GREAT BASIN

Spring

Spring

Palma Plain

Dry Lake

San Franciscquito Pass

Lake Elizabeth

STONEMANS MT

New Pass

S. Clara River

NOTE
The inclined figures refer to stations
on the line of survey.
The other figures note the elevation
above mean tide.

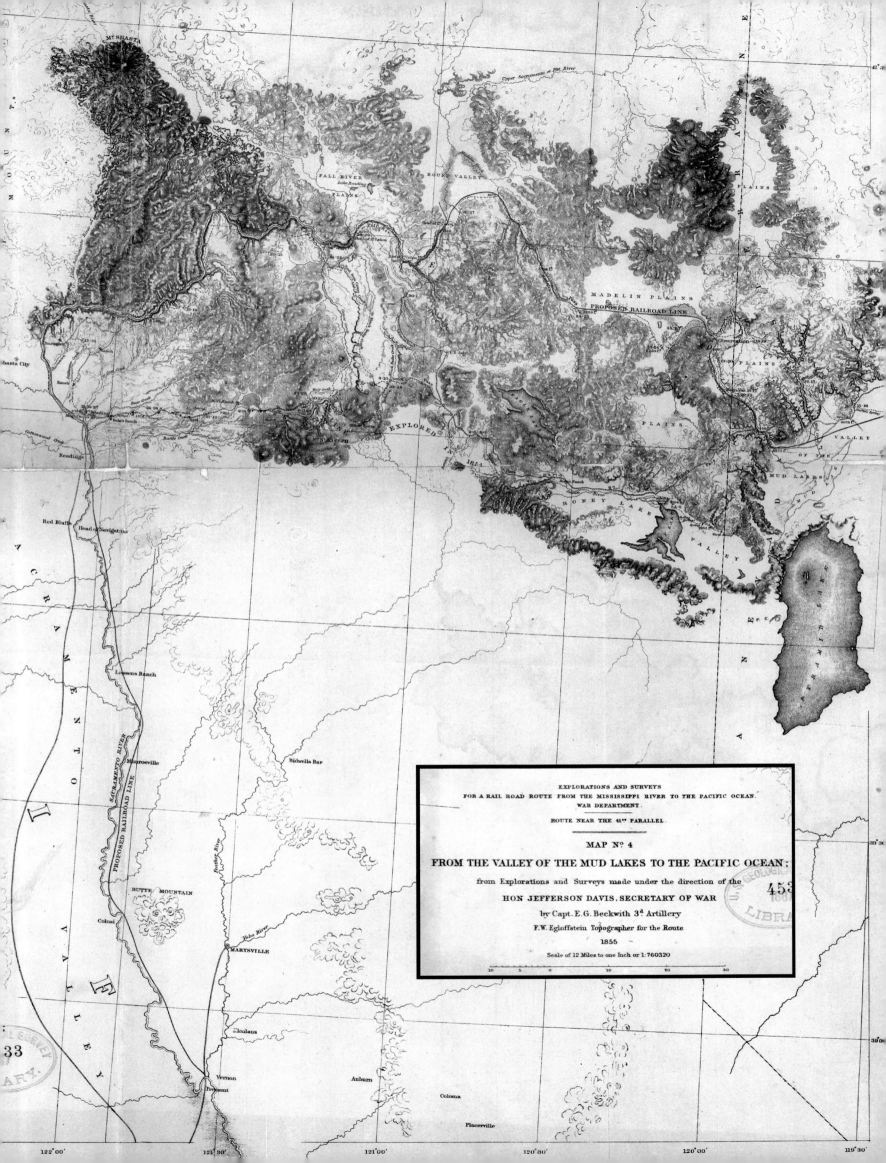

EXPLORATIONS AND SURVEYS
FOR A RAIL ROAD ROUTE FROM THE MISSISSIPPI RIVER TO THE PACIFIC OCEAN.
WAR DEPARTMENT.

ROUTE NEAR THE 41ST PARALLEL.

MAP N.º 4

FROM THE VALLEY OF THE MUD LAKES TO THE PACIFIC OCEAN;

from Explorations and Surveys made under the direction of the

HON. JEFFERSON DAVIS, SECRETARY OF WAR

by Capt. E.G. Beckwith 3.ᵈ Artillery

F.W. Egloffstein Topographer for the Route

1855

Scale of 12 Miles to one Inch or 1:760320

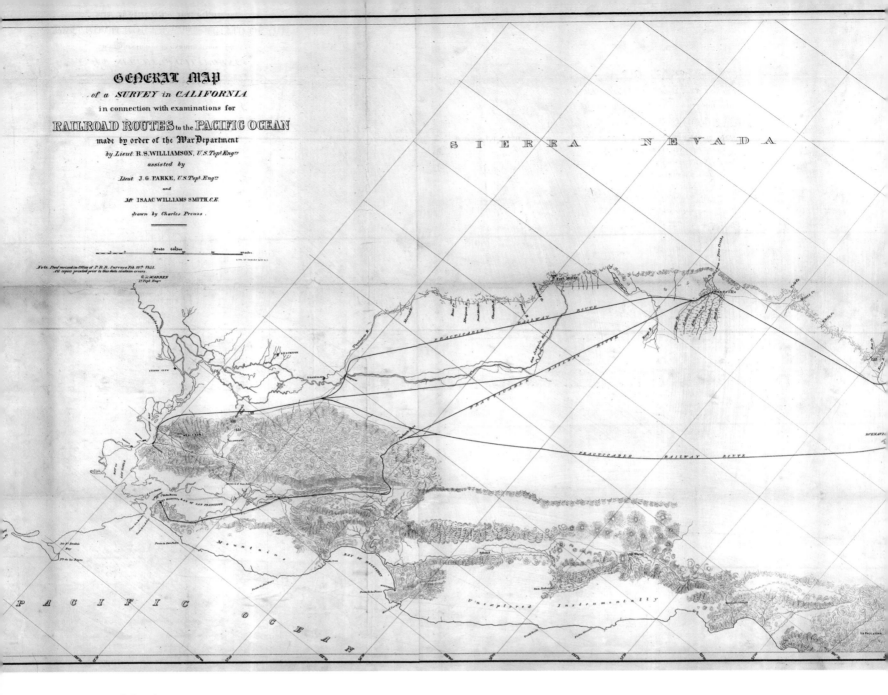

GENERAL MAP
of a SURVEY in CALIFORNIA
in connection with examinations for
RAILROAD ROUTES to the PACIFIC OCEAN
made by order of the War Department
by Lieut. R.S.WILLIAMSON, U.S.Top! Eng."
assisted by
Lieut. J.G. PARKE, U.S.Top! Eng."
and
Mr ISAAC WILLIAMS SMITH, C.E.
drawn by Charles Preuss.

**Map 215** (*above*).
Lieutenant Robert S. Williamson's map of Southern California (with north to the top left) showing his determination of possible railroad routes from San Francisco south to Los Angeles through the southern Sierra Nevada. Also shown is the survey of the impenetrable Coast Mountains east of San Diego, where no feasible railroad routes were found. A route is indicated from Fort Yuma through *San Gorgonio Pass* east of San Bernardino and to Los Angeles; then north through the San Fernando Valley and the Santa Clara Valley. The line then turns east and runs through Soledad Canyon to *New Pass,* then across the desert to *Tah-ee-chay-pah Pass* (Tehachapi Pass), then north to the Tulare Valley and on to San Francisco via several alternative routings.

survey led from Albuquerque west and crossed the Colorado River near Needles, following then the approximate route of today's Interstate 40 to the Tehachapi Pass. Whipple got his estimate of the cost of the rail line wrong, an error that put this route at a disadvantage. Nevertheless, after his estimate had been corrected, Whipple's survey came to be seen as the most likely compromise route.

In 1854, a survey of the southernmost route, along the Gila River, was carried out by Lieutenant John G. Parke. His recommendation was for a route south of the river, a route made feasible by

the acquisition of more land from Mexico by the Gadsden Purchase, negotiated by U.S. Minister to Mexico James Gadsden in late 1853.

To find a suitable route over the Sierra Nevada into the Central Valley and on to San Francisco Bay, Lieutenant Robert S. Williamson was in 1853 detailed to find passes in the south. Accompanied by Parke, he explored five possible passes, including Walker Pass, which was up to then considered to be the most likely route for a railroad. Williamson rejected it, finding only Tehachapi Pass, and Tejon Pass and the Arroyo de los Uvas to be of sufficiently mild grade.

Williamson also examined passes on the northern side of the Los Angeles Plain, discovering a pass he called, appropriately enough, New Pass (Soledad Pass, near Palmdale) and determining that Cajon Pass (north of San Bernardino) would be usable if improved by a tunnel. He also surveyed and approved San Gorgonio Pass (the location of Interstate 10, west of Palm Springs), which he thought the best pass in the Coast Range.

Williamson came to the important conclusion that there was no feasible route for a railroad between the Gila River valley and San Diego; both what he called Warner's Pass (the route between the

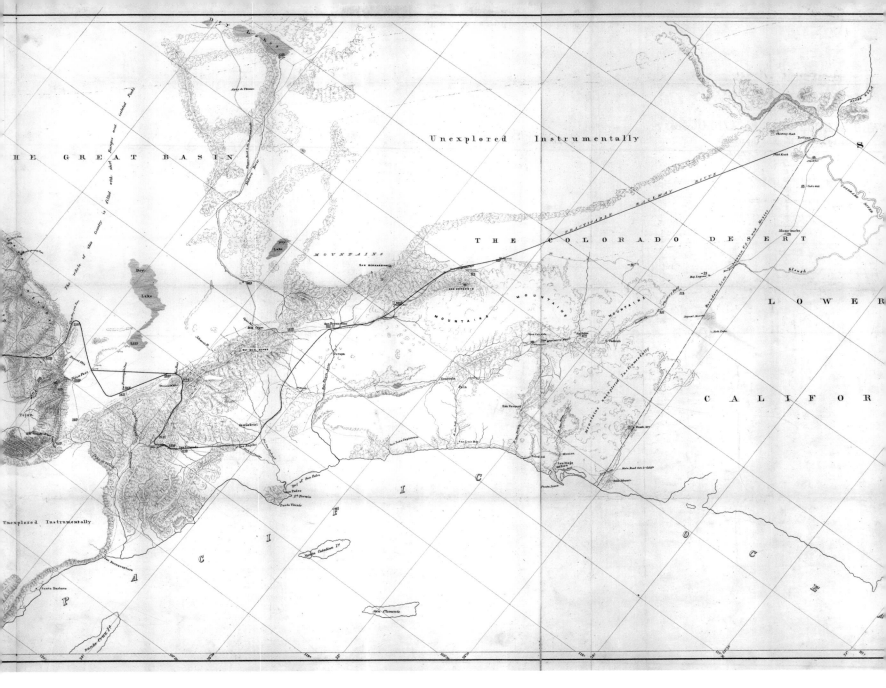

headwaters of Carrizo Creek and those of the San Dieguito River, which flows to the sea just north of San Diego) and Jacum Pass (the route through the Jacumba Mountains, roughly that of Interstate 8) were impractical for a railroad. It was a blow to the promoters of New San Diego (see page 168).

The Pacific Railroad Surveys were published in twelve handsome volumes between 1855 and 1860. But they ultimately created more confusion than existed before, because no conclusive overall route was recommended, and thus sectional interests were given a rationale to continue their bickering. The prestige of the Topographical Corps suffered, probably unfairly. The surveys were not completely wasted, however, as many of the routes were used by later railroads, although by that time California's population had grown and much less of the country remained unknown.

MAP 216 (*right*).
Contemporaneous with the Pacific Railroad Surveys, the Mexican Boundary Survey, carried out between 1848 and 1855, produced several volumes of scientific work. The mapping was under the direction of Major William H. Emory. This is part of the westernmost summary map, showing the position of the *Initial Point* located where the boundary line began—according to the Treaty of Guadalupe Hidalgo—one marine league south of San Diego. After the Gadsden Purchase of late 1853, a new boundary had to be surveyed.

# BUILDING THE
# TRANSCONTINENTAL RAILROAD

The first line of metal to connect California to the East was completed in October 1861. It was not a railroad but a telegraph wire, and in an instant communication across the continent was possible in minutes instead of months, though at considerable cost.

The telegraph put the Pony Express, which had been in operation but eighteen months, out of business. The Pony Express's relays of horses and riders had connected Sacramento with St. Joseph, on the Missouri, in ten days and was itself a vast improvement over wagon or ship.

But to transport people rather than messages a railroad was required, and the man who conceived and passionately promoted a transcontinental railroad was Theodore Dehone Judah, a railroad engineer who had been involved with the building of a number of eastern railroads in the decade before 1854. In that year he was offered the opportunity to practice his craft in California, where he became the chief engineer of the Sacramento Valley Railroad, a twenty-three-mile line between Sacramento and Folsom, California's first railroad.

Judah worked on a number of other railroad projects because the Sacramento Valley Railroad had difficulty staying in business given the decline in gold mining activity. Judah was nothing if not an optimist; his work on the Sacramento line had given him the idea that a line could be continued up and across the Sierra. He realized that only the federal government had the resources, in the form of land that could be sold, to finance such a venture, and he

made several trips—each by sea and across Panama—to promote his ideas. He produced a pamphlet with the title *A Practical Plan for Building the Pacific Railroad,* which he distributed to every member of Congress. His ideas were brilliant but his timing terrible. Sectional interests and the coming of the Civil War made the job of selling a Pacific railroad an uphill battle.

*Above.* The original Central Pacific Railroad locomotive, C.P. No. 1, *Governor Stanford,* in the California State Railroad Museum in Sacramento.

Map 217 (*below*).
Judah's plans for extensions to the Sacramento Valley Railroad, shown on a map dated September 1854. The first line to be built, to Folsom (not marked on this map) is the short line east of Sacramento along the American River. It is then shown splitting into two, with one branch going north up the Sacramento Valley and the other curving south to San Francisco, crossing the bay at two places, one marked *Ferry.*

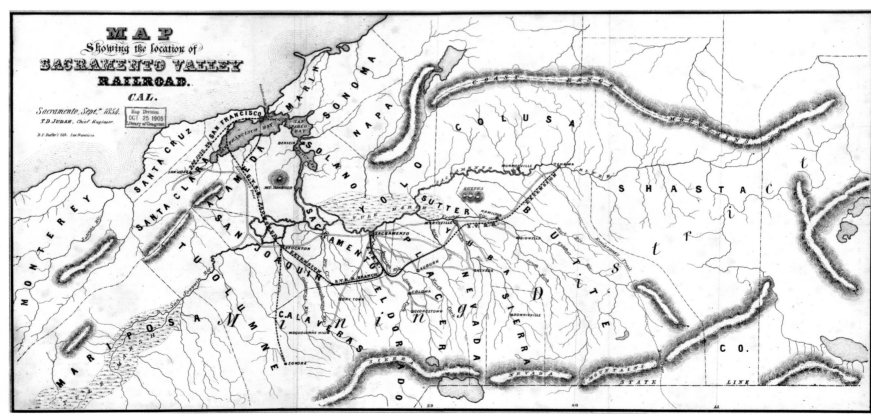

Nevertheless, in 1861 Judah persuaded four Sacramento merchants to underwrite the Central Pacific Railroad, with him as chief engineer. The merchants, later known as the "Big Four," were Amasa Leland Stanford, from 1861 to 1863 governor of California; Collis P. Huntington; Mark Hopkins; and Charles Crocker, and it was their driving desire to make money from the enterprise that drove it forward. Judah himself did not live to see his railroad built; he died in 1863 after catching yellow fever while crossing the Isthmus of Panama on one of his many trips to Washington.

A new president, Abraham Lincoln, was an avid railroad supporter, seeing clearly how it would act to bind his country, at that time fighting for its very life, together.

MAP 218 (*right*).
Judah's map presented to the directors and stockholders of the Sacramento Valley Railroad showing his survey and possible routes for the line from Sacramento to Negro Bar mining area, beside which Joseph Folsom had founded the settlement he named Granite City. Construction of the line began in February 1855, and the first train ran the full length on 22 February 1856. When Folsom died at the early age of 38, Granite City residents renamed their town Folsom.

MAP 219 (*below*).
The first railroad surveyed in California was the grandiosely named Pacific and Atlantic Railroad, surveyed between San Francisco and San Jose in 1851. There was no doubt of the pretensions of this railroad. But there is a great deal more to building a railroad than surveying the line, and this line would not be built for a few more years. The San Francisco and San Jose Railroad, a more soberly named railroad following approximately this route, was incorporated in 1859, the line was completed at the end of 1863, and the first train ran into San Francisco in January 1864. The line was acquired by the "Big Four's" Southern Pacific four years later and connected to the Central Pacific's transcontinental line.

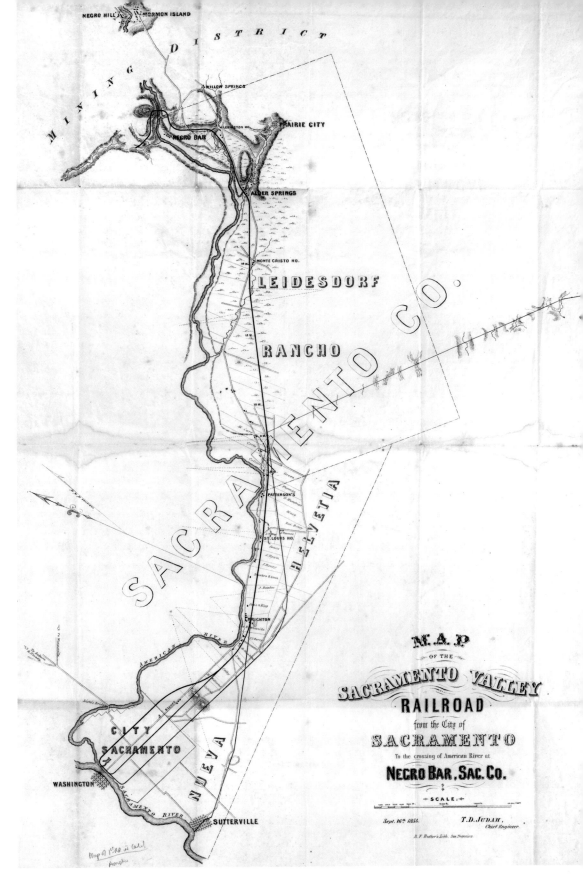

MAP OF THE SACRAMENTO VALLEY RAILROAD from the City of SACRAMENTO To the crossing of American River at NEGRO BAR, SAC. CO.

SCALE.

Sept. 16th 1854.    T. D. JUDAH, Chief Engineer.

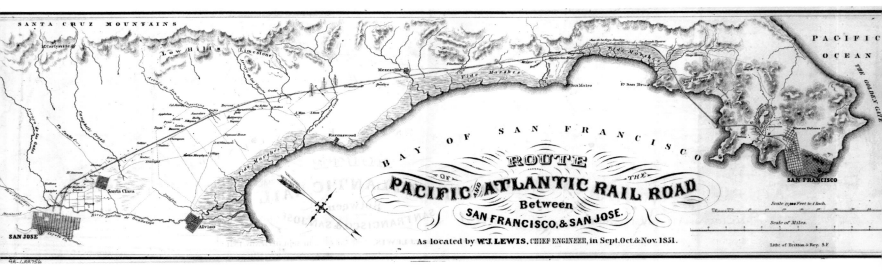

ROUTE OF THE PACIFIC AND ATLANTIC RAIL ROAD Between SAN FRANCISCO & SAN JOSE.

As located by WM. J. LEWIS, CHIEF ENGINEER, in Sept. Oct. & Nov. 1851.

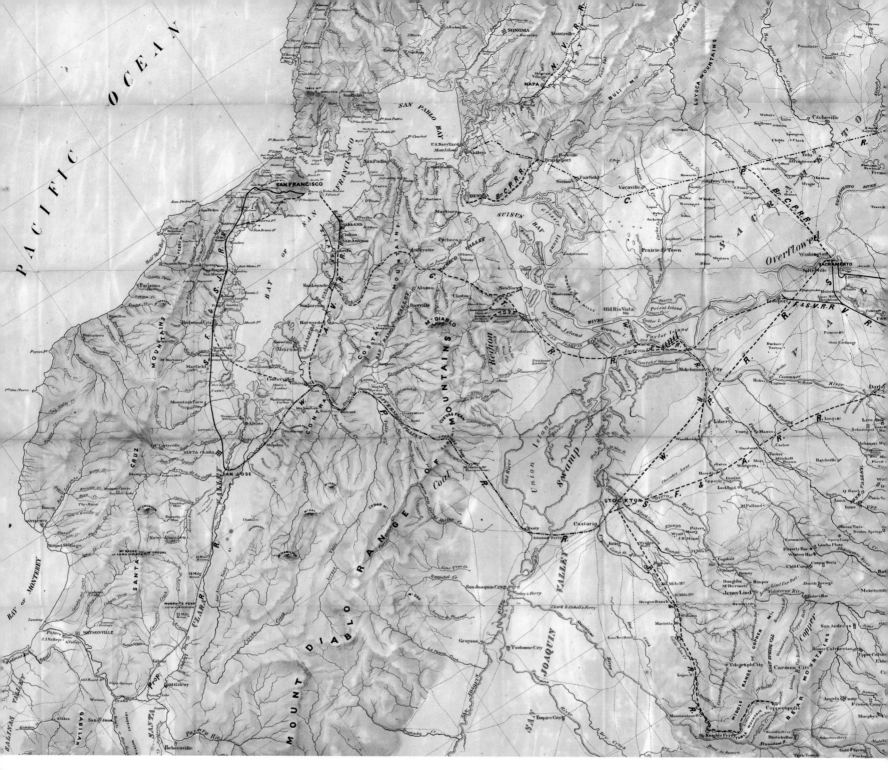

On 1 July 1862 Congress passed the Pacific Railroad Bill, which authorized the building of the transcontinental line by the Union Pacific from the east and the Central Pacific from the west as far as the California-Nevada border. The government was to give the railroads a 400-foot right of way, five alternate sections of land, checkerboard fashion, on each side of the line, for each mile of track laid, as well as financial aid. The latter was in the form of bonds, collectible every forty miles, at $16,000 per mile for flat land, $32,000 for desert, and $48,000 for mountainous terrain. Not surprisingly, this encouraged the companies to get as much land as they could classified as mountainous. The bonds, however, were a first mortgage, which discouraged other investors, who would hold a subordinate position.

The first rails were spiked in October 1863, and in May 1865 service began as far as Auburn, a distance of only thirty miles. Despite government aid, it was difficult to find investors, as it was widely thought that building a railroad across the Sierra would prove impossible. Huntington continued to lobby in Washington and managed to get the Pacific Railroad Bill amended in 1864 to give the company ten sections of land on each side of the track. Government bonds would now be issued for every twenty miles and hold a subordinate position. The government was slow issuing bonds, but the Big Four never gave up, despite the fact that the Central Pacific was virtually broke.

The other issue hampering progress was labor. In the winter of 1864–65 the Central Pacific was down to five hundred men, such was the allure of the Nevada silver mines and other promises of wealth. And so Crocker,

in charge of construction, and his deputy, James Harvey Strobridge, brought in Chinese workmen, whom they soon found performed magnificently and without complaint. At this time there were about sixty thousand Chinese people in California. Most had come to work in the gold mines and stayed on doing whatever work they could find (many in San Francisco), and Crocker had no trouble recruiting them to work on the railroad. By the end of 1865 there were seven thousand Chinese men carving a path through the Sierra, and the pace of progress picked up despite the increasingly difficult task. Huge cuts, thirteen long tunnels, and massive fills were the order of the day, all hewn and dumped manually. By the spring of 1866 there were eight thousand Chinese workers and two thousand others; the C.P.'s total workforce of ten thousand made them the largest employer in the country.

Work on the Union Pacific track west out of Omaha began in December 1863, also progressing slowly because opportunities to

Map 220 (*above*).

By 1865, the date of this map, a number of railroad projects were underway in California. The Sacramento Valley Railroad to Folsom had been completed in 1856, the San Francisco and San Jose Railroad was completed at the end of 1863, and work had begun on the Central Pacific's end of the transcontinental line in January of that same year. Progress was slow and financing tenuous, such that by June 1865 the Central Pacific line, marked *C.P. R.R.* on this map, had only reached *Clipper Gap*, forty-three miles from Sacramento, and was about to begin its assault on the Sierra. It was here that the Big Four made the decision to bring in Chinese labor.

*Far left.* From a diorama at the California State Railroad Museum: Chinese railroad construction workers hack out a toehold on the mountainside in preparation for the placing of explosives. The Chinese did most of the work of blasting a path for the railbed using black powder, up to 500 kegs per day, the cost of which was reduced by the end of the Civil War. Nitroglycerin was experimented with but caused such heavy casualties that its use was discontinued. Dynamite, available by 1866, was never used by the Central Pacific.

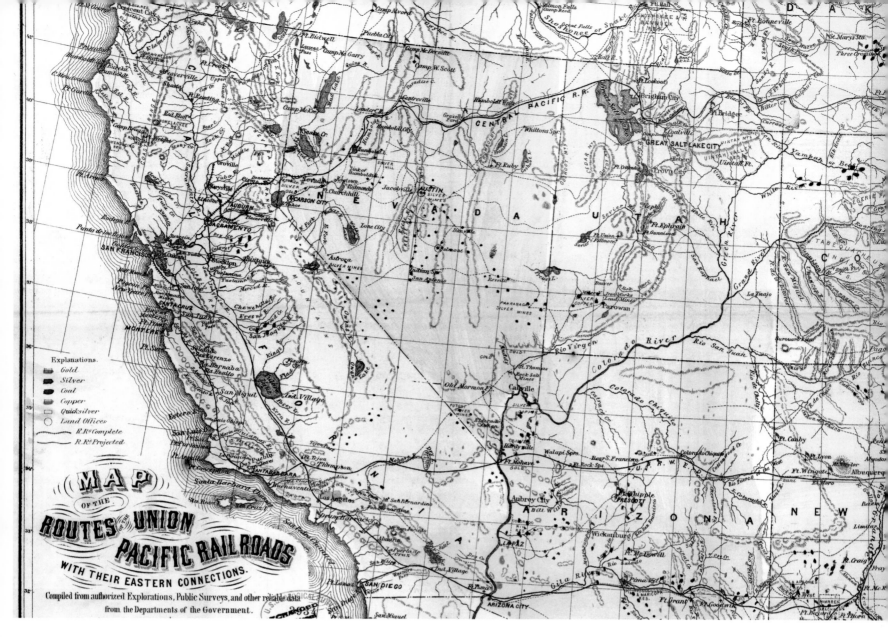

make more money from land grant manipulation overrode railroad construction considerations. But in 1866 the Casement brothers, Jack and Dan, were put in charge of tracklaying, and an ex–Union general, Grenville Mullen Dodge, assumed overall control of construction. He ran the work like a military operation, and progress accelerated.

That year, too, Collis Huntington persuaded Congress to amend the railroad bill once more to allow the Central Pacific to build as far east as it could get, rather than being limited, as it was under the 1864 bill, to 150 miles east of the California-Nevada boundary line. This created race-like conditions and piqued investor interest, for it now became clear that perhaps the transcontinental line would be completed after all.

But the going continued to be tough for the railroad in the Sierra. Drilling holes for explosives in granite by hand took an excruciatingly long time, and the Union Pacific had none of these problems and was racing west at a rate Crocker and his crew could only imagine. The cutting of the 1,659-foot-long Summit Tunnel, at the highest point of the railroad at Donner Pass—just over 7,000 feet—began while the track was still seventy-five miles away. It was designed and supervised by a young C.P. engineer, Lewis Clement. Work was hampered by deep snowfalls that made access to the tunnel mouths difficult. The tunneling went so slowly despite excavation from both ends that

MAP 222 (left).
By the size of the Union Pacific smile on the face of Mr. United States, one would think the Central Pacific had nothing to do with the transcontinental railroad instead of being the builders of the most difficult part of it. This newspaper cartoon appeared soon after the railroad was completed in 1869 and was titled *A Good Square American Smile*.

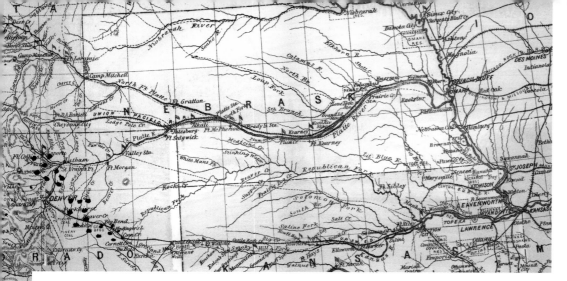

it was decided worthwhile to sink a seventy-three-foot-deep shaft near the middle and begin to work outward in either direction as well. A cannibalized locomotive was hauled up to the top of the shaft to provide a means of extracting the rock. Nitroglycerin was used for a while to speed up the tunneling process, though heavy casualties meant that the C.P. avoided its use elsewhere. The tunnel was finally broken through in August 1867. The facings of the tunnels, blasted in the dark by manpower and explosives alone and in an age long before global positioning systems and the like, were off by only two inches; a stunning feat of engineering on a tunnel so long and a tribute to Clement's skill and accuracy of measurement. There was still much to do, not least of all the clearing of debris, but then track was laid, and the first train went through on 30 November.

The bad winter weather also necessitated the building of snowsheds, also designed by Clement. Fifty miles of track, including one unbroken stretch of twenty-eight miles, were covered by snowsheds.

While work was progressing on the tunnel, men, material, and locomotives had been hauled over the mountains on the C.P.'s wagon road, the Dutch Flat Road, to begin work on the bridges, fills, and trackbed beyond, and the line had progressed from the Truckee Valley back toward the summit. With the tunnel complete, work went much faster, though in May 1867 there was a brief strike by the usually compliant Chinese workers, demanding more money; the strike failed after Crocker cut off their food supply.

As the country became flatter and easier for construction, the race to lay track before the Union Pacific did heated up. Track laid meant money in the bank. The C.P. crossed the boundary line into the new state of Nevada, created in 1864, and was responsible for the creation of Reno, the name of which (Jesse Lee Reno, a Union general) Crocker is reputed to have pulled out of a hat. Such was the competition with the Union Pacific that track was laid even after the U.P. line was reached, parallel to it, and Congress, which had reserved the right to name the meeting place, was forced to step in and set Promontary Point, north of the Great Salt Lake, as the connection point. Here on 10 May 1869, the Union Pacific and Central Pacific were joined, the last spike being driven by Leland Stanford, and the transcontinental line was a reality; California was connected to the rest of the nation. The faster pace of rail-laying toward the end, first in Nevada and then in Utah, had allowed the Central Pacific to catch up somewhat to its rival; in the end some 690 miles of track were laid by the Central Pacific and 1,060 by the Union Pacific.

## MAP 223 (right).

From a government statistical atlas of 1874 comes this map showing the distribution of Chinese people in California. Most had arrived during the gold rush and the years thereafter and are concentrated in the gold mining regions, though some would undoubtedly be in the area after working on the transcontinental railroad. The Central Pacific tried to recruit new workers in China in order to create an oversupply situation in which they could continue to dictate terms to the workers and not vice versa, as had happened for one brief period during the construction of the line when there was a short-lived strike. But, contrary to popular opinion, few Chinese came to California as a result of the C.P.'s efforts.

## MAP 221 (left).

The date of this map is 1867. Central Pacific track is shown as laid into Nevada, down the Truckee Valley. But it was not connected line. Track was not laid through the Summit Tunnel until the end of November of that year. Track had been laid in the Truckee so as not to be held up by the longer amount of time it took to create the Summit Tunnel and other trackbed around it. Union Pacific track is shown laid as far west as Cheyenne City. Track is also shown as laid between San Francisco and San Jose, the line completed in 1863. There are two other lines to the West, to Los Angeles and to San Diego, but both, on close examination, are shown only as projected rather than completed.

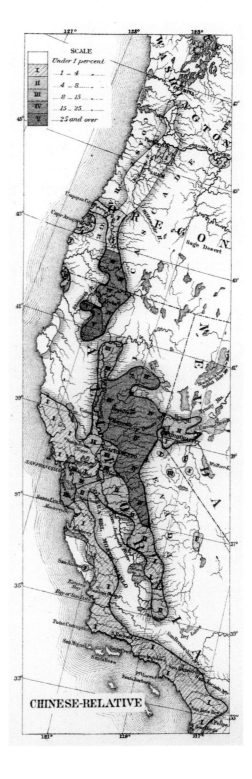

CHINESE-RELATIVE

# THE SOUTHERN PACIFIC

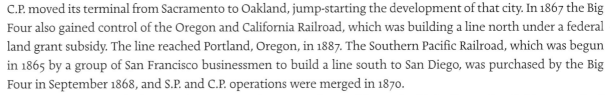

The imminent completion of the transcontinental line spawned a number of railroads within California, and many were quickly acquired by the Big Four. The Suez Canal opened in 1869 and siphoned off expected Asian trade, and so the Central Pacific needed California trade to maintain its viability.

The San Francisco and San Jose Railroad was purchased in 1867, thus completing the transcontinental line to the Pacific. In 1869 the C.P. moved its terminal from Sacramento to Oakland, jump-starting the development of that city. In 1867 the Big Four also gained control of the Oregon and California Railroad, which was building a line north under a federal land grant subsidy. The line reached Portland, Oregon, in 1887. The Southern Pacific Railroad, which was begun in 1865 by a group of San Francisco businessmen to build a line south to San Diego, was purchased by the Big Four in September 1868, and S.P. and C.P. operations were merged in 1870.

A priority was the line south to Los Angeles. Using Chinese labor to build the line, Bakersfield was reached in 1874. The Tehachapi Pass was utilized and a 3,799-foot loop—the Tehachapi Loop—had to be constructed to gain 77 feet of altitude in a tight space. Charles Crocker drove the last spike connecting San Francisco with Los Angeles near today's Palmdale on 5 September 1876 (MAP 225, below). Local Los Angeles lines had already been acquired, including the line to the harbor at Wilmington. Even before the S.P. had connected to Los Angeles, construction of a line eastward to San Bernardino had begun. With an eye to a second transcontinental line terminating at Los Angeles, the railroad built east across the desert. In the fall of 1877 the railroad reached Yuma, Arizona Territory, bridging the Colorado even before permission had been obtained from the federal government. Extension of this line plus the purchase of rail systems in Texas and Louisiana allowed the completion of the transcontinental line in 1883. In 1919 the Southern Pacific finally reached San Diego by acquiring and completing the San Diego and Arizona Railway (the route included 44 miles through Mexico), connecting the city with S.P. line in the Imperial Valley.

On the death of the Big Four the Southern Pacific passed into the control of Edward H. Harriman, who already controlled the Union Pacific, but in 1913 the federal government enforced the 1890 Sherman Anti-Trust Act, and Harriman had to give up the S.P. In 1988 the company became part of the Rio Grande Railroad System and in 1996 was finally acquired by the Union Pacific; the Southern Pacific name disappeared.

The Southern Pacific had a significant influence on the growth and development of California, encouraging (except when part of the Harriman empire) the sale of its lands, the development of agriculture, and many public irrigation projects. Yet the Southern Pacific was in its early years a company many hated; the corporate policies of the railroad often focused too much on making money. Despite the fact that the Big Four did such benevolent things as creating one of the first comprehensive industrial hospitalization and health-care insurance programs in the United States, the Southern Pacific is thought of by many as a heavy-handed corporate purveyor of unbridled capitalism with politicians and judges in its pay. This view centers on the so-called Mussel Slough affair of 1880, when the railroad tried to collect up to $40 per acre from settlers near Hanford (see MAP 245, *page 132*) after they had improved and irrigated the land. The settlers had been sold land, they thought, at the usual $2.50 *before* they improved it. The railroad violently evicted the settlers at the cost of eight lives.

*Above* and MAP 224 (*right*). Two rather opposite views of the Southern Pacific. *The Curse of California* is from an 1882 magazine, the *Wasp*, and shows the S.P. as a railroad monopoly octopus, into everything, controlling everything, and strangling the lifeblood out of anything and anybody that got in its way. MAP 224 is a large 1920s painted wooden advertising sign, of the type that would have hung in a large station, showing the Southern Pacific system, well connected and mysteriously in sunlight as the world turns and the rest of the nation is in darkness.

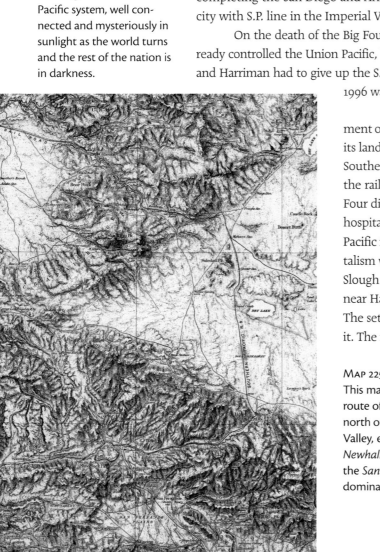

MAP 225 (*left*).
This map by army surveyor Lieutenant George Wheeler was published in 1883 and shows the route of the Southern Pacific line from Bakersfield to Los Angeles via the Tehachapi Pass, just north of which *The Loop* (the Tehachapi Loop) is marked. The line then crosses the Antelope Valley, entering the San Gabriel Mountains over *Soledad Pass* and along Soledad Canyon to *Newhall* (Santa Clarita) before turning south again, entering the San Fernando Valley through the *San Fernando Tunnel*. The route required over 8,000 feet of tunnels, all built by the predominantly Chinese workforce.

**Map 226** (*right*).

The fact that this map showing land grants to railroads was produced by a political party should immediately raise a flag of caution. The amount of land granted to railroads has been often considerably overstated, and this map puts the overstatement into visual form. The areas shown, which were indeed taken from federal government maps (and thus the official-looking certification), were granted only if previously unoccupied or unalienated, and even then only alternate sections (640 acres) were granted. Vast areas, such as virtually all the coastal lands, could not be given to the railroads because they were the subject of Mexican land grants, upheld by the United States. Where the railroads created a settlement they could own much of the land, but where they passed through an existing community, no land was granted. Naturally enough, good land tended to already be alienated, and the railroads often only actually received

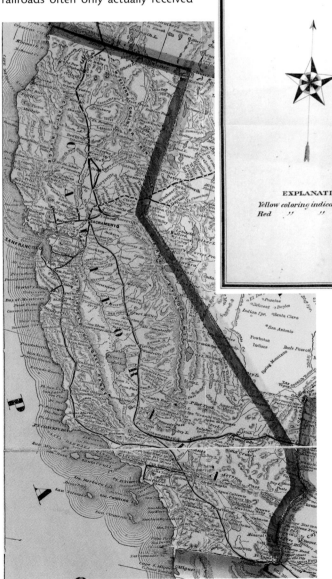

marginal land, in many cases desert land useless without irrigation. Oft-quoted figures of 11 to 12 million acres may be the total land of all types ever granted to California railroads, but this quantity was never held at any one time, as the Southern Pacific and other railroads generally sold land that they could sell right away to try to cover the costs of construction. This map was published by the California People's Independent Party, popularly known as the "Dolly Varden" Party, in 1875 as election propaganda. California pioneer John Bidwell was the gubernatorial candidate, and Romualdo Pacheco, already the Republican governor (and California's only Hispanic governor), was the candidate for lieutenant governor; neither was elected.

**Map 227** (*left*).

California railroads in 1873. Projected lines have a hairlike bristle on one side of the line. South of San Jose and Sacramento the railroads are all only projected. Within two years the Southern Pacific would reach Bakersfield, and in 1876 the S.P. line would be completed to Los Angeles. The line shown to Northern California is incorrect. It was 1887 before the Southern Pacific completed a connection to Oregon, after taking over the Oregon and California Railroad that year.

## MAP OF
## CALIFORNIA

To accompany printed argument of
### S. O. HOUGHTON
as to the rights of the
### SOUTHERN PACIFIC R.R.CO.of CAL.
to Government lands under Acts of Congress
Passed July 27.1866 and March 3.1871.
made before the
COMMITTEE ON THE JUDICIARY of the SENATE and HO. of REPs
in May 1876.

REFERENCE FOR COLORING
Central Pacific Railroad
Southern Pacific R.R. original charter line of Dec. 2nd 1865
Line of Plat filed in the General Land Office Jan.3rd 1867
Southern Pacific charter line of Oct.12'70
Texas and Pacific Line
Southern Pacific Line to connect from Tehachepe Pass with Texas and Pacific at Ft Yuma.

Scale 2,000,000 of nature
STATUTE MILES 33 TO ONE INCH
0   10   20   30   40   50   60   70   80   90   100

PREPARED BY G.W.& C.B.COLTON & Cº 172 WILLIAM St NEW YORK

RAIL ROADS
PROPOSED RAIL ROADS
STAGE ROUTES

LOWER CALIFORNIA

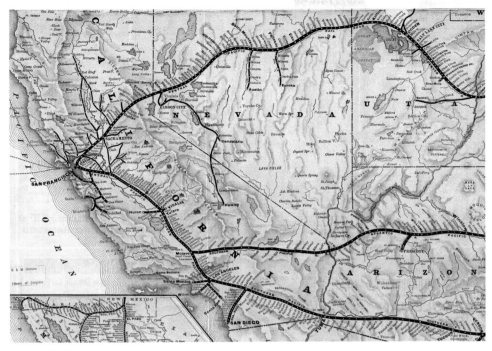

MAP 230 (*above*).

This stylized route map was published by the Atchison, Topeka & Santa Fe Railroad—the Santa Fe—in 1884. Here the Santa Fe line bears the name *Atlantic & Pacific*, an operating subsidiary of that railroad. Initially it leased the line within California from Needles to Mojave. The line to San Diego, connecting through San Bernardino to Barstow, was completed in 1885 by another Santa Fe subsidiary, the California Southern. The San Bernardino to Barstow portion of the line is not yet on this map.

MAP 232 (*right*).

The Southern Pacific published this map in 1888, superimposing climatic zones—or at least mean annual temperatures—on a system map. The map was copied from a State Board of Trade map published the same year. These kinds of maps provided information useful to prospective farmers—perhaps purchasers of S.P. lands—and tourists.

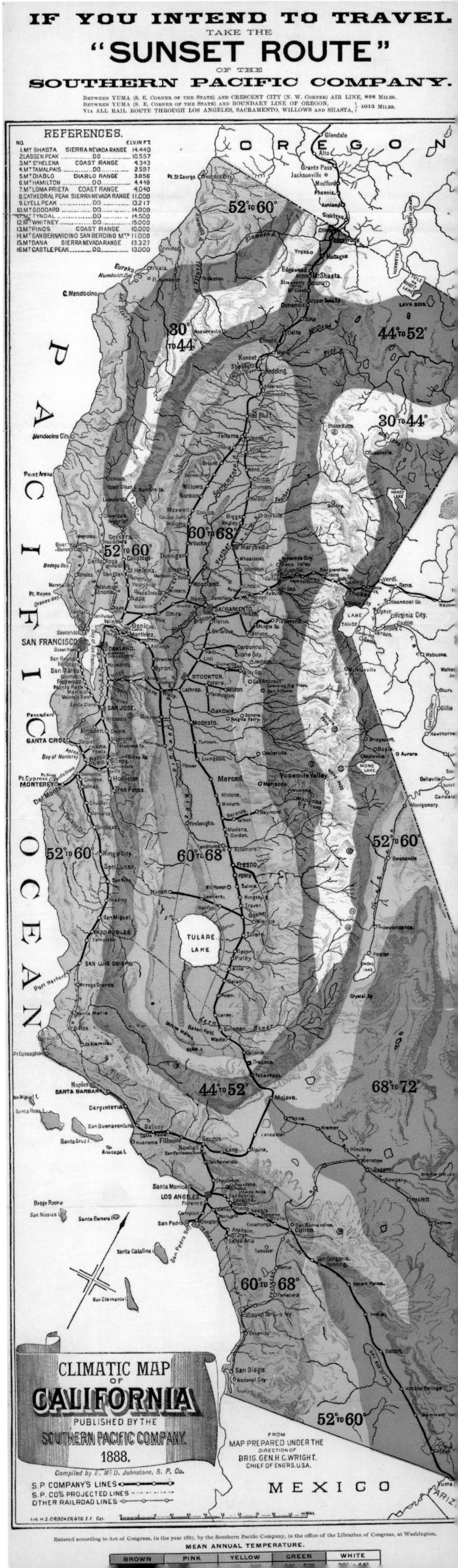

MAP 231 (*above*).

Quite a few candidates ran for political office by harnessing the popular public backlash against the Southern Pacific in the first part of the twentieth century. This one was used by Hiram Johnson in the 1910 gubernatorial election. A lawyer, Johnson had come to public prominence in 1908 when he took over the prosecution of a notorious graft case in San Francisco after the previous prosecutor had been gunned down. Tellingly, in the 1910 hustings, Johnson toured California by horse. Johnson was elected and served as governor of California from 1911 to 1917. By the 1910 election, so unpopular was the Southern Pacific that many candidates for public office found it necessary to espouse an anti–Southern Pacific attitude in order to be elected.

MAP 228 (*left*).

The Southern Pacific created this map in 1876 to try to establish its rights to government land grants based on its chartered line both built and unbuilt.

MAP 229 (*left, inset*).

This map was an accurate representation of completed railroads by 1879. Los Angeles, already with some local railroads, had been connected to the Southern Pacific line from the north in September 1876, and the southern line reached Yuma the following year.

# "THE GLOBE"

**Panama-Pacific International Exposition**

**San Francisco 1915**

**Western Pacific**
**Denver & Rio Grande**
**Missouri Pacific**
**St. Louis, Iron Mountain & Southern**

**1915**

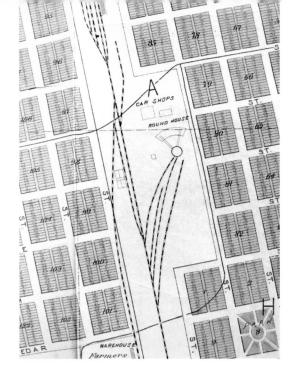

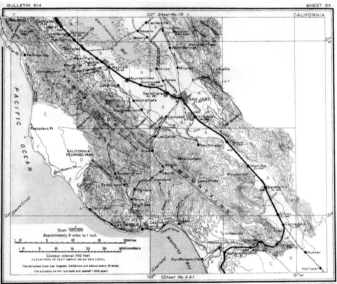

**MAP 233** (*above*).
All the railroads recognized that the 1915 Panama-Pacific International Exposition in San Francisco would be good for traffic. This advertising poster showed all their routes to California.

**MAP 234** (*left*).
One of a series of maps published in 1915 by the United States Geological Survey to show topographic details along the Southern Pacific's various routes. This one shows the line north and south of San Jose and the route through the Santa Cruz Mountains to the coast.

**MAP 235** (*above*).
In a layout that was repeated many times in smaller California communities, the street plan of the City of Tulare is shown laid out surrounding the Southern Pacific station. Tulare was but one of a number of towns spawned by the S.P. as the line reached down the San Joaquin Valley in the 1870s that were encouraged by the railroad to develop the value of its land grant.

**MAP 236** (*below*).
A Southern Pacific route map, 1892. This seems to have been aimed principally at the growing tourist trade—note the engraving at bottom left of the *Interior of tourist sleeping car*—and the cover (*inset*) emphasizes the Sunset Route, from New Orleans to Los Angeles, on which the famous *Sunset Limited* was inaugurated in 1894.

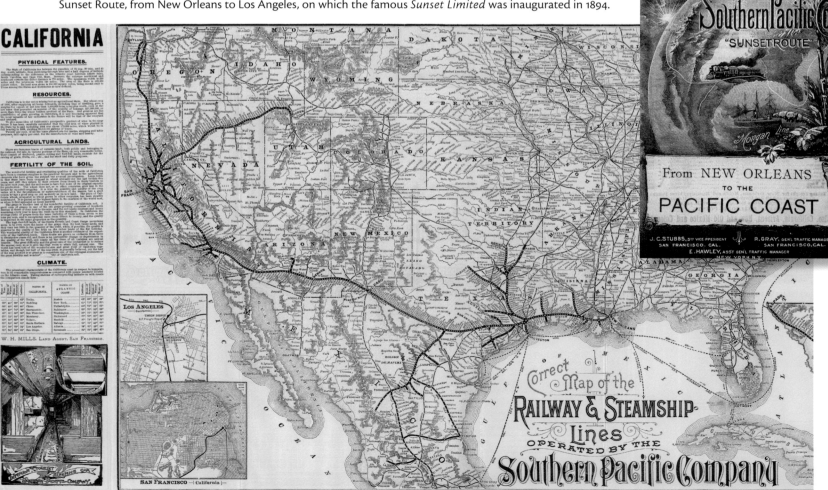

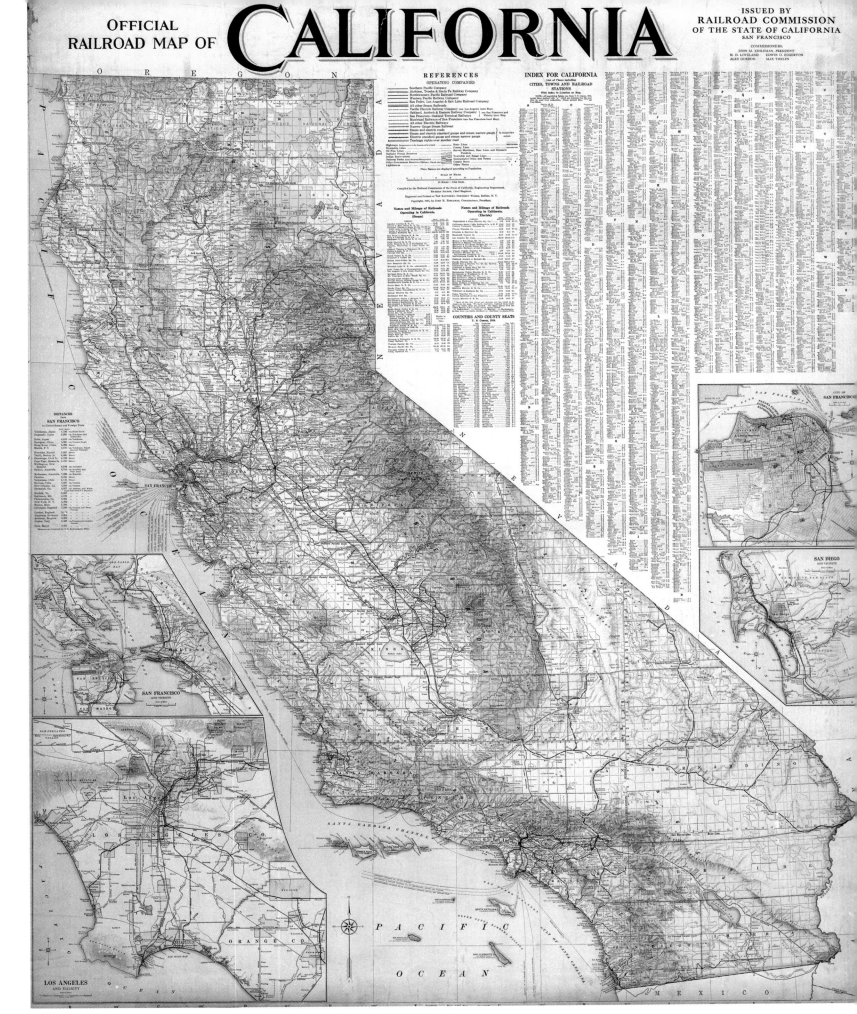

Map 237.
The Railroad Commission of the State of California was created as part of a revised constitution in 1879. Many of its individual commissioners were under the effective control of the Southern Pacific. This detailed and large (approx. 4 x 5 ft.) map of the state railroad system was published in 1915.

# A GEOLOGICAL SURVEY

The first California Geological Survey was created in 1853, but a professional geological survey was not commissioned until 1860, when Josiah Dwight Whitney, who had been engaged in geological surveys in the East and was considered one of the foremost geologists of his day, was appointed state geologist and commissioned to carry out an accurate and complete survey of the state.

The California legislators who approved the survey thought that they were getting a road map to where the next gold would be found, but the survey was intended to be much more comprehensive. Whitney gathered a small group of specialists and produced an ambitious survey with much new information about California. The survey was suspended in 1868 when the California legislators who had appointed Whitney became dissatisfied with the scope of the survey.

Whitney remained state geologist until 1874, and he even privately funded publication of the final volumes of the survey.

The survey was the first to describe and map Kings Canyon, (later a national park; see page 190), and Whitney was one of the first to advocate protection for the Yosemite Valley, writing an influential travel guide, *The Yosemite Book,* in 1865. The valley was set aside as a state park in 1864 and made a national park in 1890 (see page 190). Whitney seems to have been a controversial type. He became embroiled with John Muir over the origins of the valley, insisting that it was created by subsidence rather than by glaciers, as Muir thought (correctly). Nevertheless, the California Geological Survey is remembered for the vast amount of pioneering scientific data it collected; Mount Whitney, the highest mountain in the lower forty-nine, is named after its leader.

**MAP 238** (*left*).
The Pacific Railroad Surveys of 1853–56 included much work on geology and botany. William P. Blake, who was with Lieutenant Robert Williamson in 1853, produced this map, one of the earliest of the geology of the central part of California; it was published in 1855 with Williamson's report. Blake was a contemporary rival of Josiah Whitney and differed with him over ideas ranging from the antiquity of man to the origin of the Yosemite Valley.

**MAP 239** (*right*).
A grand and detailed topographical map published in 1874 by Whitney's California Geological Survey, a compendium using his own data and all else that was available.

**MAP 240** (*right, inset*).
The American Association for the Advancement of Science requested in 1872 that Congress publish the accumulated knowledge from government expeditions, and in 1874 the first geological map of the United States was published. This is the western portion of that map, which, within the state boundaries, used information from the California Geological Survey.

**MAP 241** (*right, bottom*).
Part of a map of the central part of California published by the California Geological Survey in 1873. The south fork of *King's River* is shown, between Fresno and *Independence,* in the Owens Valley. Around the head of the Kings River are mountains named after the members of the survey: *Mt. [Clarence] King; Mt. [James] Gardner* (now Mt. Gardiner); and *Mt. [William] Brewer.* Mt. Whitney is off the part reproduced here but can be seen on MAP 373, *page 194.*

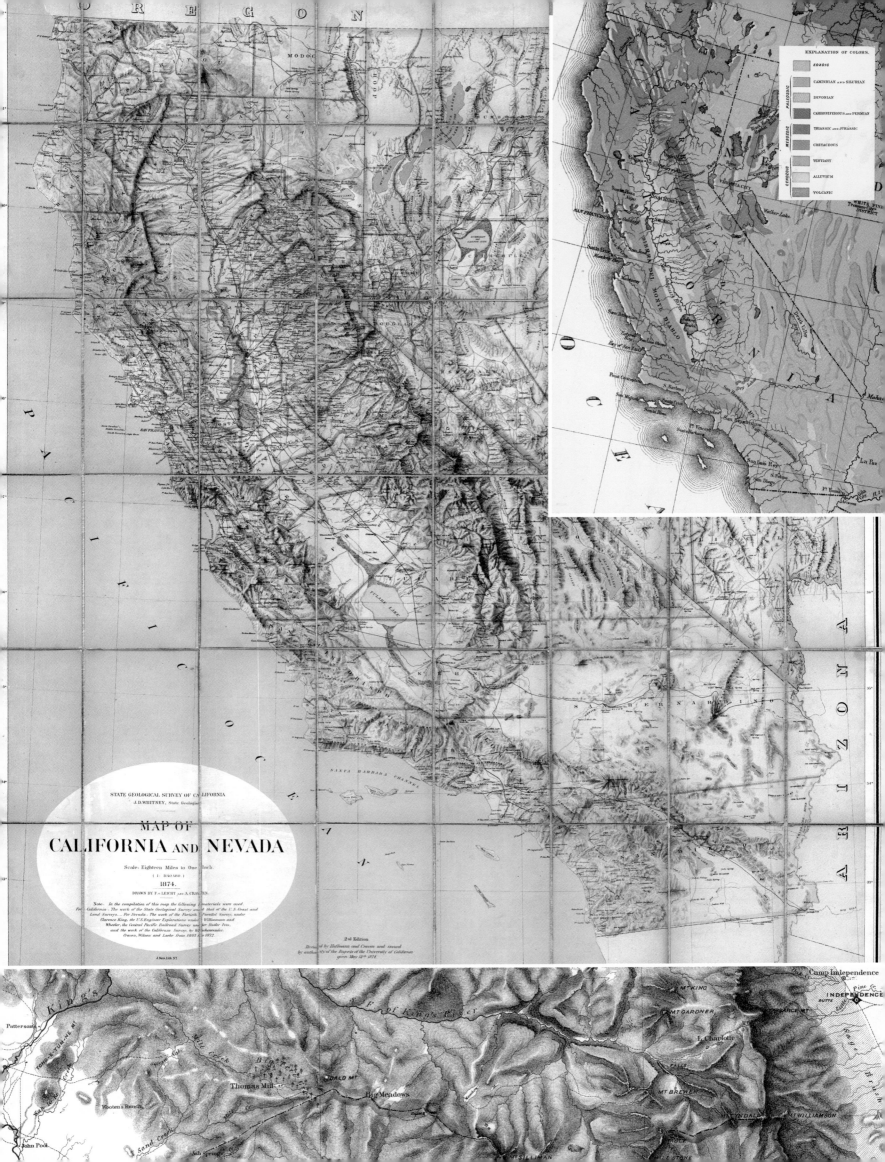

# WATER, WINE, AND ORANGES

Water has always been the key to unlocking the riches of California's land. With water, a vast range of fruits and vegetables could be grown in the felicitous climate, and the growth of powerful marketing organizations, at first backed by the railroads, was all that was necessary to propel California to its position as the food larder of the nation, and its wine cellar too.

Many of California's early irrigation projects were land colonies, where larger blocks of land were purchased and, after irrigation canals were dug, allocated to settlers for cultivation. One of the earliest and best-known was the Mormon colony at San Bernardino. In the Sacramento Valley, John Bidwell had well over a thousand fruit trees and 15,000 vines on his rancho as early as 1857, but since much of the Central Valley was at first successfully farmed without irrigation, projects did not get under way on any scale in the Central Valley until the 1870s. Indeed, during the 1870s to 1890s the valley was the breadbasket of Europe. In 1881 some 559 ships loaded a single season's grain harvest. Also, artesian wells could be dug in many areas, and at first there was adequate water pressure available without pumping, the technology for which was insufficient until about 1900, when electricity began to be available.

Rivers issuing from the Sierra Nevada, such as the Tule and the Kings, which flowed to Tulare Lake, and the Kern, which flowed to Buena Vista and Kern lakes (MAP 243, *right*), were diverted through multiple channels early on, to spread the water out over more land. The system is well illustrated by MAP 246, *page 133*, which shows the irrigation canals from the Kern River south of Bakersfield. It was here that in 1886 a legal precedent was established that would be of enormous importance: that riparian rights (the right of the adjacent landowners to a river's water), established when California adopted English Common Law in 1850, overrode appropriation, the principle, followed until then in much of the West, that the first user of water had a right to its continued use, even to irrigate land away from the river. This court decision (Lux vs. Haggin) could have proved disastrous for landowners away from rivers and led quickly to the Wright Act of 1887, which provided a process by which farmers could form an irrigation district and legally obtain river water. Forty-nine districts were organized in the following eight years. This act (later the California Irrigation District Act) was amended to cover all manner of special situations.

*Above left.* The carefully orchestrated advertising of California as an untapped Eden, the *Cornucopia of the World,* was well illustrated by this beautiful poster published by the California Immigration Commission in 1883. The apparent easy availability of farmland and the favorable climate (*without cyclones or blizzards*) are emphasized and clearly worded to appeal to farmers in the South and Midwest.

MAP 242 (*left*).
This map, from an 1867 survey, shows the considerable area in the delta of the Sacramento and San Joaquin rivers (the area shaded with horizontal lines) that was subject to flooding. Much of this land has been reclaimed for agricultural use, other than areas left deliberately as wetland.

MAP 243 (*right*).
This federal government map from 1873 shows potentially irrigable lands, finished and proposed irrigation canals, and the flood zones of the Central Valley. It was published by the Board of Commissioners on Irrigation as a summary of its survey of the valley to determine the state of irrigation and what might be achieved. The southern part may be compared to the more detailed map of irrigation channels shown in MAP 246, *page 133*.

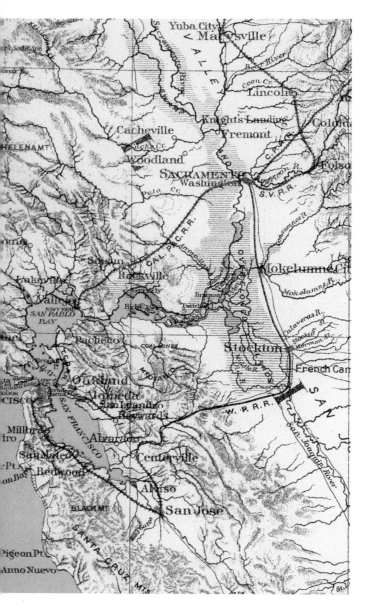

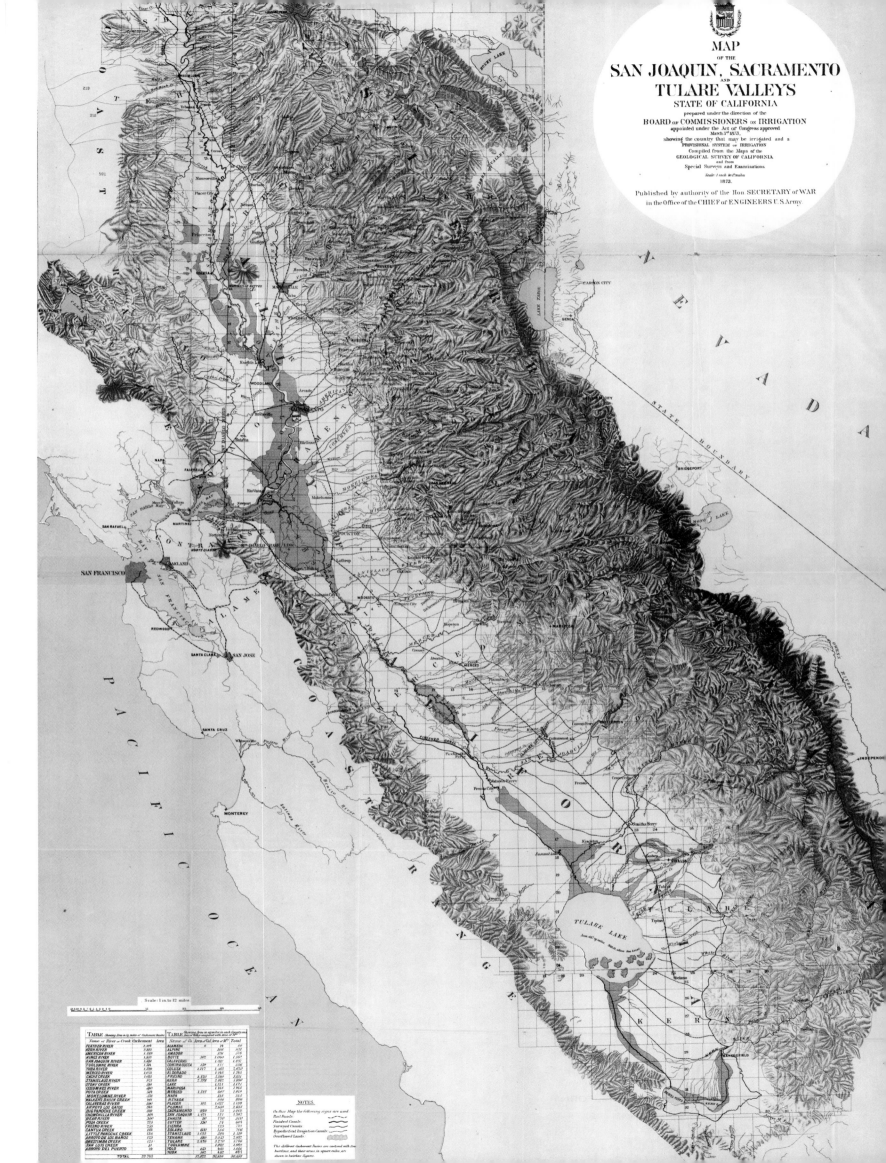

# MAP
## OF THE
# SAN JOAQUIN, SACRAMENTO
### AND
# TULARE VALLEYS
## STATE OF CALIFORNIA

prepared under the direction of the
### BOARD OF COMMISSIONERS ON IRRIGATION
appointed under the Act of Congress approved
March 3rd 1873,
showing the country that may be irrigated and a
PROVISIONAL SYSTEM OF IRRIGATION
Compiled from the Maps of the
GEOLOGICAL SURVEY OF CALIFORNIA
and from
Special Surveys and Examinations
Scale 1 inch to 12 miles
1873.

Published by authority of the Hon. SECRETARY of WAR
in the Office of the CHIEF of ENGINEERS U.S. Army.

MAP 244 (*right*) and
MAP 245 (*below*).

Two views of the Tulare Valley and Tulare Lake. MAP 244 is from an 1850 military survey and shows the area in its pre-irrigation state. An extensive area of floodland extends north and south of Tulare Lake. MAP 245 shows the area forty-two years later. Many irrigation canals have been created to spread the water from the Kern River over the productive sedimentary soils deposited by the river over many centuries before. The Southern Pacific track is shown, as is *Hanford*, site of the infamous Mussel Slough incident of 1880 (see page 122).

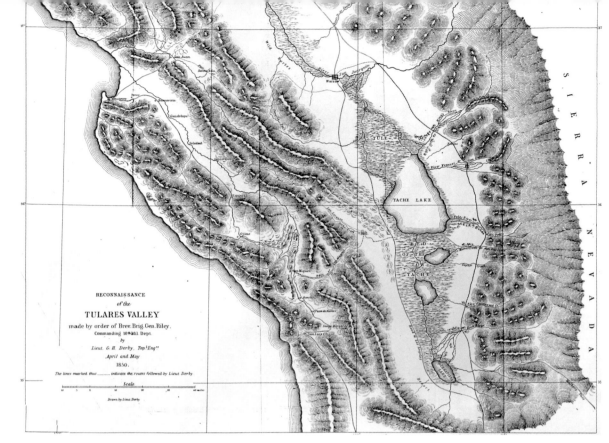

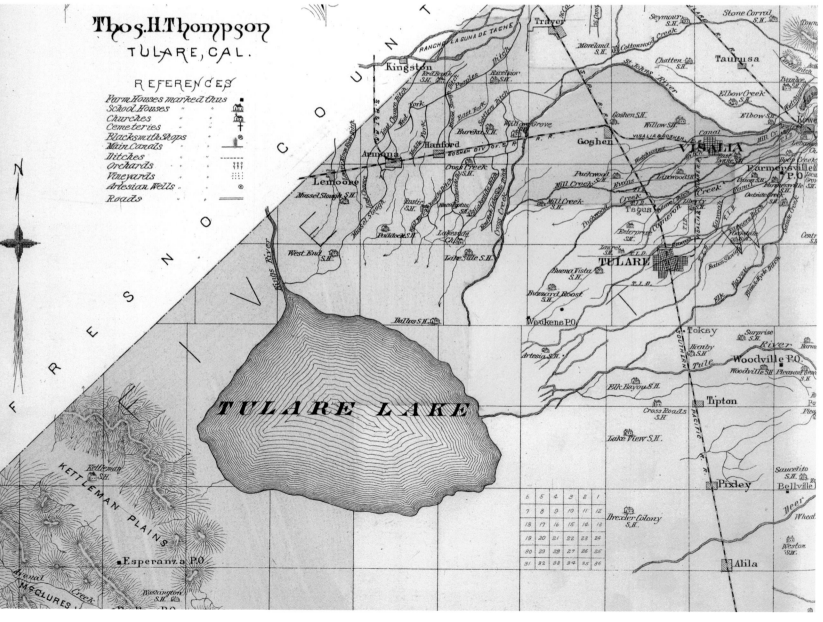

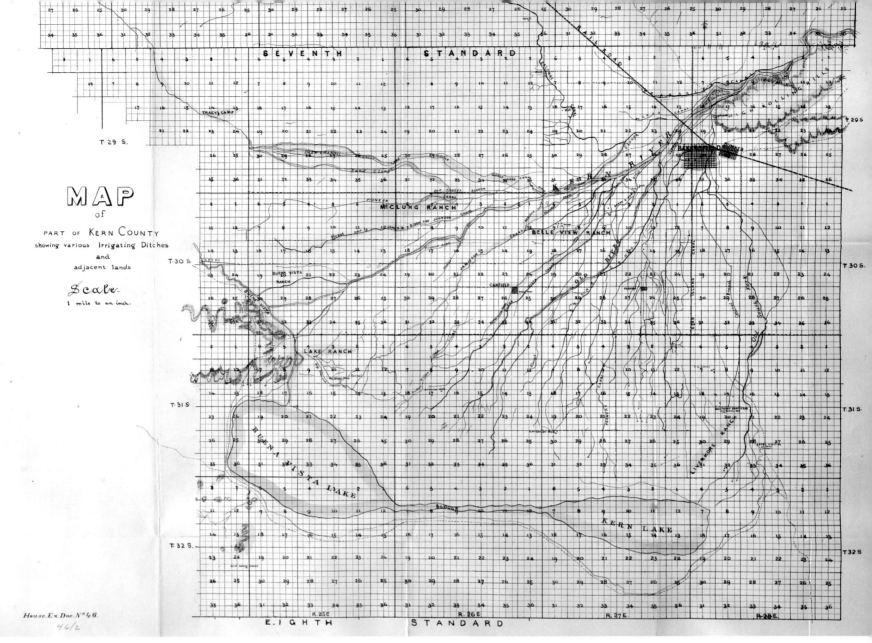

MAP
of
PART OF KERN COUNTY
showing various Irrigating Ditches
and
adjacent lands

*Scale*
1 mile to an inch.

House Ex Doc N° 46.
46/2

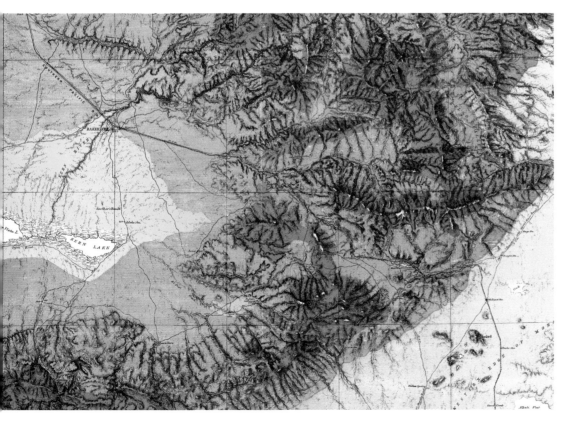

MAP 246 (*above*).
Irrigation canals, many of which are improved natural sloughs, fan out from the Kern River in this detailed 1877 map. Bakersfield was founded in 1863 by Colonel Thomas Baker, who moved to the area specifically to begin reclamation of the frequently flooded lands of the Kern River. The digging of canals allowed for better control of the flooding and provided a distribution network for gravity-fed irrigation water.

MAP 247 (*left*).
This is the area in its wider context at the southern end of the Central Valley. The map is a land-use map; the beige-colored area is agricultural with irrigation; the green horizontal-lined area is grazing land, some of which would later be irrigated and become crop lands; dark green is timbered land; and brown-pink is arid land. The contrast between the Central Valley, the mountains surrounding it, and the arid lands to the east is quite distinct. The map was published in 1879 and is from surveys by George Wheeler, the last of the great Army surveyors of the West. Note the line of the Southern Pacific through the Tehachapi Pass.

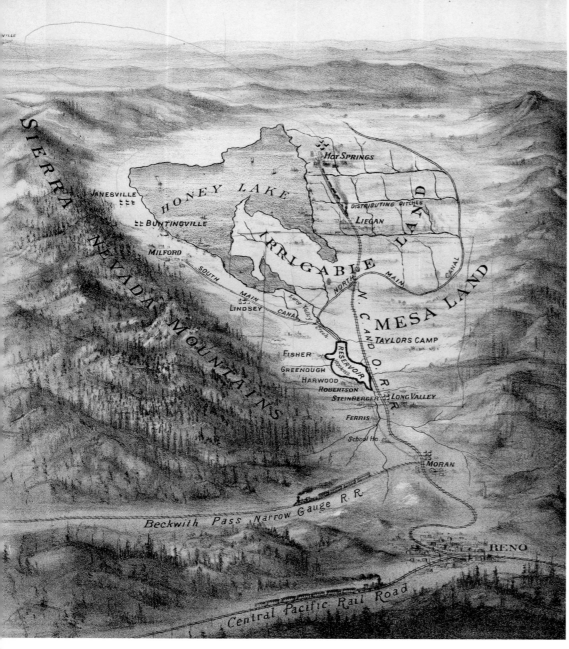

MAP 248 (*left*).
In a project typical of many small schemes, the Honey Lake Valley Land and Water Company planned in 1891 to use gravity-fed water from the lake to make land in the otherwise arid Honey Lake Valley agriculturally usable. This bird's-eye map was likely produced to interest investors or farmers in the land. The valley straddles the Nevada boundary in northeastern California.

MAP 249 (*left, bottom*).
Green on this map shows the irrigated area of the Sacramento–San Joaquin delta in 1920. The map was published in 1922 by the U.S. Department of Agriculture in cooperation with the California State Water Commission and other state agencies. Other parts of this large, four-sheet map are reproduced on the following pages.

MAP 250 (*right*).
This *Unique Map of California* is certainly just that. It was produced in 1888 for promotional purposes for the Southern Pacific and the State Board of Trade and incorporates separate maps showing soils, temperature, and the relative size of the state compared to eastern and midwestern states. On the main map each county's area is given together with its agricultural products, and the map is topped off with views of landmarks and the bounty of the state.

*Below.*
*From Desert to Garden, From Worthlessness to Wealth* was the title of a promotional booklet published in 1902 by a magazine called *California Homeseeker*.

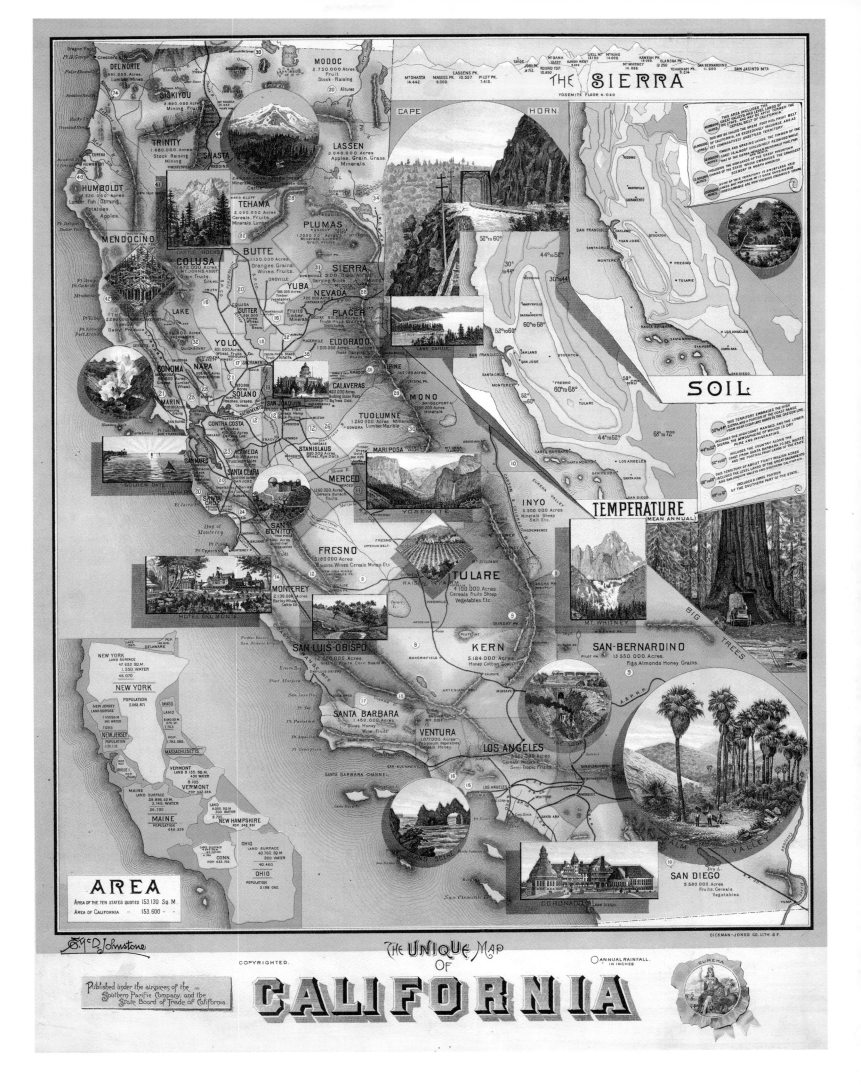

THE UNIQUE MAP OF

# CALIFORNIA

COPYRIGHTED.

○ ANNUAL RAINFALL. IN INCHES

Published under the auspices of the Southern Pacific Company, and the State Board of Trade of California.

DICKMAN-JONES CO. LITH. S.F.

Map 251 (right), Map 252 (below), and Map 253 (far right).
Further areas of California shown on the 1922 map (with 1920 information) published by the U.S. Department of Agriculture in cooperation with the California State Water Commission and other state agencies. The map legend is shown at the bottom of Map 253 (far right), which shows the southern San Joaquin and Tulare valleys. This map may be compared with the earliest maps of the same area on the previous pages. Map 251 (right) shows the northern San Joaquin Valley, and Map 252 (below) shows the Los Angeles basin region. In the Central Valley, especially since the completion of the California Aqueduct down the west side of the valley in 1968, just about all agriculturally usable land—the green and brown on these maps—is now irrigated. The main difference between what these 1920 maps depict and what exists today is that some areas have gone out of agricultural production altogether, because of the expansion of the urban areas. Thus on Map 251 and Map 253, all the brown-colored areas are irrigated, but much larger areas around Bakersfield, Fresno, Modesto, and Stockton are now urban. Likewise, on Map 252, the reduction of the irrigated area, shown here in the middle of what is now the urban area of Los Angeles, is even more marked. Such a map brings home the realization that thousands of square miles of once-productive agricultural land is now obliterated by houses and malls, industry and freeways.

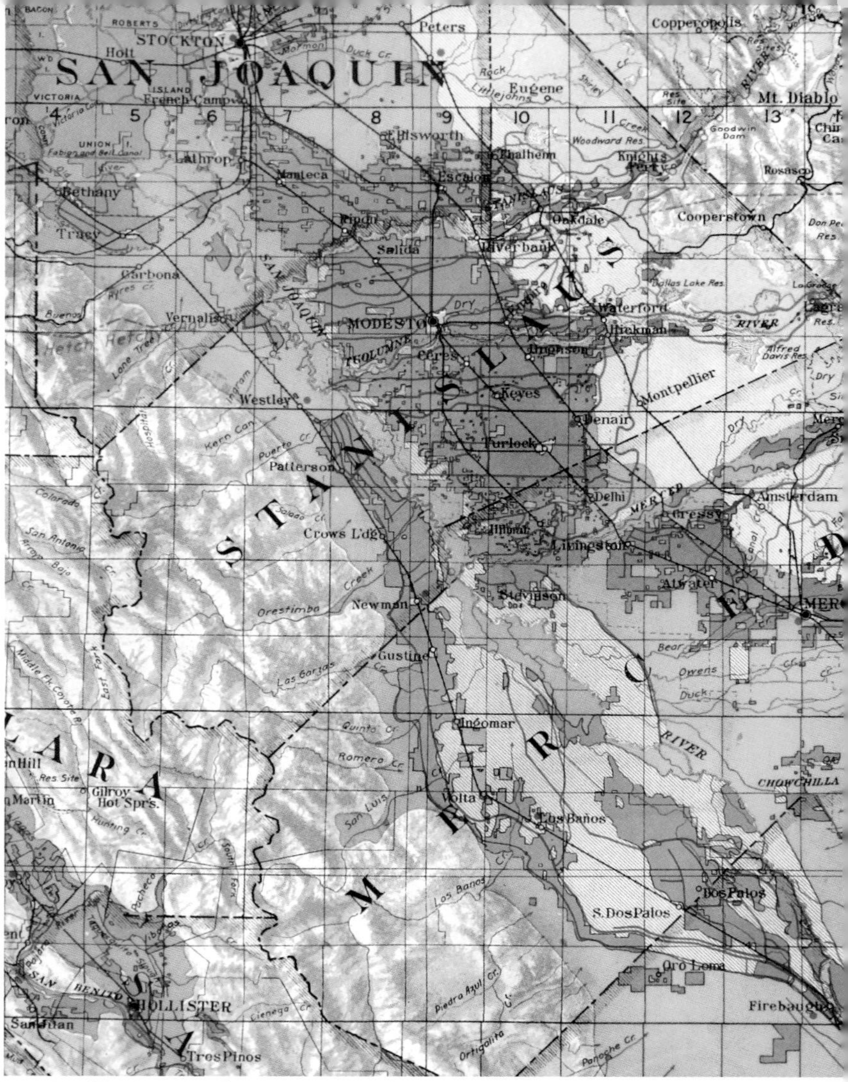

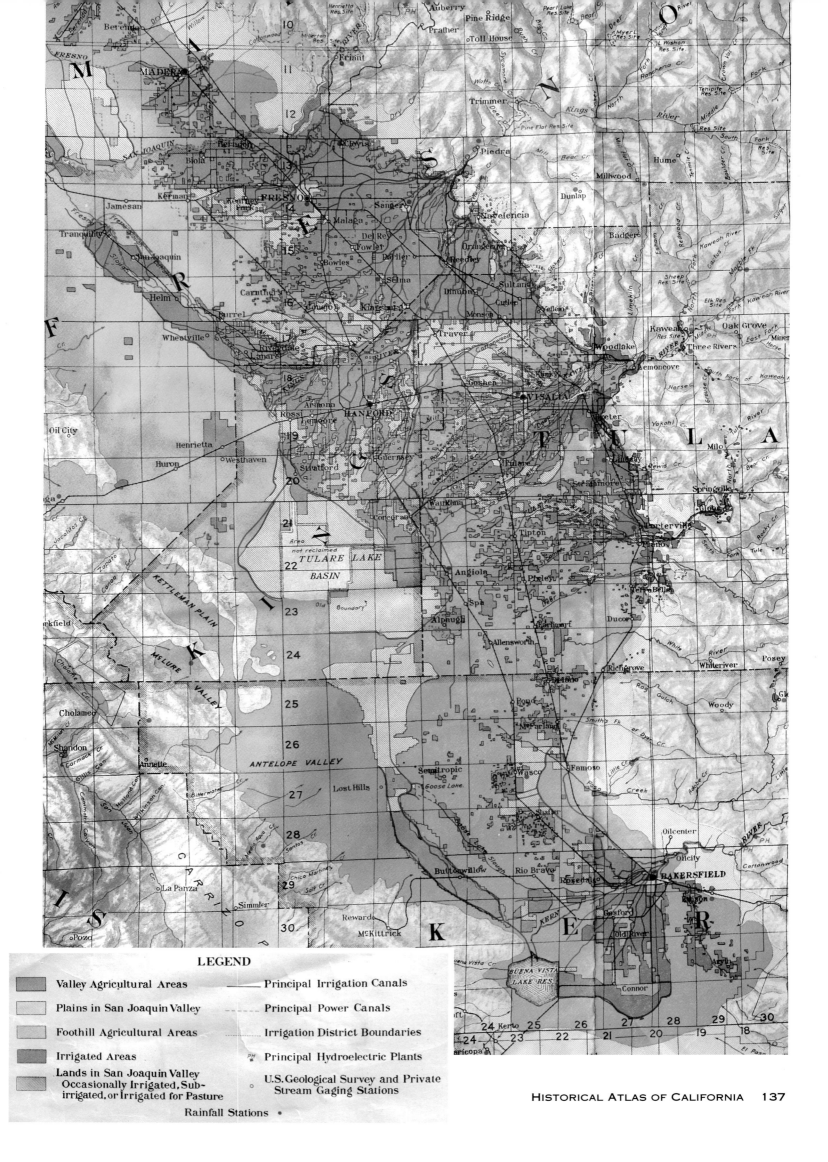

## LEGEND

Valley Agricultural Areas

Plains in San Joaquin Valley

Foothill Agricultural Areas

Irrigated Areas

Lands in San Joaquin Valley
Occasionally Irrigated, Sub-
irrigated, or Irrigated for Pasture

Rainfall Stations •

Principal Irrigation Canals

Principal Power Canals

Irrigation District Boundaries

Principal Hydroelectric Plants

U.S. Geological Survey and Private
Stream Gaging Stations

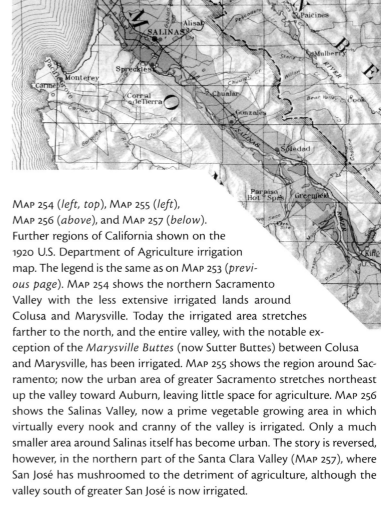

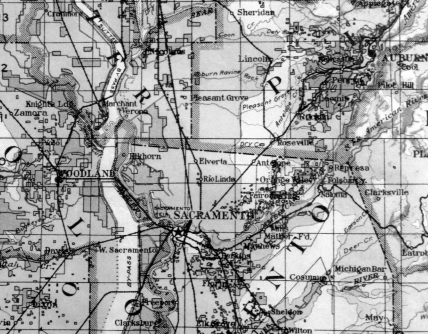

Map 254 (*left, top*), Map 255 (*left*),
Map 256 (*above*), and Map 257 (*below*).
Further regions of California shown on the
1920 U.S. Department of Agriculture irrigation
map. The legend is the same as on Map 253 (*previous page*). Map 254 shows the northern Sacramento
Valley with the less extensive irrigated lands around
Colusa and Marysville. Today the irrigated area stretches
farther to the north, and the entire valley, with the notable exception of the *Marysville Buttes* (now Sutter Buttes) between Colusa
and Marysville, has been irrigated. Map 255 shows the region around Sacramento; now the urban area of greater Sacramento stretches northeast
up the valley toward Auburn, leaving little space for agriculture. Map 256
shows the Salinas Valley, now a prime vegetable growing area in which
virtually every nook and cranny of the valley is irrigated. Only a much
smaller area around Salinas itself has become urban. The story is reversed,
however, in the northern part of the Santa Clara Valley (Map 257), where
San José has mushroomed to the detriment of agriculture, although the
valley south of greater San José is now irrigated.

The first large-scale irrigation system in California
was initiated in 1871 by the San Joaquin and Kings River
Canal Company, whose namesake canal was forty miles
long by 1873 and serviced an area a hundred miles north
of Mendota on the west side of the valley. A federal government report the following year recommended that
government aid be provided for surveys and planning
but that actual work should be carried out by regulated
private companies. The report also recommended that
land be given perpetual rights to its water.

Recognition of the need for a coordinated plan for
the use of water in the Central Valley, coupled with the
depletion of ground water, led in the 1920s to the development of the Central Valley Project, and nearly a million
dollars were spent on studies. Work was finally authorized
in 1933, but the Depression prevented financing, and the
project was taken over by the federal Bureau of Reclamation in 1935. For flood control and irrigation purposes the
project's principal components were the Shasta Dam, on
the Sacramento, completed in 1945; the Friant Dam, on the

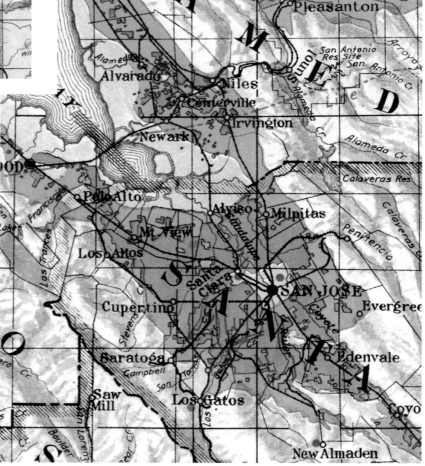

*Above.*

This U.S. Bureau of Reclamation photograph from the 1940s shows the practice of furrow irrigation in the Central Valley.

MAP 258 (*right*).

The root cause of the water problem in California was illustrated in this 1932 map, from a report of a joint legislative water committee. It shows the relative abundance of water in the north and the scarcity of it in the south, both in relation to area. Hence the need to transport water from north to south.

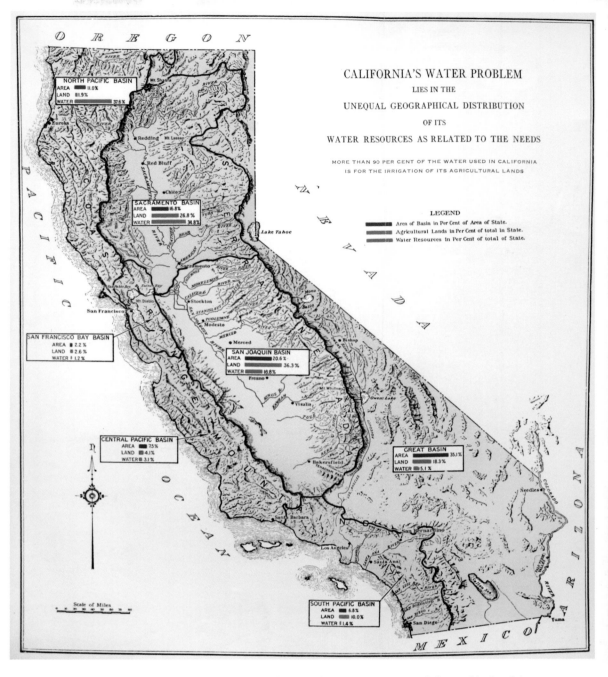

San Joaquin, completed in 1945, which diverts water into the Madera Canal, completed the same year, and the Friant-Kern Canal, completed in 1949; and the Delta Mendota Canal, completed in 1951, which runs down the west side of the San Joaquin Valley, replacing with delta water that lost from the San Joaquin River by diversion into the Madera and Friant-Kern canals under a complex legal swap arrangement.

The State Water Project was authorized in 1960. Water is transported from Northern California, principally from the Oroville Dam on the Feather River, a tributary of the Sacramento, south via the California Aqueduct to the Los Angeles Basin. This requires a number of pumping stations and includes a 2,000-foot lift over the Tehachapi Mountains. Urban and industrial uses take 70 percent of this water, with the remaining 30 percent going to agricultural use. With the help of this and all the other irrigation projects, California now has well over eight million acres of irrigated land.

Perhaps the most dramatic example of the changes wrought by irrigation is the Imperial Valley, adjacent to the Mexican border. This land was once emphatically desert (MAP 259 and MAP 260, *overleaf*), with rainfall of about two inches a year, and is now totally reliant on water transported from the Colorado River.

Imperial Valley is a former extension of the Gulf of California cut off by the natural delta building of the Colorado River, and hence much of its area is below sea level.

The first irrigation was the work of the California Development Company, which in 1900–1902 constructed a canal from the Colorado; this project was only a viable proposition because a gravity-flow route could be found through Mexico. A concession was secured from the Mexican government, and a Mexican subsidiary was set up to carry out the work in Mexico. Water was sold to purchasers of public and railroad lands in the valley. The area under irrigation increased rapidly, reaching 400,000 acres by the end of the second decade of the twentieth century.

Flood control was a problem, however. In the fall of 1904, the company cut a bypass channel around the point at which the river was diverted because silting had reduced the amount of water entering the canal. An early flood on the Gila River in December suddenly crashed through the gap, and, after several more floods, in April 1905 the entire flow of the Colorado River was flowing into Imperial Valley, creating a large inland lake, the Salton Sea. Numerous attempts were made to close the breach.

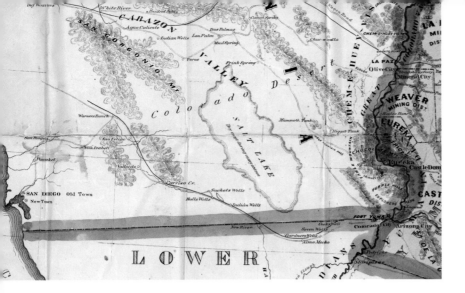

**MAP 259** (*above*).
An 1865 map of the southern boundary region of California shows a large *Salt Lake Dry except during rainy season* stretching across the Colorado Desert. The trail (double line) and proposed railroad route (single line) dip into Mexico to follow the line of oases, most shown as *Wells*.

**MAP 260** (*above right*).
This map by Army surveyor Robert Williamson was drawn in 1867 but not published until 1895. It depicts a smaller but more explicit *Dry Lake* and notes *Valley 70' below the Ocean*. Here only the existing trails are marked, with dashed lines, following the wells. The *Colorado Desert* straddles the international boundary.

**MAP 261** (*below*).
A relief map of the Imperial Valley produced by the U.S. Reclamation Service (under the direction of Joseph B. Lippincott, who was soon to feature in the saga of the bringing of water to Los Angeles; see page 194) and published in January 1905. The map was found in a package together with **MAP 262** and **MAP 263**.

In September 1906 the Southern Pacific Railroad, owner of considerable tracts of land in the valley, took over the task of trying to redivert the river's flow. The railroad used every available freight-car to transport rock to the scene, dumping it onto brush and willow mattresses, and eventually gaining on the river. On 10 February 1907 the Colorado again flowed to the Gulf of California, leaving the Salton Sea, now 35 miles long and 40 feet deep, as a permanent reminder of the river's force.

The Imperial Irrigation District was formed in 1911 and acquired rights from the California Development Company. Consideration was given as early as 1912 to the building of a canal that would be entirely on American soil, but it was not until 1928 that construction of the All-American Canal, together with the Boulder Dam (later

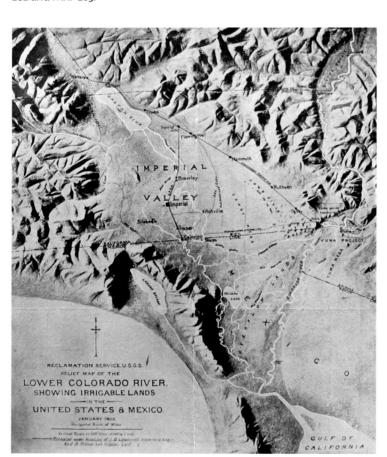

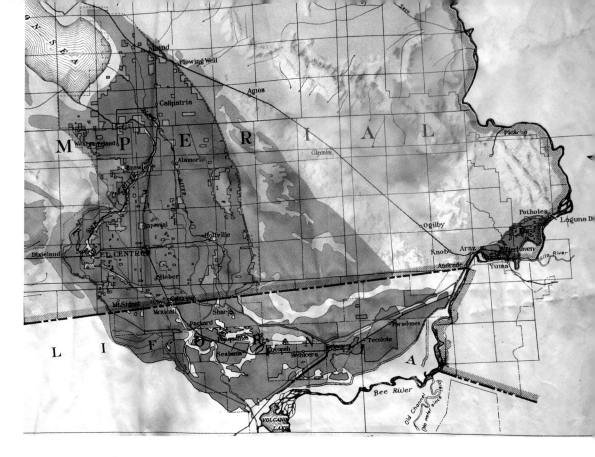

MAP 262 (*below left*) and MAP 263 (*below*). These two maps were in the investor's information package with MAP 261, issued about 1907 by a the Imperial Investment Company, part of the Imperial Land Company, a subsidiary of the California Land Company. Imperial Valley was named after the land company. The Imperial Canal (now the Alamo Canal) is shown, though not named, on both maps, running through Mexico before reentering the United States at Calexico. This is the canal built by the California Development Company in the first years of the twentieth century to begin the extensive irrigation of the Imperial Valley, and this canal was in the 1930s replaced by the All-American Canal. The California Development Company was soon in financial trouble. The Imperial Canal was beginning to silt up at an alarming rate, and a diversion canal was built to try to remedy this problem. In the winter of 1905, however, the volume of water coming down the Colorado was too great for the system to handle; the canal was breached, and the entire flow of the river diverted into the valley, forming the Salton Sea. It took two years to repair the damage, but the Salton Sea, although reduced in size, remained. Note on MAP 263 the *Southern Land Grant Boundary Line Southern Pacific*; the railroad was active in the promotion of irrigation in the valley, realizing that its land was nearly valueless without water.

the Hoover Dam), and the Imperial Dam (which would divert water into the canal), was authorized by the Boulder Canyon Project Act. The All-American Canal was constructed by the Bureau of Reclamation in the 1930s, and the first water flowed along it to the Imperial Valley in 1940. In 1942 the canal became the sole water source for the valley.

Other than water, agriculture in California benefited from the development or introduction of new varieties of fruits and vegetables suited to the climate and soils; the development of transportation to markets in the East, and in particular the invention of refrigerated rail cars; and the savvy marketing of the state's produce as the bounty of a tropical paradise.

Probably the best-known introduced fruit was the Washington Navel orange. Seedlings were sent to Washington, D.C., from Brazil by federal government horticulturalists and planted in Riverside by Elizabeth and Luther Tibbets in 1870, revolutionizing the fruit growing of that area in an instant. The Washington Navel would become the original sun-kissed orange—Sunkist.

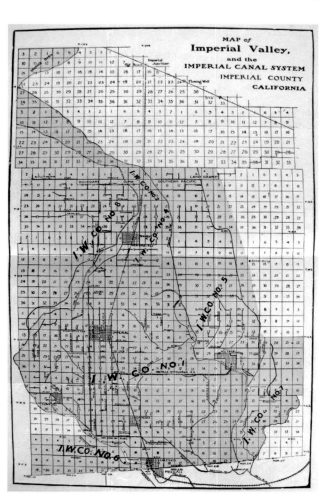

MAP 264 (*above*).
The U.S. Department of Agriculture's irrigation map of California, drawn in 1920 and published in 1922, shows the extent of irrigated lands in the Imperial Valley and across the border in Mexico at that time. The line of the Imperial Canal (Alamo Canal) is clearly shown, diverting from the Colorado just below Yuma, running through Mexico and back into California at Calexico.

MAP 265 (*right*).
Constructed by the federal government during the 1930s, although authorized in 1928, and included as a Public Works Administration (PWA) program, the All-American Canal was completed in 1940 and two years later became the sole water source for the Imperial Valley. This is part of a PWA pictorial map published in 1935 to show the public what the government was doing to help end the Depression.

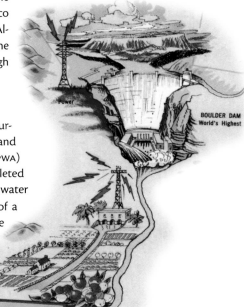

Map 266 (above).
Map showing the lands of the Placer County Citrus Colony in 1887 around the then small settlements of Rocklin and Loomis, now part of the urban area of greater Sacramento. Note the *Line of Central Pacific Railroad*; the two semicircles adjacent to the line in Rocklin probably depict the roundhouse that the railroad located there to service additional locomotives for the Sierra crossing. The other settlements shown, Penryn and Newcastle, still exist but are small. Placer County became known for its soft fruit.

Map 267 (right).
A rather simpler map, this time of American Colony in Tulare County, served the same purpose as the Placer County map. It is dated 1892.

MAP OF
AMERICAN COLONY
TULARE COUNTY
Located on S.W.¼ Sec 28 T.19 S.R.24 E.
Scale 10 Chains to the Inch.

| J.C.&M. Gifford 10 Acres | S. C. Gifford 10 Acres | D. W. Madden 10 Acres | D. W. Madden 10 Acres |
|---|---|---|---|
| M.C.Hunt 10 Acres | V. S. Johnson 10 Acres | J. J. Madden 10 Acres | D. W. Madden 10 Acres |
| A. T. Clippenger 10 Acres | C.F.Hall 10 Acres | John Sweeney 10 Acres | D. W. Madden 10 Acres |
| L.E. Fleshman 10 Acres | D. B. Anderson 10 Acres | W. L. Gifford 10 Acres | D. W. Madden 10 Acres |

**VALENCIAS**

**GOLDEN SCEPTRE** BRAND

GOLDEN SCEPTRE QUALITY

**RIALTO ORANGE CO.**
RIALTO, SAN BERNARDINO CO. CALIFORNIA.

FONTANA CITRUS LANDS

Rialto Orange Grove—sold two years ago for $1500 an acre—now worth over $2000.

Rialto oranges being of superior size, and free from blemish, command top prices at local packing houses and in Eastern markets.

SANTA FE ROUTE

MAP 268 (*above*) and MAP 269 (*right*). Orange groves were being touted as a good investment in 1910 when the land of the Fontana Development Company, next to that of the Rialto Orange Company (crate label, *left*) was offered for sale. The green-colored lots on MAP 269 have already been sold and planted with oranges. "The average increase in valuation of Rialto Orange Land (adjoining Fontana Citrus Lands)," read the sales material on the margins of this map, "during the last five years, was approximately One Hundred Percent—and anyone who purchased during that period could now sell at a substantial advance."

MAP 270 (*below*).
This rather spectacular 1915 pictorial map advertises the agricultural and residential glories of Fresno County as *Mid-California's Garden of the Sun*. It shows clearly, though in exaggerated form, the basin nature of the Central Valley, surrounded on all sides by mountain ranges.

Pictorial Map of
FRESNO COUNTY
and
MID-CALIFORNIA'S
GARDEN of the SUN

# CALIFORNIA & ARIZONA SHIPPING POINTS

## FOR CITRUS FRUITS MARKETED BY THE 14,500 GROWER-MEMBERS OF THE

# CALIFORNIA FRUIT GROWERS EXCHANGE

## INDEX

| | | | | | |
|---|---|---|---|---|---|
| Algoso .......O-16 | Corona ......Q-15 | Glendale, Ariz. .M-11 | Lemon ......P-11 | Orosi ......K-15 | Santa Barbara ..O-10 |
| Alhambra .....P-14 | Coronado .....T-16 | Glendora .....P-15 | Lemon Cove..L-16 | Oroville ......L-12 | Santa Monica ..Q-13 |
| Alta Loma ....P-15 | Covina .......P-15 | Goleta ......O-10 | Lemon Grove..T-17 | Ortonville .....P-11 | Santa Paula ..P-12 |
| Anaheim .....Q-14 | Crafton ......P-17 | Goodale ......L-16 | Lemoore ......L-14 | Oxnard ......P-12 | Saticoy ......P-12 |
| Arlington .....Q-16 | Cucamonga ...P-15 | Gridley ......L-12 | Liberty ......N-10 | Pacoima ......P-13 | Selma ......K-14 |
| Avalon ......R-14 | Delano ......M-15 | Hamilton City..K-11 | Limeo ......P-12 | Pasadena .....P-14 | Shafter ......N-15 |
| Azusa ......P-15 | Del Mar ......T-16 | Hanford ......L-14 | Lindsay ......L-16 | Perris ......Q-15 | Simi ......P-12 |
| Bakersfield ...O-16 | Dinuba ......K-15 | Hemet ......M-17 | Lisko ......L-16 | Phoenix ......N-11 | Strathmore ..L-16 |
| Balboa ......R-14 | Downey ......Q-14 | Highgrove ....Q-16 | Long Beach ..Q-14 | Piru ......O-12 | Success ......L-16 |
| Banning .....Q-17 | Duarte ......P-14 | Highland .....P-16 | Los Angeles ..Q-14 | Placentia ....Q-15 | Sunkist ......F-16 |
| Beaumont ....Q-17 | East Highlands .P-16 | Hillgrove .....Q-14 | Magnolia ....Q-16 | Pomona ......P-15 | Sunland ......M-16 |
| Beverly Hills ..P-13 | East Pasadena ..P-14 | Hollywood ....P-13 | McFarland ....N-15 | Ponca ......M-16 | Sunny Hills ..Q-14 |
| Brea ......Q-15 | (Lamanda Park) | Huntington | Mentone ......P-17 | Porterville ....L-16 | Tapo ......P-12 |
| Briggs ......P-12 | East Whittier ..Q-14 | Beach ......R-14 | Merryman .....N-16 | Port Hueneme..P-11 | Tempe ......N-12 |
| Bryn Mawr ...Q-16 | Edison ......O-16 | Inglewood ....Q-13 | Mesa ......N-12 | Prenda ......Q-16 | Terminus ....K-16 |
| Burbank .....P-14 | El Cajon .....T-17 | Irvine ......Q-15 | Mira Loma ...Q-15 | Puente ......Q-15 | Terra Bella ..M-16 |
| Cairns ......L-15 | Elderwood ....K-16 | Ivanhoe ......L-15 | Miramar ......P-10 | Redlands .....Q-17 | Tolleon ......N-11 |
| California | El Monte ......P-14 | Kathryn ......Q-15 | Mission ......P-13 | Redondo Beach .R-13 | Tulare ......L-15 |
| Hot Springs..M-17 | Elsinore ......R-16 | Keith ......Q-12 | Montalvo ......P-11 | Reedley ......K-15 | Tustin ......Q-15 |
| Camarillo ....P-12 | Escondido .....S-17 | Kerrville .....R-17 | Montebello ...Q-14 | Rialto ......P-16 | Ultra ......M-16 |
| Canoga Park ..P-13 | Etiwanda .....P-16 | Kevet ......Q-15 | Montecito .....O-10 | Richgrove .....L-16 | Upland ......P-15 |
| Carpinteria ...O-10 | Exeter ......L-16 | Kimball ......P-11 | Moor Park ....P-12 | Rivera ......Q-14 | Venice ......Q-13 |
| Casa Blanca ..Q-16 | Fallbrook ....R-16 | Kingsburg ....K-14 | Naranjo ......K-16 | Riverside .....Q-16 | Ventura ......O-11 |
| Chandler .....N-12 | Famoso ......N-15 | Laguna Beach ..R-15 | Narod ......Q-16 | San Bernardino .P-16 | Villa Park ..Q-15 |
| Charter Oak ..P-15 | Fillmore ......O-12 | La Habra .....Q-15 | National City ..T-17 | San Clemente ..R-15 | Visalia ......L-15 |
| Chatsworth ...P-13 | Fontana ......P-16 | La Jolla ......T-16 | North Hollywood.P-13 | San Diego ....T-16 | Vista ......S-16 |
| Chico ......K-12 | Fowler ......K-14 | Laguna Beach ..R-15 | North Pomona ..P-15 | San Dimas ....P-15 | Walnut ......Q-15 |
| Chula Vista ..T-17 | Frances ......Q-15 | Lamanda Park ..P-14 | Oceanside .....S-16 | San Fernando ..P-13 | Wasco ......N-15 |
| Citro ......P-15 | Fremont ......K-14 | (East Pasadena) | Ojal ......O-11 | San Gabriel ..P-14 | Whittier ......Q-14 |
| Claremont ....P-15 | Fullerton .....Q-15 | La Mesa ......T-17 | Olive ......Q-15 | San Jacinto ..Q-17 | Willows ......L-10 |
| Colton ......Q-16 | Garden Grove ..Q-15 | La Patera .....O-10 | Ontario ......P-16 | San Juan | Wilmington ..Q-13 |
| Compton .....Q-14 | Giant Forest ..K-16 | Las Lomas ....P-14 | Orange ......Q-15 | Capistrano ..R-15 | Wirta ......P-12 |
| Corcoran .....L-14 | Glendale, | Lateen ......P-14 | Orange Cove ..K-15 | San Pedro ....Q-13 | Woodlake ....K-15 |
| Corning ......K-10 | California ....P-14 | La Verne .....P-15 | | | |
| | | Leffingwell ....Q-14 | Orland ......K-10 | Santa Ana ..Q-15 | Yorba Linda ..Q-15 |

# Sunkist ORANGES · LEMONS GRAPEFRUIT

And likely the best-known developer of locally suited varieties of vegetables was Luther Burbank, a pioneer of agricultural science who moved to Santa Rosa in 1874. He developed more than eight hundred varieties and strains of plants, including the Russet Burbank ("Idaho") potato; the freestone peach; 113 varieties of plums and prunes; 50 varieties of lily: the Flaming Gold nectarine; the Santa Rosa plum; and the Shasta daisy. His work inspired the passage of the federal Plant Patent Act of 1930, four years after his death.

In Southern California, the orange rapidly became king. In 1877 pioneer grower William Wolfskill shipped the first railroad carload of oranges east, to St. Louis. Twelve years later California was shipping 1.2 million boxes of oranges eastward by rail, and by 1909 14.5 million boxes were being shipped. In 1870 the state had 30,000 orange trees; by 1920 there were 10 million, which produced 22 million boxes of fruit.

It was at times too much of a good thing. In the early 1890s there developed a glut of oranges on the market. Agents began to only handle oranges on consignment, thus placing all financial risk in the hands of the growers. In August 1893 about a hundred growers got together and created the Southern California Fruit Exchange to market their oranges; they immediately managed to obtain higher prices than individual growers. In 1905 the organization changed its name to the California Fruit Growers Exchange to reflect the fact that central California growers had joined. The next year the exchange created a timber supply company to manufacture crates, as wood was in short supply after the 1906 San Francisco earthquake. Today the organization owns 360,000 acres of California's forests as a result.

A major breakthrough occurred in 1908, when the name "Sunkist" began to be used in advertising. It was the first time a perishable food product had been advertised, and it was phenomenally successful as a means of selling the dream of a tropical paradise to less-blessed easterners. Here was a way everyone could share in California's sunshine and the fruits of Eden. Sunkist became part of six million orange and a million lemon crate labels and created a culture of consumption for commercially produced citrus fruit.

The organization became adept at advertising of all types. Added to the embodiment of sunshine and good health, freshness and the nutritional value of oranges were emphasized; recipes were regularly provided, and figures from Greek mythology were employed in ads. The California Fruit Growers Exchange changed its corporate name to Sunkist Growers in 1952, thus consolidating itself with the brand they had made so famous. Sunkist eventually marketed three quarters of all oranges grown in California. The gold so eagerly sought by the Forty-niners had been found again in the soil.

The other agricultural industry for which California is well known is that of wine making. Father Junípero Serra is credited with planting the first vines in California, at the San Diego mission. His "Mission Grape" variety dominated until about 1880, when grape varieties introduced by Agoston Haraszthy, a Hungarian merchant, took over. Haraszthy introduced about three hundred varieties and is thought of as the founder of the California wine industry.

MAP 271 (left).
By the 1930s the California Fruit Growers Exchange had 14,500 member-growers in California and Arizona. (Due to consolidation it now has about 6,000 members.) This rare pictorial map is a poster supplied to member-growers listing shipping points. Plain maps with information are made more palatable for wall display by the inclusion of the pictorial map. The Sunkist brand became so well known that in 1952 the exchange changed its corporate name to Sunkist Growers. "Your good opinion of Sunkist is our most valuable asset," said one ad. The map is rare because of the rough use these maps likely received as a working information sheet. This map has been electronically restored.

Right, bottom center.
An 1888 advertisement for Fresno as the Fruit Center of California, *Home of the Raisin Grape. HERE IS THE PLACE TO MAKE MONEY where Nature is prodigal with her favors*, touts the ad.

MAP 274 (right).
Another Sunkist advertising poster-map, likely published in 1943 to commemorate the fiftieth anniversary of the California Fruit Growers Exchange. Varieties of oranges and lemons are shown at bottom right, while scenes of citrus production cover what would otherwise have been Nevada.

MAP 272 (above).
A 1940s Sunkist crate label for lemons featuring a map of California.

MAP 273 (above).
This orange crate label and brand name emphasizes the Pacific Ocean with a map view of a grove complete with pier, perhaps at Santa Monica.

**FRESNO**
The Home of the Raisin Grape.

THE FRUIT CENTER OF CALIFORNIA.

The Apricot, Nectarine, Pomegranate, Fig, Prune, Peach, Pear, Plum, Quince, Apple, Orange, Olive, Almond and the Grape flourish equally well in this County.  HERE IS THE PLACE TO MAKE MONEY where Nature is prodigal with her favors.  Plenty of Land.  Plenty of Water.  Soil Fertile.  Climate Healthful.  Come to FRESNO, and be satisfied.

**Map 275** (*above*).

The State Agricultural Society of California was created in 1854 and has held a State Fair every year since, except for the war years and immediately after, 1942–48. The fair moved around the state at first, but in 1909 a permanent site was found in Sacramento, an 80-acre site on Stockton Boulevard, expanded to 155 acres in 1937. This is the site shown on this poster. This site continued to be used until 1967 when the fair moved to the 350-acre Cal Expo site, which continues to be used today. This innovative poster shows a map of California with its counties crammed with their local agricultural produce. The 1941 fair, which this poster advertises, was the last until 1949.

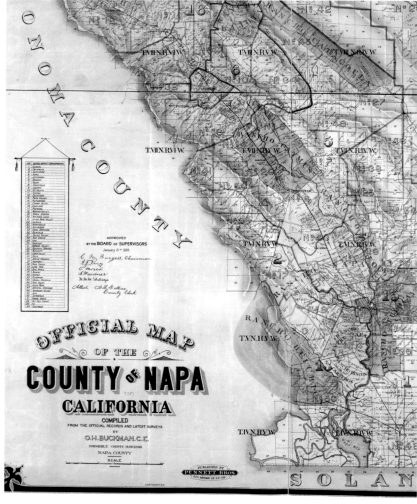

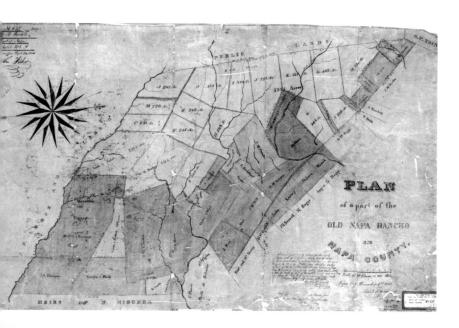

Map 278 (*right*) and Map 279 (*below, center*).
This pictorial poster map of the wine country of California was commissioned from artist Ruth Taylor by the Wine Advisory Board in 1942, though it had earlier appeared in a book of similar pictorial maps of the United States published by the artist. Concerned, perhaps, that the pictorial map alone would not convey the detail required for the public to actually find the wine growing areas, the Wine Advisory Board also issued Map 279 in the advertising package. Here the wine growing regions of the state are shown in light green, and roads and cities are also shown. Despite the depiction of so many wine growing areas, those beyond the premium areas of the Napa and Sonoma valleys were better known for commercial grape production and grapes grown for raisins. As early as 1888, Fresno was already advertising itself as the home of the raisin grape (see page 145).

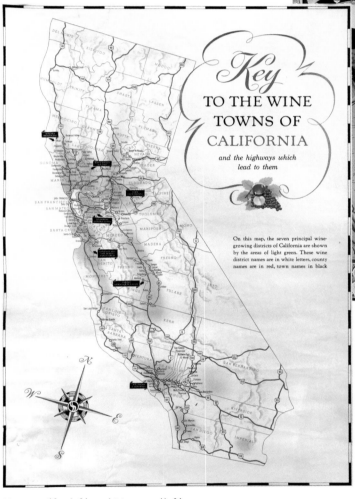

Map 276 (*far left*) and Map 277 (*left*).
Most of the Napa Valley, being prime agricultural land, was claimed as ranchos during the Mexican period. Map 276 is an 1852 plan of part of the Rancho Napa, just west of the City of Napa, on Map 277 at the branch of Napa Creek and the Napa River. The city was incorporated in 1872. Note that Map 276 is oriented with north approximately to the right and that the site of the City of Napa is just off the bottom edge of the map. The pattern of land holdings shown on this map is seen also on Map 277. Today the area is covered with many specialty wineries including Phoenix Vineyards on the old rancho lands, which produces a wine named Rancho Napa. Map 277 is a county map, dated 1895, showing land holdings.

Californian vine rootstocks resistant to the root louse phylloxera saved the European wine industry in the late nineteenth century when Europe was attacked by this pest, itself introduced from North America about 1860. Prohibition (1919–33) all but destroyed the California wine industry. After that, wine quality was generally quite low, and it was not until the 1960s that world-class California wine began to be made. In 1976, at a now-famous wine competition held in Paris, California wines won out over the finest from France, and their reputation was forever assured.

Premium wineries became concentrated in the valleys north of San Francisco, principally in those of Napa and Sonoma. Much of the land here was originally Mexican ranchos, but by 1970 many were growing other crops. There was a great revival of the premium wine industry following the triumph in Paris, and today each of the two valleys count over two hundred active wineries of all sizes, just a few of which could date their heritage back to before the beginning of the nineteenth century. And California wine, like the even more widely available California oranges, is synonymous with the good life in Eden.

# THE RISE OF URBAN CALIFORNIA

The considerable natural endowments of California plus four key factors—immigration, railroads, water, and streetcars—allowed people to aggregate, industrialize or trade, and find profit or find employment in urban areas that would develop into the vast urban conglomerations we see today.

California has always been a place to which migrants aspire. The railroads allowed them to follow the rainbow west in far larger numbers than would otherwise have been possible, and the railroads are what allowed Californians to take advantage of the enormous market for their products in the East. And without water the cities would soon have outgrown themselves, but the enterprise and the technology were there to transport water considerable distances to allow continued growth of urban areas. The water projects themselves are described on page 194. Streetcars, long before the automobile, allowed what we would today call suburban living and shaped the cities in the form of their rail lines.

## 1. LOS ANGELES

The ink was hardly dry on the Treaty of Guadalupe Hidalgo officially making California American when the *ayuntamiento* (town council) of Los Angeles asked Lieutenant Edward Otho Cresap Ord to survey the pueblo and its land grant of four leagues square and prepare a detailed plan (MAP 282, *right*). The residents, of whom there were about 1,600 at this time, needed to have their land holdings confirmed, and the council wanted to be able to sell land to fund its expenses. This was not possible without a map, and so Ord had been authorized to offer his services to prepare one. A number of the officers of the Topographical Engineers were allowed to do this, it being hard in those gold rush times to provide enough money from Army sources to pay for everyday expenses. William Warner's map of Sacramento was prepared in much the same way (MAP 194, *page 99*). So strapped for money was Los Angeles that the pueblo had to borrow to pay Ord for his survey, a loan to be repaid when lots were sold. Ord's map was the first survey of Los Angeles; previous

*Above.*
Los Angeles City Hall, completed in 1928, and until 1964 by ordinance the tallest building in the city at 32 floors.

MAP 280 (*below*).
This *diseño* (see page 68) of the Mexican Rancho de San José de San Gabriel, drawn in the 1840s, shows the rancho covering most of the western part of the Los Angeles basin.

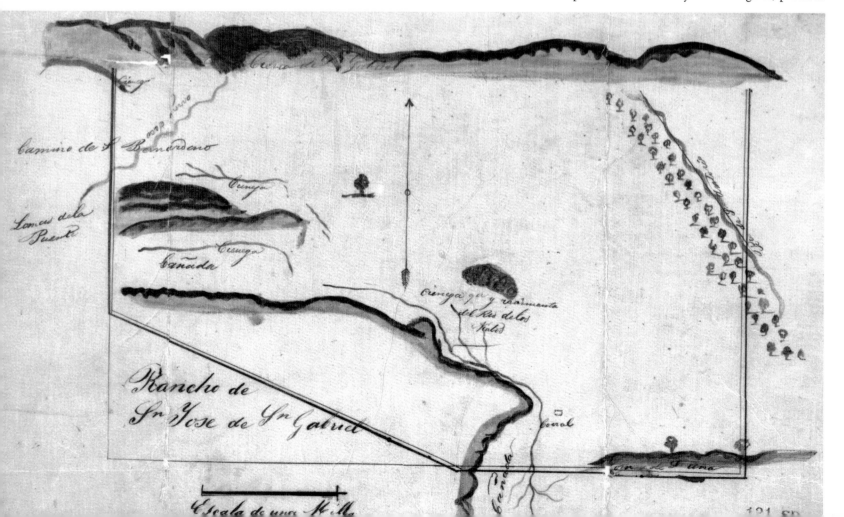

MAP 281 (*right*).
The Los Angeles basin as shown on the Pacific Railroad Survey survey done by Lieutenant John G. Parke in 1854 and 1855.

MAP 282 (*below*).
The first survey of the City of Los Angeles, by Lieutenant Edward O.C. Ord, carried out in 1849. This is one of three copies; the original has been lost. The original pueblo, with existing buildings shown, is at center right. Agricultural lots are shown with dots; some irrigation ditches are also shown. Ord also drew a sketch map of the larger region in 1849, and this is shown as MAP 408, *page 212*.

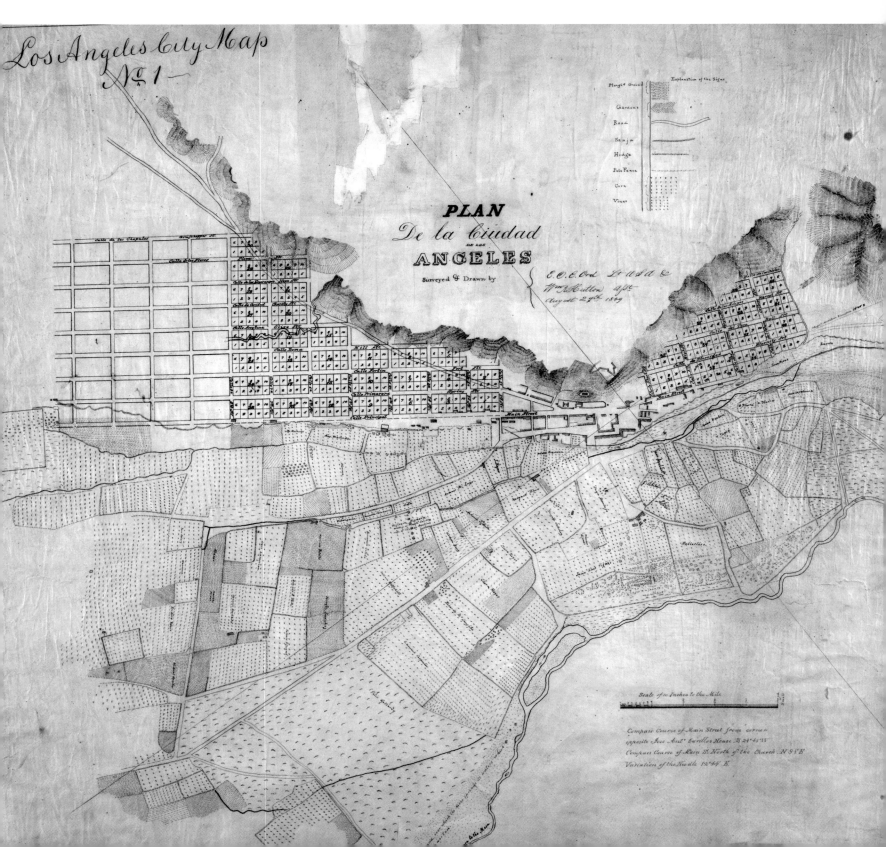

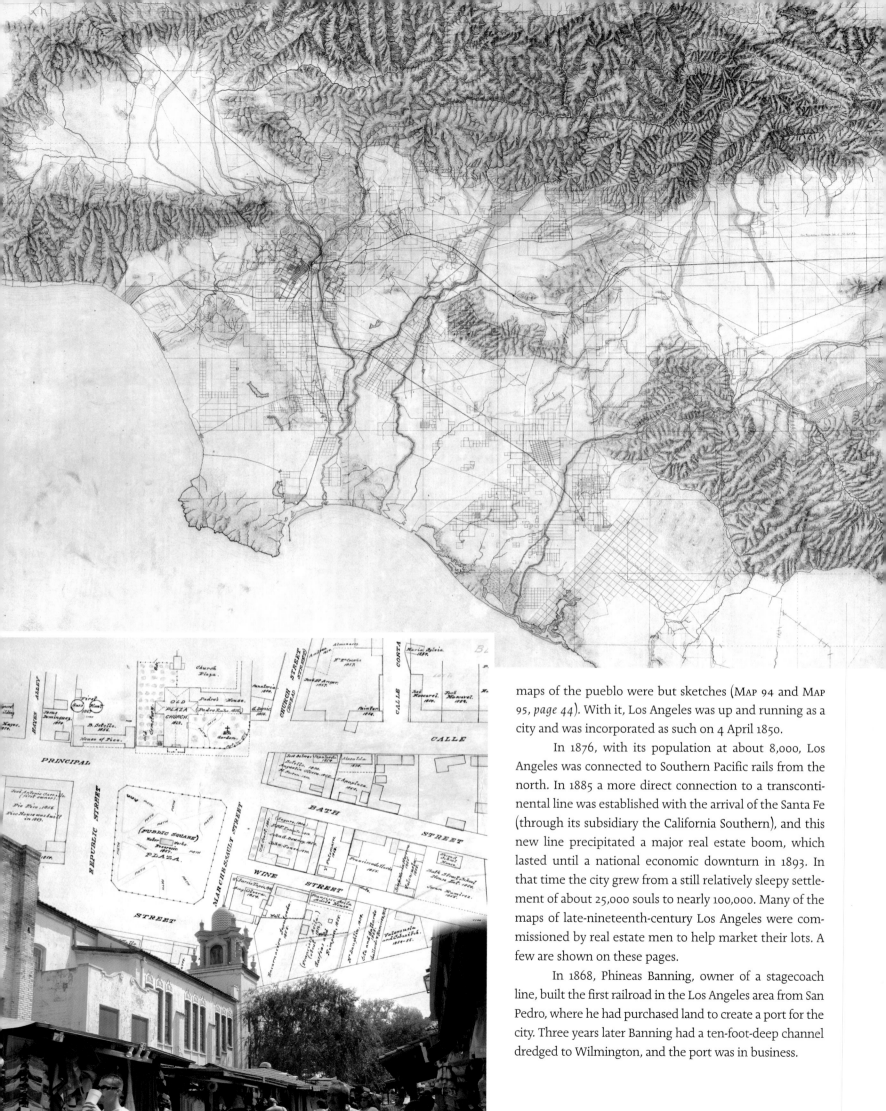

maps of the pueblo were but sketches (Map 94 and Map 95, *page 44*). With it, Los Angeles was up and running as a city and was incorporated as such on 4 April 1850.

In 1876, with its population at about 8,000, Los Angeles was connected to Southern Pacific rails from the north. In 1885 a more direct connection to a transcontinental line was established with the arrival of the Santa Fe (through its subsidiary the California Southern), and this new line precipitated a major real estate boom, which lasted until a national economic downturn in 1893. In that time the city grew from a still relatively sleepy settlement of about 25,000 souls to nearly 100,000. Many of the maps of late-nineteenth-century Los Angeles were commissioned by real estate men to help market their lots. A few are shown on these pages.

In 1868, Phineas Banning, owner of a stagecoach line, built the first railroad in the Los Angeles area from San Pedro, where he had purchased land to create a port for the city. Three years later Banning had a ten-foot-deep channel dredged to Wilmington, and the port was in business.

**Map 283** (*left*).
The Los Angeles basin was a developing agricultural area with scattered urban areas when this detailed map was drawn in 1880 by William Hammond Hall, the first state engineer. The Southern Pacific tracks enter Los Angeles from the north, and Phineas Banning's railroad, now part of the S.P., connect the harbor at San Pedro with the city.

**Map 284** (*left, bottom*).
The center of Los Angeles as it was in 1873. *Wine Street,* leading to the central plaza, was renamed Olvera Street in 1877 after local judge Agustin Olvera. The area was restored in 1930 and remains today the historic core of Los Angeles, with twenty-seven designated historic buildings. The photograph is of Olvera Street, looking west toward the plaza.

**Map 285** (*right*).
*Sunset,* on land near today's UCLA, was a subdivision of Rancho San José de Buenos Ayres and was offered for sale in 1887. The rancho had been sold by John Wolfskill to the Santa Monica Land and Water Company for $438,000 in 1886, and that company laid out the town of Sunset. The project failed, however, and in 1891 the land reverted to Wolfskill. Hence no street names survive today, except, of course, the famous Sunset Boulevard.

The railroad was sold to Collis P. Huntington's Southern Pacific when that company threatened otherwise to bypass Los Angeles altogether, but the railroad did not gain control of Banning's port. Instead, in 1893 the Southern Pacific built a line to Santa Monica, where a long wharf was constructed. A tug-of-war for federal funding for port expansion then followed, and Huntington pulled every string he could—and he

**Map 286** (*right*).
Land was offered for sale in the 1870s from Abel Stearns's ranchos. Stearns, from Massachusetts, had in the 1830s become a prosperous trader in hides, tallow, and liquors. A naturalized Mexican, he married into a wealthy Mexican family and soon began to accumulate considerable land holdings, which made him the wealthiest citizen of Southern California. His holdings, shown here, included much of today's Huntington Beach, Santa Ana, Garden Grove, and Anaheim.

# ·LOS· ANGELES, CAL.

·LOOKING SOUTH-WEST TO PACIFIC OCEAN·
·1887·

# LOS ANGELES, CAL.

Population of City and Environs 65,000.

Published by SOUTHERN CALIFORNIA LAND CO., 344 N. Main Street. 1891

**Map 287** (*above left*).
This bird's-eye map of Los Angeles in 1887 is interesting because it shows the city just before the real estate boom that began that year. The view is from approximately over Elysian Park looking south to Palos Verdes and Catalina Island beyond.

**Map 288** (*left, bottom*).
A classic bird's-eye-view map of Los Angeles published in 1891. Subscriptions would have been sold to the businesses illustrated around the perimeter of the map, and there is every probability that money also changed hands from the owners of the houses shown larger than life on the map, for the bird's-eye map was a prestigious way to show off where you lived and the size of house you could afford, as well as a medium for advertising your business.

**Map 289** (*above*).
This is Los Angeles in 1894, at the end of the first major real estate boom. The unusual double view gives a superb feel for the city at that time. The top map shows the original site between the Los Angeles River and the mountains, while the bottom view looks south toward the Pacific and gives a good idea of the land available for expansion in that direction.

had many of them—to secure the funding for his port at Santa Monica. Despite his best efforts, a federal commission awarded the funds to San Pedro, and work on a long breakwater there began in 1899. The port in 1907 became the Port of Los Angeles, after being connected in 1906 to the city by a long, thin strip of land, the so-called shoestring addition (Map 296, *page 157*). Los Angeles has grown immensely by simple annexation of territory, a process encouraged by the city's ability to offer water.

The city's growth was all but guaranteed by the discovery of oil, first found within the city limits just north of downtown, near today's Dodger Stadium, in 1892 (see page 212), and soon oil rigs intermingled with housing tracts.

Another real estate boom began about 1905 and lasted eight years. This period coincided with the building of William Mulholland's Los Angeles Aqueduct, which gave the city the water to continue its growth and at the same time the leverage to induce other municipalities to annex themselves to Los Angeles. The most spectacular was the addition of the San Fernando Valley in 1915 (Map 296, *page 157*).

The streetcar system was highly influential in shaping Los Angeles as the nineteenth century turned over to the twentieth (see page 180). The Los Angeles network of the Pacific Electric, owned by Collis Huntington's nephew Henry Huntington, was begun in 1901 and became at its peak the largest electrically operated railway in the world. By about 1915, however, a new factor was competing with the streetcar and would free development from lines of steel—the automobile. Los Angeles was destined to become a city dependent on the automobile like no other (see page 211).

Map 290 (*above, top*).
San Pedro Harbor in 1905, showing the dredged channel. The cities of San Pedro and Wilmington adjacent to the harbor became part of Los Angeles in 1909. This was a real estate sales maps and bears notations in ink about lots available and sold.

*Above.*
Celebrations marking the awarding of federal funding to San Pedro as Los Angeles's harbor in 1899 were advertised with this poster, complete with a bird's-eye view of the breakwaters to be constructed.

Map 291 (*right*).
A rather beautifully illustrated real estate map produced in 1887 showing lands in the San Fernando Valley offered for sale. The land would be subdivided again and offered for sale during the real estate boom of the first part of the following century (see Map 294, *overleaf*).

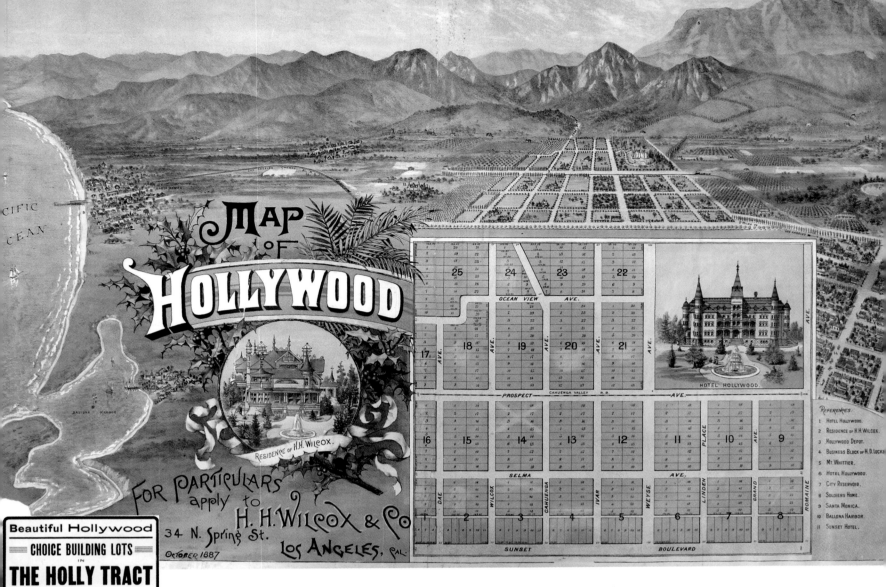

Map 292 (*above*).

One of the most innovative of the real estate sales maps of the late-1880s boom was this map for what has become one of the most internationally famous parts of Los Angeles—Hollywood. Produced in 1887, the map combines the necessary plan of lots with a bird's-eye map of the surroundings, although this image takes considerable license with the reality of what can actually be seen from Hollywood. In 1886 Harvey Henderson Wilcox, an immigrant from Kansas who had made a fortune in real estate, purchased 160 acres west of Los Angeles and laid out a town, registering the plan in February 1887. His wife, Daeida Wilcox, came up with the name "Hollywood," after hearing it used on a trip back East and liking the sound of the word. This map was printed in October 1887 as a marketing aid. Hollywood succeeded where many other developments did not and by 1900 had 500 inhabitants; in 1903 it was incorporated as a municipality. The coming of a quick streetcar connection to Los Angeles in 1904 sped growth, but the supply of water was becoming a problem, and so in 1910 Hollywood voted to be annexed to its larger neighbor with the water supply from the Owens Valley (see page 194). The name of the main street, *Prospect Ave.*, shown on the map, was changed to Hollywood Boulevard. The advertisement, *left*, dates from 1887, the same year as the map.

Map 293 (*left*).

This bird's-eye map of San Gabriel, just east of Los Angeles, shows the principally agricultural appearance of the region in 1893.

155

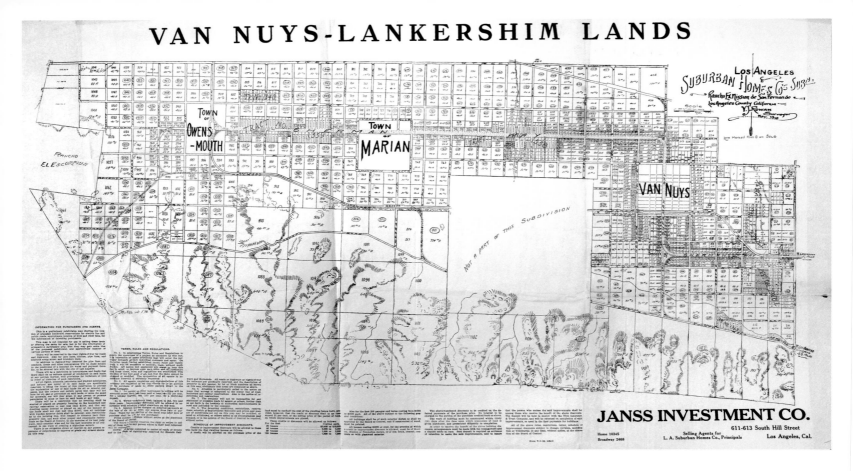

# VAN NUYS-LANKERSHIM LANDS

**JANSS INVESTMENT CO.**

**Map 294** (*above*).

A 1912 real estate map offering lots for sale in the San Fernando Valley. Isaac Lankershim and Isaac Newton Van Nuys farmed here in the 1870s. Lots were being sold in 1912 starting at $350. The *Town of Owensmouth* is now Canoga Park, the name having been changed in 1930. The area was annexed to Los Angeles in 1917, lured by the prospect of acquiring water.

**Map 295** (*below*).

This 1909 bird's-eye is of the more limited area of the city center, near the end of the second major land boom. Complete with highrise buildings, Los Angeles is clearly beginning to look like a modern city.

**Map 296** (*right*).

The city engineer of the City of Los Angeles had this map made in 1916 showing all the annexations to the city to that date. The city's original four leagues square is shown as the yellow square at center right. Los Angeles got its access to the ocean in 1906 with the creation and annexation of the *Shoestring Addition* shown due south of the city center to San Pedro. The 1915 annexation of the San Fernando Valley, which historian Kevin Starr referred to as the city's local Louisiana Purchase, added 108,732 acres in 1915 and far more than doubled the city's size at the stroke of a pen. (The city encompassed 77,317 acres beforehand). Annexations did not stop with the eighteen shown on this 1916 map. By the end of the century there had been—amazingly—over 260 more. Most were accomplished because of Los Angeles's superior access to water (see page 194).

LOS ANGELES —1909—

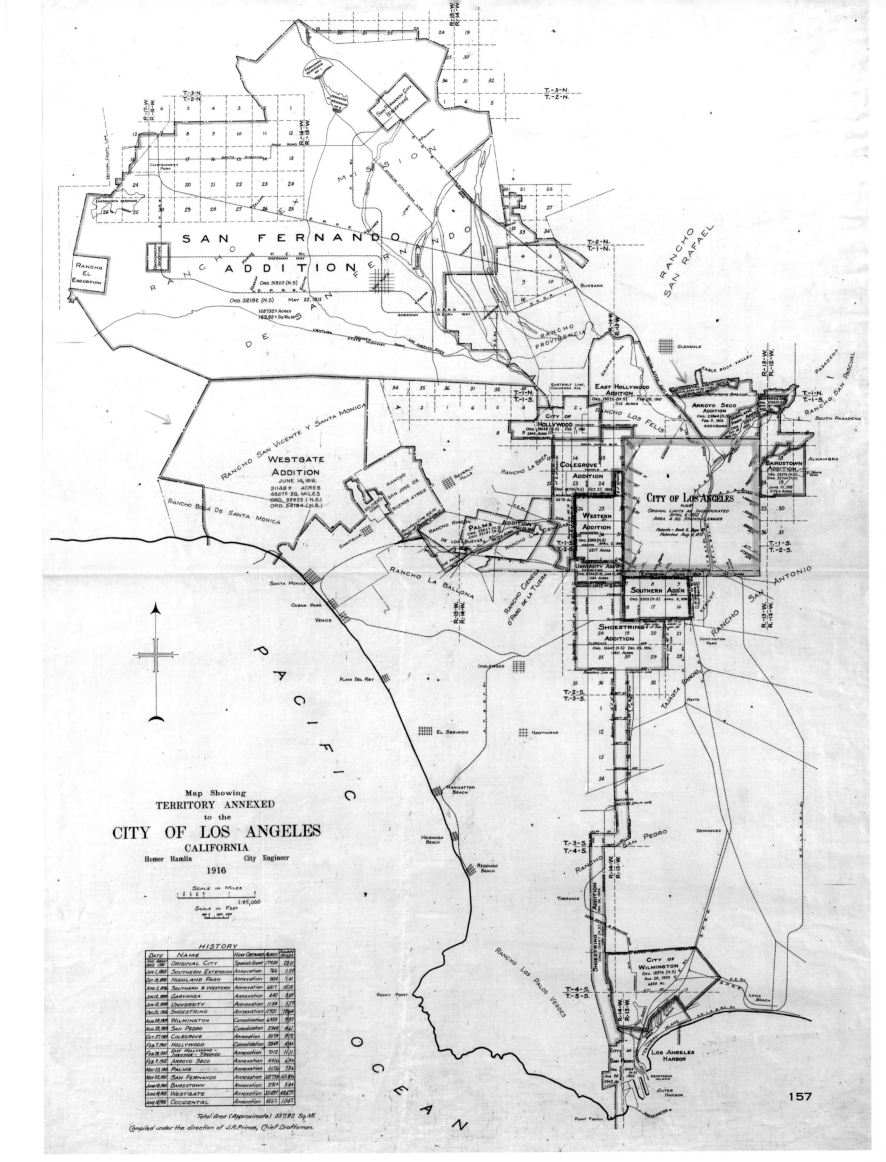

Map Showing
TERRITORY ANNEXED
to the
CITY OF LOS ANGELES
CALIFORNIA

Homer Hamlin    City Engineer
1916

Scale in Miles

1:55,000

Scale in Feet

HISTORY

| Date | Name | How Obtained | Acres | Square Miles |
|---|---|---|---|---|
| Inc. Grant 1850-1781 | Original City | Spanish Grant | 17934 | 28.01 |
| Jun. 1, 1859 | Southern Extension | Annexation | 766 | 1.20 |
| Oct. 18, 1895 | Highland Park | Annexation | 904 | 1.41 |
| Apr. 2, 1896 | Southern & Western | Annexation | 6517 | 10.18 |
| Jun. 12, 1899 | Garvanza | Annexation | 440 | 0.69 |
| Jun. 13, 1899 | University | Annexation | 1134 | 1.77 |
| Dec. 26, 1906 | Shoestring | Annexation | 11931 | 18.64 |
| Aug. 28, 1909 | Wilmington | Consolidation | 6358 | 9.93 |
| Aug. 28, 1909 | San Pedro | Consolidation | 2948 | 4.61 |
| Oct. 27, 1909 | Colegrove | Annexation | 5579 | 8.72 |
| Feb. 7, 1910 | Hollywood | Consolidation | 2848 | 4.45 |
| Feb. 28, 1910 | East Hollywood – Ivanhoe - Tropico | Annexation | 7112 | 11.11 |
| Feb. 9, 1912 | Arroyo Seco | Annexation | 4416 | 6.94 |
| May 22, 1915 | Palms | Annexation | 4672 | 7.30 |
| May 22, 1915 | San Fernando | Annexation | 108732 | 169.89 |
| June 10, 1915 | Bairdstown | Annexation | 2176 | 3.44 |
| June 14, 1916 | Westgate | Annexation | 31149 | 48.67 |
| June 14, 1916 | Occidental | Annexation | 665 | 1.04 |

Total Area (Approximate) 337.92 Sq. Mi.

Compiled under the direction of J. R. Prince, Chief Draftsman.

# 2. THE SAN FRANCISCO BAY AREA

With its magnificent harbor, the Pacific end of the first transcontinental rail link, San Francisco *was* California until Los Angeles, relatively belatedly, began its growth. San Francisco was officially overtaken by Los Angeles in size sometime between 1910 and 1920.

San Francisco Bay, superb as it was as a harbor "able to hold all the navies of the world," nevertheless had shoaling mudflats that made it difficult to bring ships in to unload. To overcome this problem, extensive filling occurred, beginning with Yerba Buena Cove during the gold rush (MAP 301, *overleaf*). There was for a time some confusion—eventually worked out through the courts—as to whether San Francisco's four square leagues included the reclaimed land, since the original pueblo grant of land was said to begin at the bay—but the bay had now moved eastward. Silting of the bay was one of the reasons hydraulic mining was ordered stopped in 1884. In 1874 a survey of the entire bay was carried out to determine areas that might be reclaimed (MAP 300, *overleaf*). Mission Bay, a large but very shallow inlet at the southern end of the San Francisco wharves, was to be one such infill. In 1867 an earth dike, Long Bridge, cut off the bay almost entirely, and in 1869 fill from Second Street, being cut through Rincon Hill, was dumped into Mission Bay. This large, marshy inlet was almost completely filled in by 1895, much of it with garbage. The land was taken over by the Southern Pacific as railyards; today this area is being redeveloped into a campus for UCSF and other uses. Infill of mudflats around the bay has continued (see page 216 and page 234), although in modern times there has been a greater sensitivity to the ecological value of the wetlands, and several areas have been preserved as National Wildlife Refuges.

One of the more successful mayors of San Francisco, which, like many large cities at this time, suffered from considerable political chicanery, was James D. Phelan, elected in 1896. When he left office in 1901 he became interested in remaking the city in the grand style of the "city beautiful" movement then in vogue. He hired Daniel Burnham, a famous architect and city planner, to draft a plan for the beautification of the city. Only a few parts of his plan—for example a waterfront boulevard, the Embarcadero, circling the city—were implemented. Burnham's plans (shown on page 188), were revived in the wake of the 1906 earthquake and fire (see page 182), which would have provided an excellent opportunity for a new beginning. But it was not to be.

MAP 297 (*below*).
The magnificent setting and the vibrant business community of San Francisco have led to the production of many bird's-eye maps of the city. This is one of the earliest and was published in 1864.

MAP 298 (*right, top*).
A view from the Pacific shore looking east, this 1868 bird's-eye shows that wharfage on the bay has been extended southward. A trestle, called Long Bridge, has been constructed across Mission Bay (at center), the precursor to the infill of this shallow inlet. The state had authorized a toll road across Mission Bay as early as 1851. Across the bay, long wharves have been built at Oakland and Alameda.

MAP 299 (*right, bottom*).
An 1877 bird's-eye view to the south. In the distance is Mission Bay, with Long Bridge cutting it off from San Francisco Bay.

*Above left.*
San Francisco City Hall, rebuilt after the earthquake and fire of 1906.

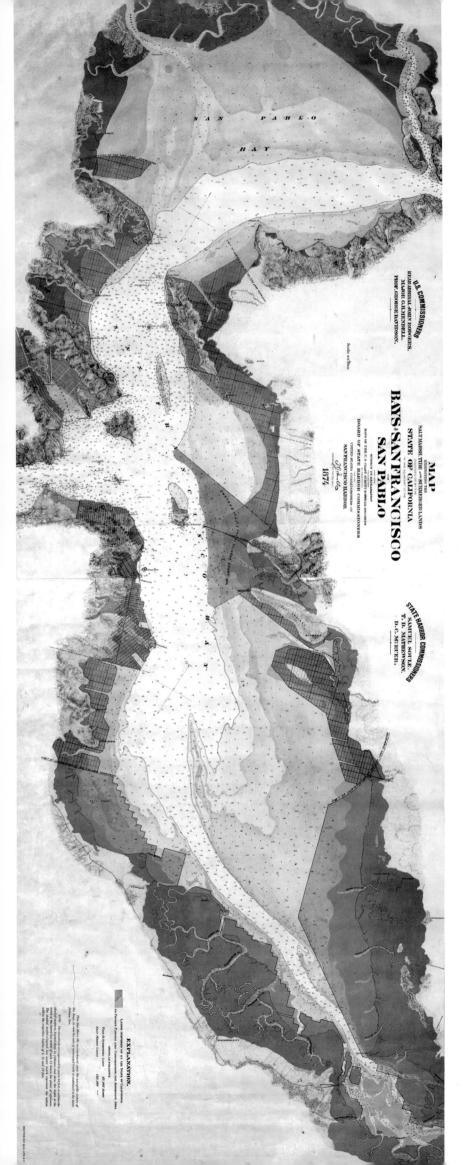

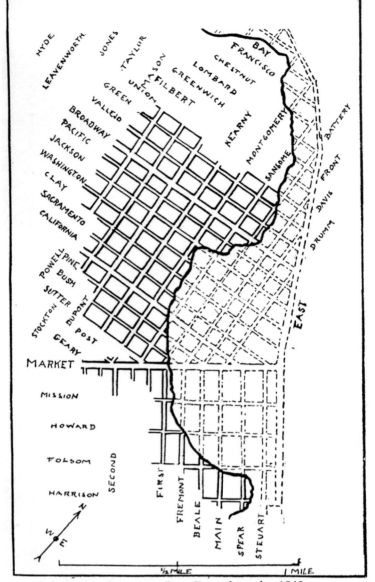

Map Showing San Francisco in 1849
Dotted Lines Show Present Streets beyond Old Shore Line

MAP 300 (*left*).
A very large and detailed map of the mudflats reclaimed and potentially able to be reclaimed around the shores of San Francisco Bay, from a survey carried out in 1874. The key is at bottom left. Of note is Mission Rock, just off Mission Bay, which is shown apparently more infilled than it actually was by this time. The rock was eventually surrounded and became part of Pier 50.

MAP 301 (*above*).
Published in 1906, this map shows the shoreline of San Francisco as it was in 1849 and at present (that is, 1906). The entire shore has been extended, not just within the cove.

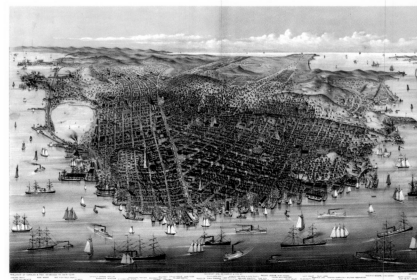

THE CITY OF SAN FRANCISCO.
BIRDS EYE VIEW FROM THE BAY LOOKING SOUTH-WEST.

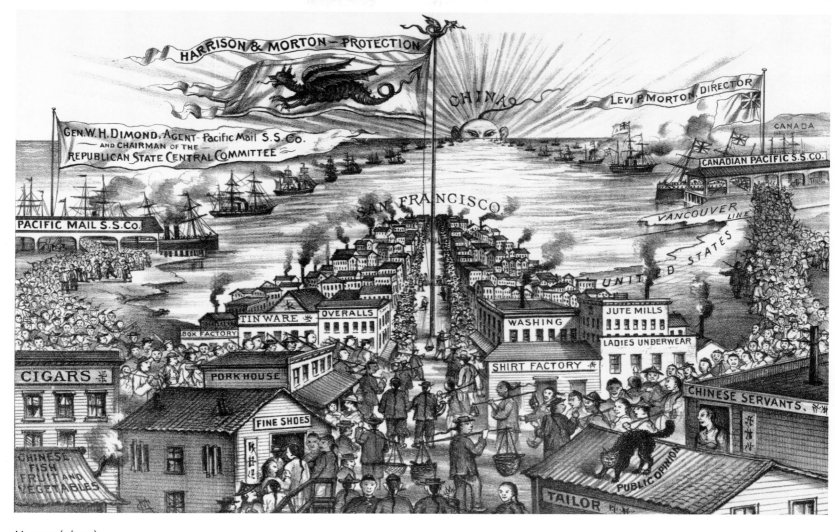

**MAP 303** (*above*).
Antagonism against Chinese immigrants was an ongoing fact of life in San Francisco and the rest of California until after World War II. The Chinese labored in the gold mines and were later employed by the Central Pacific and the Southern Pacific to build the critical transcontinental line and the line south to Los Angeles across the Tehachapi Mountains. Their willingness to work hard for lower pay than EuroAmericans caused friction; in the 1870s the Chinese were the focus of race riots and other mob activity, which culminated in the federal Chinese Exclusion Act of 1882, which al-lowed only a limited number of male adults into the United States. Nonetheless, the Chinese were popularly viewed as pouring into California to work at all manner of jobs that might otherwise employ EuroAmericans. This map-based cartoon-like drawing, clearly designed to inflame, appeared in the early 1890s and depicts streams of Chinese people entering San Francisco via the Pacific Mail Steamship Company directly, and via the Canadian Pacific Steamship Company from Vancouver, Canada. A pony-tailed *China* lurks on the horizon.

**MAP 304** (*right*).
A real estate sales map of San Francisco published in 1890. Many of the city streets and lots shown laid out on the west side of the city were not yet occupied. The boundaries of some of the ranchos are shown. Also shown is Golden Gate Park, created in the years after 1870, when the park was first surveyed. The park was immensely popular with the city's inhabitants, and close to 50,000 people—about 20 percent of the entire city population—are known to have visited the park, by streetcar, on some holiday weekends by the mid-1880s.

**MAP 302** (*left*).
Probably the most reproduced of the old San Francisco bird's-eye maps is this one, originally published in 1878. This shows Mission Bay, completely enclosed but not yet filled.

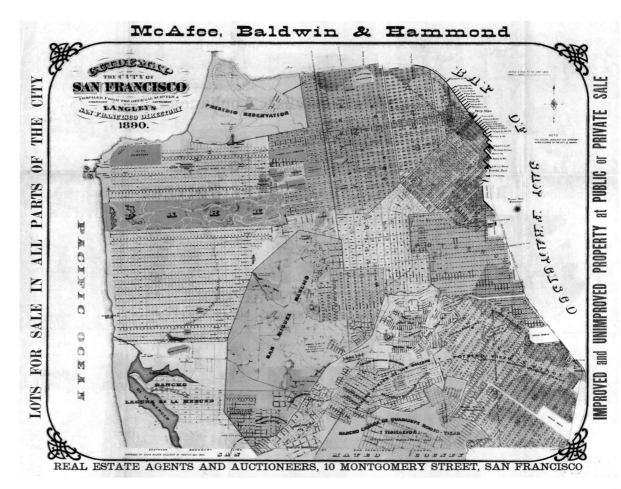

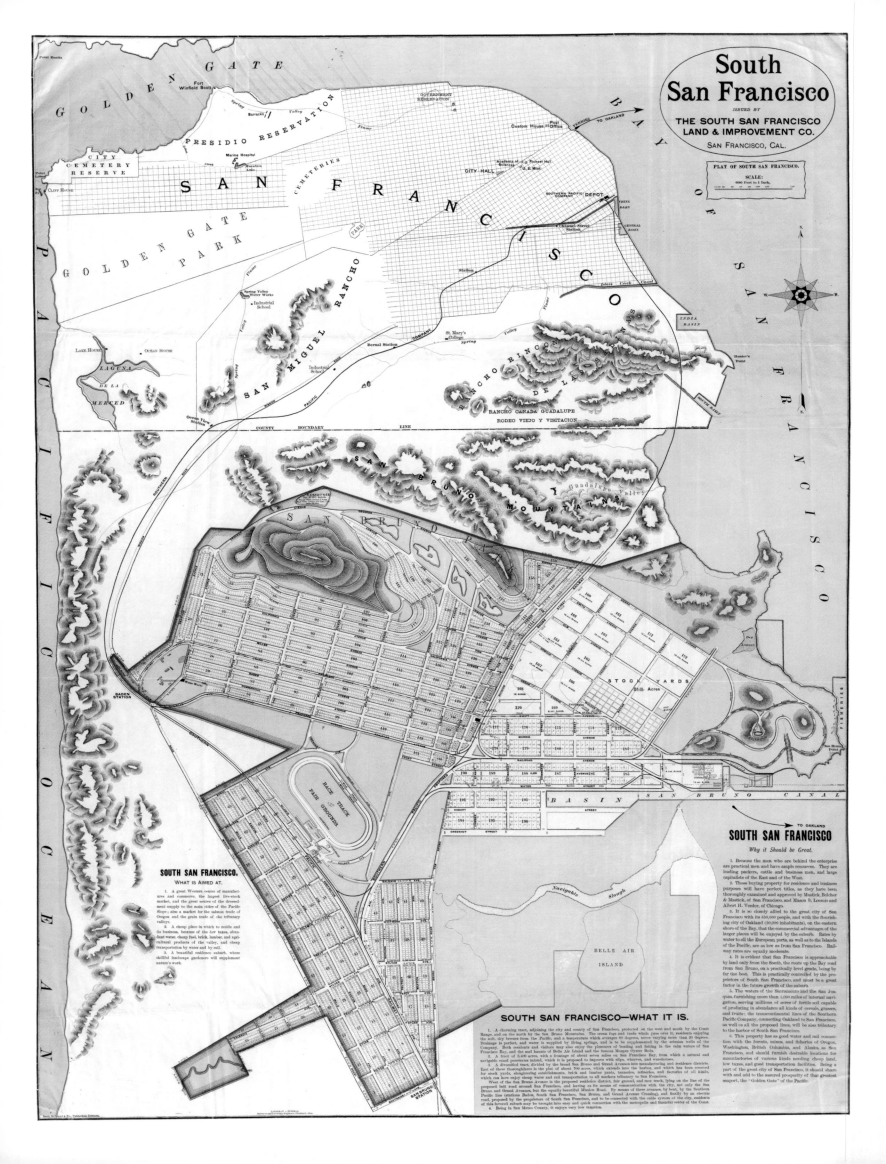

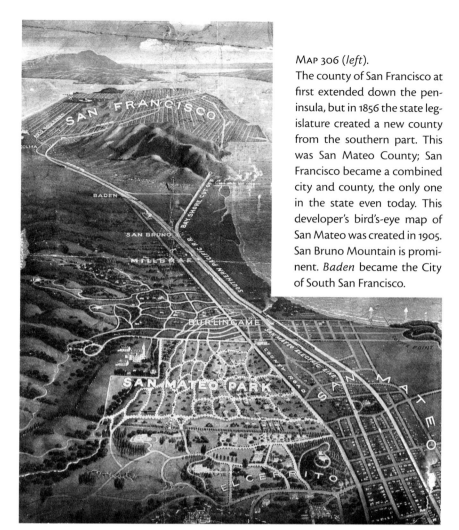

Map 306 (*left*).
The county of San Francisco at first extended down the peninsula, but in 1856 the state legislature created a new county from the southern part. This was San Mateo County; San Francisco became a combined city and county, the only one in the state even today. This developer's bird's-eye map of San Mateo was created in 1905. San Bruno Mountain is prominent. *Baden* became the City of South San Francisco.

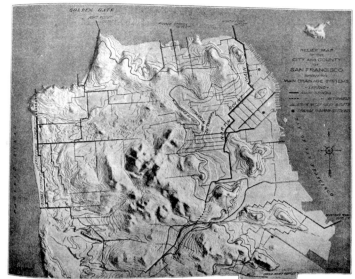

Map 307 (*above*).
Interesting for the way relief is depicted—it may be a photograph of a three-dimensional model—is this 1915 map of a proposed main sewer system for San Francisco, which was to replace a previous unsanitary, inadequate, and uncoordinated system.

Across the bay, the City of Oakland began as a small settlement named Contra Costa but was incorporated as Oakland in 1852, the name deriving from the oak trees that grew extensively in the area. The Central Pacific built the Long Wharf at Oakland Point as the terminus of the transcontinental railroad. The city grew after the 1880s, aided by an extensive streetcar system (see pages 177–78).

Lake Merritt, shown front and center on Map 309, *next page,* was originally an arm of San Francisco Bay and is shown as such on Map 300, *page 160,* and Map 310, *page 166.* It is still tidal, since it is connected to the bay by a narrow channel. The slough was donated to the city in 1867 by local resident Samuel Merritt. As a magnet for migratory birds, in 1869 it became the first National Wildlife Refuge in the United States.

A measure to create a consolidated San Francisco Bay metropolitan area, controlled from San Francisco, was on a state ballot in 1912. The idea was scuttled by the concerted efforts of Oakland politicians, who saw no reason why a greater Oakland could not become the premier port of the

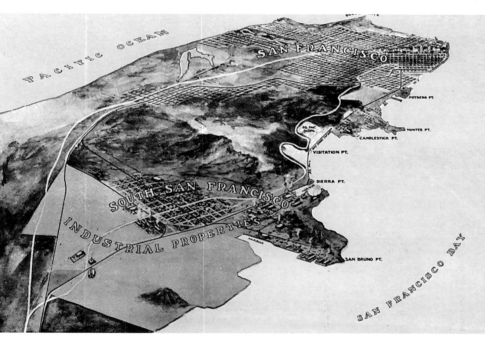

Map 305 (*left*).
The land that would become South San Francisco was first part of the old Rancho Buri-Buri (see Map 149, *page 70,* and Maps 417–20, *page 216*). The land was purchased in 1890 for the establishment of stockyards (seen near *San Bruno Point* on the map) by a meat packer. The South San Francisco Land and Improvement Company was formed to attract other companies and develop the property; this map was used to market lots. Two residential tracts have been laid out on the west side. One of the streets is named *Swift Avenue,* after the meat packer involved, Gustavus F. Swift, whose meat packing empire survives today. The name of South San Francisco was selected by Swift, following a pattern used elsewhere for his plants and yards, similarly located in "South Chicago" and "South Omaha."

Map 308 (*above, left*).
A later attempt to market South San Francisco used this 1920 bird's-eye map to emphasize the proximity to San Francisco. Originally marketed as "The Industrial City," South San Francisco was incorporated in 1908, and the city today still uses this moniker.

*Below* is the one-time federal prison on the island of Alcatraz, in San Francisco Bay.

OAKLAND TRIBUNE

OFFICE: 413, 415, 417 EIGHTH ST.

RESIDENCE OF J.T. BARRACLOUGH, ESQ.
PIEDMONT

FIRST UNITARIAN CHURCH

D.F. OLIVER, ARCHITECT.
MACDONOUGH BLDG, OAKLAND,

PACIFIC COAST LUMBER & MILL CO.
COR. GROVE & SECOND STS.
WHITE CEDAR, REDWOOD & DOUGLAS FIR LUMBER,
MOULDINGS & MILL WORK.

CALIFORNIA BANK

HALL OF RECORDS

SWETT SCHOOL
TWELFTH AVE. S. EAST NINETEENTH ST. EAST OAKLAND

COAL BUNKERS—FRANKLIN ST. WHARF.
JAMES P. TAYLOR
OFFICE: 455 NINTH ST.

JUDSON MFG. CO.
FACTORIES AT EMERYVILLE.
H.E. BOTHIN, PRESIDENT.

POLYTECHNIC BUSINESS COLLEGE

GRANT SCHOOL
COR. BROADWAY & PROSPECT ST.

LAKE MERRITT

OAK CALIFORNIA

SNYDER BUILDING.
A.J. SNYDER & CO.
REAL ESTATE

THEO. GIER CO.

CENTRAL BANK BUILDING.
OFFICES OF MERCHANTS' EXCHANGE.

FIRST CONGREGATIONAL CHURCH

WILLIAM J. DINGEE
REAL ESTATE
OFFICE: 303 BROADWAY, COR. 8TH ST.

LAYMANCE

REAL ESTATE CO.

RESIDENCE OF E.M. WALSH ESQ.
LINDA VISTA TERRACE
D.F. OLIVER, ARCHITECT.
MACDONOUGH BLDG., OAKLAND.

COR. GROVE &
HOBART STS.
ST FRANCIS DE SALES CHURCH

JEFFERSON &
TENTH STS.
CHABOT OBSERVATORY

TWELFTH &
JEFFERSON STS.
OAKLAND HIGH SCHOOL

ALAMEDA CO.
COURT HOUSE
BROADWAY
BETWEEN

WEST &
SEVENTEENTH STS.
LAFAYETTE SCHOOL

OFFICE BUILDING
COR. THIRTEENTH &
CLAY STS.
OAKLAND GAS, LIGHT & HEAT CO

PUBLIC LIBRARY
14TH & GROVE STS.

COR. BROADWAY &
FOURTEENTH ST.
MACDONOUGH BUILDING

COR. HARRISON &
FOURTH STS.
HARRISON SCHOOL

MAP OF OAKLAND, CALIFORNIA,
SHOWING PROPERTIES OF
THE REALTY SYNDICATE

PACIFIC OCEAN

SAN FRANCISCO    GOLDEN GATE

SAN FRANCISCO BAY

AND
RNIA

PUBLISHED BY
F & H. SODERBERG.

HOMES BUILT ON EASY TERMS.
OFFICE,
1070 BROADWAY.
WM P. TODD. REAL ESTATE

FIRST PRESBYTERIAN CHURCH.

CITY HALL
OAKLAND.

REAL ESTATE
& INSURANCE
BROKER
OFFICE,
454 9TH ST
GEO. B.M. GRAY.

THE REALTY SYNDICATE

MUTUAL L. & LITH. CO. S. F

Pacific coast. The city had better railroad connections, after all, and these had been enhanced in 1909 with the arrival in Oakland of the last railroad from the East, the Western Pacific.

Just to the north, the new University of California found a location for a campus in 1868. Its predecessor, the College of California, had been established in Oakland in 1855 to escape the sins of San Francisco, but a decade later Oakland seemed to have been rivaling its neighbor across the bay in the debauchery department, and the college sought out a new peaceful, rural location. The name for the place was suggested by San Francisco lawyer and mining magnate Frederick Billings. Looking toward the Golden Gate he was reminded of the words of eighteenth-century Irish philosopher Bishop George Berkeley that became the paean of American continental conquest—"westward the course of empire takes its way"—and so he named the new town after its author. The University of California's Berkeley campus opened in 1873.

At the southern end of San Francisco Bay was San José, founded in 1777 as the Spanish pueblo of San José de Guadalupe (see page 45). The south bay, too, became the home of a prestigious university, that of Leland Stanford Junior, today adjacent to Palo Alto, which was opened in 1891 by Leland Stanford, one of the "Big Four" of the Central and Southern Pacific railroads. San José (now the largest city in Northern California, having overtaken San Francisco in the 1980 with the growth of Silicon Valley; see page 232) was founded as a city in 1850, even before the new state was granted admission to the Union. For many decades, despite the best efforts of promoters (such as those who created MAP 314, *right*), the city grew quite slowly and had only 21,500 inhabitants by the beginning of the twentieth century.

MAP 309 (*previous pages*).
A superb bird's-eye map of Oakland in 1900, looking west across San Francisco Bay to its rival city San Francisco. Lake Merritt, now cut off from the bay except for a narrow channel, is prominent in the foreground.

MAP 310 (*above*).
Oakland, shown in a composite of maps from an 1878 county atlas. The site of the original city, founded in 1852, is shown as the Original Town, in yellow. Lake Merritt is an arm of the bay, and only a bridge connects its two banks.

MAP 311 (*below*).
A bird's-eye map of Berkeley in 1909. The University of California, which opened its doors at this location in 1873, is shown at front, center.

MAP 312 (*right, top*).
A bird's-eye map of San José in 1875. The view is to the north.

MAP 313 (*right, center*).
This bird's-eye map of the Bay Area, viewed from the south, was published as a promotional postcard in 1915 by the San José Chamber of Commerce.

BERKELEY

## Map 314 (right).
Moses Davis and W.S. Chapman created this idyllic plan they called Poplar City, with poplar trees lining every block to create shade, to market lots between San José and Santa Clara in 1876. Two of the named streets are Davis and Chapman, and both still exist, as does the basic street grid, now part of San José immediately south of the airport. Davis is now adjacent to the line of Interstate 880.

## Map 315 (below).
A classic bird's-eye map of San José, published in 1901. At the top is a tiny map showing the lines of the Southern Pacific Railroad on another perspective map, of California viewed from over the Pacific Ocean. Despite the best efforts of the artist, it is evident that there are many lots yet to be developed; the population of the city at this time was 21,500 persons.

# 3. San Diego

San Diego was incorporated as a city in 1850, encompassing all the original pueblo of 1834 (MAP 154 and MAP 155, *page 73*). A settlement had grown up on the banks of the San Diego River downstream from the mission, but the magnificent harbor of San Diego Bay had been completely overlooked because there was difficulty finding water there.

Soon after the American annexation of California, a boundary surveyor, Andrew B. Gray, realized the potential and interested a San Francisco financier, William Heath Davis, in the idea of establishing a city on the bay. The pair purchased a 160-acre tract on the waterfront from the city trustees and laid out lots and built a wharf. They called it New San Diego (MAP 317, *below*). Water initially had to be hauled from the river, until some wells were drilled for an easier supply. The federal government was convinced to establish an army barracks in the new town, and the wood for it was shipped from the East by sea. Likewise, Davis bought a shipment of prefabicated wooden houses in Portland, Maine. In 1851 Davis experienced heavy financial losses from a fire in San Francisco and could no long support New San Diego; the settlement languished. Most of the people moved back to the Old Town, taking their houses with them. The wharf was rammed by a steamer in 1853 and not repaired, and then in 1861–62 troops stationed at the barracks ran out of fuel and were forced to use wood from the wharf. New San Diego, once so promising, had all but disappeared.

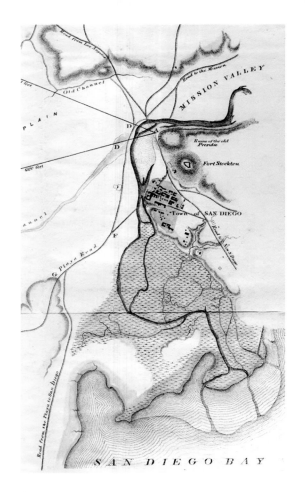

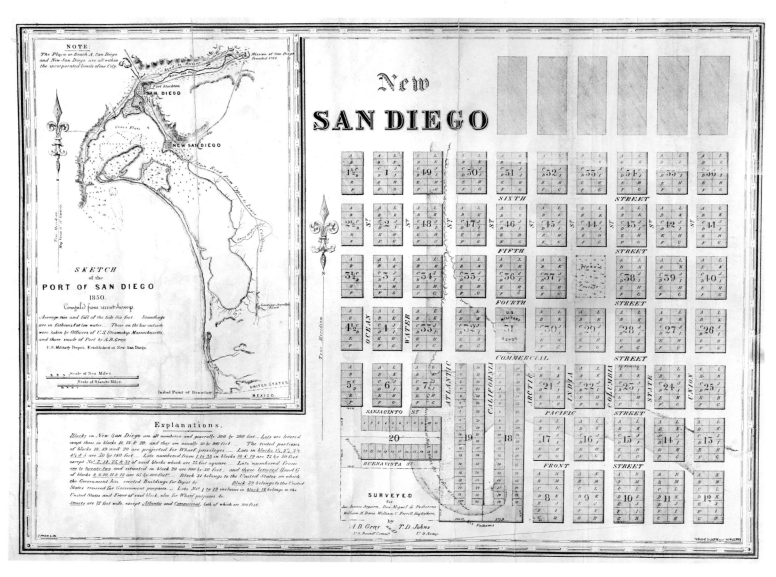

MAP 316 (*left, top*).
This map of the original settlement of San Diego and environs was published in 1853 as part of a U.S. Army report on the possibility of diverting the San Diego River to Mission Bay.

MAP 317 (*left, bottom*).
The plan for New San Diego as envisaged by Andrew Gray in 1850. The inset shows the location of New San Diego, on San Diego Bay, in relation to the original settlement of San Diego, on the San Diego River.

MAP 318 (*right*).
Alonzo Horton's addition to the plan for New San Diego, 1867. The inset map shows its location immediately east and north of Gray's original plan. Blocks were made short, with no alleys (because Horton disliked them as places where trash would accumulate), in order to create more of the valuable corner lots. The T-shaped wharf was not completed until 1869, but it extended into deep water, thus assuring its use by larger steamers. The *City Park* was set aside at Horton's suggestion and is now Balboa Park.

MAP 319 (*below*).
The same plan as MAP 317 from the 1870s, here showing the ownership of lots, including those sold to investors or assigned to the United States government.

Then in 1867 Alonzo Erastus Horton arrived in San Diego. He had been a successful real estate entrepreneur in Wisconsin (where he founded Hortonville, today still a village of 2,600 inhabitants) who came to the Southwest looking to improve his ailing health. Horton immediately saw an opportunity and purchased a large tract of land adjacent to the original New San Diego, although he had to pay $10 to get an election called so that trustees who could authorize the sale could first be elected. Horton bought a total of 960 acres of what is now downtown San Diego for the princely sum of $265.

Yet the locals thought he was mad. The settlement had failed once and surely would do so again. But this time it was different. Horton was a skilled businessman and returned to San Francisco, where he sold many of the lots at a considerable profit. He interested ex–Civil War General William Rosecrans to such an extent that the general offered him $250,000 for his land. Horton refused to sell but was now certain he was on to a good thing. By 1870, only three years after Horton had first arrived, the population of San Diego was officially 2,300, and there were 915 occupied houses and 69 businesses.

A railroad connection with the East was critical to San Diego's continued growth. The Texas and Pacific Railway was chartered in 1871 to establish this link, and it caused a real estate boom, but the railroad failed. It was not until 1885 that a line was completed by the California Southern Railroad (a subsidiary of the Santa Fe) connecting to existing

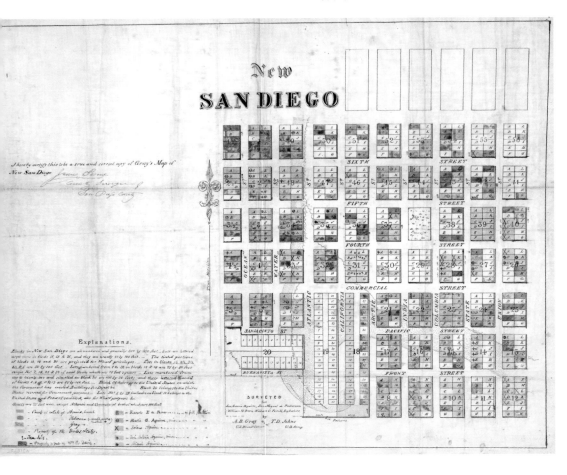

lines at Barstow. The route was problematic, and many washouts occurred, leading to the building of a coastal line by the California Southern, which opened in 1888. Yet another connection was made in 1919 when the San Diego and Arizona Railway was completed to Southern Pacific lines at Seeley, but this railroad ran partly through Mexico, as it was impossible to locate an eastbound route north of the border.

San Diego experienced a real estate boom in the second part of the 1880s, set off by the first railroad completion and ending abruptly in 1888. Across the bay, a group of investors formed the Coronado Beach Company and began developing a resort community, Coronado (MAP 321, *below*). They announced plans to build a grand hotel (the Hotel del Coronado, which still exists), laid on a ferry service, and then subdivided the land, selling 350 lots on a single day (13 November 1886) at between $500 and $1,600 each, realizing $110,000, exactly what they had paid to purchase the entire peninsula.

The real estate market collapsed soon thereafter, and many of the recent immigrants left, but the future of San Diego was now assured. It had a railroad, water supply (which would later be much increased by water from the Colorado River; see page 203), a superb harbor on a coast with so few good harbors, and a forgiving climate.

MAP 320 (*above*).
An 1876 bird's-eye map of San Diego from the northwest. The gap between North Island and Coronado, seen across San Diego Bay (and at far left on MAP 321, *below*), was filled in during 1943–44 to create more space for a U.S. naval base.

MAP 321 (*below*).
An 1886 bird's-eye map of the subdivision of the Coronado Beach Company, which would become the City of Coronado. On the Pacific shore is a representation of the hotel the investors would build, the now world-famous Hotel del Coronado, which opened on 19 February 1888, just as the real estate market collapsed.

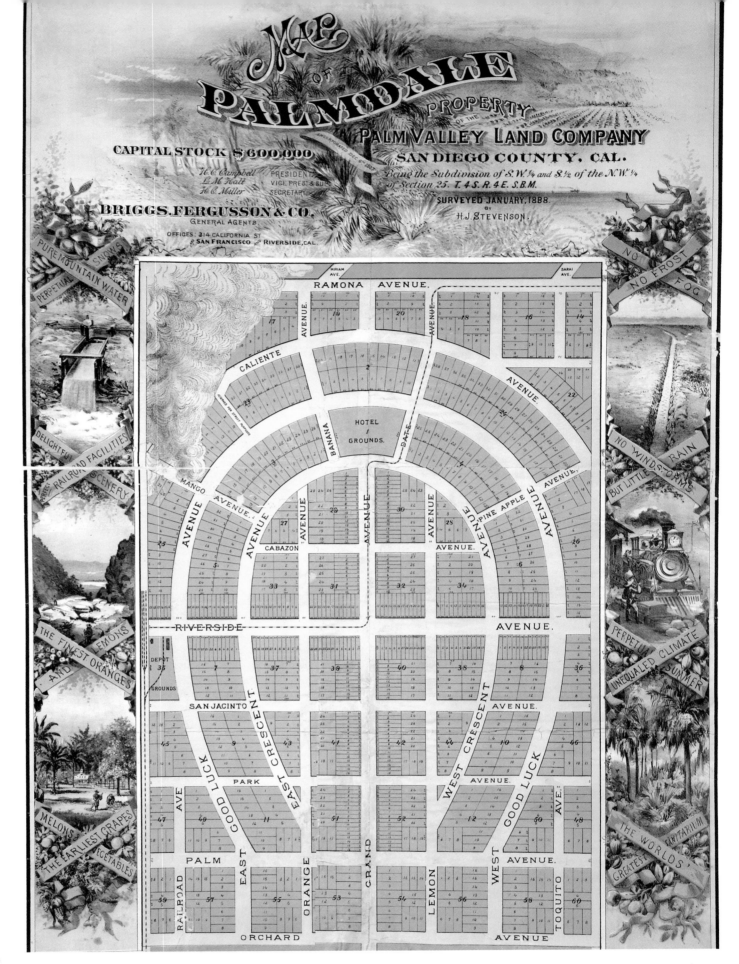

MAP 322.

This is one of the finest real estate sales maps out of many that were produced for the various land booms in California. The marginal illustrations extol *Pure Mountain Water, Perfect Railroad Facilities, The Finest Oranges,* and the *Earliest Grapes; No Windstorms, No Frost,* and *Perpetual Summer.* The street plan, laid out in a horseshoe shape, includes *Good Luck Avenue,* in among other streets of fruit. This was Palmdale, San Diego County, surveyed in January 1888—unfortunate timing for the promoters, who had clearly put a lot of thought into their creation, for Palmdale never left the drawing board. The area shown on this map is now in Palm Springs in Riverside County, about two miles southwest of the airport. The southwest corner is a right-angled bend in Highway 111, but no trace of the innovative street pattern remains, although the highway does deviate from due north to pass around the mountain edge shown at top left.

# 4. SACRAMENTO

Sacramento, which became the California capital in 1855, had, like Los Angeles, been laid out by an Army topographical engineer during the gold rush, this time William Warner (see MAP 194 and other details of the city's early history on page 99). The city dealt with its flooding problem with fill, raising the level of the land so that first floors of houses became basements. As the capital, growth was all but assured.

After the beginning of the nineteenth century, much of the rich agricultural land to the east of the city was populated and farmed, especially for citrus fruits; one suburb is Citrus Heights. In 1909 Daniel W. Carmichael purchased 2,000 acres north of the American River and established a colony system, bringing in immigrants from the East to become part of the community, water and farm the land, and not coincidentally provide him with a return on his investment. Adjacent Fair Oaks, named for its oak trees, likewise was sold off as a "sunset colony" for citrus farming.

The enterprises suffered a setback during the Depression of the thirties when there was a massive freeze, killing many of the trees. Today the suburbs of Sacramento have spread over virtually all this land, and the area is home to some of the most desirable residential real estate in the state.

MAP 323 (*left, top*).
A black-and-white, but nevertheless classically beautiful, bird's-eye map of Sacramento from the last decade of the nineteenth century. The view is to the east, with the Sacramento River in the foreground and the American River at center to left. The commercial buildings and private residences that no doubt subscribed to the map's publication do not preclude one image of the State Capitol at top, center.

MAP 324 (*left, bottom*).
The area shown in this U.S. Geological Survey map, surveyed in 1901 and published the following year, is now completely covered by the cities that make up metropolitan Sacramento. The Southern Pacific rail line south of the American River follows the route of the Sacramento Valley Railroad (see page 117), while the line to the north is that of the Central Pacific's transcontinental.

MAP 325 (*below*).
One of the original agricultural colonies that were established in the Sacramento area was that of Carmichael, seen in this 1909 map used to allocate and sell lots. The location is just north of *Del Paso* on the topographical map (MAP 324).

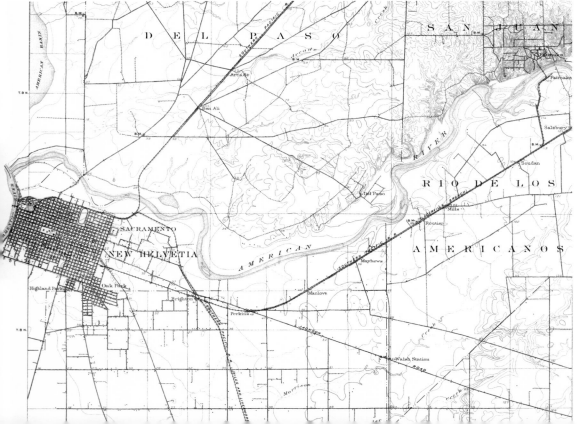

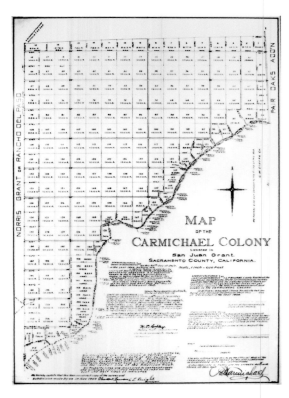

# 5. OTHER CITIES

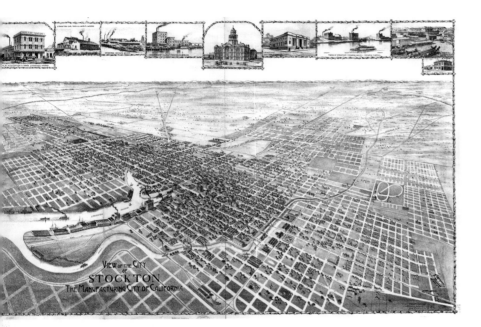

MAP 326 (*left*).
A bird's-eye map of Stockton, *The Manufacturing City of California*, in 1895. Stockton, named after Commodore Robert F. Stockton, was founded in 1849 and was incorporated as a city the following year.

MAP 327 (*right*) and MAP 328 (*below*).
Fresno is the Spanish word for the ash tree, and so the name was a natural choice for the city that grew on the banks of the mountain ash–lined Fresno Creek. The Southern Pacific established a station here in 1872 on the line it was building to Los Angeles, and the community grew up around the station, as did many on the rail line in the Central Valley. MAP 327 shows the city, with lots surrounding the station, in 1886. Fresno was incorporated as a city in 1895. It was an agricultural center and bills itself still as "the raisin capital of the world." The classic bird's-eye (MAP 328) shows Fresno in 1901. See also MAP 270, *page 143*.

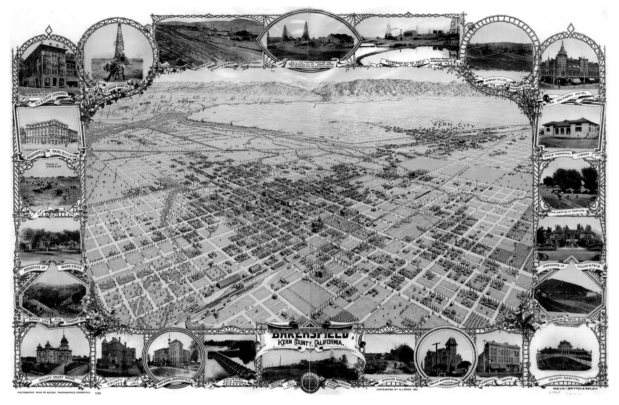

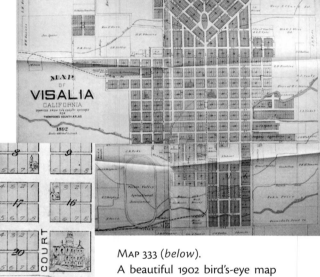

## Map 329 (*above*).

Another superb bird's-eye map, of a then quite small community of Bakersfield in 1901. Bakersfield was founded in 1863 by the friendly Colonel Thomas Baker, who moved to the area to begin reclamation of the frequently flooded lands of the Kern River (see Map 246, *page 133*). Bakersfield was incorporated as a city in 1874 but then reversed the incorporation two years later in order to get rid of a city marshal. The city was incorporated again in 1898.

## Map 330 (*above, right*).

The underlying engine of urban growth was immigration, both from the East and from foreign countries. This map of California, in Italian, but with the map title still in English, formed part of a brochure distributed in Italy in 1910.

## Map 331 (*right, and inset*).

Visalia, like many of the Central Valley communities, grew up around the railroad station. This map is from an 1892 subscription atlas. Individual houses were depicted oversize (*inset*) if, of course, their owners had paid to subscribe to the atlas. The city grew from Fort Visalia, built in 1852 to guard against Indian attacks.

## Map 333 (*below*).

A beautiful 1902 bird's-eye map of Eureka, on the northern coast.

## Map 332 (*below*).

A finely engraved bird's-eye of Santa Barbara in 1877. Santa Barbara grew up around its mission (see Map 92, *page 44*), was a Mexican pueblo, and was incorporated as a city in 1850.

## Map 334 (*right*).

This was the first map of Humboldt County, created in 1853. The map, published in 1865, included insets of the two cities: Eureka, incorporated in 1856, and Arcata, incorporated in 1858. The area's residents ruthlessly removed Indians they thought to be in their way; perhaps as many as two hundred Wiyot were murdered on Gunther Island in Humboldt Bay in 1860, an incident known as the Humboldt County Massacre.

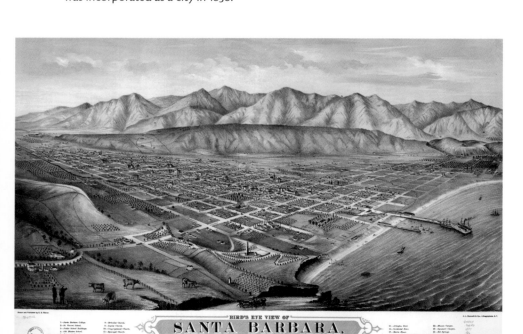

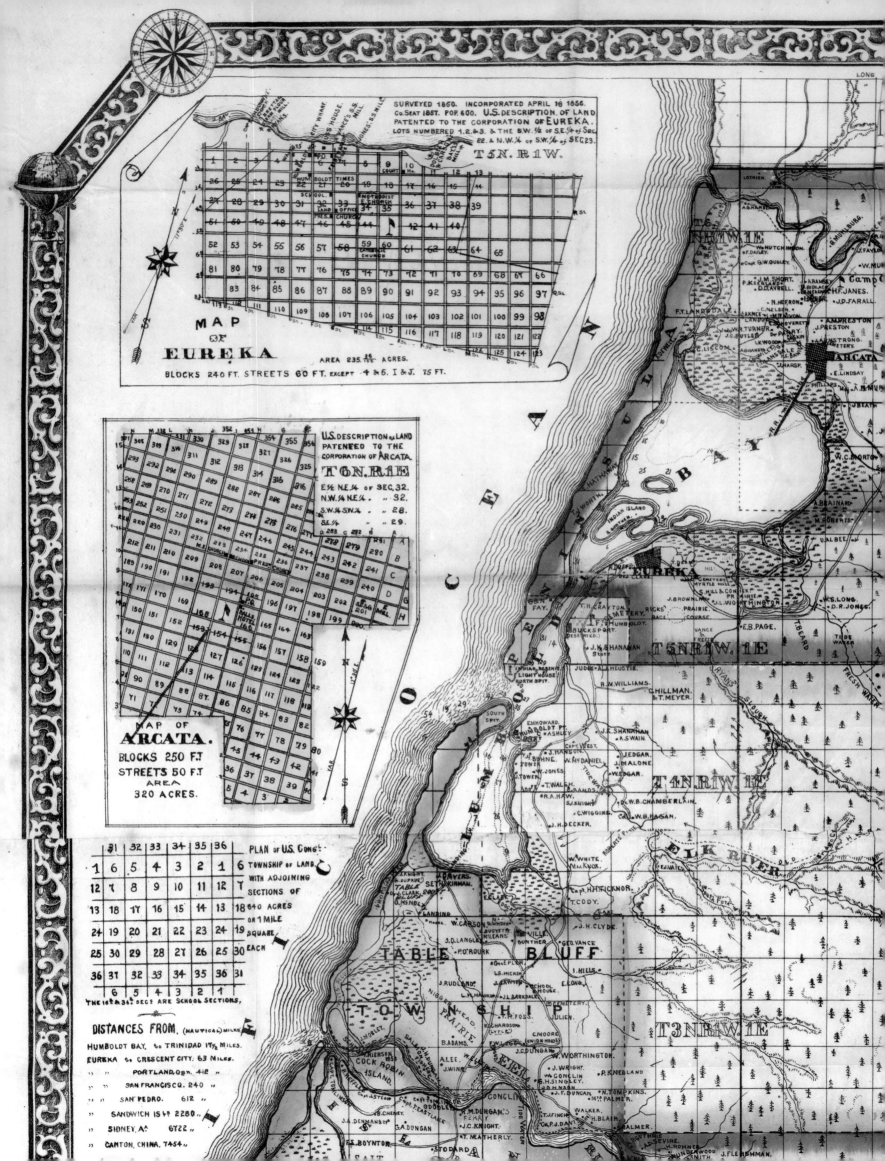

# Rails for Growth

Urban growth would not have occurred the way it did were it not for the streetcar. In the days before the automobile attained widespread popularity the only way what we would today regard as suburbs could exist was if a streetcar line served the area. In many cities the streetcar preceded development and was necessary for that development. In recognition of this relationship, landowners often paid streetcar companies to build a streetcar line; the value of the land leaped with the public accessibility the line immediately bestowed. And longer-distance commuting only became possible with the interurban, a sort of cross between a train and a streetcar that ran in the streets in the cities but on dedicated tracks elsewhere.

In San Francisco public rail transit began particularly early with the introduction of cable cars, an invention of Andrew Hallidie, an ingenious engineer who owned the California Wire Rope and Cable Company. Indeed, it was the world's first commercially successful cable car that first ascended Nob Hill on 1 August 1873. The cable car allowed landowners to develop land otherwise inaccessible by virtue of steep slopes and sparked localized real estate booms along cable lines. Other cable lines opened between 1877 and 1890, and Map 335 (*below*) represents the heyday of cable in the city. Now amalgamated within the San Francisco Municipal Railway (Muni) system, the cable cars have survived only because of their value as a tourist attraction.

The first electric streetcars in the Bay Area began to run in 1891, only three years after they had first been demonstrated in Richmond, Virginia, and San Francisco's first streetcar ran a year later. Their value as people movers and facilitators of land development in the two decades thereafter cannot be overemphasized. The Twin Peaks Tunnel, completed in 1918 (Map 338, *overleaf*) allowed the Muni to build a direct line from downtown to serve the southwestern part of San Francisco, which led to the development of this area.

In the East Bay, a streetcar line was constructed between Oakland and Berkeley, where the University of California had opened its doors in 1873. Various streetcar companies were amalgamated in the late nineteenth century and early twentieth by Francis Marion "Borax" Smith—

MAP 335 (*below*).
An 1890 map of the cable railways of San Francisco. There are a number of different cable car companies whose lines are represented. Co-operation on a map such as this was possible because no cable route competed with any other. The black map has been overprinted with red advertising.

*Above, left* is an aging streetcar running on the Market Street route in 2006.

MAP 336 (*right*).
This informative map shows the Bay Area routes of both electric and steam commuter interurban rail lines of several companies, plus those of the ferries, in 1923 or 1924. The Key (black circles) and Southern Pacific (black dots) stops are listed. In San Francisco the lines of the electric Market Street Railway and the steam Southern Pacific are shown.

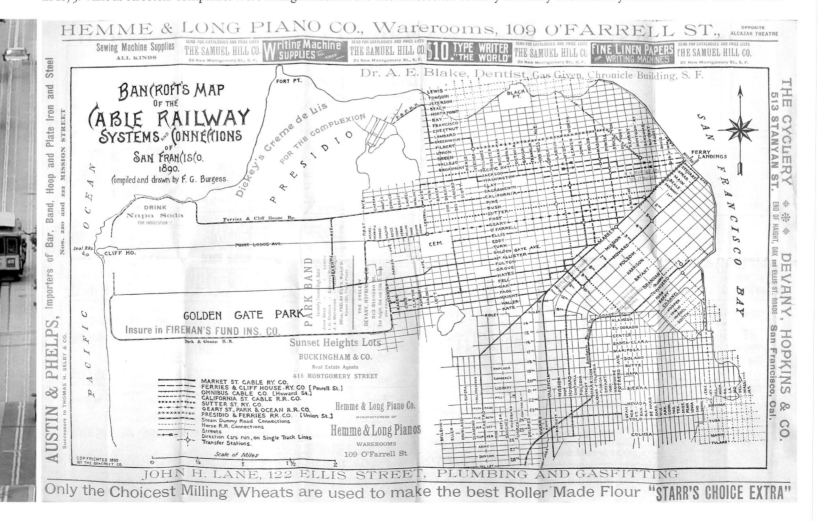

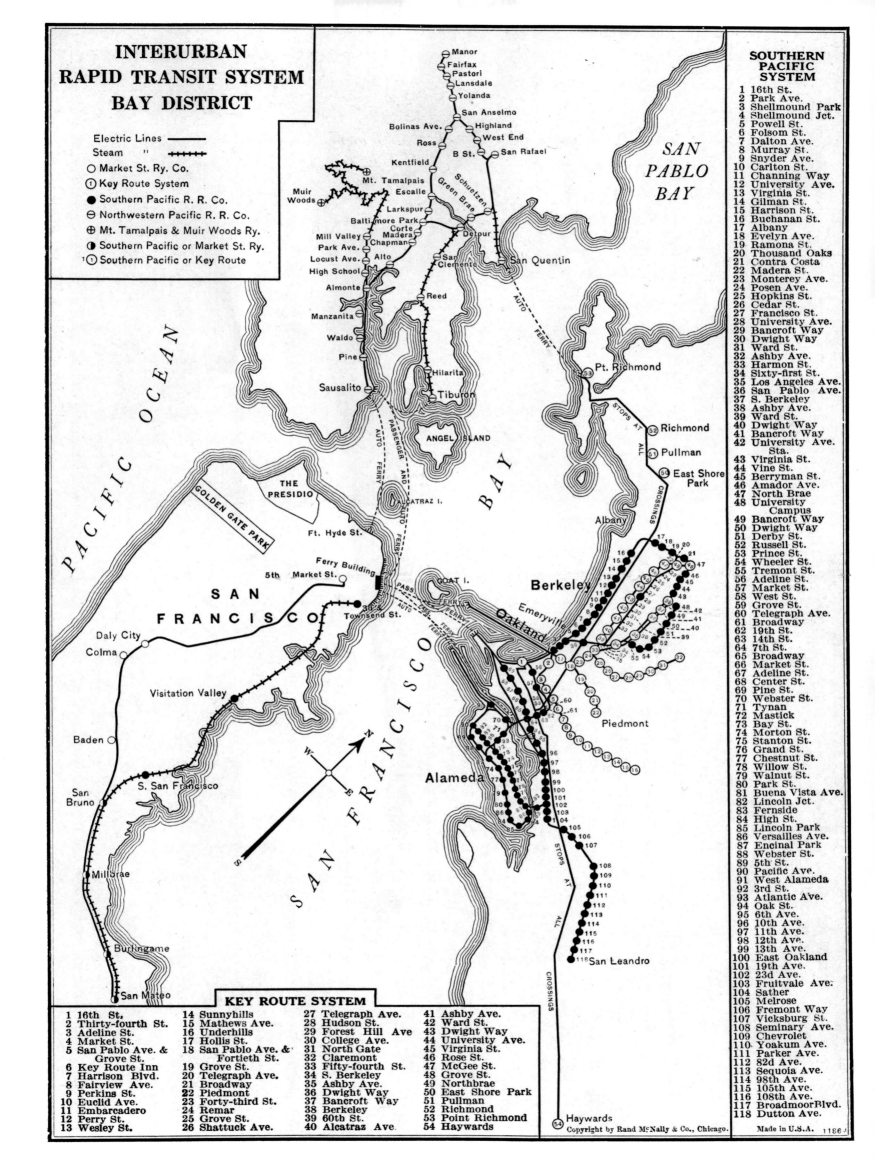

# INTERURBAN RAPID TRANSIT SYSTEM BAY DISTRICT

Electric Lines ———
Steam " +++++
○ Market St. Ry. Co.
① Key Route System
● Southern Pacific R. R. Co.
⊖ Northwestern Pacific R. R. Co.
⊕ Mt. Tamalpais & Muir Woods Ry.
◐ Southern Pacific or Market St. Ry.
¹① Southern Pacific or Key Route

## SOUTHERN PACIFIC SYSTEM

1 16th St.
2 Park Ave.
3 Shellmound Park
4 Shellmound Jct.
5 Powell St.
6 Folsom St.
7 Dalton Ave.
8 Murray St.
9 Snyder Ave.
10 Carlton St.
11 Channing Way
12 University Ave.
13 Virginia St.
14 Gilman St.
15 Harrison St.
16 Buchanan St.
17 Albany
18 Evelyn Ave.
19 Ramona St.
20 Thousand Oaks
21 Contra Costa
22 Madera St.
23 Monterey Ave.
24 Posen Ave.
25 Hopkins St.
26 Cedar St.
27 Francisco St.
28 University Ave.
29 Bancroft Way
30 Dwight Way
31 Ward St.
32 Ashby Ave.
33 Harmon St.
34 Sixty-first St.
35 Los Angeles Ave.
36 San Pablo Ave.
37 S. Berkeley
38 Ashby Ave.
39 Ward St.
40 Dwight Way
41 Bancroft Way
42 University Ave. Sta.
43 Virginia St.
44 Vine St.
45 Berryman St.
46 Amador Ave.
47 North Brae
48 University Campus
49 Bancroft Way
50 Dwight Way
51 Derby St.
52 Russell St.
53 Prince St.
54 Wheeler St.
55 Tremont St.
56 Adeline St.
57 Market St.
58 West St.
59 Grove St.
60 Telegraph Ave.
61 Broadway
62 19th St.
63 14th St.
64 7th St.
65 Broadway
66 Market St.
67 Adeline St.
68 Center St.
69 Pine St.
70 Webster St.
71 Tynan
72 Mastick
73 Bay St.
74 Morton St.
75 Stanton St.
76 Grand St.
77 Chestnut St.
78 Willow St.
79 Walnut St.
80 Park St.
81 Buena Vista Ave.
82 Lincoln Jct.
83 Fernside
84 High St.
85 Lincoln Park
86 Versailles Ave.
87 Encinal Park
88 Webster St.
89 5th St.
90 Pacific Ave.
91 West Alameda
92 3rd St.
93 Atlantic Ave.
94 Oak St.
95 6th Ave.
96 10th Ave.
97 11th Ave.
98 12th Ave.
99 13th Ave.
100 East Oakland
101 19th Ave.
102 23d Ave.
103 Fruitvale Ave.
104 Sather
105 Melrose
106 Fremont Way
107 Vicksburg St.
108 Seminary Ave.
109 Chevrolet
110 Yoakum Ave.
111 Parker Ave.
112 82d Ave.
113 Sequoia Ave.
114 98th Ave.
115 105th Ave.
116 108th Ave.
117 Broadmoor Blvd.
118 Dutton Ave.

## KEY ROUTE SYSTEM

1 16th St.
2 Thirty-fourth St.
3 Adeline St.
4 Market St.
5 San Pablo Ave. & Grove St.
6 Key Route Inn
7 Harrison Blvd.
8 Fairview Ave.
9 Perkins St.
10 Euclid Ave.
11 Embarcadero
12 Perry St.
13 Wesley St.
14 Sunnyhills
15 Mathews Ave.
16 Underhills
17 Hollis St.
18 San Pablo Ave. & Fortieth St.
19 Grove St.
20 Telegraph Ave.
21 Broadway
22 Piedmont
23 Forty-third St.
24 Remar
25 Grove St.
26 Shattuck Ave.
27 Telegraph Ave.
28 Hudson St.
29 Forest Hill Ave
30 College Ave.
31 North Gate
32 Claremont
33 Fifty-fourth St.
34 S. Berkeley
35 Ashby Ave.
36 Dwight Way
37 Bancroft Way
38 Berkeley
39 60th St.
40 Alcatraz Ave.
41 Ashby Ave.
42 Ward St.
43 Dwight Way
44 University Ave.
45 Virginia St.
46 Rose St.
47 McGee St.
48 Grove St.
49 Northbrae
50 East Shore Park
51 Pullman
52 Richmond
53 Point Richmond
54 Haywards

Copyright by Rand McNally & Co., Chicago.

Made in U.S.A.
1186 J

KEY ROUTE & S.F. FERRIES TO
BERKELEY. OAKLAND AND ALAMEDA.

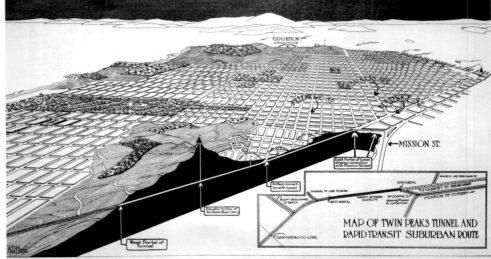

← MISSION ST.

MAP OF TWIN PEAKS TUNNEL AND
RAPID TRANSIT SUBURBAN ROUTE

This Twin Peaks Tunnel Will Make Available for Homesites a Vast and Now Inaccessible Area Ideally Situated for Residence
Purposes, and Capable of Housing 400,000 People

**LEGEND**
1 PARK-PRESIDIO DISTRICT
2 SUNSET           "
3 PARKSIDE         "
4 INGLESIDE TERRACES
5 WESTWOOD PARK
6 ST. FRANCIS WOOD
7 WEST PORTAL PARK
8 FOREST HILL
9 CLAIRMONT COURT
10 MISSION DISTRICT
11 POTRERO          "

*Municipal Railway Lines*
OF
SAN FRANCISCO. CAL.
—1920—

These lines cover 65 miles of single track. The total street railway track mileage in the City is
321 miles. The Municipal Railway mileage is 20 per cent of the total.

MAP 337 (*above, left*).
The ferry terminal building, for Key and Southern Pacific ferries, shown on part of a bird's-eye map of San Francisco dated 1912.

MAP 338 (*above*).
The Twin Peaks Tunnel, completed in 1918, allowed the San Francisco Municipal Railway access to the southwestern suburbs. This cutaway planning map dates from 1913.

MAP 339 (*left*).
"Muni" system map, 1920. Note the newly completed Twin Peaks Tunnel at center. Mileage figures are given under the map.

MAP 340 (*below, left*).
Oakland's Key System in 1941, after the completion of the Bay Bridge. The inset map shows the loop taken off the bridge into downtown San Francisco. Only interurban lines are shown, not streetcar lines.

*Below, top.* The car ferry *Eureka,* now an exhibit in the San Francisco Maritime National Historical Park.
*Below, bottom.* Automobiles disembarking from the Berkeley ferry on the San Francisco waterfront, The photographer recorded the time: 5.35 *P.M.,* 14 June 1931.

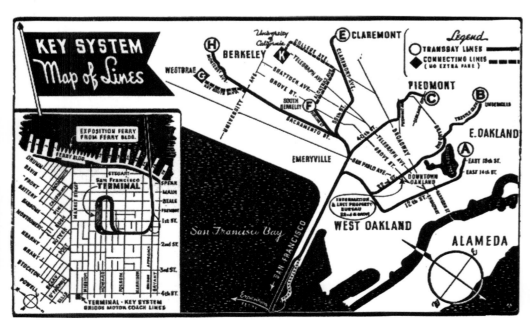

KEY SYSTEM
*Map of Lines*

*Legend*
○ TRANSBAY LINES
◆ CONNECTING LINES
(NO EXTRA FARE)

H BERKELEY
K
G WESTBRAE
E CLAREMONT
F
PIEDMONT
C
B
E. OAKLAND
A
EMERYVILLE
DOWNTOWN OAKLAND
WEST OAKLAND
ALAMEDA

EXPOSITION FERRY
FROM FERRY BLDG.

San Francisco TERMINAL

San Francisco Bay

TERMINAL · KEY SYSTEM
BRIDGE MOTOR COACH LINES

who had made a fortune mining the mineral for which he is nicknamed—to create what became the Key System. His San Francisco, Oakland, and San Jose Railway began service in 1903, running from Berkeley to the company ferry pier. His manager came up with the idea of using a stylized map to show this and various other routes. The company's advertising touted it as a "key" route, the name the system used after 1938 until its demise in 1958 (Map 340, *left, bottom*).

The first large-scale ferries across San Francisco Bay were those of the Central Pacific. The landmark San Francisco Ferry Building was completed in 1898 (Map 337, *left, top*), surviving the earthquake and fire of 1906 to continue today as a ferry terminal, albeit with a much reduced service. The rise of the automobile and the completion of the Golden Gate and Bay bridges in the 1930s (see page 222) hastened the demise of the streetcar and interurban in the Bay Area and sealed the fate of the ferries.

The longest interurban in North America was the Sacramento Northern Railway (Map 341, *right*), owned by the Western Pacific Railway. It began in 1913 as the Oakland, Antioch, and Eastern Railway, a 93-mile line from San Francisco to Sacramento. This was purchased by and added to the Sacramento Northern, then running from Sacramento to Chico, in 1928. Whole trains were carried across Carquinez Strait on a special ferry, the *Ramon*. Passenger service lasted until 1941.

All cities and aspiring cities needed the streetcar to facilitate their growth. Cities ranging from Eureka to San Diego, from San José to Santa Cruz; the Napa Valley; Stockton (which had a 53-mile interurban link to Sacramento); Fresno, Bakersfield, and Santa Barbara all had streetcar systems at one time. Almost all were eventually killed by the automobile. In San Diego, John D. Spreckels (later builder of the San Diego and Arizona Railway; see page 170) established a network of five streetcar routes in 1892, a system that lasted until 1949.

Map 341 (*above, right*).
A system map of the Sacramento Northern Railway in 1939, at the peak of its geographical coverage, but only two years before the line shut down passenger services. At its peak the Sacramento Northern had one of the longest, if not the longest, interurban runs in the world, 185 miles from San Francisco to Chico. At *top* is a typical Sacramento Northern electric train photographed in 1939, approaching Oakland from the east. At *right* is a modern Sacramento Regional Transit Metro train in central Sacramento; part of its route uses the old right-of-way of the Sacramento Northern.

MAP 342 (*above*).

Thaddeus S.C. Lowe, who had invented the observation balloon during the Civil War, retired to Los Angeles in 1887 and decided to build an electrically operated incline railway up Echo Mountain. A hotel and observatory were built at the summit, and Pacific Electric streetcars ran to the base of the incline railway by a precipitous and spectacular route. A fire in 1936 destroyed the tourist attraction.

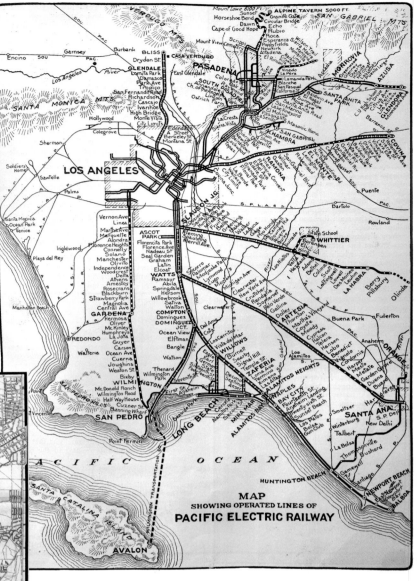

MAP 343 (*above*).

The Huntington Pacific Electric system in January 1911, just before it was sold to the Southern Pacific.

MAP 344 (*left*).

The streetcar systems of central Los Angeles, 1908. Henry Huntington's Los Angeles Railway Company's routes (*Yellow Cars*) are listed at bottom left, and his Pacific Electric lines are listed bottom right.

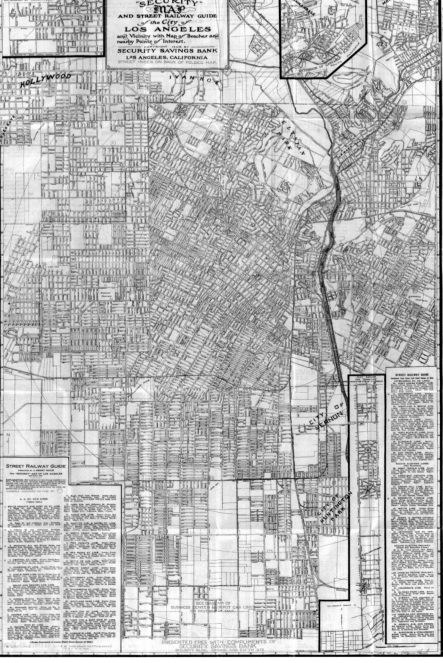

In Los Angeles, the first interurban line, between downtown and Pasadena, opened in 1895, and Henry Huntington incorporated the first Pacific Electric Railway in 1901; the company's first new line was built to Long Beach. In 1911 Huntington sold out to the Southern Pacific, which consolidated its lines as the new Pacific Electric—always known by its popular moniker, the "Red Cars." Huntington in turn gained exclusive control of the streetcar system of central Los Angeles, the Los Angeles Railway, known as the "Yellow Cars." Until that time the Southern Pacific had controlled part of Huntington's Pacific Electric, its intense competitor. At their peak, the two systems dispatched more than 2,000 streetcars and interurbans every day.

In 1949 the state Public Utilities Commission approved a plan to replace 200 streetcars with 200 buses on eleven of P.E.'s seventeen routes as the first part of a $4.5 million "modernization plan." It was the beginning of the end; Los Angeles's love affair with the automobile had overtaken the streetcar.

MAP 345 (*right*).
This map of all rail lines in the Los Angeles region in 1912 reveals a complex network—one that would one day be completely replaced by an almost equally complex network of freeways.

MAP 346 (*below*).
The interurban lines (only) of the new Southern Pacific–owned Pacific Electric are shown, unusually but interestingly, on a regional relief map of the Los Angeles basin. The map is dated 1920.

*Below.*
A reconstructed Pacific Electric Red Car runs for tourists on the new streetcar line in the Port of Los Angeles.

# THE BURNING OF SAN FRANCISCO

MAP 347 (*above*).
This rather superb bird's-eye map color print of San Francisco at the height of the 1906 conflagration was rushed into print soon after the fire. The Ferry Building, at bottom, was untouched.

MAP 348 (*below*).
A map and engraving of one of the six fires that ravaged San Francisco in 1849–51. The result of arson, this one occurred on 4 May 1850 and consumed several blocks before it could be contained with dynamite and rope.

Most American cities experienced devastating fires during their formative years, and San Francisco was no exception; indeed, the city was destroyed by fire more times than any other major city. Primitive firefighting methods and principally wooden construction combined to create ideal conditions for a conflagration.

Six major fires occurred in the space of nineteen months in 1849–51, at least two the result of arson. The speedy use of dynamite and rope—to pull buildings down—saved the city from total devastation several times, although a fire on 3–4 May 1851 consumed three quarters of the city. Each time the city was rebuilt, with ever-increasing construction of wells, reservoirs, water tanks on roofs, and more organization of fire companies.

The fire menace seemed to have at last been contained, but all was for naught when a major earthquake struck a now much larger city in the early hours of Wednesday, 18 April 1906, for not only did the quake tip stoves and break gas lines, which began fires, but it also broke the water supply lines in a thousand places, removing almost completely the means with which the fire might be quickly contained. The earthquake reduced large areas of the city to rubble, and the fire finished the job, resulting in a scene of devastation the likes of which have rarely been seen, before or since.

Although fires began in many buildings, the coalescing firestorm that destroyed the city in general terms began south of Market Street and in the Hayes Valley area west of City Hall, and over the next three days it worked its way north, burning itself out on Saturday, 21 April, just to the north of Telegraph Hill, which itself escaped the fire. The course of the fire is better described with the help of contemporary maps such as MAP 349, MAP 350, and MAP 351 (*right*).

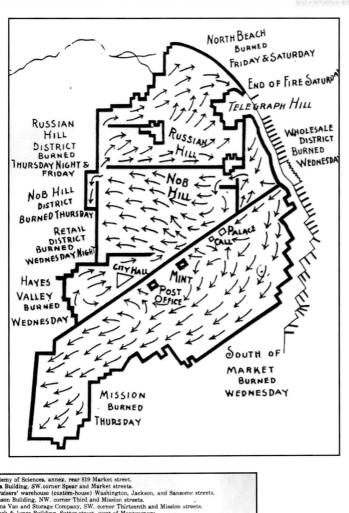

NORTH BEACH
BURNED
FRIDAY & SATURDAY

END OF FIRE SATURDAY

TELEGRAPH HILL

WHOLESALE DISTRICT BURNED WEDNESDAY

RUSSIAN HILL DISTRICT BURNED THURSDAY NIGHT & FRIDAY

RUSSIAN HILL

NOB HILL

NOB HILL DISTRICT BURNED THURSDAY

RETAIL DISTRICT BURNED WEDNESDAY NIGHT

HAYES VALLEY BURNED WEDNESDAY

CITY HALL    MINT    POST OFFICE    PALACE    CALL

SOUTH OF MARKET BURNED WEDNESDAY

MISSION BURNED THURSDAY

**MAP 349** (*left*).
This map from a 1906 book shows the progress of the fire by day and illustrates the way the fire moved in general from south to north between Wednesday and Saturday, 18–21 April.

**MAP 350** (*right*).
This map shows where fires started (top map) and the situation at 3 A.M. on the second day (bottom map). A considerable area of the southern part of the city has been destroyed in less than twenty-four hours.

**MAP 351** (*below*).
From a government report issued in 1907 comes this informative map detailing the location of firefighting water supply lines, cisterns and tanks. It also shows principal fissures in the streets, and the downtown part of the city built principally of brick.

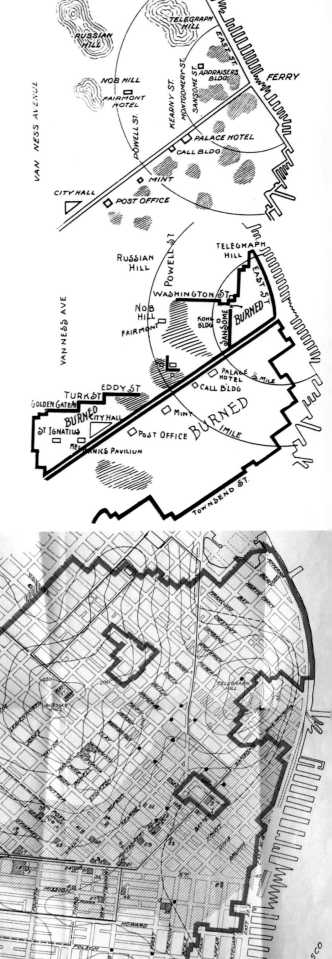

RUSSIAN HILL / TELEGRAPH HILL / NOB HILL / FAIRMONT HOTEL / VAN NESS AVENUE / POWELL ST. / KEARNY ST. / MONTGOMERY ST. / SANSOME ST. / EAST ST. / APPRAISERS BLDG / FERRY / PALACE HOTEL / CALL BLDG / CITY HALL / MINT / POST OFFICE

RUSSIAN HILL / TELEGRAPH HILL / WASHINGTON ST. / POWELL ST. / EAST ST. / NOB HILL / FAIRMONT / KOHL BLDG / SANSOME / BURNED / VAN NESS AVE / TURK ST / EDDY ST / GOLDEN GATE AV / BURNED / ST IGNATIUS / CITY HALL / MECHANICS PAVILION / PALACE HOTEL / CALL BLDG / MINT / POST OFFICE / BURNED / TOWNSEND ST. / ½ MILE / 1 MILE

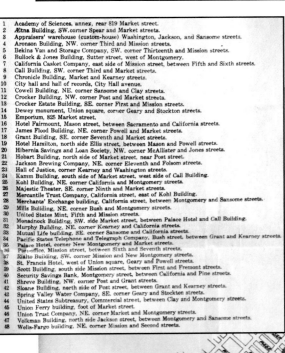

1  Academy of Sciences, annex, rear 819 Market street.
2  Ætna Building, SW. corner Spear and Market streets.
3  Appraisers' warehouse (custom-house) Washington, Jackson, and Sansome streets.
4  Aronson Building, NW. corner Third and Mission streets.
5  Bekins Van and Storage Company, SW. corner Thirteenth and Mission streets.
6  Bullock & Jones Building, Sutter street, west of Montgomery.
7  California Casket Company, east side of Mission street, between Fifth and Sixth streets.
8  Call Building, SW. corner Third and Market streets.
9  Chronicle Building, Market and Kearney streets.
10  City hall and hall of records, City Hall avenue.
11  Cowell Building, NE. corner Sansome and Clay streets.
12  Crocker Building, NW. corner Post and Market streets.
13  Crocker Estate Building, SE. corner First and Mission streets.
14  Dewey monument, Union square, corner Geary and Stockton streets.
15  Emporium, 825 Market street.
16  Hotel Fairmont, Mason street, between Sacramento and California streets.
17  James Flood Building, NE. corner Powell and Market streets.
18  Grant Building, SE. corner Seventh and Market streets.
19  Hotel Hamilton, north side Ellis street, between Mason and Powell streets.
20  Hibernia Savings and Loan Society, NW. corner McAllister and Jones streets.
21  Hobart Building, north side of Market street, near Post street.
22  Jackson Brewing Company, NE. corner Eleventh and Folsom streets.
23  Hall of Justice, corner Kearney and Washington streets.
24  Kamm Building, south side of Market street, west side of Call Building.
25  Kohl building, NE. corner California and Montgomery streets.
26  Majestic Theater, SE. corner Ninth and Market streets.
27  Mercantile Trust Company, California street, east of Kohl Building.
28  Merchants' Exchange building, California street, between Montgomery and Sansome streets.
29  Mills Building, NE. corner Bush and Montgomery streets.
30  United States Mint, Fifth and Mission streets.
31  Monadnock Building, SW. side Market street, between Palace Hotel and Call Building.
32  Murphy Building, NE. corner Kearny and California streets.
33  Mutual Life building, SE. corner Sansome and California streets.
34  Pacific States Telephone and Telegraph Company, Bush street, between Grant and Kearney streets.
35  Palace Hotel, corner New Montgomery and Market streets.
36  Post-office, Mission street, between Sixth and Seventh streets.
37  Rialto Building, SW. corner Mission and New Montgomery streets.
38  St. Francis Hotel, west of Union square, Geary and Powell streets.
39  Scott Building, south side Mission street, between First and Fremont streets.
40  Security Savings Bank, Montgomery street, between California and Pine streets.
41  Shreve Building, NW. corner Post and Grant streets.
42  Sloane Building, north side of Post street, between Grant and Kearney streets.
43  Spring Valley Water Company, SE. corner Geary and Stockton streets.
44  United States Subtreasury, Commercial street, between Clay and Montgomery streets.
45  Union Ferry building, foot of Market street.
46  Union Trust Company, NE. corner Market and Montgomery streets.
47  Volkman Building, north side Jackson street, between Montgomery and Sansome streets.
48  Wells-Fargo building, NE. corner Mission and Second streets.

———— Principal distribution mains.
‒‒‒‒‒ Salt-water system.
∙∙∙∙∙∙ Old shore line.
▬▬▬▬ Boundary line of burned district.
///////// Principal earthquake breaks in streets.

▨▨▨ District covered largely by brick structures.
●  ●  ●  Cisterns in service.

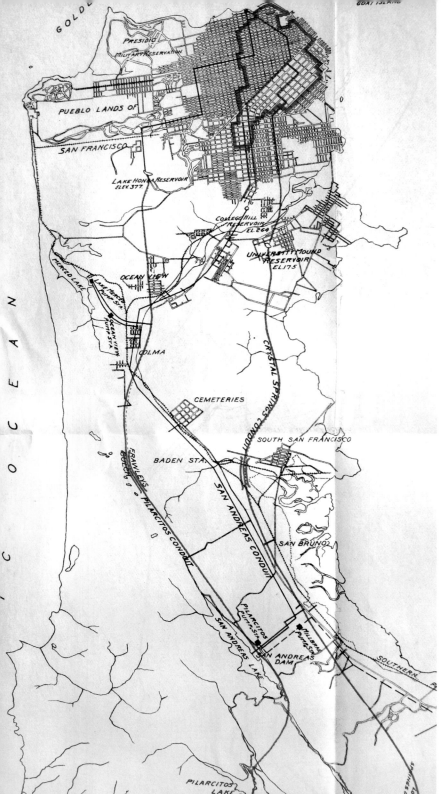

Army units from the Presidio were quickly called in to assist, and others followed later in the day; they began dynamiting buildings around the U.S. Mint (shown on MAP 349). But neither dynamiting nor the several stands made by the fire department were able to contain the conflagration. Mayor Eugene E. Schmitz issued a now infamous proclamation declaring that all looters would be shot on sight, which was certainly going beyond his legal powers.

At the time 478 deaths were reported, as city officials thought that publicizing a higher death toll would destroy the precious real estate values and hinder efforts to rebuild the city. Nowadays the number of deaths is thought to be in excess of three thousand and perhaps as high as six thousand. Many deaths in the city's Chinatown were unreported for purely racial reasons. Other deaths were reported from other locations around the bay, especially Santa Rosa and San José, and Stanford University suffered much damage.

The Army assisted with the setting up of a number of refugee camps, which included a vast city of quickly erected huts at the Presidio itself. MAP 355, *overleaf*, shows the location of these camps within the city. Half of the refugees fled across the bay to Oakland.

Government and private corporations such as insurance companies and construction firms initiated exhaustive analyses in the days, months, and years following the quake. They wanted to determine exactly what had happened so that a recurrence, in San Francisco or in other cities, could be prevented. Construction experts from the giant Roebling Company, which among other projects had built New York's Brooklyn Bridge, examined many buildings to determine which had withstood the shaking the best, finding that reinforced concrete was by far superior. This survey led to revision of construction techniques so that reinforced concrete was used in future. And geologists from universities and the U.S. Geological Survey reaped so much data from the quake that they essentially created a new science—seismology.

Never before had so many cameras been on the spot to record events. A horde of photographers went out into the streets to detail the devastation and the firefighting, which included several attempts by the Army to blow up buildings in the path of the fire

MAP 352 (*above*).
A United States Geological Survey report on the earthquake and fire published in 1907 contained this map showing two main water conduits into the city and where they broke; the ruptures rendered them ineffective for firefighting purposes in the city.

MAP 353 (*right*).
The San Francisco chief engineer issued a report on 18 July 1906 with this map detailing the location of broken water service pipes; multiple breaks are shown as streets with black lines, whereas individual breaks are black dots. Over 23,200 breaks were counted. A marginal note indicates that some of the water line breaks were actually caused by the dynamiting of buildings.

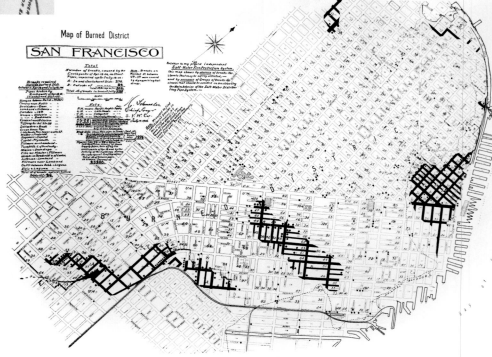

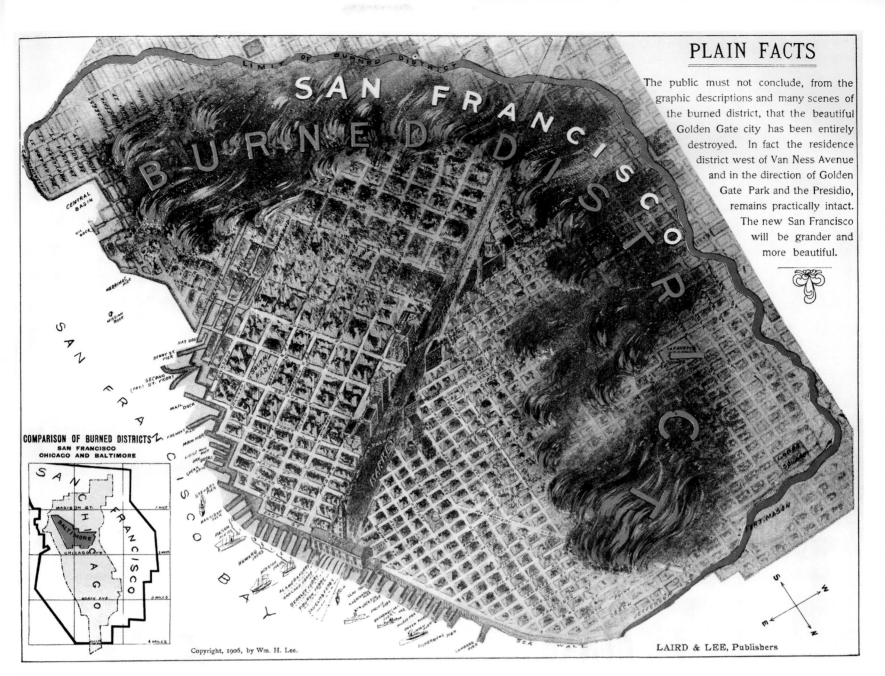

The public must not conclude, from the graphic descriptions and many scenes of the burned district, that the beautiful Golden Gate city has been entirely destroyed. In fact the residence district west of Van Ness Avenue and in the direction of Golden Gate Park and the Presidio, remains practically intact. The new San Francisco will be grander and more beautiful.

SAN FRANCISCO BURNED DISTRICT

COMPARISON OF BURNED DISTRICTS
SAN FRANCISCO
CHICAGO AND BALTIMORE

Copyright, 1906, by Wm. H. Lee.

LAIRD & LEE, Publishers

THE DOOMED CITY
BY
FRANK THOMPSON SEARIGHT

A THRILLING HISTORY
OF
SAN FRANCISCO'S DESTRUCTION
WITH ILLUSTRATIONS FROM
ORIGINAL PHOTOGRAPHS

Map 354 (*above*).
One of the most graphic maps to appear in the aftermath of the earthquake and fire was in a book by Frank Thompson Searight called *The Doomed City* (*left*). It illustrates very well how a map can be "jazzed up" for popular consumption, all in the name of selling books. Despite its immediate appeal, the map actually contains far less information than other maps such as those from government reports. The map does, however, offer an inset at bottom left showing the comparatively much smaller areas of other great fires, in Baltimore in 1904 and Chicago in 1871.

to create firebreaks. With and without photographs, hundreds of publications leapt from the presses of the nation to feed a voracious public appetite for information on the disaster; the American public at the time, of course, having no other source of information but that in print. Books were rushed into print with titles designed, tabloid-like, to attract purchasers. One such popular title was "a thrilling history" entitled *The Doomed City,* which included the dramatized map reproduced here (Map 354, *above*).

The earthquake and the fire together destroyed over 80 percent of San Francisco and was one of the worst natural disasters to hit the United States. But a city destroyed became a city reborn, a city remade. A plan advocated before the quake by famous early city planner and architect Daniel Burnham was resuscitated (see maps on page 188); what better time to create a modern city of grand boulevards and parks and civic buildings than when the city was in ruins and the canvas empty? Yet the overall plan was not implemented in the rush to rebuild, mainly because landowners did not want the city to expropriate their land, but many minor features

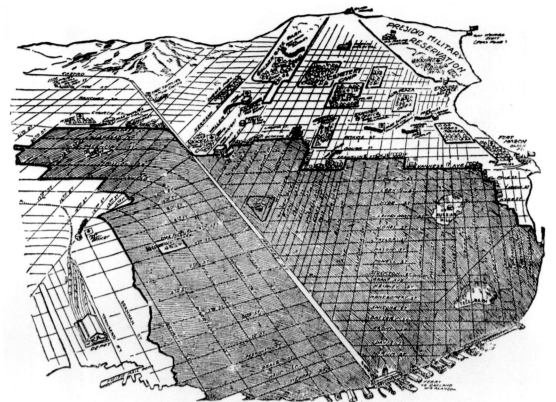

MAP OF SAN FRANCISCO SHOWING BURNED DISTRICT

MAP 355 (*left*).
Relief camps were set up almost immediately to house the stream of refugees from the fire. This seems to be the only map that illustrated their location, beyond the burned area, shown shaded gray. Golden Gate Park (top, center) and the Presidio (top, right) were two of the principal camps and are shown here complete with little tents and a Red Cross flag. The camp at the Presidio became a veritable city of wooden huts.

of the Burnham plan did see the light of day: the Embarcadero, a waterfront boulevard; the Coit Tower atop Telegraph Hill; a neoclassical civic center; and more arterial thoroughfares.

Reconstruction was swift. MAP 358 (*right*) shows the remarkable progress that had been made only two years later; by 1915 rebuilding was effectively complete, and the city hosted the Panama-Pacific International Exposition. Although ostensibly to celebrate the opening of the Panama Canal, the exposition was also a good opportunity to recognize the phoenix city of San Francisco's rise from the ashes.

Yet despite this success, San Francisco was never to be the same again. Until the fire, the city had been preeminent in the commercial life of California, but after, it lost ground to Los Angeles. In the thirty years between 1900 and 1930 San Francisco and the Bay Area more than doubled in size, but its rival to the south grew ten-fold.

MAP 356 (*above*).
Surveying requires the establishment of exact locations from which to begin triangulation (see page 106), and these are normally marked by survey monuments ranging from concrete or stone obelisks to brass markers flush with the ground. Remeasurement of these established points allowed scientists to plot the movement of the earth after both the 1868 Hayward earthquake and the 1906 San Francisco one. This map, published in 1907, shows the result.

MAP 357 (*right*).
This map of the distribution of apparent shaking of the ground was published in a 1908 atlas of maps and seismograms accompanying a report of the State Earthquake Investigation Commission. Its author was Andrew Lawson, a University of California geology professor who, more than any other individual, was responsible for establishing the new science of seismology. The degree of shaking varied depending on the nature of the ground; most damage occurred on loose silt and reclaimed land.

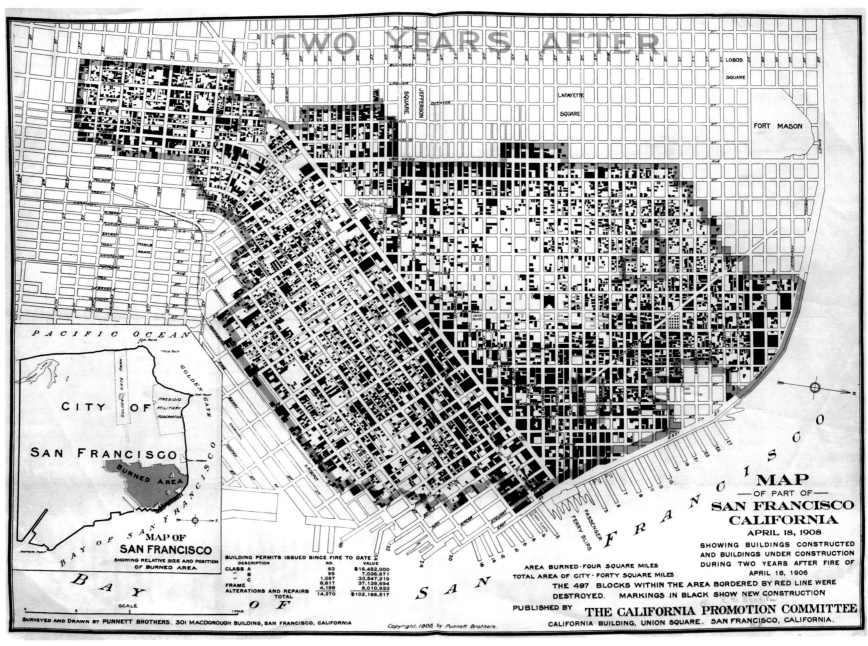

MAP
—OF PART OF—
SAN FRANCISCO
CALIFORNIA
APRIL 18, 1908

SHOWING BUILDINGS CONSTRUCTED
AND BUILDINGS UNDER CONSTRUCTION
DURING TWO YEARS AFTER FIRE OF
APRIL 18, 1906

THE 497 BLOCKS WITHIN THE AREA BORDERED BY RED LINE WERE
DESTROYED.   MARKINGS IN BLACK SHOW NEW CONSTRUCTION

PUBLISHED BY   THE CALIFORNIA PROMOTION COMMITTEE
CALIFORNIA BUILDING, UNION SQUARE, SAN FRANCISCO, CALIFORNIA.

AREA BURNED · FOUR SQUARE MILES
TOTAL AREA OF CITY · FORTY SQUARE MILES

| BUILDING PERMITS ISSUED SINCE FIRE TO DATE | | |
| --- | --- | --- |
| DESCRIPTION | NO. | VALUE |
| CLASS A | 63 | $16,452,000 |
| " B | 95 | 7,036,671 |
| " C | 1,097 | 33,547,219 |
| FRAME | 8,817 | 37,139,694 |
| ALTERATIONS AND REPAIRS | 4,198 | 8,010,933 |
| TOTAL | 14,270 | $102,186,517 |

MAP OF SAN FRANCISCO
SHOWING RELATIVE SIZE AND POSITION OF BURNED AREA

SURVEYED AND DRAWN BY PUNNETT BROTHERS, 301 MACDONOUGH BUILDING, SAN FRANCISCO, CALIFORNIA

Copyright, 1908, by Punnett Brothers.

## MAP 358 (*above*).

Although not to the Burnham plan, the speed of reconstruction was remarkable. This map was published by the "California Promotion Committee"—in reality a San Francisco promotion committee—to show the new buildings completed and under construction exactly two years after the 1906 earthquake and fire. A table giving the value of building permits is at bottom left, with an inset map that seems to try to minimize the burned area, a distinct contrast with some of the popular maps on these pages, which do precisely the opposite. The damage was minimized to attract new investment.

## MAP 359 (*left*).

Part of a proposal to ensure a similar tragedy not happen again: the new water mains and a proposed backup fire protection system.

## *Right.*

Boundless optimism seemed to mark San Francisco's rebound from the cataclysm. This "Resurrection Number" of the *New San Francisco Magazine* (the "New" referring to the city, not the magazine) shows the California bear growling at the—presumably American—eagle.

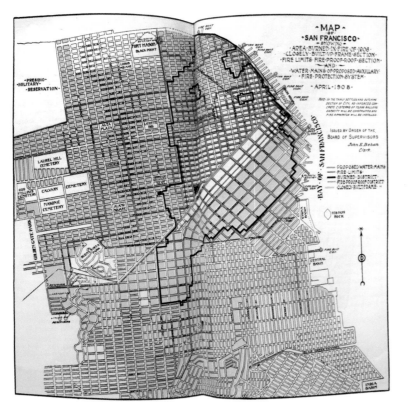

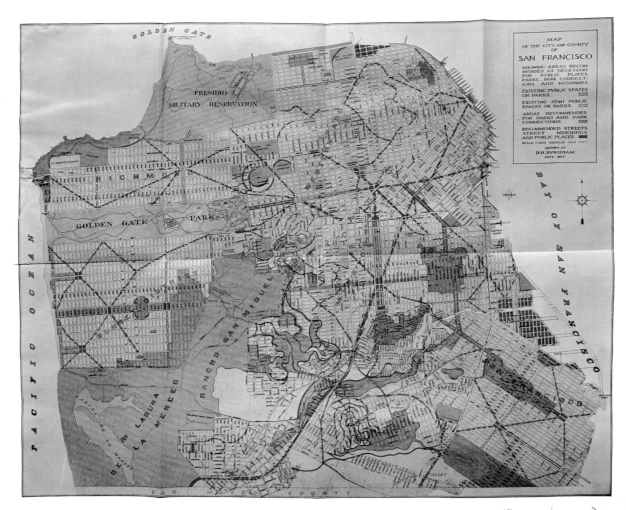

MAP 360 (*left*).
Daniel Burnham's proposal for the revamping of San Francisco, with boulevards, vistas, squares, and a coherent urban design. It was a great idea but before its time; the "city beautiful" movement, to which Burnham contributed, was only just beginning to register on the consciousness of civic officials and the public. A plan to move Chinatown away from the city center also failed, and the neighborhood was simply rebuilt in the form it was before, albeit with structurally superior buildings. The racially oppressed Chinese community actually benefited from the fire in one way: at the time Chinese persons were only allowed into the United States if they could prove an existing relative. With the destruction of City Hall and the Hall of Records by the fire, thousands of San Francisco resident relatives were claimed, allowing far more immigration than would otherwise likely have been possible.

MAP 361 (*below*) and MAP 362 (*below, bottom*).
From the Burnham plan, a bird's-eye-view map of the proposed boulevards for San Francisco and a more detailed bird's-eye view of the concept of grand boulevards.

MAP 363 (*right*).
The Burnham plan in its regional context; a map from the 1905 report.

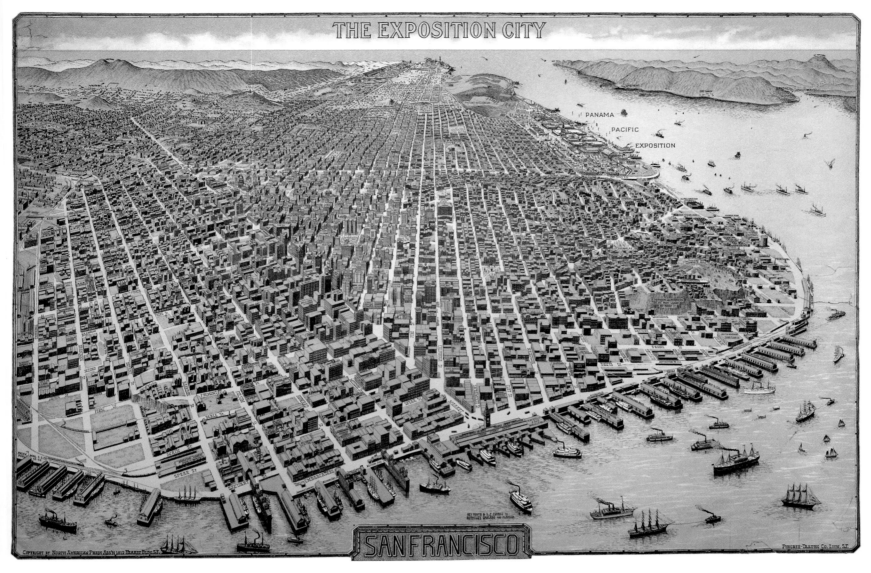

SAN FRANCISCO

**MAP 364** (*above*).
No evidence of the 1906 disaster is apparent on this stunning 1912 bird's-eye map of San Francisco—now touted as *The Exposition City*—published by the North American Press Association. The *Panama Pacific Exposition* is shown as it would be three years later on its site along the shore of the Golden Gate.

**MAP 365** (*left, bottom*).
In the same manner that cities bid for the Olympic Games today, several cities bid for the Panama-Pacific International Exposition that was held in 1915. San Diego even held a rival exposition when it did not win the official one. In the typical racist tone of the day, this map was included in a document advocating San Francisco as the venue. A railroad-sponsored map advertising the exposition is shown as MAP 233, *page 126.*

*Below.*
San Francisco fog was an ideal medium for the playing of lights—modern *electric* lights—into the night sky of the Panama-Pacific International Exposition. At left is a 435-foot-high "Tower of Jewels" covered with pieces of cut glass. A celebration of the opening of the Panama Canal was widely perceived as a celebration of the recovery of San Francisco.

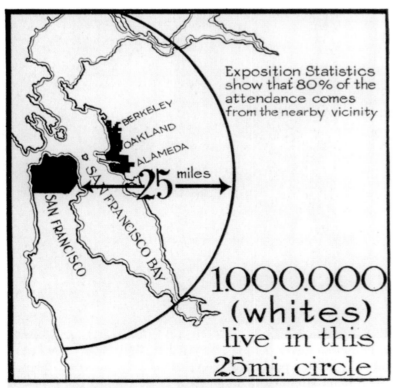

Exposition Statistics show that 80% of the attendance comes from the nearby vicinity

BERKELEY
OAKLAND
ALAMEDA

25 miles

SAN FRANCISCO

SAN FRANCISCO BAY

1,000,000 (whites) live in this 25mi. circle

Attendance is what makes an Exposition a financial success

# WILDNESS FOR THE PEOPLE

It did not take long after California became an American state for tourists to discover the wonders of the High Sierra despite the region's inaccessibility. When the first photographs of the Yosemite Valley were produced in 1859 many more could see for themselves that the arduous trip would prove worthwhile.

Commercial interest nevertheless threatened the valley, especially logging of the sequoia (which was later found not to be worthwhile due to the splintering quality of the wood, unlike the coast redwood) and overgrazing, especially by sheep. In 1864 Abraham Lincoln signed a bill protecting the Yosemite Valley and the Mariposa Grove of big sequoias, conveying it to California as a state park. This action preceded the establishment of the first national park, Yellowstone, eight years later (where the federal government had to take responsibility since the area was not in a state). The original Yosemite Grant, the state park, is shown in MAP 366, *below*.

Of particular concern was the preservation of the "big trees." California's first true national park was created in September 1890.

This was the Sequoia National Park, which protected the area around the 2,200-year-old General Sherman Tree, at 275 feet high and 36½ feet in base diameter considered the world's largest living organism. A month later the smaller General Grant National Park was created just to the north, again to protect a grove of big trees. The same bill also created the Yosemite National Park (MAP 369, *overleaf*) around, but not including, the original Yosemite Grant.

In 1892, famous preservationist-naturalist John Muir founded the Sierra Club and became its president. The club's primary objective was to protect the new Yosemite park, and its first public action was to defeat a proposal to once again reduce the park's boundaries.

Muir and the Sierra Club lobbied the federal government to include the state's Yosemite Grant as part of the national park, as the state was not controlling grazing. In 1903 Muir camped in the park with president Theodore Roosevelt, taking the opportunity to convince him of the wisdom of this move. Three years later Roosevelt signed a bill making Yosemite a single national park.

Sequoia, Yosemite, and General Grant national parks were managed by the Army until 1916, when the National Park Service was created.

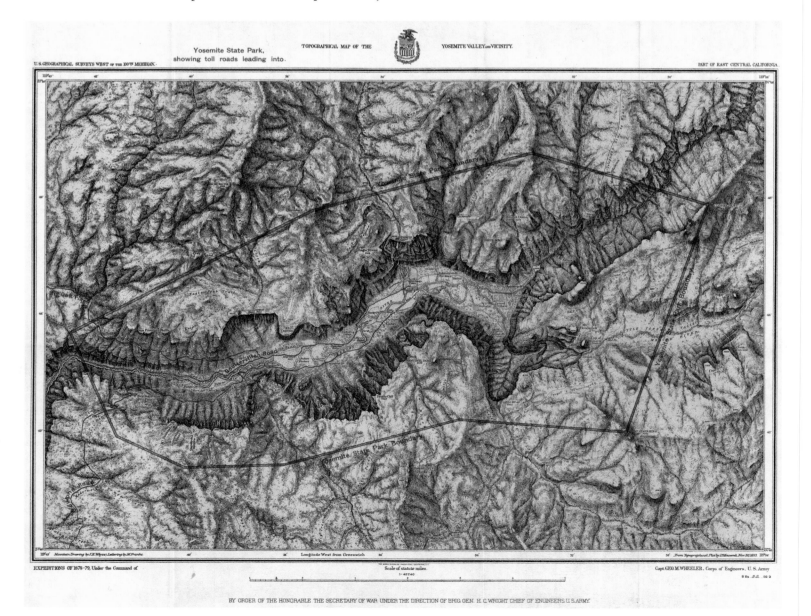

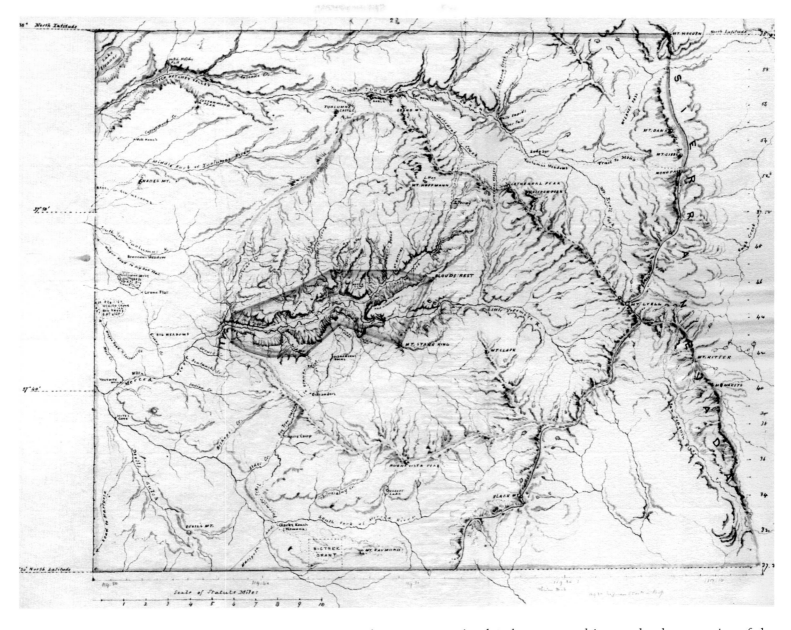

Kings Canyon National Park was created in 1940 by the expansion of the smaller General Grant National Park. Sequoia and Kings Canyon are adjacent and are managed as a single park. California's Sierra national parks now cover an area of over 2,500 square miles and are visited by almost five million people each year.

MAP 366 (*left*).
*Yosemite State Park Boundary* (the red line) defines the extent of the Yosemite Grant on this 1883 map from the surveys of Lieutenant George Wheeler.

MAP 367 (*above*).
John Muir drew this map in 1890 showing his proposal for the boundaries of an expanded federally controlled park. The actual boundaries established that year closely followed his recommendations (MAP 369, *overleaf*).

MAP 368 (*right*).
The *Eighth Annual Report of the U.S. Geological Survey* published in 1889 contained this nicely engraved map of the Lyell Glacier and the much smaller McClure Glacier, on the northeast slope of Mt. Lyell at the southeast edge of Yosemite National Park. Needless to say, the size of the glacier is today much reduced, but it is still the second largest in the Sierra. At 13,114 feet, Mt. Lyell is the highest mountain in Yosemite.

*Above, left.*
The artistic cover of *The Yosemite,* the book John Muir wrote about the national park he helped create. The book was published in 1912.

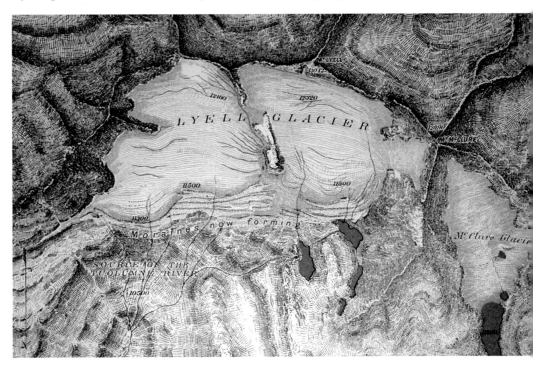

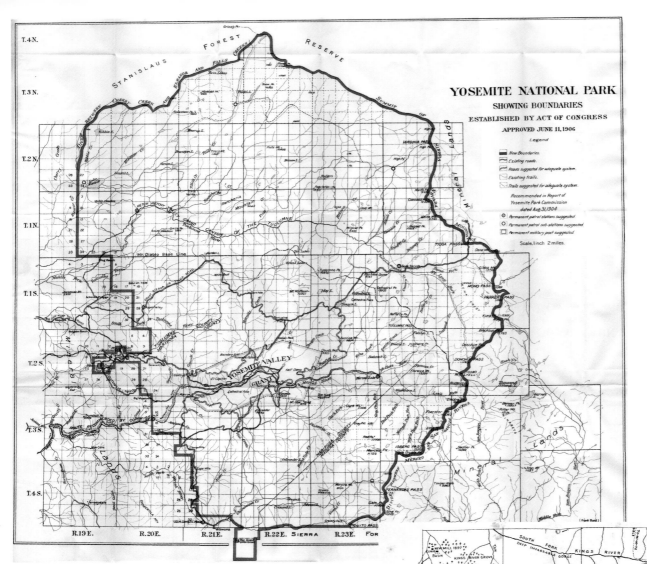

YOSEMITE NATIONAL PARK
SHOWING BOUNDARIES
ESTABLISHED BY ACT OF CONGRESS
APPROVED JUNE 11, 1906

Legend

☐ New Boundaries.
☐ Existing roads.
☐ Roads suggested for adequate system.
☐ Existing trails.
☐ Trails suggested for adequate system.

Recommended in Report of
Yosemite Park Commission
dated Aug. 31, 1904
⊙ Permanent patrol stations suggested
○ Permanent patrol sub-stations suggested
☐ Permanent military post suggested

Scale, 1 inch 2 miles.

MAP 369 (*left*).
Yosemite National Park in 1906. The red line shows the park boundaries as they were adjusted slightly in that year from the 1890 boundaries, the original expansion from the grant, which included only the Yosemite Valley (MAP 366, *previous page*). The 1890 boundaries were more rectilinear, and thus less sensitive to the realities of the topography.

MAP 372 (*right*).
Famous California artist and mapmaker Jo Mora drew this pictorial bird's-eye map—or "carte," as he and collectors preferred to call it—of the Yosemite Valley, published in 1931. A color version of this map was produced ten years later. Jo Mora died in 1947; subsequent modifications were made to the map by others in Mora's style to reflect changes in the national park.

MAP 370 (*right*).
This map was attached to the *Report of the Acting Superintendent of Sequoia and General Grant National Parks, California*, dated 15 October 1903. The acting superintendent at the time was one Captain Charles Young of the Ninth Cavalry, which was based at the Presidio of San Francisco. One of the recommendations in the report was "the purchase as soon as possible of all the private lands in the General Grant and Sequoia National Parks." The report also stated that "it does not seem advisable to further extend the system of roads and trails until the purchase of the private lands is completed."

MAP 371 (*below*).
General Grant National Park as depicted on a 1927 U.S. Geological Survey topographic map. The park was created in 1890 and absorbed into the larger Kings Canyon National Park in 1940.

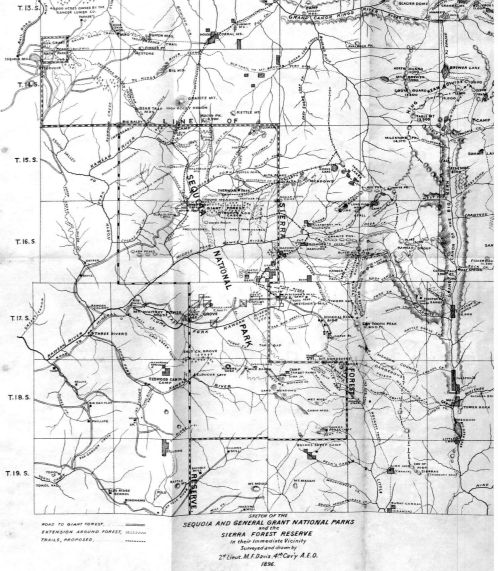

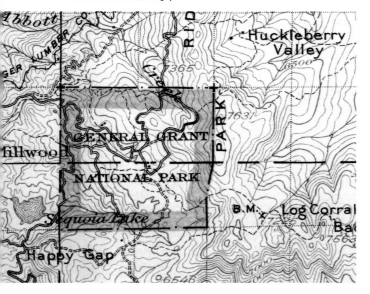

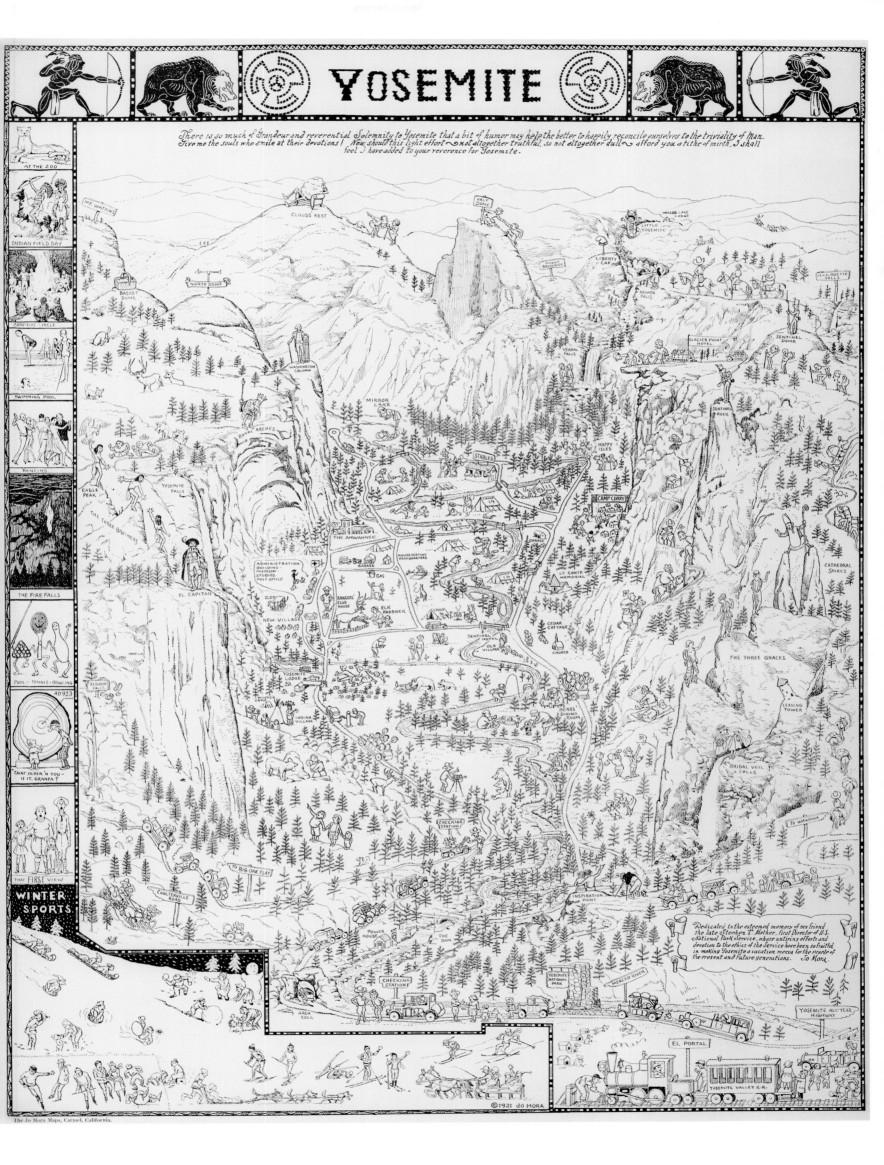

# BRINGING WATER TO THE CITIES

MAP 374 (*right*).
A map of the entire Los Angeles Aqueduct, then under construction, produced by the Los Angeles Department of Water and Power in 1908. The water supply line, shown in red, originates at the Long Valley Reservoir (at top), and bypasses Owens Lake for the Haiwee Reservoir, which is higher than Owens Lake. The latter, now dry, has been the subject of recent attempts at rehabiliation.

MAP 375 (*far right*).
This unusual photomosiac map of the line of the Los Angeles Aqueduct appeared in the *Construction of the Los Angeles Aqueduct Final Report* published by the City of Los Angeles in 1916. It is oriented similarly to MAP 374 and may be compared to that map to identify features.

*Above.* Watched by thousands of excited Angelenos, water from Owens Lake emerges from Tunnel No. 108 and plunges down the "aerating cascade" into the San Fernando Valley on 5 November 1913.

MAP 373 (*below*).
The California Geological Survey map dated 1873 shows Owens Lake and its valley as it was long before Los Angeles became interested in its water. The map also shows Mt. Whitney, named for Josiah Whitney (see page 128).

It was inevitable that once cities like San Francisco, Los Angeles, and San Diego began to grow substantially, they would run out of water, for San Francisco has hardly any river catchment area to call its own, and Los Angeles and San Diego are in the more arid south. Early on civic leaders began to cast their eyes farther afield in search of sources of water, and when at the end of the nineteenth century the technology became available in the form of electrical pumps, long, interregional conduits could be considered without the constraint that the water would have to flow downhill all the time. Also necessary were reservoirs, to enable seasonal variations in supply to be evened out.

In Los Angeles, the legendary William Mulholland was the visionary engineer who convinced the city fathers that it was feasible to pipe water from the Owens Valley, 220 miles to the north. Owens Lake was in an interior enclosed basin, and a start had been made on a federally funded irrigation system for local farmers. Fred Eaton, mayor of Los Angeles from 1898 to 1900, in cahoots with the federal reclamation agent, Joseph B. Lippincott (see MAP 261, *page 140*), bought up large tracts of land that he was able to resell to the city along with their water rights. The trio were responsible for making the Los Angeles Aqueduct politically, financially, and technically feasible. Ultimately it was a battle between the concept of the greatest good for the greatest number—the urban residents of Los Angeles—and the rights of minorities—the farmers of the Owens Valley, who never really had a chance; Eaton persuaded President Theodore Roosevelt to cancel the Owens Valley irrigation system.

The voters of Los Angeles approved the issuance of a $23 million bond in 1907, and construction began on the aqueduct in 1908. Some 100,000 workers were employed fabricating, excavating, and laying the 223-mile long, 12-foot-diameter steel pipe, two hydroelectric plants, and 170 miles of power lines. As the work progressed, a railroad was built to transport men and materials, and 215 miles of roads were also constructed. The aqueduct was completed in 1913 with the release of the first water from Owens Lake into the San Fernando Valley (*photo, top, left*).

Capacity was increased in 1940 when the aqueduct was extended forty miles north into the Mono Lake water system. In 1970 construction was completed on a second Los Angeles

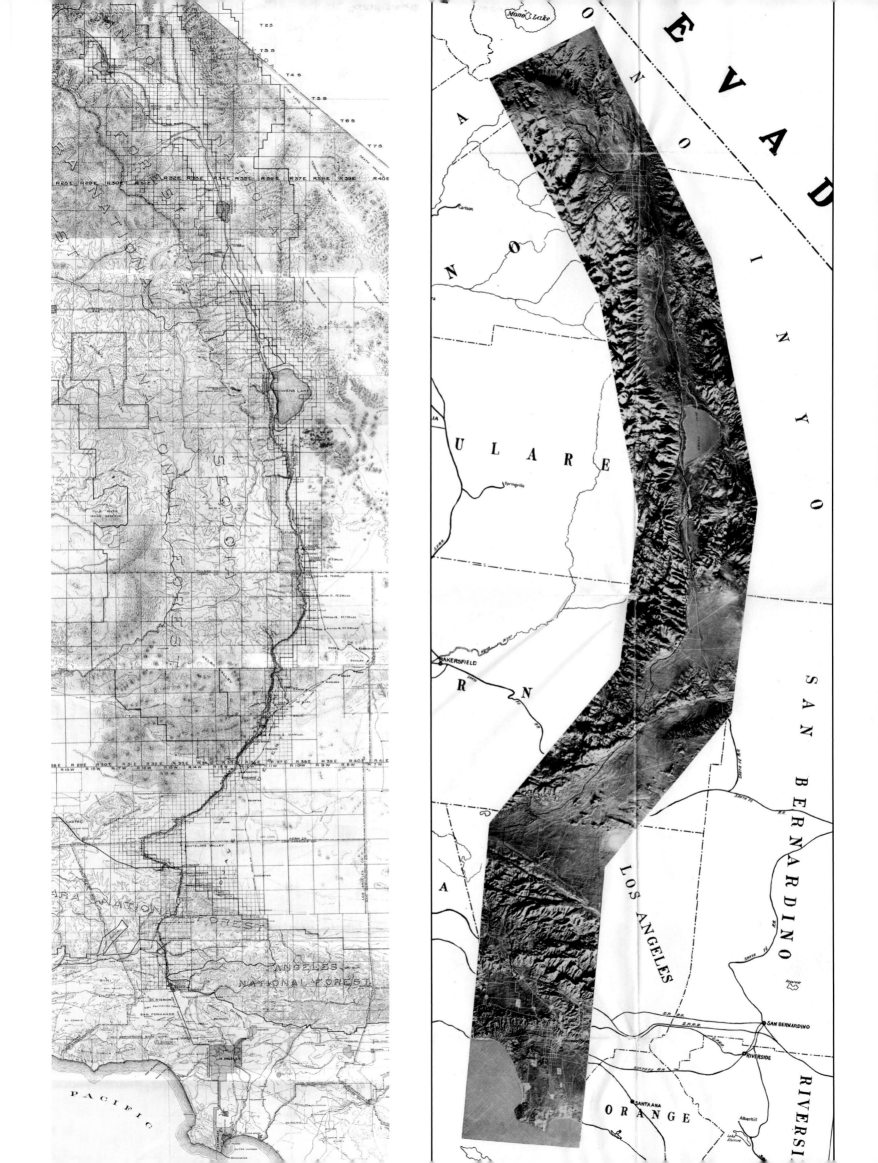

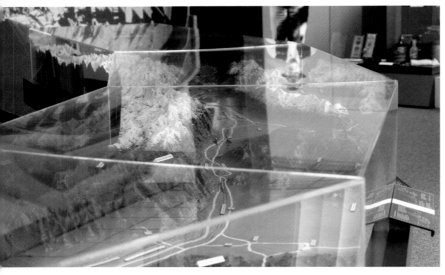

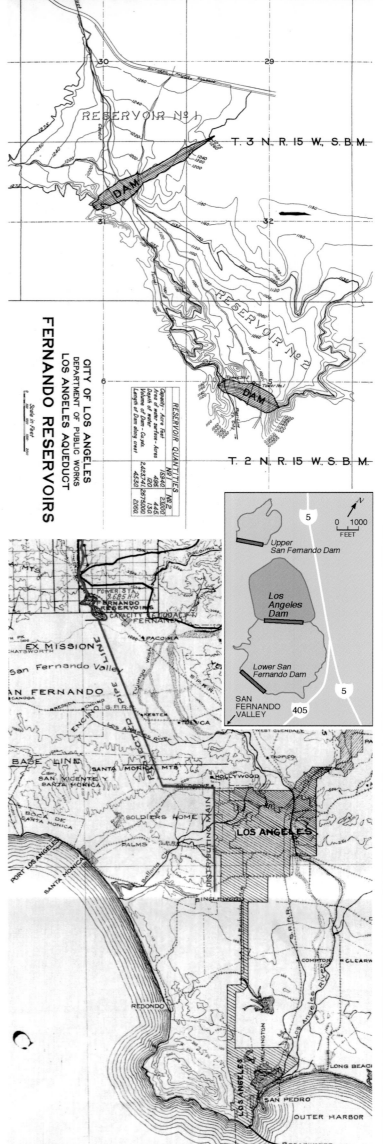

CITY OF LOS ANGELES
DEPARTMENT OF PUBLIC WORKS
LOS ANGELES AQUEDUCT

# FERNANDO RESERVOIRS

Scale in Feet

| RESERVOIR QUANTITIES | | |
|---|---|---|
| | № 1 | № 2 |
| Capacity - Acre Feet | 15840 | 24000 |
| Area of water surface - Acres | 495 | 445 |
| Depth of water | 120 | 130 |
| Volume of Dam - Cu.yds. | 2423741 | 2675000 |
| Length of Dam along crest | 4530 | 2060 |

**Map 376** (*above, both photos*).
Not content with a mere photomosaic, Mulholland had his employees construct this relief map of the route of the Los Angeles Aqueduct, now on display at the Los Angeles Department of Water and Power. Unfortunately the map has been permanently sealed in an acrylic case that makes it next to impossible to photograph properly.

Aqueduct, which ran on a similar line to the first and doubled the water capacity. The aqueduct still provides some 60 percent of the water supply of Los Angeles.

William Mulholland, who had never been formally trained as an engineer and had been hired initially to work as a ditchdigger for the water department, is today lauded for his vision and skill, but for many years his reputation suffered because of the 1928 collapse of a dam he designed, the St. Francis Dam in San Francisquito Canyon just to the north of Santa Clarita (Map 380 and Map 381, *far right*). It has been more recently determined, however, that Mulholland was not to blame for the dam's collapse because it was caused by failure of an old landslide on the dam's eastern edge, a landslide that would have been impossible to detect with 1920s technology. A similar catastrophe was narrowly averted in 1971 when the Lower San Fernando Dam partially failed during an earthquake (Map 377, Map 378, and Map 379, *right*); fortunately there was enough time for the evacuation of the downstream area and the rapid reduction in the level of water in the reservoir.

Early San Francisco's water was supplied by the Spring Valley Water Company, formed in 1858. The company purchased water

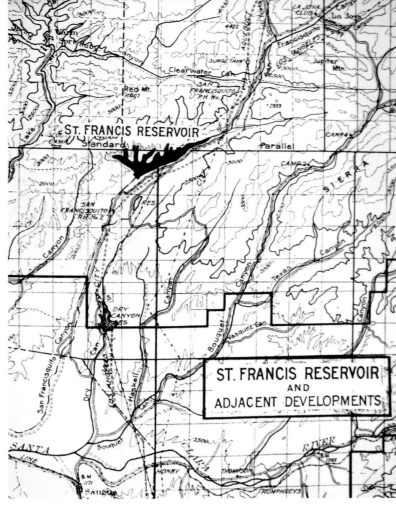

**Map 377** (*left, top*).
The San Fernando Reservoirs were the end point of the Los Angeles Aqueduct, and from the lower dam distribution pipes spread out across the city. This is the map from the 1916 report on the aqueduct. The Lower San Fernando Dam failed during the 1971 San Fernando earthquake when the top 30 feet of the earth-fill collapsed downward, leaving only a thin earth wall between 15 million tons of water and 80,000 people downstream.

**Map 378** (*left, center, inset*).
After analyzing records from the 1971 earthquake, engineers realized that shaking near the epicenter—which was near the dam in this case—was much stronger than previously allowed for in structural designs. A new dam, called the Los Angeles Dam, was built in 1975–76 between the original upper and lower San Fernando dams. The new dam was about three times stronger than the old ones. The old dams were left in place as water retention basins only. The 1994 Northridge earthquake tested the new dam, and it passed with flying colors. Designed to withstand severe shaking, it suffered only a few surface cracks. The map shown is a modern U.S.G.S. map.

**Map 379** (*left, bottom*).
The position of the San Fernando dams in relation to Los Angeles is shown on this 1908 map, an enlarged detail of **Map 374**, *page 195*.

**Map 380** (*above right*) and **Map 381** (*below*).
Between 1924 and 1926, the St. Francis Dam was constructed in San Francisquito Canyon, north of Saugus, to create an additional reservoir for water from the Los Angeles Aqueduct, which ran through the canyon. During construction Mulholland twice had the height of the dam raised above its original design height. Two leading geologists had examined the site and found it sound, but unknown to them and to Mulholland (and in fact impossible to detect given the state of technology in the 1920s), the eastern flank of the dam had been attached to an ancient rockslide. Just before midnight on 12 March 1928 the dam collapsed, sending a wall of water, said to have been 78 feet high, downstream, destroying everything in its path and leaving a 70-foot-deep layer of mud and debris in many places. More than 500 people were killed. These two maps, showing the location of the dam and its detailed position in the canyon, are from a report to the governor of California ordered after the disaster.

The photo, *above left*, shows all that was left of the dam the day after its collapse.

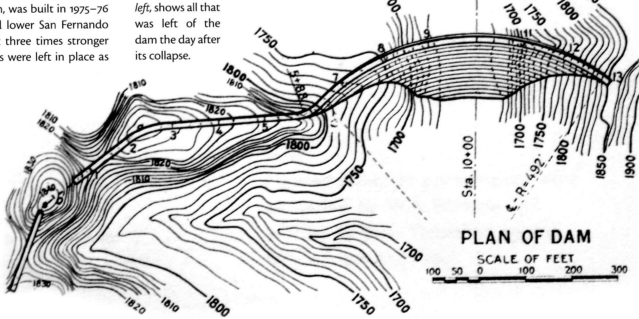

PLAN OF DAM

SCALE OF FEET

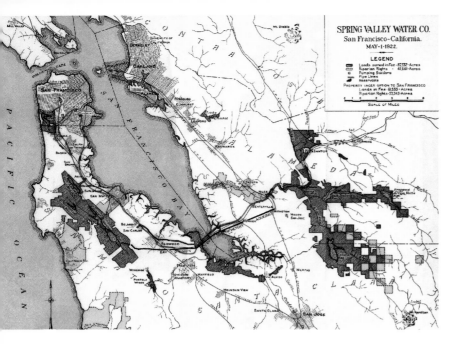

Map 382 (above).
The water supply system of the Spring Valley Water Company in 1922. The red lines are the pipelines serving San Francisco from the East Bay. The *Sunol Water Temple* is marked just to the right of *Niles*. Company-owned land is red, water rights land, yellow. San Francisco purchased the company outright in 1930. To the south of the water temple the *Calaveras Res.[ervoir]* is shown. Formed by the largest earth-fill dam in the world, it was completed in 1925, three years after its appearance on this map.

Map 383 (below).
The proposed line of the Hetch Hetchy Aqueduct, from a 1915 report.

rights in a number of local areas, including the East Bay, and in 1910 completed the well-known Sunol "Water Temple" atop the junction of several water lines just south of Pleasanton (Map 382, *above*). Many had blamed the company for not being able to provide the water necessary to deal with the great fire of 1906. San Francisco purchased the company in 1930.

San Francisco's engineers had long realized that water for the city would eventually have to be found further afield. The first scheme, an idea floated in 1864, appears to have been to pipe water from Lake Tahoe, and indeed its promoters listed the ability to deal with a large fire as one of its virtues. San Francisco mayor James D. Phelan had in 1901 made an application to the federal Department of the Interior, under whose jurisdiction the valley fell, to dam the Hetch Hetchy Valley in Yosemite National Park. He had been refused. In the aftermath of the fire, San Francisco applied again and set off a multi-year fight with John Muir and the Sierra Club. Muir fought tooth and nail. "Dam Hetch Hetchy! As well dam for water-tanks the people's cathedrals and churches," famously exclaimed Muir, "for no holier temple has ever been consecrated by the heart of man."

But Muir's campaign was to no avail. The promise of higher land values defeated him, and the voters approved a bond issue in 1910. The federal government granted San Francisco the water rights to the valley in 1913, passing the Raker Act, which provided that no private profit was to be allowed. The dam was completed in 1923, named for Michael M. O'Shaughnessy, the chief engineer of the city who was responsible for the project and who had been appointed in 1912 by the then newly elected and popular James Rolph Jr., who became the longest-serving mayor of San Francisco (1912–31).

It was not until 1934, however, that the first Sierra water was delivered by the 167-mile-long Hetch Hetchy Aqueduct to San Francisco, such had been delays, cost overruns, and necessary refinancings. The East Bay cities had in the meantime become fed up with waiting and constructed their own Mokelumne Aqueduct to that river, north of the Tuolumne and well clear of the national park.

By this time Los Angeles was again in the process of obtaining more water. In 1923 Mulholland devised a plan to bring water no

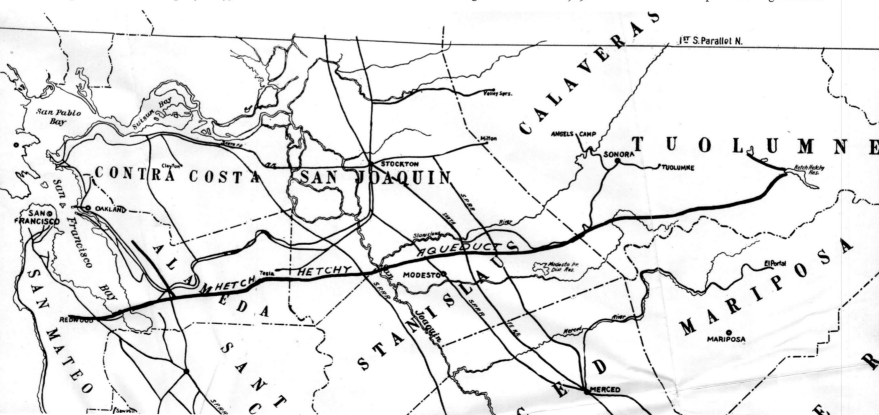

**Map 384** (*above*).
An excellent bird's-eye map of the Hetch Hetchy Aqueduct, then under construction, from a 1930 brochure explaining the project to the public.

**Map 385** (*below*).
This 1910 map shows the proposed locations of the Hetch Hetchy reservoir site in the Grand Canyon of the Tuolumne River in Yosemite National Park, and also the site of Lake Eleanor, a subsidiary reservoir also connected to the Hetch Hetchy Aqueduct. The shaded areas are land owned by San Francisco at the time. The thick red line is the boundary of the national park. The map formed part of a submission by the city to the federal Department of the Interior in February 1910.

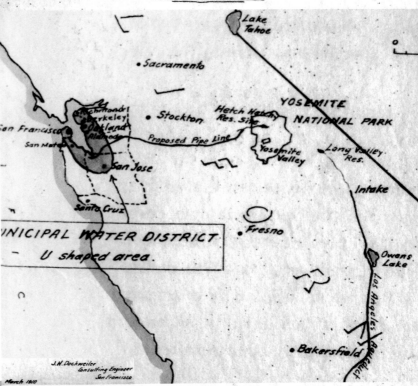

**Map 386** (*above*).
The line of the Hetch Hetchy Aqueduct to a proposed Municipal Water District encompassing all the San Francisco Bay municipalities is shown on this 1910 map. It also shows the boundary of Yosemite National Park and the northern part of the Los Angeles Aqueduct, then under construction. Partly because of opposition from conservationists including John Muir and the Sierra Club, San Francisco would take a lot longer to complete its project than Los Angeles had. The O'Shaughnessy Dam for the Hetch Hetchy Reservoir was not completed until 1923, and the first water did not reach the city until 1934.

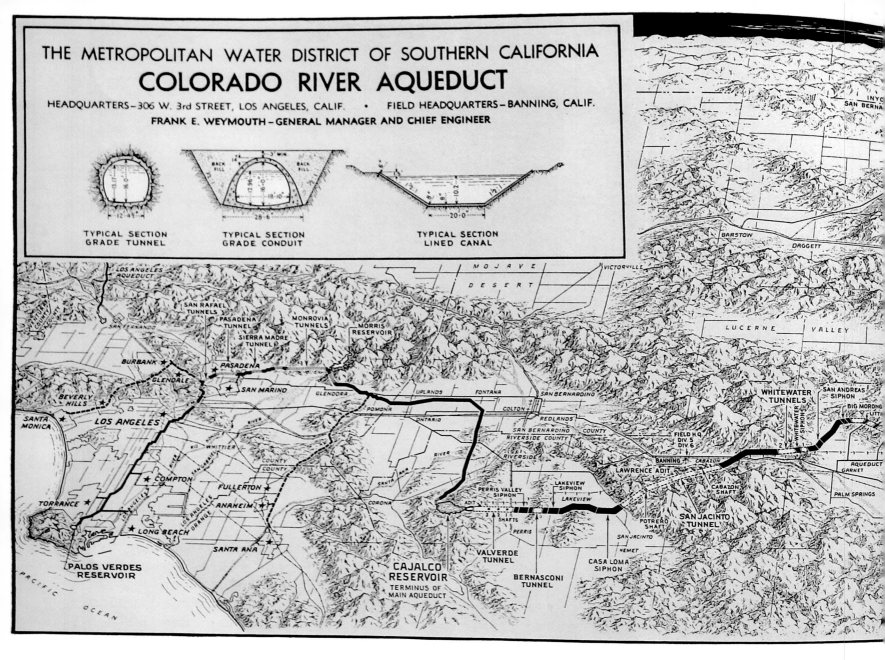

THE METROPOLITAN WATER DISTRICT OF SOUTHERN CALIFORNIA
# COLORADO RIVER AQUEDUCT
HEADQUARTERS—306 W. 3rd STREET, LOS ANGELES, CALIF. • FIELD HEADQUARTERS—BANNING, CALIF.
FRANK E. WEYMOUTH—GENERAL MANAGER AND CHIEF ENGINEER

TYPICAL SECTION GRADE TUNNEL • TYPICAL SECTION GRADE CONDUIT • TYPICAL SECTION LINED CANAL

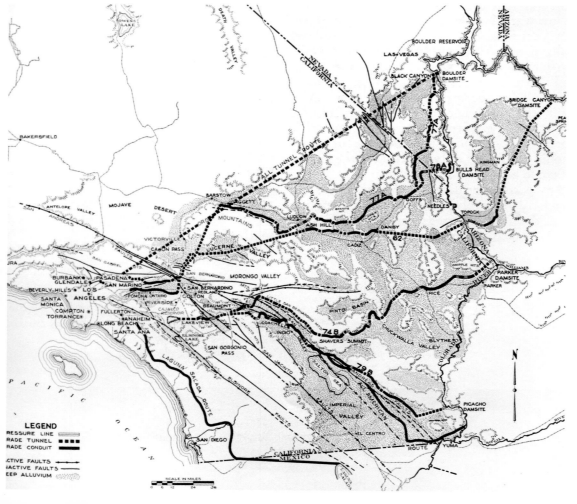

less than 270 miles from the Colorado River. After considering a number of possible routings (MAP 388, *left*), and making models of the topography to be crossed (MAP 390, *overleaf*), Mulholland determined that the most practicable route was from the great bend of the Colorado fifteen miles north of Parker, Arizona. From here the water would be pumped in tunnels over the initial high ground to enjoy a gravity flow until it was pumped up once more over mountains, a procedure repeated several times. MAP 387, *above,* shows the entire route of the aqueduct and gives a good idea of the technical difficulty of the route.

During the planning it became clear that the costs would exceed what Los Angeles could itself afford, and other cities naturally wanted what they saw as their share of Colorado water, so the Metropolitan Water District of Southern California was created

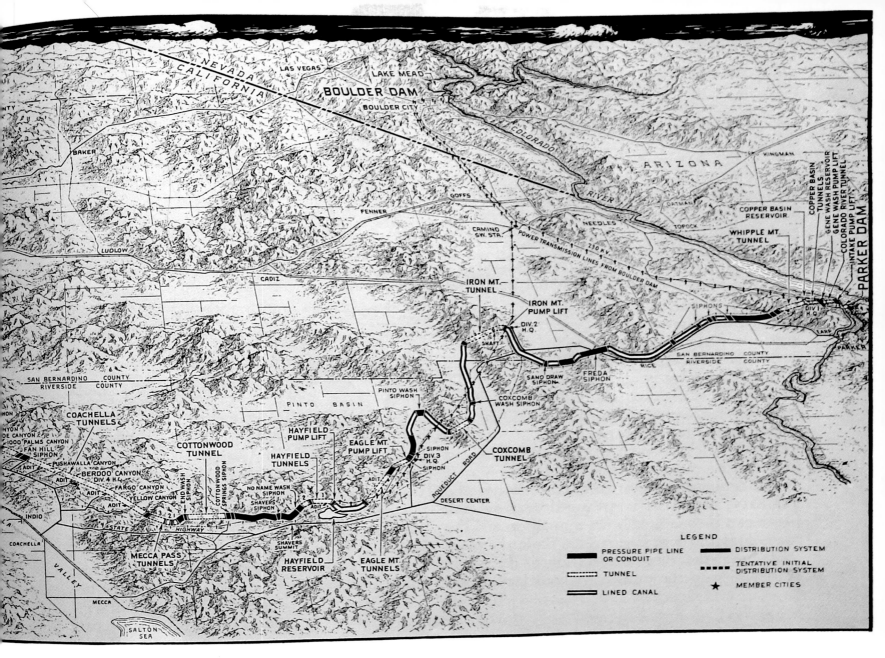

MAP 387 (*above*).
A superb bird's-eye map of the Colorado Aqueduct, from the 1939 report of the Metropolitan Water District.

MAP 388 (*left*).
From the same report came this map showing all the alternative routings for the aqueduct that had been considered, including one, the Lagunas-Salada Route, that would have extended the Alamo Canal, which passed through Mexico and was itself superseded by the All-American Canal to the Imperial Valley (see page 140). Even an extension of the All-American had been considered.

MAP 389 (*right*).
The general construction plan for the Parker Dam, which created Lake Havasu, from which the Colorado Aqueduct begins.

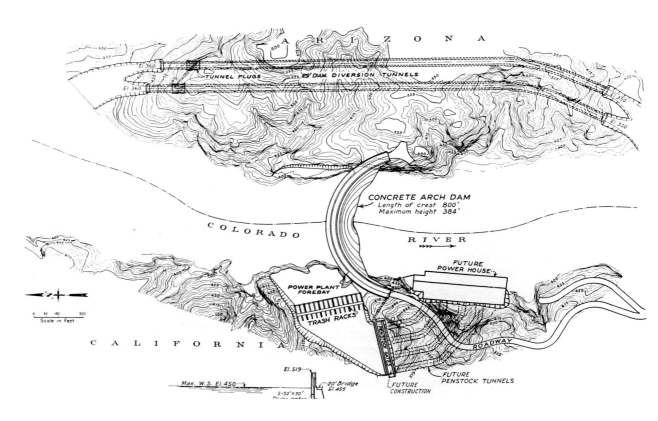

MAP 390 (*above*).

This map-scale model was used to plan the route of the Colorado Aqueduct. The section shown is from the Colorado River west to Eagle Mountain (for reference to locations see MAP 387, *previous page*). Successive layers cut around the contours create relief. *ABCD* is the Colorado. The Parker Dam is at *B*. The diversion is made at *E*, two miles above the dam, by a pump lift of 291 feet to Gene Wash Reservoir, and then another 303 feet to Copper Basin Reservoir; both are shown in white just to the left of *E*. From *E* to *F* the aqueduct is in a tunnel, but beyond *F* the aqueduct is on the surface.

The pumped height was determined by the height of saddles *G* and *H*. Another pump is at Iron Mountain, at *I*, and Iron Mountain Tunnel runs from *I* to *J*. *J* is a further high point and determined the pump height at *I* (144 feet). A fourth pumping plant, at Eagle Mountain, at *L*, lifts water 438 feet. The model illllustrates why the diversion point was at *E* rather than a nearer point on the river such as *C* or *D*: the line as constructed allows much longer distance to be covered along the contours. The model also illustrates why planning such a project might be expected to take many years.

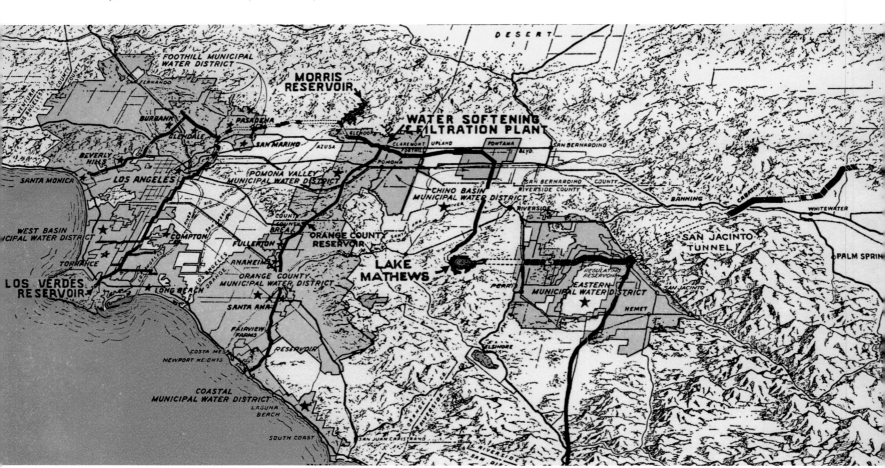

MAP 392 (*above*).
The southern part of the San Diego Aqueduct, an extension of the Colorado Aqueduct completed in 1947. This map is from the 1953 report of the Metropolitan Water District of Southern California.

in 1929; it ensured that the Colorado Aqueduct would supply water to most of urban southern California.

The Boulder Dam, after 1947 known as the Hoover Dam, was constructed between 1931 and 1936, and the secondary Parker Dam was completed in 1938, creating Lake Havasu behind it. Construction of the Colorado Aqueduct, which begins two miles north of the Parker Dam, began in 1933 and was completed, with a delivery of water to Pasadena, in June 1941.

Before his death in 1935, Mulholland lived to see construction of his idea begin. Today, because of the research that showed the collapse of the St. Francis Dam not to be a result of any negligence on his part, his reputation has been somewhat rehabilitated, and the Los Angeles Department of Water and Power refers to him in their publications as the builder of the Los Angeles Aqueduct and the father of the Colorado Aqueduct.

The latter aqueduct consists of 92 miles of tunnels; 84 miles of buried conduit and siphons (which carry water across intervening valleys); 63 miles of canals; 5 pumping plants; and 2 reservoirs. The aqueduct is credited with making possible the industrial growth that occurred in the Los Angeles basin during and after World War II.

In 1944 the explosive growth of San Diego, as a Pacific harbor critical to the war effort, led to water shortages, and authorization was given for the emergency extension of the aqueduct to San Diego from a point near Hemet. The San Diego Aqueduct was completed in 1947 with the first release of water from the regulating San Jacinto Reservoir.

Further water for cities now comes from the State Water Project, built in the 1960s and early 1970s. The 444-mile-long California Aqueduct, the main line of which was completed in 1972, brings water from north to south. Only about 20 percent of this water is supplied to urban areas, with the rest going to agriculture (see page 139).

MAP 391 (*left*).
The water distribution system had expanded but, alas, the standard of cartography had declined by 1953, the date this map appeared in a Metropolitan Water District of Southern California annual report. The line to the south is the San Diego Aqueduct.

MAP 393 (*below*).
The small San Jacinto Reservoir is at the top of this 1953 map; it regulates the flow of water to San Diego. Also at the top is Lake Mathews, the western terminus of the Colorado Aqueduct.

*Above* is a view of the San Diego Aqueduct.

# FROM BIKE PATHS TO FREEWAYS

It seems almost unbelievable now, but in the closing decades of the nineteenth century a near social revolution was wrought by the lowly bicycle. Technological innovations, especially the pneumatic tire, patented by John Boyd Dunlop in 1888, had by 1890 resulted in a universally rideable bicycle not unlike the modern machine.

In April 1884 Thomas Stevens set off from San Francisco and arrived in Boston four months later, having become the first transcontinental bicyclist. Two years later he arrived back in San Francisco having circumnavigated the world. Clearly here was a new mobility machine to be reckoned with.

In 1894, during a railroad strike, an enterprising merchant in Fresno set up a bicycle messenger service between that city and San Francisco. Relays of six or seven riders went back and forth, Pony Express–style. This was perhaps the first example of rails being usurped by the road; there would be many more to come.

The bicycle has been credited with a major advance in the emancipation of women as thousands threw out their bustles and corsets and took to the road. And the rise of the bicycle's popularity led to a demand for paved roads that was easily transferred to the new automobilists when cars began to appear on California's roads at the beginning of the twentieth century.

The automobile, unlike the bicycle, initially required a significant investment to purchase and considerably more technical expertise to run. Nevertheless, its sheer convenience, especially once Henry Ford started mass-producing his cars for everyman, ensured its success. The Ford Motor Company was established in 1903, and the Model T was introduced five years later, with a price of $825. By 1916, after the introduction of assembly lines in 1913, the price had dropped to $325. The era of mass automobile transportation was under way.

In 1896 the state legislature created the Department of Highways, which began to designate state highways. The first was the Lake Tahoe wagon road. Automobile owners soon grouped together to lobby for better roads. Both the Automobile Club of California, in San Francisco, and the Automobile Club of Southern California were created in

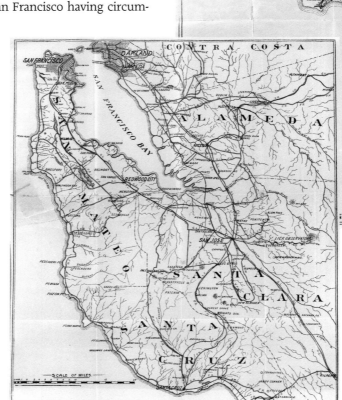

MAP 394 (*above*) and
MAP 395 (*left*).
These two maps, published in 1896, depict recommended bicycle routes around Los Angeles and the Bay Area. Many of these routes are not paved but merely considered by the publisher to be the least rutted and thus most rideable for bicycles.

MAP 396 (*right*).
Serving the bicyclist market was big business in its day, as this elaborately produced map—complete with marginal advertisements—attests. Even hotels were offering special rates to bicyclists, and a riding school can teach you how to cycle. The roads shown here are classified as good to very poor, and their grades, very significant for cyclists, are shown from level to mountainous. The map was published in 1895, at the height of the bicycle craze.

*Below.*
Modern freeway driving, the way it was meant to be. This is Interstate 80 between Vallejo and Fairfield.

## MAP OF CALIFORNIA ROADS FOR CYCLERS

**EXPLANATORY**

| | |
|---|---|
| ——— | RAILROADS |
| ——— | RAILROADS PROPOSED |
| ——— | BICYCLE ROADS |

Condition
G......GOOD
F......FAIR
P......POOR
V.P....VERY POOR

Grade
L......LEVEL
R......ROLLING
H......HILLY
M......MOUNTAINOUS

Endorsed by Geo. H. Strong.
(Rep. Consul-L.A.W. 1893)
H.F. Wynne
Pres. Cal. Cycling Club 1895.
Published and Copyrighted by
Geo. W. Blum
San Francisco Cal.

SCALE OF MILES

This Map Engraved by the CALIFORNIA PHOTO-ENG. CO. Wasp Bldg. 513 Market St. S.F.

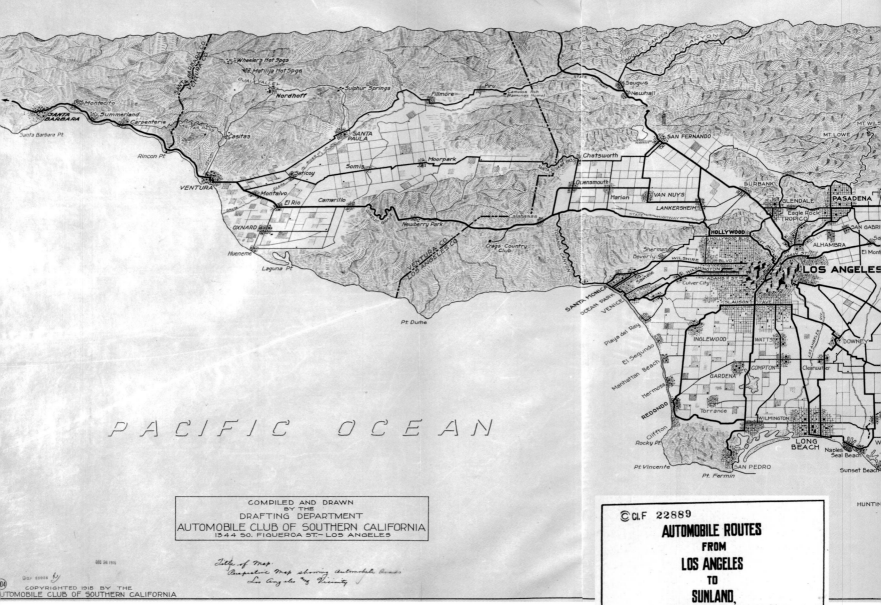

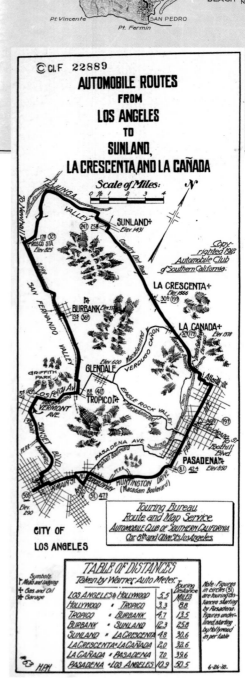

1900, two years before the national American Automobile Association. Bonds were passed in 1909 and again in 1919, largely as a result of automobile club lobbying, to finance road improvement, but it was the passage of a gasoline tax in 1923 that finally allowed for continuous funding of better roads. A new state highway numbering system began in 1917 after the creation of the California Highway Commission.

Increasing demands for better and better roads ushered in the era of freeways. The first freeway, the Arroyo Seco Freeway from Los Angeles to Pasadena, was opened on 30 December 1940. About this time the Automobile Club of Southern California issued a report calling for the construction of four hundred miles of divided highways covering Los Angeles. "Imagine driving your car on an exclusive express highway through the congested Los Angeles metropolitan area without a stop or hindrance," the report said. Many Angelenos still imagine this, many years after a network of freeways was actually built. In an 1941 exhibition ". . . Now We Plan,"

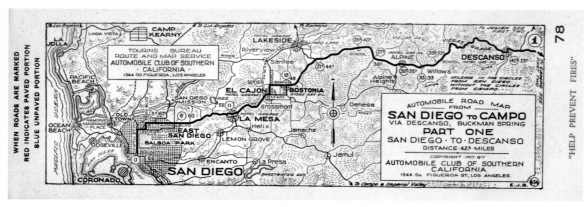

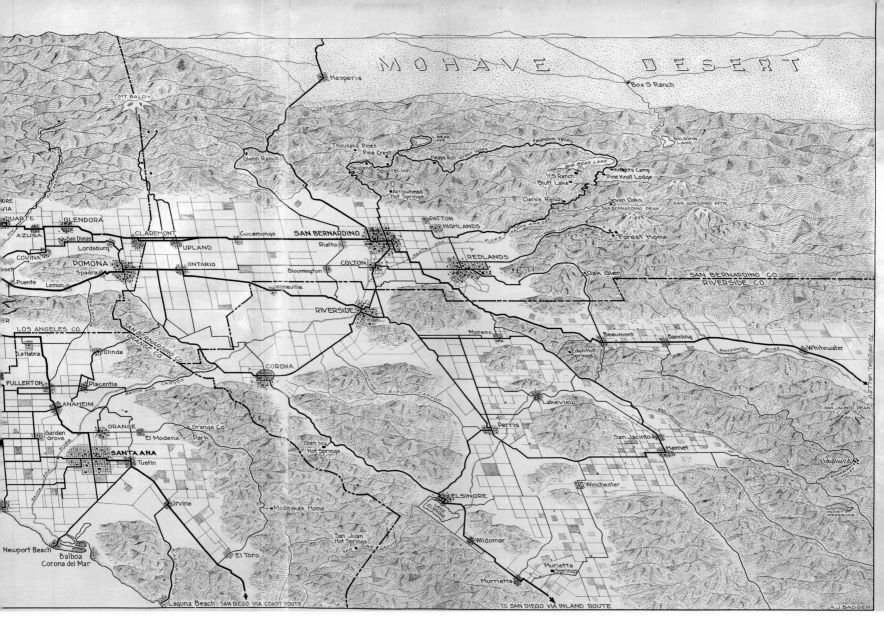

MAP 397 (*above*).
A map of automobile roads in the Los Angeles region published in 1915 by the then fifteen-year-old Automobile Club of Southern California.

MAP 398 (*far left*) and
MAP 399 (*left*).
In the early days of motoring it was very easy to get lost simply by missing a turn at some critical intersection. Auto clubs and other organizations often issued these route cards as a ready reference for the harried motorist. MAP 398 depicts a route from San Diego to Descanso, published in 1917, while MAP 399 shows a round-trip jaunt from Los Angeles in 1912. Both were published by the Automobile Club of Southern California.

MAP 400 (*right*).
Long-distance driving remained an adventure for decades. Here is a 1915 advertising map showing the route down the West Coast from Vancouver, B.C., to San Diego, complete with requisite overnight stops at the sponsoring hotels.

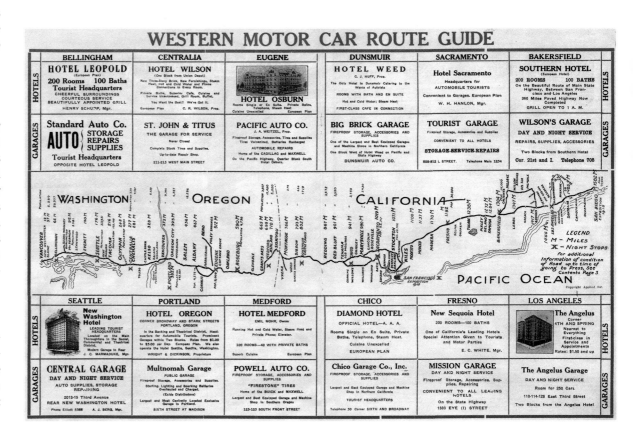

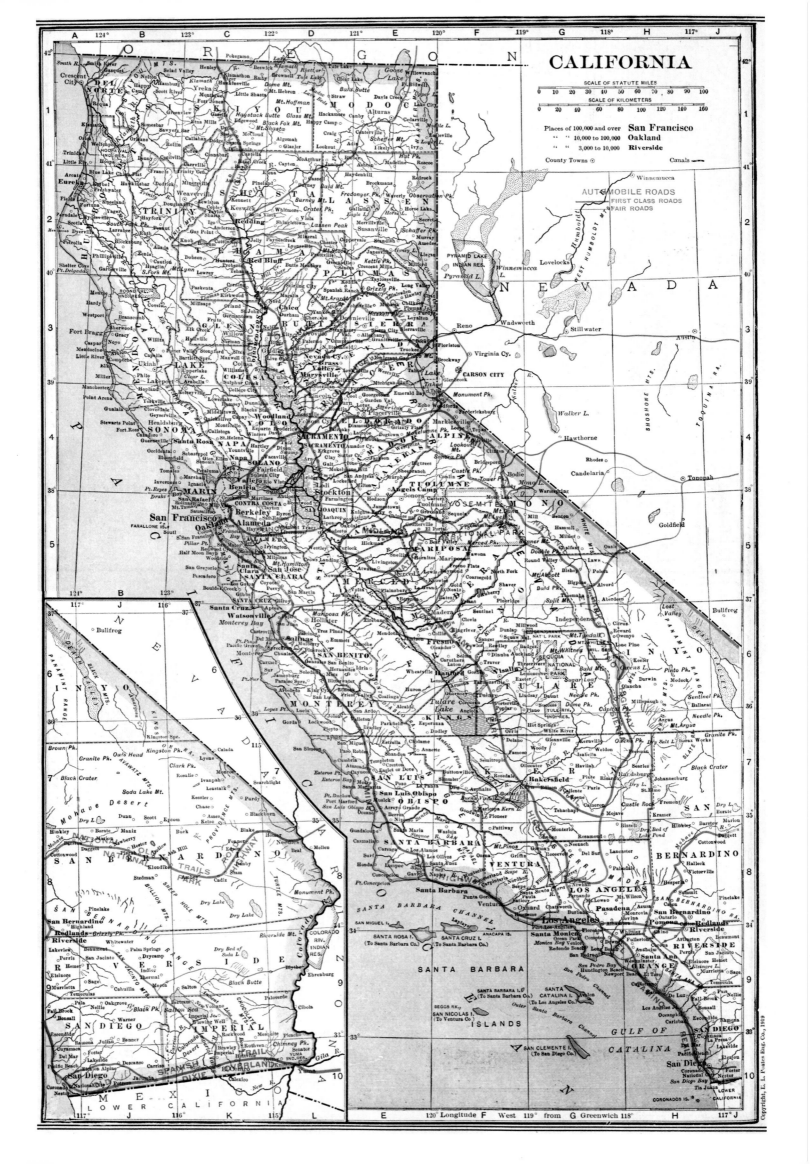

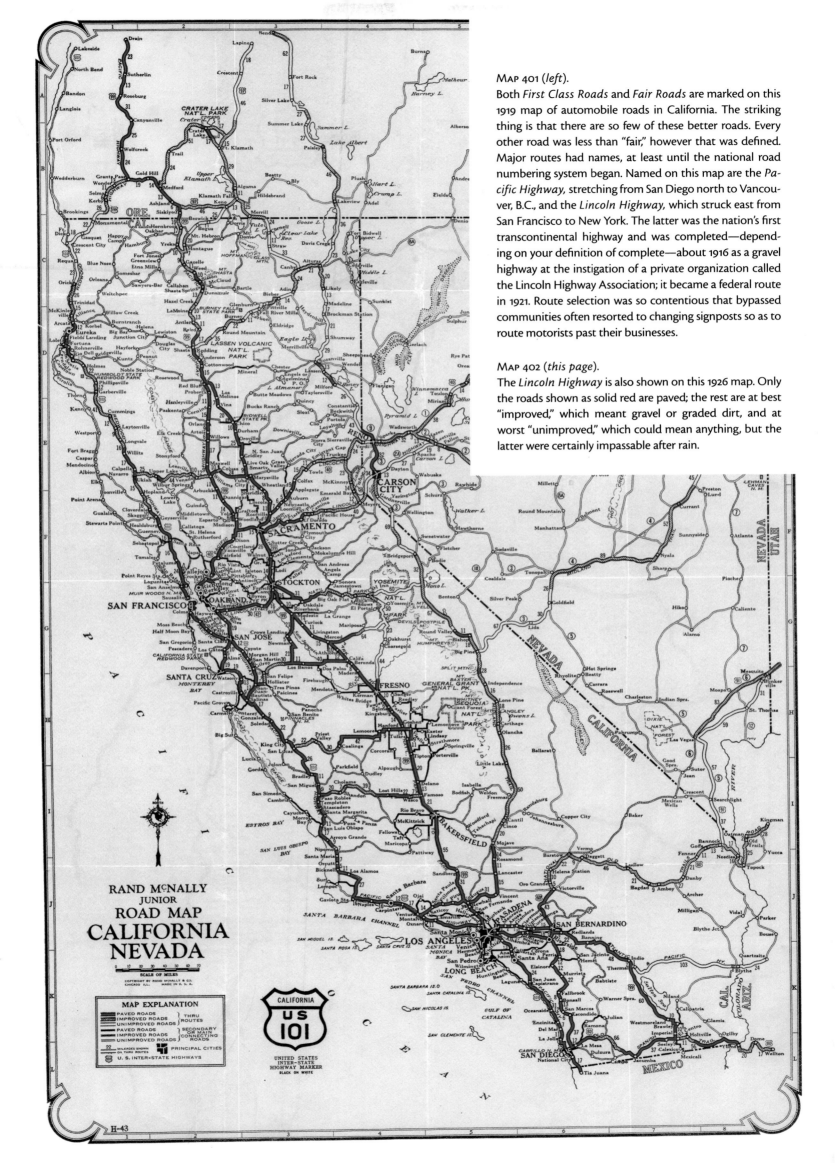

**Map 401** (*left*).
Both *First Class Roads* and *Fair Roads* are marked on this 1919 map of automobile roads in California. The striking thing is that there are so few of these better roads. Every other road was less than "fair," however that was defined. Major routes had names, at least until the national road numbering system began. Named on this map are the *Pacific Highway*, stretching from San Diego north to Vancouver, B.C., and the *Lincoln Highway*, which struck east from San Francisco to New York. The latter was the nation's first transcontinental highway and was completed—depending on your definition of complete—about 1916 as a gravel highway at the instigation of a private organization called the Lincoln Highway Association; it became a federal route in 1921. Route selection was so contentious that bypassed communities often resorted to changing signposts so as to route motorists past their businesses.

**Map 402** (*this page*).
The *Lincoln Highway* is also shown on this 1926 map. Only the roads shown as solid red are paved; the rest are at best "improved," which meant gravel or graded dirt, and at worst "unimproved," which could mean anything, but the latter were certainly impassable after rain.

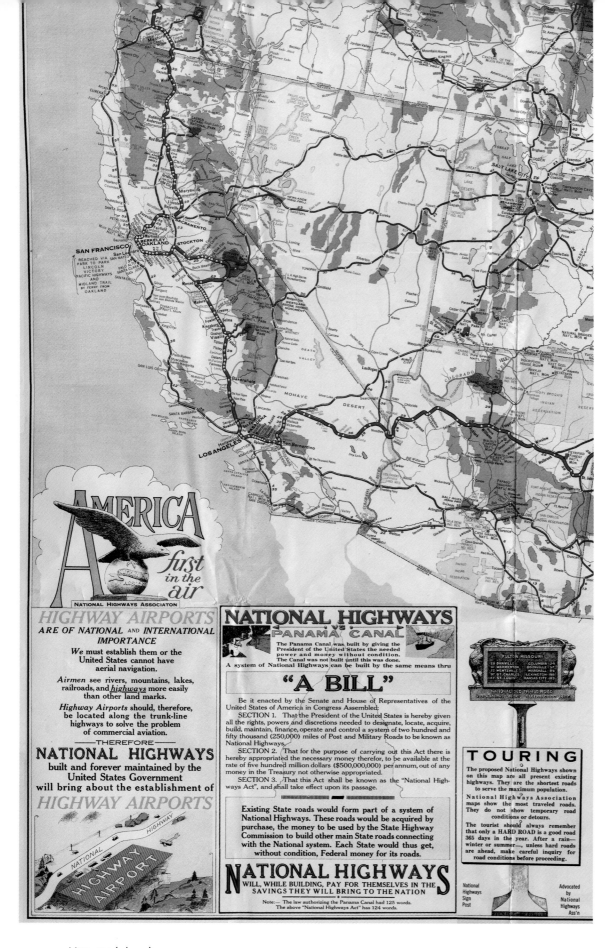

the city's future was inexorably linked to the automobile and the freeway.

After World War II the Los Angeles Regional Planning Commission developed a master plan for a proposed freeway system crisscrossing the urban area, and the Automobile Club of Southern California also published its own ideas for a freeway system for Los Angeles. Both agencies used the somewhat euphemistic term "parkway."

In San Francisco a similar relatively dense network of freeways was proposed in 1948 by that city's planning department and refined in 1951 and 1955 as the "Trafficways Plan." In a city with much less room than Los Angeles, the citizens of San Francisco demonstrated much less enthusiasm for freeways than their southern brethren. In 1959 the city's Board of Supervisors passed a resolution opposing seven out of ten freeway routes. One was the waterfront Embarcadero Freeway, which had incited huge protests during its construction and was never finished. Indeed, in 1985 the board voted to tear it down, though no action was taken until it was weakened by the Loma Prieta earthquake of 1989 (see page 234), after which it was quickly demolished.

Clearly freeways were not without flaws. Traffic engineers have estimated that on average Angelenos spend time equivalent to four days a year stuck in traffic, and jams seem unavoidable despite state-of-the-art information on traffic volumes from sensors embedded in the roadway and available instantaneously on the Internet. And it is no mistake that the California Department of Transportation (Caltrans) now includes rail transport in its responsibilities. San Francisco went on to develop an alternative to freeways, the Bay Area Rapid Transit (BART) line, but Los Angeles's effort at rail rapid transit (Metro) remains short, inconvenient, and relatively little used.

MAP 403 (*above*).
This map was headed *Good Roads Everywhere* and was published by the National Highways Association in 1925. The organization, created in 1913, lobbied effectively for paved highways on a federal as well as a state level—for "a paved United States in our day." It also advocated the creation of highway airports—shown in the panel at bottom left—so that pilots could use the road network for visual navigation and be able to find airports. Beginning in 1925 the federal agriculture department, then responsible for highways, began to introduce the federal system of road numbering to replace named highways, but this numbering is not shown on this map.

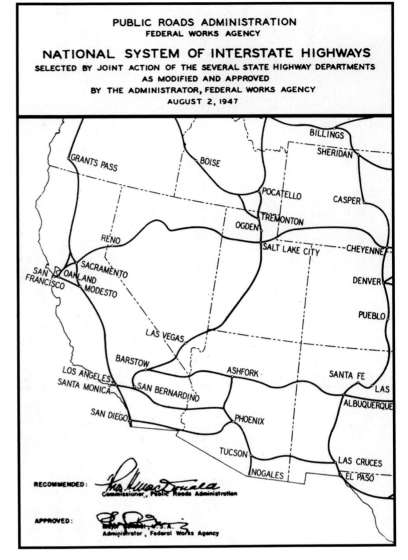

MAP 404 (*above*).

The freeway master plan for Los Angeles adopted by the Regional Planning Commission in 1947. All of the darker, thicker black lines are proposed freeways, or parkways, as the commission generally preferred to call them. A comparison with a modern road map of Los Angeles shows that a number of the routes were followed when the freeway system was built.

MAP 405 (*right*), MAP 406 (*below*), and MAP 407 (*below, right*).

These three maps are from a report published by the Bureau of Roads of the U.S. Department of Commerce in 1955 known as "the Yellow Book" from the color of its cover. Its proper title was *General Location of National System of Interstate Highways,* and it contained national and city maps showing federally funded interstates approved in August 1947 with additions and adjustments to September 1955. MAP 405 is the western part of the national map, MAP 406 is the Bay Area map, and MAP 407 is the Los Angeles map from the report. President Dwight D. Eisenhower, who had been impressed by the military value of the German autobahns during World War II, signed the Federal Highways Act in June 1956, which created the "National System of Interstate and Defense Highways" and authorized the spending of $25 billion to create 41,000 miles of superhighways—roads that could be used to evacuate cities in the event of a nuclear attack; hence the use of the term "defense" in their name.

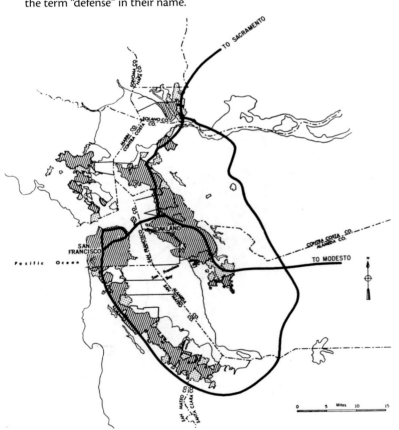

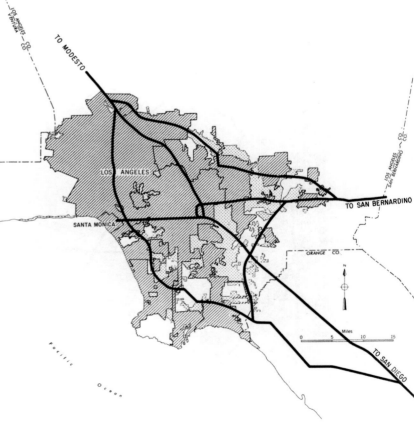

# POWER FOR A NEW ECONOMY

The value of all the oil found in California now vastly exceeds the value of all the gold, and yet while the gold rush continues to receive much attention from historians, the state's oil discoveries are hardly touched upon in most standard histories.

Tar oozing naturally from the ground had been used for centuries by the native people as caulking for canoes or as a glue. George Vancouver had recorded an oil slick in the Santa Barbara Channel in 1793. By 1855, several San Francisco streets were paved with asphalt, and oil was distilled for use in lighting and lubrication in Los Angeles by 1860. But whale oil prevailed into the 1890s. The first commercial sale of refined oil from a California well took place in 1865, from a well drilled in Humboldt County. Oil was discovered and drilling began in the McKittrick-Cymeric field, thirty miles west of Bakersfield, in 1887, and in the Los Angeles basin in 1889. By the end of the first two decades of the twentieth century no fewer than twenty-eight separate oil fields had been located in the Los Angeles region. In 1921 came a big strike at Signal Hill, with a capacity of 250,000 barrels a day. Signal Hill, completely surrounded by Long Beach, incorporated in 1924 to avoid annexation by Long Beach and an accompanying tax on its oil. By this time not only had the market for oil been vastly increased with the development of the automobile (which first appeared on the scene in California in 1898), but the Panama Canal, completed in 1913, allowed easier shipment of oil to eastern markets. MAP 409, *below*, shows that even in 1906, oil wells covered central Los Angeles.

An early oil field was the Kern River field near Bakersfield, an extension—in a big loop—of the McKittrick and Sunset fields (MAP 410, *right*). Oil was discovered here in 1899. The prospectus for the New Amsterdam Oil Company, which published MAP 410, demonstrated the dramatic rise of the oil industry. According to

*Above.* A gusher on the cover of a 1910 series of oil field maps, of which one is shown as MAP 412, *overleaf.*

MAP 408 (*below*).
An 1849 map drawn by Edward Ord, who produced the first survey of Los Angeles the same year (see MAP 282, *page 149*), showed a *Pitch Spring* to the west of the city. This was the now well-known La Brea Tar Pits, where seeping bitumen gave an early indication of the wealth of oil in the Los Angeles basin.

MAP 409 (*below*).
The Los Angeles oil field in 1906. The map covers an area about four miles long, between downtown and what is today Dodger Stadium to the Los Angeles River, shown at right. Each black dot is an active oil well; black circles are wells not pumping oil at the time the map was made. The dense mass of oil wells ensured that many people literally had a well in their backyard. By the 1920s local ordinances sometimes required oil derricks to be covered on the side nearest a dwelling—to protect the house from being covered with oil if things got out of control.

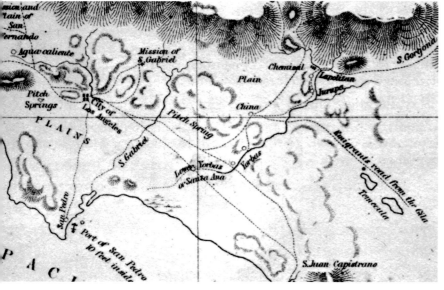

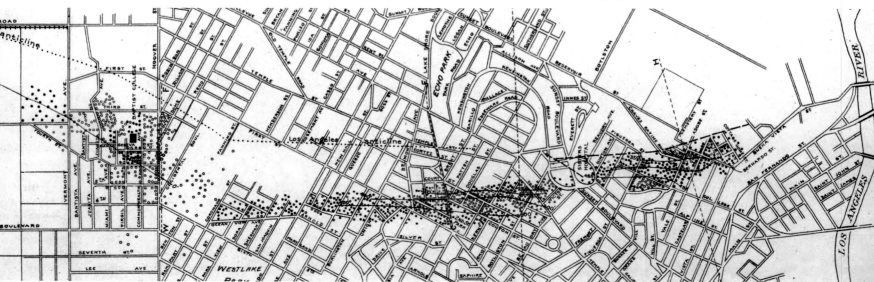

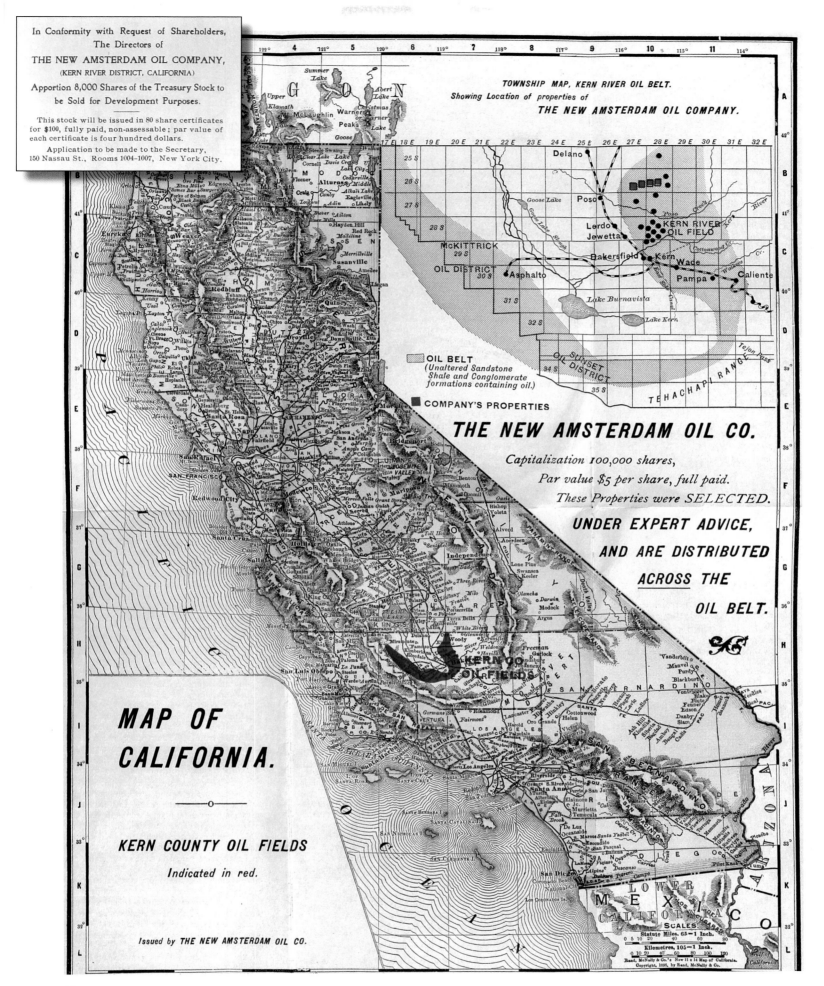

TOWNSHIP MAP, KERN RIVER OIL BELT.
Showing Location of properties of
THE NEW AMSTERDAM OIL COMPANY.

OIL BELT
(Unaltered Sandstone
Shale and Conglomerate
formations containing oil.)

COMPANY'S PROPERTIES

THE NEW AMSTERDAM OIL CO.

Capitalization 100,000 shares,
Par value $5 per share, full paid.
These Properties were SELECTED.

UNDER EXPERT ADVICE,

AND ARE DISTRIBUTED

ACROSS THE

OIL BELT.

MAP OF
CALIFORNIA.

KERN COUNTY OIL FIELDS

Indicated in red.

Issued by THE NEW AMSTERDAM OIL CO.

Map 410.
Issued by the New Amsterdam Oil Company to entice prospective investors for its drilling in the Kern River oil field in 1901, this map, showing the location of the wells on a state map and a detail oil field map (inset), came complete with an order form for shares attached to the back. "California has no real coal deposits," stated the accompanying prospectus, "and petroleum comes to revolutionize the State's industries, being the cheapest fuel in the world." Most of the presumed future consumption of oil was attributed to railroads, many of which did later change to oil.

its prospectus, in 1887, the State Mining Bureau made a reconnaissance of the petroleum industry in California and found only four companies actually engaged in what it termed petroleum mining. In July 1900, however, the same agency found two hundred and fifty. From 1905 to 1928 California was the largest oil producing region in the country.

California continues to produce both oil and gas, being the fourth-highest producing state in the nation. Today oil wells are still concentrated in the south, in the southern Central Valley, in Ventura, Los Angeles, and Santa Barbara counties, and offshore. Gas fields are mainly in the northern Central Valley.

MAP 411 (*right*).
This map showing Southern California oil fields in 1910 was the general location map in the package of maps of which the illustration on page 212 is the cover. The oil fields shown are mainly still in production today. Missing are the coastal fields of the Los Angeles Basin of which Signal Hill was the largest. These were discovered in 1921–22.

OIL FIELDS
OF
CALIFORNIA.
BARLOW & HILL
BAKERSFIELD, CAL.
Copyright, 1910

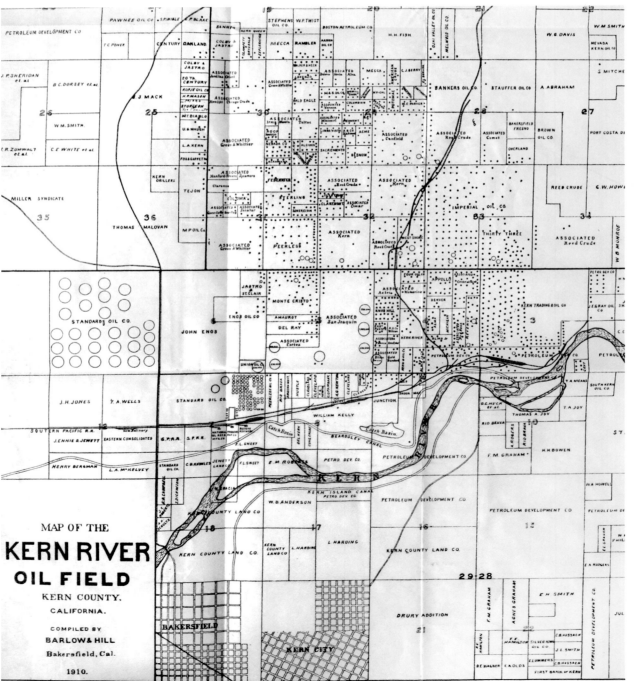

MAP OF THE
KERN RIVER
OIL FIELD
KERN COUNTY,
CALIFORNIA.
COMPILED BY
BARLOW & HILL
Bakersfield, Cal.
1910.

MAP 412 (*left*).
One of the detailed oil-field maps from the 1910 Barlow and Hill package was this one of the Kern River field, near Bakersfield, shown at bottom left. The claims and lands of individual oil companies are indicated. Each black dot is an oil well, with large circles representing storage tanks. Barlow and Hill must have had a thriving business producing these maps required by the oil companies, for if their ad (*below*) is to be believed, they corrected the maps daily.

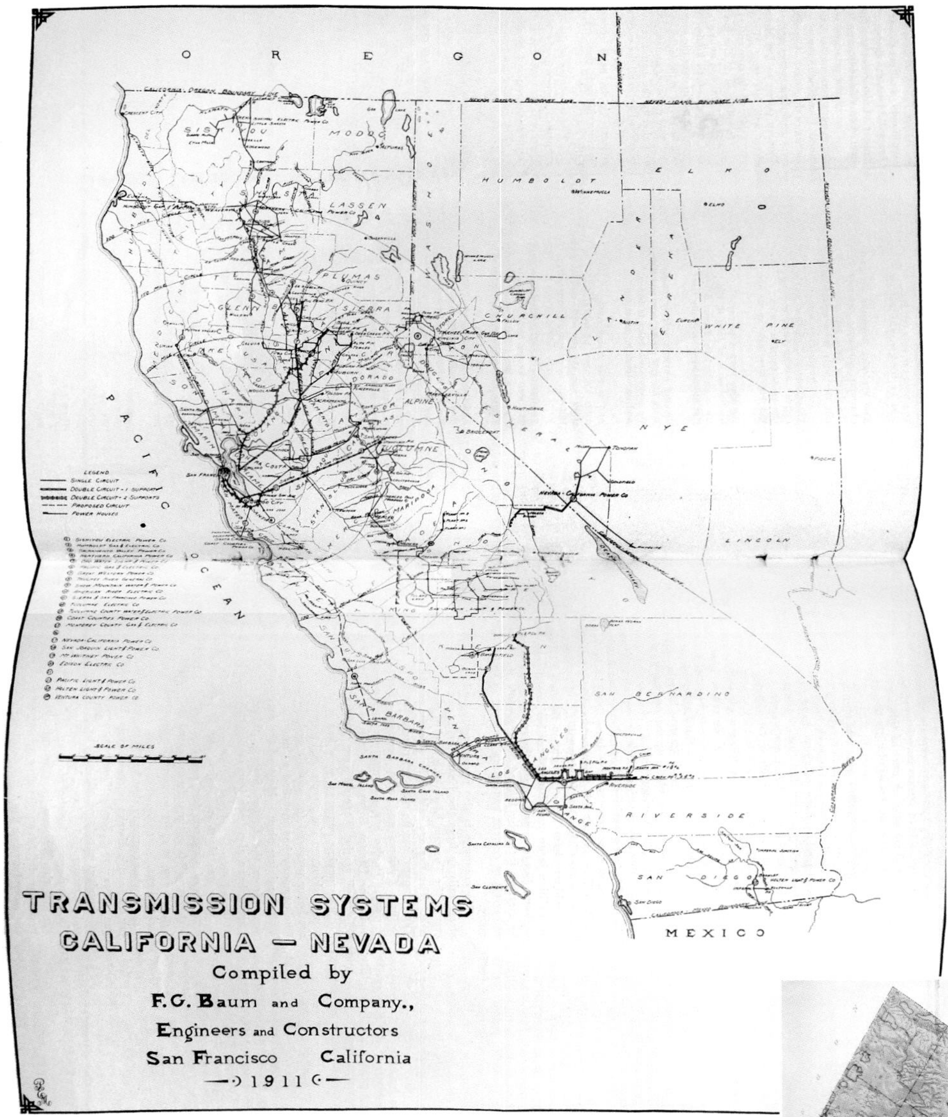

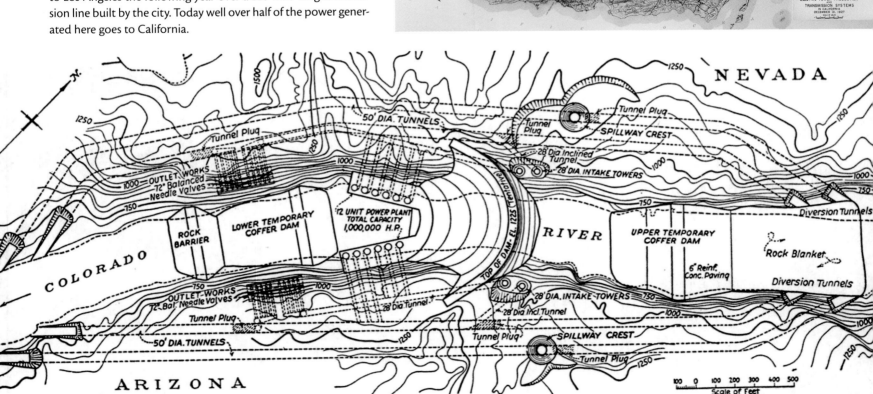

The extensive efforts to redistribute California's water from north to south and east to west also allowed the production of hydro-electric power, which was distributed via an increasingly complex electrical powerline grid. Due to California's right to its allocation of Colorado River water, a share of the power generated at the various dams also flows to the state. Most notably, 58 percent of the electricity from the Hoover Dam (Map 415, *below*), located between Nevada and Arizona, flows to California. Power also flows south and west from dams of the Central Valley Project and the State Water Project, primarily aimed at flood control and irrigation, and from dams for urban water uses (see pages 138–39 and pages 194–203).

Map 413 (*left*).
Given that electrical power only gained widespread use about 1900, it is perhaps surprising that the electricity transmission network in California in 1911, shown here, is so extensive. California was an early world leader in electricity use. Most of the electricity is generated from hydro-electric plants.

Map 414 (*below*).
This is the California electricity transmission network seventeen years later, in 1927. Both hydro and thermal generating stations are shown as squares (see legend). The map comes from a report on the feasibility of the Kennett Dam, which was completed in 1945 as the Shasta Dam.

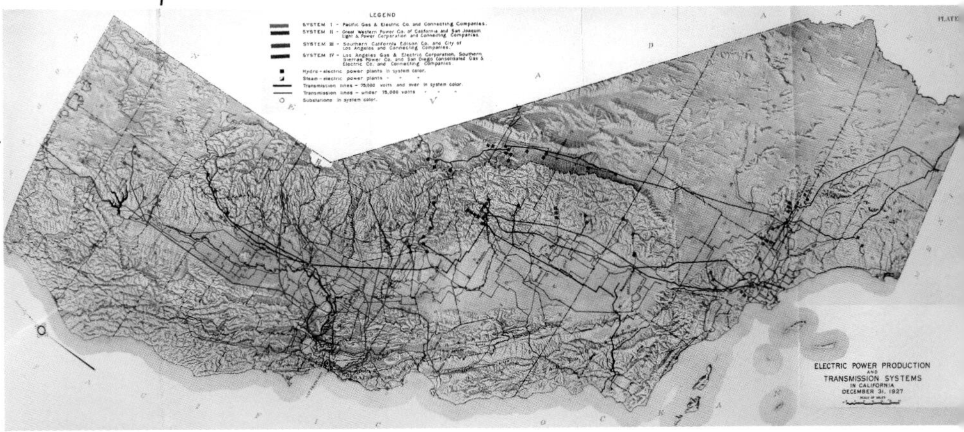

Map 415 (*below*).
A plan of the Hoover Dam, originally the Boulder Dam, on the Colorado River in 1931, the year construction began. Temporary coffer dams are shown, upstream and downstream of the main structure. Completed in 1935, the dam began sending electricity to Los Angeles the following year over a 226-mile-long transmission line built by the city. Today well over half of the power generated here goes to California.

# OF AIRPORTS AND AIRLINES

In San Diego in 1883, John L. Montgomery made the first controlled flight in a fixed-wing aircraft—a glider. In 1950 the City of San Diego named Montgomery Field, a general aviation airport about seven miles north of downtown, after its pioneer aviator. In 1925, Ryan Airlines inaugurated the nation's first daily scheduled, year-round air passenger service, from San Diego to Los Angeles. And when Charles Lindbergh began his record-setting first solo transatlantic flight in May 1927, he began from San Diego, where his aircraft, the *Spirit of St. Louis,* had been built by the Ryan Aeronautical Corporation.

Lindbergh, who was seen by an estimated three million people as he flew 22,350 miles around America promoting civil aviation, is credited with getting dozens of cities to build proper airports. Not least was San Diego (Map 425, *overleaf*). Encouraged by Lindbergh, the city opened the San Diego Municipal Airport on the site of the present international airport in August 1928. It was the first AAA-rated (for all types of aircraft) airport in the United States.

In San Francisco, Crissy Field, the Presidio airfield, was named after Major Dana Crissy, one of a number of military pilots who set out to fly across the continent in October 1919 and who died in the attempt. Even before becoming an official airfield, Crissy had been the site of aerobatic stunts, including those performed for the 1915 Panama-Pacific International Exposition (see page 189).

Two weeks before Charles Lindbergh's solo transatlantic flight, the city opened Mills Field Municipal Airport, a 150-acre island barely reclaimed from the mud flats of the bay. The land had been leased for three years from landowner Ogden L. Mills and quickly graded to fill in the uneven surface (Map 421, *right*).

Map 416 (*above*).
The first international air meet in the United States took place in 1910, with many aviation pioneers attending. One, Louis Paulhan, set a new world record at the meet by staying in the air for over an hour.

Map 417 (*left*), Map 418 (*below, left*), Map 419 (*below, center*), and Map 420 (*below, right*).
This sequence of four maps shows the evolution of San Francisco International Airport. Map 417 is a copy of a *diseño* dated 1864, when the owner of Rancho Buri-Buri (see also Map 149, *page 70*) tried to assert his continued ownership under American rule. It shows the shallow wetlands along the shore of San Francisco Bay more or less as they had been for centuries, as does Map 418, a U.S. Geological Survey topographic map surveyed between 1892 and 1899, although South San Francisco has now appeared. Map 419, a U.S.G.S. topographic map dated 1939–42 shows the area reclaimed for use as the first airport, Mills Field. The final map, Map 420, also a U.S.G.S. map, shows the expanded airport as it was in 1978. The land reclaimed for the airport is as it is today, and the runways are the same, but today's terminal complex is not yet present; the latter was completed in 2000.

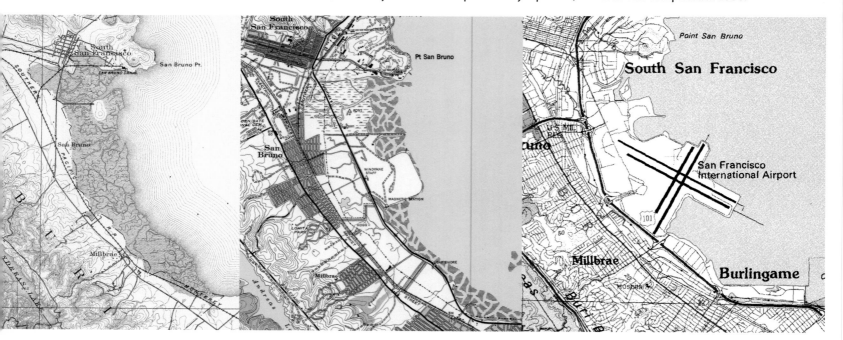

So sure was Mills that the arrangement would be temporary that he added restrictions in the contract on the plants allowed for landscaping so that the land could revert to cow pasture. Runways of rolled rock fill covered with two inches of earth were prepared. The airport's first major commercial customer was Boeing Air Transport. However, the first air-mail flight was canceled due to heavy fog, and Boeing, disgusted, moved its operations to the new Oakland Municipal Airport across the bay (MAP 423, *overleaf*)—not an auspicious start for Mills Field. The *San Francisco Chronicle* called the new airport "the world's prize mud hole." The state of the airport can be judged from the fact that Lindbergh himself, testing a heavy new plane for possible transcontinental service, got stuck in the mud on landing. It was not the sort of publicity the airport craved. Nonetheless, the airport was well located, and two years later the city purchased the site, and a larger area surrounding it, from Ogden Mills—on a ten-year installment plan.

Improvements were stymied by the onset of the Depression, and a 1930 bond issue was voted down. In 1935 Pan Am began to use the airport for its "China Clipper"

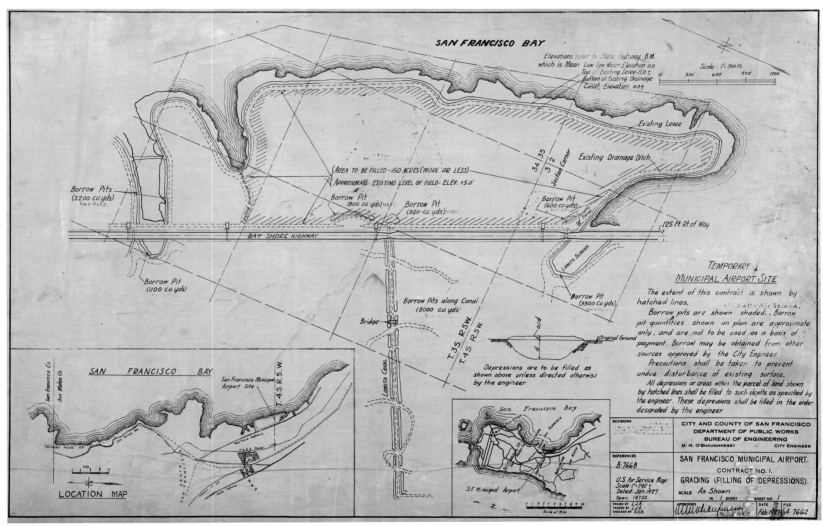

flying boat service across the Pacific. Men working for federal relief during the Depression converted much of the mud into concrete runways. By 1940 a considerable area of mud flats had been filled out into the bay to create a larger airport, and by 1949 it had achieved much the shape it has today, though runways would be considerably lengthened to accommodate jets.

It was planning for the new jet age that resulted in the expansion of many airports. One was Los Angeles (MAP 424, *overleaf*). That city had purchased a site in 1927 and converted it into dirt

MAP 421 (*above*).
The original site of San Francisco International Airport, Mills Field, on reclaimed land on the mud flats of the bay. This map was part of the first grading contract awarded by the city to fill in depressions and level the land sufficiently to allow the aircraft of the day to land safely. Note that the document is labeled *Temporary Municipal Airport Site*. At *top* is an appropriately aerial photo of the site; the wet and marshy nature of the terrain is apparent. The contract, with this map, was approved in February 1927.

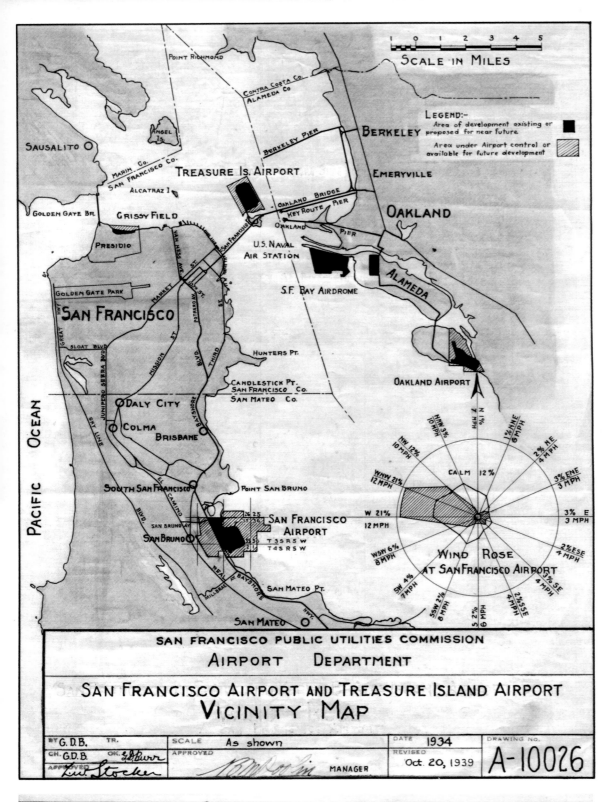

**OAKLAND MUNICIPAL AIRPORT**
1000 ACRES PRESENT OPERATIONS AREA
COMBINED PRESENT AND
FUTURE OPERATIONS AREA....1700 ACRES
ADDITIONAL AREA FOR AVIATION
INDUSTRIAL DEVELOPMENT.......700 ACRES
TOTAL.................2400 ACRES
PRESENT RUNWAYS AND TAXIWAYS SHOWN IN
BLACK AND WHITE

landing strips. Called Mines Field after the real estate agent who arranged the sale, the airport that would in 1941 become Los Angeles International was officially opened in 1930. Commercial jet travel came to Los Angeles and San Francisco in 1959 with the debut of the Boeing 707, which was to revolutionize air travel the world over. The first transcontinental jet service was inaugurated by American Airlines and the 707 on 25 January that year.

An intrastate airline, Pacific Southwest (PSA), was founded in San Diego in 1949, with a Douglas DC-3 flying once a week from San Diego to Oakland via Burbank. PSA flew until 1987 when it merged with U.S. Airways. Another regional airline, Air California (after 1981 AirCal), is fondly remembered by many a child who was whisked into Orange County Airport for a visit to Disneyland. The airline was founded in 1967 and for nearly twenty years provided low-cost service to a number of the state's smaller airports. AirCal was acquired by American in 1986.

MAP 422 (*left, top*).
Produced by the San Francisco Public Utilities Commission in 1934 and undated to 1939, this map is a summary of all airport facilities around the bay. *San Francisco Airport* was still Mills Field at this date. The city's earliest landing facility at *Crissy Field* is at the top of the peninsula, and *Oakland Airport* and *S.F. Bay Airdrome* are on the East Bay, along with the naval air station. Treasure Island, created from dredged fill for the Golden Gate International Exposition in 1939 and 1940 (see pages 224–25), was leased to Pan Am as an airport for its "Clippers" on Pacific routes but was preempted by the Navy with the approach of war and became a naval base in 1941.

MAP 423 (*left*).
Oakland had big plans for its municipal airport, as this postcard, dated about 1946, shows. The airport was first built in 1927 and opened late that year, dedicated by Charles Lindbergh. The airport has become the low-cost airline base for central California, and it is an important center for air freight.

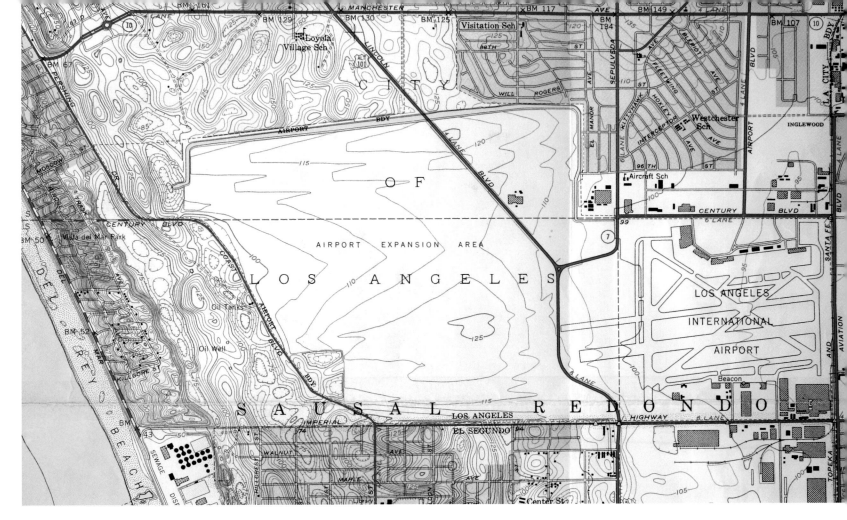

MAP 424 (*above*).
This portion of a U.S.G.S. topographic map, surveyed in 1947 and published in 1950, shows Los Angeles International Airport as it was at that time with a considerable area to the west prepared for expansion. It is instructive to compare this map with a modern one. Today the airport area extends east beyond *Aviation Blvd* (at right; this is the parking area) to the San Diego Freeway and controls the land to the ocean. *Sepulveda Boulevard* passes under the runways in a tunnel, *Coast Blvd* has disappeared, and a residential subdivision along [Playa] *Del Rey Beach,* built after this map was made, is abandoned. *Century Blvd* leads to the present terminal complex, and Interstate 105 is aligned along Imperial Highway, ending at Sepulveda.

MAP 425 (*below*).
A proposal for an airport at San Diego, 1927–28. The airport as built had traditional runways rather than the innovative paved circle shown here, which was designed to allow an approach from any angle. San Diego Municipal Airport, on this site, was praised by Lindbergh for its proximity to downtown, but this very fact now means the airport has outgrown this location and will have to be moved, possibly to the nearby Miramar Air Force Base. San Diego International is the second busiest single-runway commercial airport in the world, behind only Gatwick Airport, near London, England.

MAP 426 (*below*).
In 1979, Air California, the nearest thing the state ever had to its own airline, produced this innovative map of its routes on the front of a timetable brochure. The map, in leaving out all information other than the routes themselves, allows the map to be schematic, with the distances and direction between airports only roughly correct. The effect is nevertheless easy to understand.

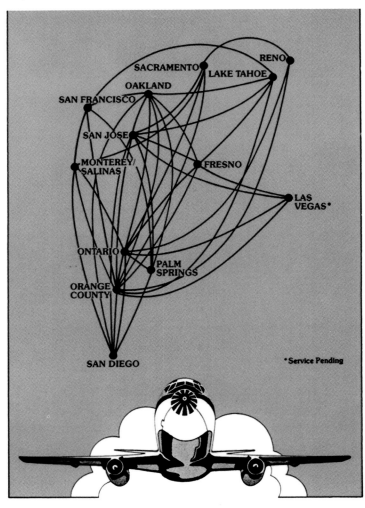

# BOOM AND BUST

By the 1920s oil, and the demand for it in California and elsewhere, had created prosperity in the state, especially in the south. Everybody, it seemed, wanted automobiles and land, and the growing industrial infrastructure and its accompanying employment allowed an unprecedented increase in the state's population. In the decade of the twenties the population increased by 67 percent and stood at 5.7 million people in 1930.

Times were good, and everyone seemed to be making money, not least of all those investing heavily in stocks. Then came the reckoning; the stock market lost 40 percent of its value in September and October 1929, and by July 1932 had lost 89 percent. Banks failed, workers lost their jobs, and families were evicted from their homes. Then the Dust Bowl years on the Plains drove farmers from their land, and many headed for California, where California's own advertising had for years been telling them the living was easy. So many came that they had nowhere to go and nowhere to live. Shantytowns, dubbed Hoovervilles, after a president who the unemployed thought was not doing enough to save them from their plight, sprang up around the cities.

A new president, Franklin D. Roosevelt, was elected in 1933 promising a "new deal for the American people." Federal programs came to California. The California Pacific International Exposition (MAP 427 and MAP 428, *this page*) was held in San Diego using funds from the Works Progress

MAP 427 (*above*) and MAP 428 (*below*). The California Pacific International Exposition was held in Balboa Park in San Diego in 1935, in the depths of the Depression, to promote the city and create employment. Open for just over a year, the exposition attracted 7.2 million visitors and employed 2,700 people, half of whom were federal relief workers. Some of the buildings have been rebuilt and remain in the park.

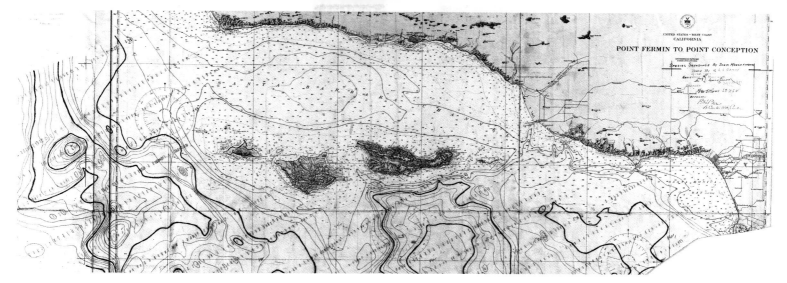

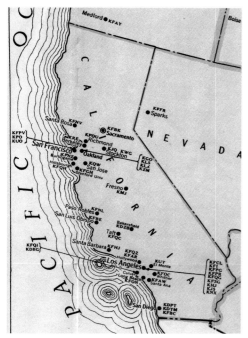

MAP 430 (*above*).
California radio broadcasting stations in 1930.

## MAP 429 (*above*).

This very unusual map demonstrates the advances made in technology by the 1920s. It is the first map of the seabed off California made by sonar, which uses sound to map the morphology of the sea bed. This map is a small part of a much larger one in seven irregular sheets made by cutting and pasting U.S. Coast and Geodetic Survey charts stretching from San Diego to San Francisco. The part shown here covers Point Conception (at top) to Santa Monica Bay (at right). Seabed contours have been drawn. These are based on the sonar soundings made in 1922 by USS *Hull* with the "Sonic Depth Finder or Rangefinder," as it was called. The map is now in the U.S. National Archives in Washington, D.C.

## MAP 431 (*right*).

Part of a map published by the Public Works Administration (PWA) in 1935 to show the public what was being done to fight the Depression. Projects in California included the Alameda County Courthouse and roads and trails in Yosemite National Park. It also included the All-American Canal (see an enlarged part of this map, MAP 265, page 141).

## MAP 432 (*below*).

This bird's-eye map of California, with the viewpoint from west to east, was produced as part of a brochure for tourists in 1936.

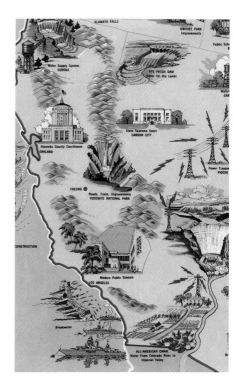

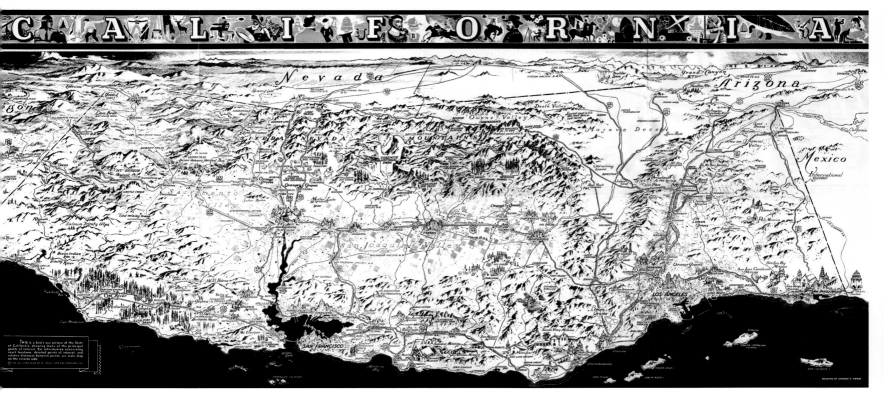

Administration (WPA), monies that were intended for the arts and all types of artists on relief. There were hundreds of smaller WPA projects in California. The Public Works Administration (PWA) dispensed funds for major capital projects, a number of which were built in the state (MAP 431, *previous page*).

California author and later Nobel Laureate John Steinbeck published his Pulitzer Prize–winning novel, *The Grapes of Wrath,* in 1939, a story constructed around the social and class upheaval caused by the mass migration of "Okies" to California, an upheaval that no federal program would solve but that would take a world war to end.

Not all was doom and gloom, however. In the Bay Area three major projects were completed in the 1930s that would change the face of the region dramatically: the Golden Gate Bridge, the Bay Bridge, and Treasure Island, the latter created from sand and silt dredged up from the bottom of the bay.

The idea of a bridge across the Golden Gate had been raised as early as 1872 by railroad builder and entrepreneur Charles Crocker. In 1916 the idea was revived by newspaper editor James Wilkins, and San Francisco city engineer Michael O'Shaughnessy polled engineers nationwide as to its feasibility and cost. Most said it was impossible. Others thought it would cost over $100 million. One bridge designer, Joseph Baermann Strauss, said it was feasible and could be built

MAP 433 (*below*).

The twenties and thirties were the heyday of the new entertainment industry, which had moved in to southern California to take advantage of its year-round production abilities. Studios such as MGM, Universal, and Warner Brothers purchased land around Hollywood for their movie productions, and in their wake Hollywood became the home of hundreds of movie stars. The public, of course, was fascinated with everything about the stars, and maps such as this one, printed in 1938 and literally sold on street corners, guided gawkers hoping for a glimpse of their favorite. Radio had begun in California in 1912, when station KQW in San José had begun regular broadcasts, but the medium was embraced by the entertainment industry in the thirties. Television broadcasting began in 1936 with a series of weekly sound broadcasts by radio station KHJ synchronized with images broadcast from W6XAO. The radio programs reached an audience of some 800,000, whereas the television images reached only about 1,500 who had built homemade television sets. True commercial television would have to await the end of the war; KTLA in Los Angeles, the first commercial television station, began broadcasting in 1947.

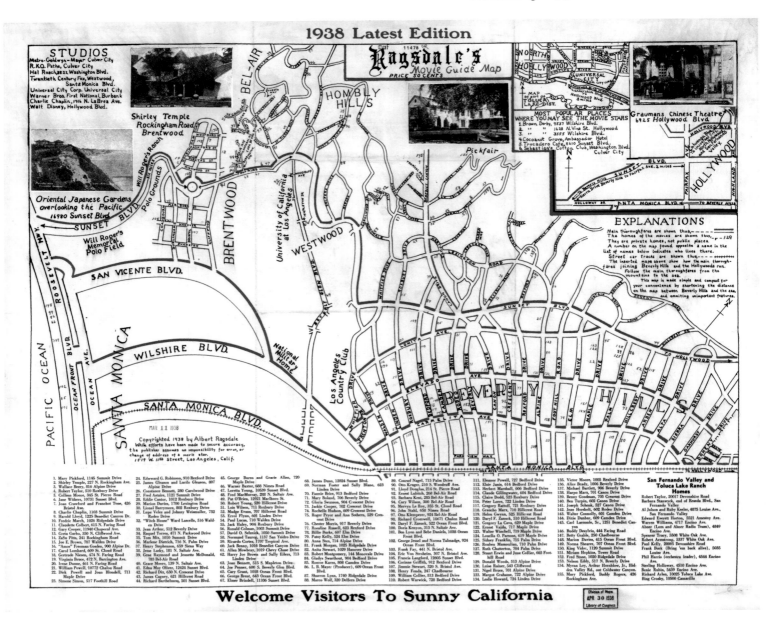

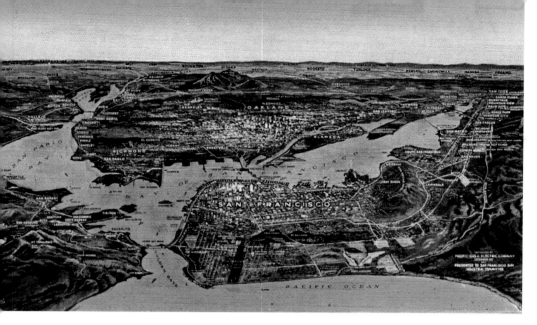

Map 434 (*above*).
This excellent bird's-eye general map of the Bay Area from the west was a postcard published in time for the Golden Gate International Exposition. Both of the bay's new bridges are shown.

Map 435 (*below*).
The Golden Gate Bridge is touted as the *Southern Gateway to Redwood Empire* on this 1938 tourist road map.

for $25–30 million. Construction began in 1933, and the bridge was opened to pedestrian traffic on 27 May 1937 and to vehicles the following day (Map 435, *above,* and Map 437, *below*). At that time it was the longest suspension bridge in the world. Almost concurrently the San Francisco–Oakland Bay Bridge was built. Construction also began in 1933 and was completed in November 1936, six months ahead of the Golden Gate. Of combined suspension and cantilever design, the bridge's lower deck contained track for the interurban trains (see pages 178–79).

Conceived as an airport for San Francisco, Treasure Island, likely named for the gold-laden sand and silt that had washed into the bay and been used in its construction, first hosted the Golden Gate International Exposition of 1939 and 1940 (Map 440, *overleaf*) before being preempted by the military for a naval base with the coming of war.

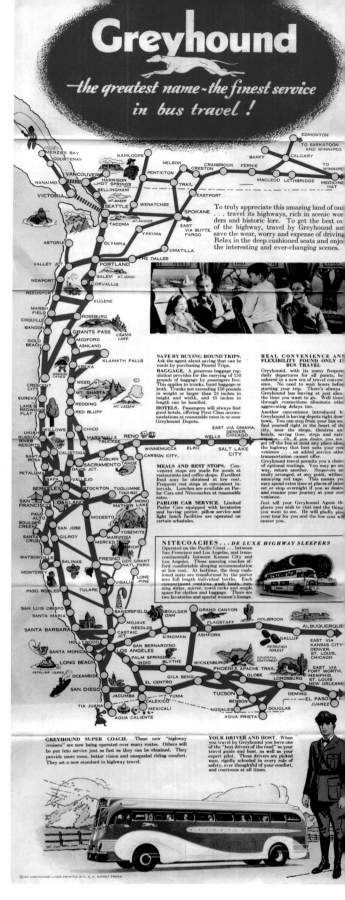

Map 436 (*above*).
A Greyhound Bus map published about 1940.

Map 437 (*left*).
A sort of map-photo combo hardly qualifying for the title of map at all, this image was published before the Bay Bridge was finished and shows it, with Treasure Island and the Golden Gate in the distance, superimposed on an aerial photo of the bay. The U.S. Fleet has also been drawn in.

MAP 438 (*left*).
A tourist road map of the "Redwood Empire" opened up for easier access by the Golden Gate Bridge. This attractive map complete with views was published in 1938.

MAP 439 (*below*).
A pictorial map of the Bay Area published by the Bank of America in 1939 for the Golden Gate International Exposition, shown on Treasure Island. Prominent in the foreground is an incoming China Clipper, a Pan Am flying boat; Pacific service had begun out of San Francisco Airport in 1935 and was to be transferred to Treasure Island after the fair, but the coming of war led the Navy to take over the island instead.

**OFFICIAL GUIDE BOOK**
25¢

**GOLDEN GATE INTERNATIONAL EXPOSITION**
ON SAN FRANCISCO BAY

*Above.*
Could it be Queen Calafia herself who graces the art deco cover of the official guidebook to the Golden Gate International Exposition, which contains a map of the newly reclaimed Treasure Island (MAP 440, *right*)? Or perhaps it was intended to be San Francisco—Mistress of the Pacific, a personification used at the turn of the century? Whoever it was meant to be, the art is superb.

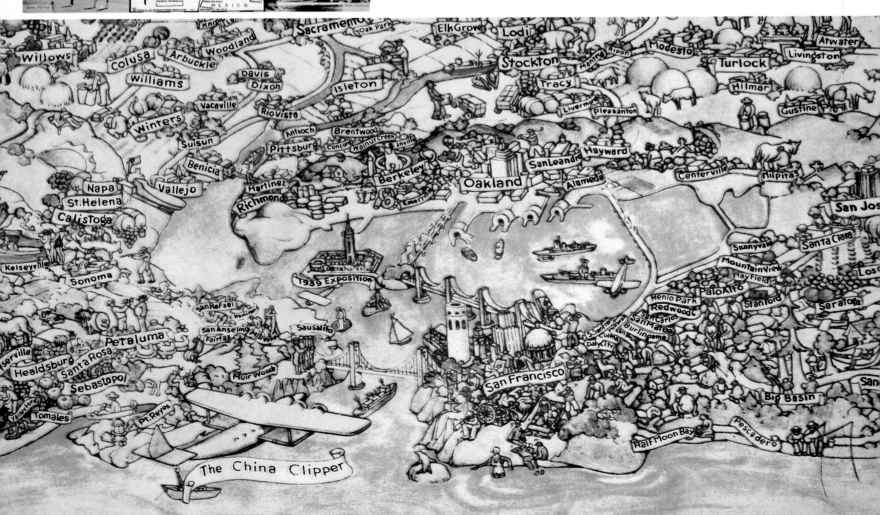

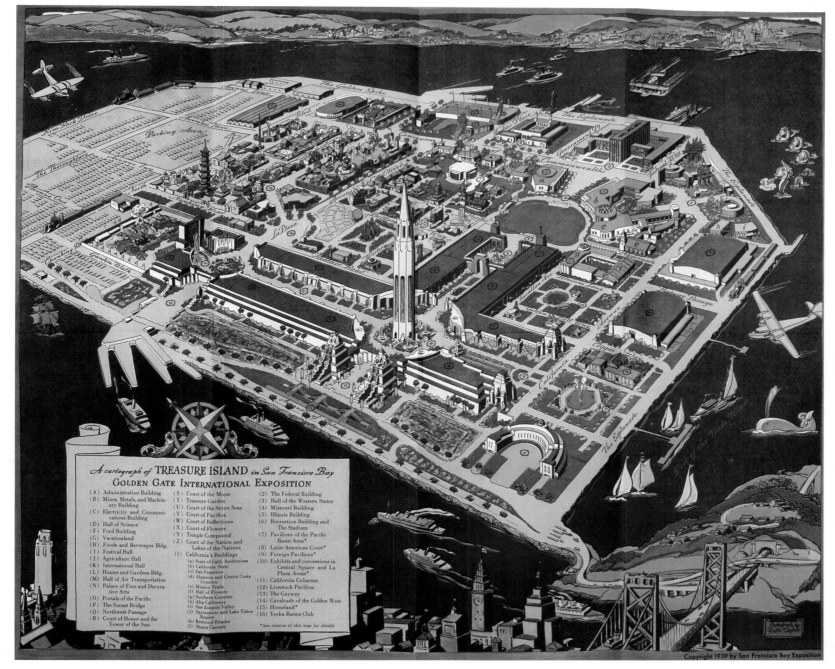

A cartograph of TREASURE ISLAND in San Francisco Bay
GOLDEN GATE INTERNATIONAL EXPOSITION

(A) Administration Building
(B) Mines, Metals, and Machinery Building
(C) Electricity and Communications Building
(D) Hall of Science
(F) Ford Building
(G) Vacationland
(H) Foods and Beverages Bldg.
(I) Festival Hall
(J) Agriculture Hall
(K) International Hall
(L) Homes and Gardens Bldg.
(M) Hall of Air Transportation
(N) Palace of Fine and Decorative Arts
(O) Portals of the Pacific
(P) The Sunset Bridge
(Q) Northwest Passage
(R) Court of Honor and the Tower of the Sun

(S) Court of the Moon
(T) Treasure Garden
(U) Court of the Seven Seas
(V) Court of Pacifica
(W) Court of Reflections
(X) Court of Flowers
(Y) Temple Compound
(Z) Court of the Nation and Lakes of the Nations
(1) California's Buildings
　(a) State of Calif. Auditorium
　(b) California State
　(c) San Francisco
　(d) Alameda and Contra Costa Counties
　(e) Mission Trails
　(f) Hall of Flowers
　(g) Southern Counties
　(h) Alta California
　(i) San Joaquin Valley
　(j) Sacramento and Lake Tahoe Region
　(k) Redwood Empire
　(l) Shasta Cascade

(2) The Federal Building
(3) Hall of the Western States
(4) Missouri Building
(5) Illinois Building
(6) Recreation Building and The Stadium
(7) Pavilions of the Pacific Basin Area*
(8) Latin-American Court*
(9) Foreign Pavilions*
(10) Exhibits and concessions in Central Square and La Plaza Areas*
(11) California Coliseum
(12) Livestock Pavilion
(13) The Gayway
(14) Cavalcade of the Golden West
(15) Homeland*
(16) Yerba Buena Club

*See reverse of this map for details*

Copyright 1939 by San Francisco Bay Exposition

MAP 440 (*above*).

Here's a new word: *cartograph*. That is what the creator of this map from the official guidebook to the Golden Gate International Exposition called this bird's-eye map. In the foreground is the prominent *Tower of the Sun*. A large proportion of the island's surface is devoted to parking, just as it likely would be today. The artificial Treasure Island, from 1941 a military installation, reverted to public control in 1996.

MAP 441 (*below*).

This detailed bird's-eye map of the Bay Area was published as a poster by utility company Pacific Gas and Electric in 1943.

# CALIFORNIA AT WAR

Europe had been at war for over two years, but many in the United States still thought America could avoid war when the Japanese staged their surprise attack on Pearl Harbor in the early morning of 7 December 1941. What President Roosevelt termed "a day of infamy" suddenly jerked the nation, and California, into action; if it could happen to Honolulu it could happen to San Francisco or Los Angeles.

Enemy aircraft were thought to be approaching Southern California right away. Partial blackouts were organized almost immediately, often with stiff penalties for showing a light. Reports flowed in of imminent attack both by sea and by air. On 10 December unidentified planes were reported approaching the south coast, and Army command ordered a complete blackout, which lasted for several hours, for the whole area from Bakersfield to San Diego. The release of the casualty figures from Pearl Harbor added to the sense of impending doom—2,251 killed and 1,119 wounded.

But there were no attacks on land—although the first ship was torpedoed off Eureka on 19 December—until, on 23 February 1942, a Japanese submarine, I-17, surfaced just west of Santa Barbara and fired twenty-four shells at the oil installations at Ellwood; most missed, but the attack was front page news the next morning.

Then, at seven the next evening the Navy received a warning from Washington of an imminent air attack on Los Angeles. About midnight radar screens, then very much in their infancy and difficult to interpret, picked up an unidentified object 120 miles west of the city, and at three in the morning something thought to be a balloon was sighted over Santa Monica. Anti-aircraft batteries opened fire, and in the course of the night, many others opened fire, all over the region. What they were actually shooting at has never been satisfactorily determined. Clouds, perhaps. Some have taken the opportunity to claim it was UFOs, but as was determined after the war, there were no Japanese planes over California that night. The headline in the *Los Angeles Times* the next morning was "L.A. Area Raided!" And, on the front page in a subheading: "Fifth-Column Acts Reported During Raid." The incident, dubbed the Battle of Los Angeles, is an indication of the high state of tension and paranoia that had descended on the United States in the months following Pearl Harbor over the possibility of a Japanese invasion and goes a long way toward explaining the order to relocate all persons of Japanese origin away from the coast.

President Roosevelt had signed the order a week before the phantom battle. Executive Order 9066 authorized the designation of "military areas" from which "any or all persons" may be excluded

MAP 442 (*below*).
A map from a newspaper report the day after the supposed "Battle of Los Angeles" showing *Where anti-aircraft guns opened up*, despite a lack of enemy aircraft.

MAP 443 (*below*).
Plan of the sixteen-inch gun emplacements in Battery Imperial, in Coronado. The battery was part of a complex named Fort Emory in December 1942 in honor of William Hemsley Emory, the Army engineer responsible for many of the early maps of the region, including the Mexican Boundary Survey (see pages 83 and 115).

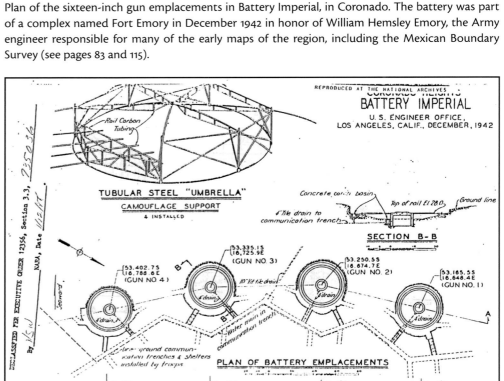

WHERE ANTI-AIRCRAFT GUNS OPENED UP—Map spots areas (1) about Los Angeles where anti-aircraft guns opened up and searchlights sought out either a plane or a blimp. The object moved down the coast from Santa Monica and disappeared south of the Signal Hill oil fields. All of Southern California was blacked out. At Goleta (2) a submarine previously had fired 25 shells into an oil field.

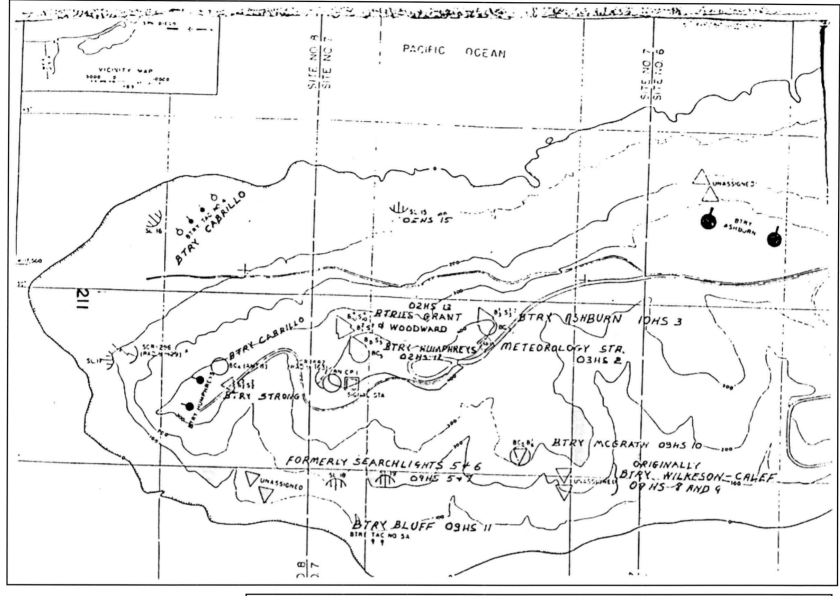

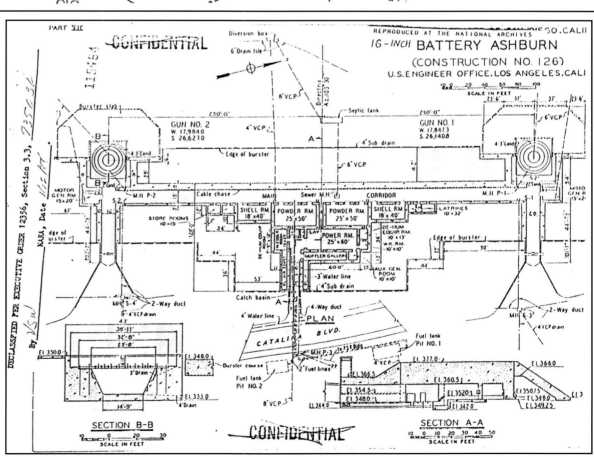

**Map 444** (*above*).
An Army map of the battery locations on Point Loma, at the entrance to San Diego Harbor. Note that north is to the right, so the guns are facing more or less out to sea.

**Map 445** (*right*).
Plan of the gun emplacements at Battery Ashburn, part of the first Rosecrans complex on Point Loma. These were the only guns to be casemated in concrete. The location of the battery can be seen at top right on Map 444.

*Above left.*
One of the massive sixteen-inch guns at Battery Ashburn. The figure gives some notion of their size. It seems likely that the photo was taken after war's end, since it is unlikely the army would have permitted photos to be taken of its gun emplacements during the war.

at the discretion of the military commander. In reality it applied only to persons of Japanese origin, whether American citizens or not. The officer in charge of implementing the order was General John Lesesne DeWitt. He initially sought to persuade Japanese Americans to relocate away from the coast voluntarily, but this approach was soon superseded by forcible relocation. All Japanese Americans were required to report to assembly centers from which they were allocated to one of ten relocation centers set up throughout the West (Map 447, *right*).

"Relocation center" was the official government term, but some historians maintain they should properly be called "concentration camps," an emotionally loaded term that evokes the conditions in such camps in Germany or, worse, Japan, during the war; but the American camps were certainly not remotely of that caliber. Two centers were established in California: at Tule Lake in the north and Mazanar in the Owens Valley (Map 446, *below,* and Map 447, *right*).

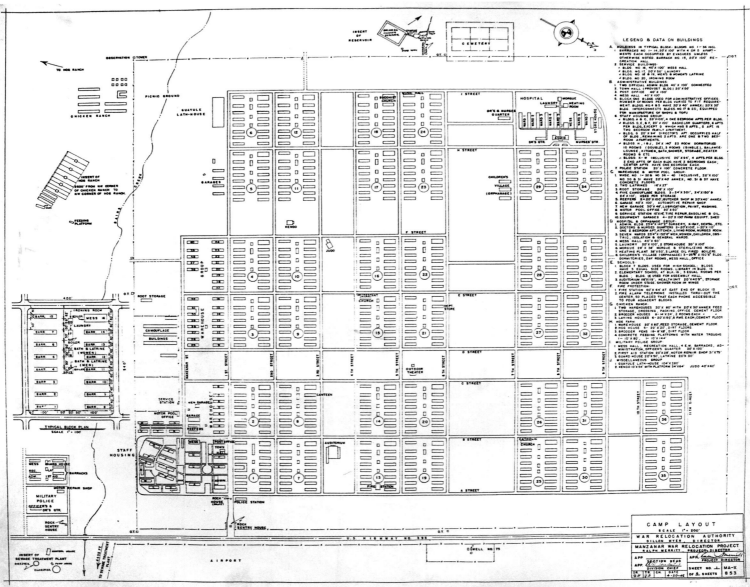

Map 446 (*above*).
Plan of the Mazanar Relocation Center in the Owens Valley, one of the two relocation camps in California. It is a veritable city of huts and housed 10,000 Japanese Americans. *Above right* is a striking photograph of the camp taken in July 1942 by a War Relocation Authority (WRA) photographer.

Map 447 (*right*).
From a federal government report, *Japanese Evacuation from the West Coast, 1942,* comes this map, which shows by color codes the areas from which persons were allocated to specific relocation centers, not only for California but also for Washington and Oregon.

# JAPANESE EVACUATION PROGRAM

## WESTERN DEFENSE COMMAND AND FOURTH ARMY
## WARTIME CIVIL CONTROL ADMINISTRATION

## RELOCATION CENTER DESTINATIONS

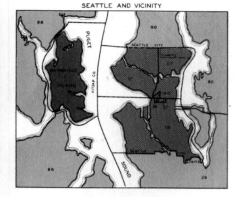

SEATTLE AND VICINITY

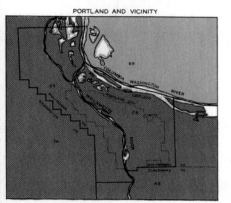

PORTLAND AND VICINITY

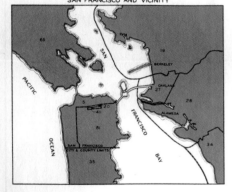

SAN FRANCISCO AND VICINITY

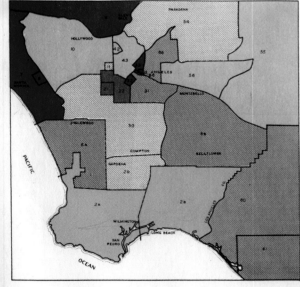

LOS ANGELES AND VICINITY

MILITARY AREA 1 — MILITARY AREA 2

SACRAMENTO AND VICINITY

### LEGEND

- — — EXCLUSION AREA BOUNDARY LINES
- 100 EXCLUSION AREA ORDER NUMBERS
- ⊛ ASSEMBLY CENTERS
- ⊛ RELOCATION CENTERS

- CENTRAL UTAH
- COLORADO RIVER
- GILA RIVER
- GRANADA
- HEART MOUNTAIN
- JEROME
- MANZANAR
- MINIDOKA
- ROHWER
- TULE LAKE

WESTERN DEFENSE COMMAND AND FOURTH ARMY
WARTIME CIVIL CONTROL ADMINISTRATION
STATISTICAL DIVISION

### E X P L A N A T O R Y   N O T E - III

THIS IS NUMBER III OF A SERIES OF THREE MAPS. 10 PERMANENT RELOCATION CENTERS WERE CONSTRUCTED BY THE ARMY IN 7 STATES. THE COLOR SCHEME IS DESIGNED TO SHOW THE ULTIMATE RELOCATION CENTER DESTINATION OF EACH EVACUEE POPULATION GROUP MOVED FROM THE EXCLUSION AREAS OUTLINED ABOVE. EACH RELOCATION CENTER HAS BEEN ASSIGNED A DISTINCTIVE COLOR. SO FAR AS SOUND LOGISTICS PERMITTED, THE CONTROLLING CONSIDERATIONS IN THE DEVELOPMENT AND EXECUTION OF THE PLAN OF MOVEMENT TO ULTIMATE DESTINATION WERE: CHARACTER OF POPULATION; COMMUNITY BALANCE; PRESERVATION OF COMMUNITY AND FAMILY UNITS.

*Above.*
R.B. Cozzens, assistant director of the War Relocation Authority, symbolically wipes relocation centers from the map in January 1945, after the relocation program had been canceled. The map appears to be the same as MAP 447 (*previous page*). Over four years, 93,000 Japanese Americans had been "relocated" by the program.

MAP 448 (*left, top*).
Released by the federal government in March 1942, this map shows the areas from which aliens and Japanese Americans would be excluded (the coastal zone) and where they may be permitted to remain with conditions imposed by the military (the lined shaded area). Special restricted zones (black triangles) are military installations, power stations, or reservoirs.

MAP 449 (*left*).
Surveyed between 1937 and 1942, this U.S.G.S. topographic map, a composite of two sheets, shows Mare Island, where the Napa River flows into San Pablo Bay. This was the site of the U.S. Navy's critical shipbuilding facility during the Second World War.

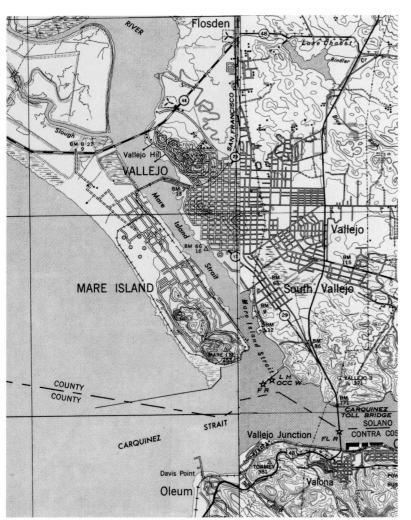

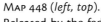

Federal money poured into California during the war. The Bay Area became the leading shipbuilding region in the nation; The Mare Island Naval Shipyard (MINS) in Vallejo (MAP 449, *left*) employed as many as 46,000 people and turned out hundreds of naval vessels. Richmond saw its population quadruple as 75,000 workers arrived, including a significant number of black persons from the Deep South. The Henry J. Kaiser's shipyard in Richmond built 486 of the critical Liberty ships, 441-foot-long cargo ships built to the same design for speed of construction; they took an average of only forty-eight days to build. Another major shipyard was Marinship, in Marin County. By 1945 San Francisco Bay was collectively the largest port in the United States.

Southern California also had its share of shipbuilding, with the California Shipbuilding Corporation on Terminal Island in Los Angeles Harbor. Kaiser, who had difficulties obtaining enough steel for his shipyards, built a new steel mill at Fontana; he had wanted to establish it on the coast for ease of transportation, but the government had insisted he build

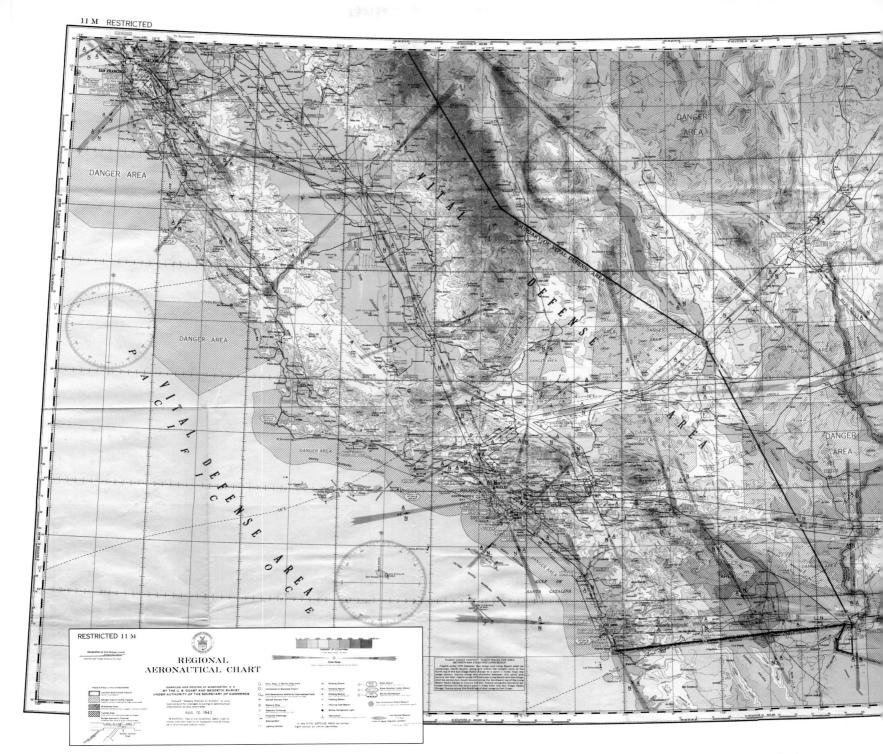

MAP 450 (*above*).
This *restricted* aeronautical chart, a map for pilots, dated 12 August 1943, shows much of Southern California as a *Vital Defense Area* in which the only civilian aircraft allowed were scheduled flights. The map is clearly an update from an earlier version for, at top, the lightship *San Francisco* is depicted twelve miles west of the Golden Gate, but the ship was actually removed at the beginning of hostilities and not reinstated until October 1945. Note the key, *above, inset*.

it eight miles inland in case of Japanese attack. The mill went into operation in the final days of 1942 and produced steel throughout the war; it closed in 1984.

The Los Angeles region became a critical aircraft manufacturing center, with such companies as Douglas, Lockheed, Northrop, and North American; Consolidated-Vultee and Ryan were in San Diego. The latter city's growth bulged 75 percent between 1942 and 1945 thanks to the aircraft builders and the Navy. Indeed, all Southern

California was changed forever as nearly a million aviation and other war matériel workers streamed into the region between 1939 and 1945, and many of them, now well trained and with high expectations for their standard of living, decided to stay after victory over Japan was achieved on 14 August 1945.

Many lost their defense industry jobs after 1945, including thousands of women who had joined the workforce for the duration of the war. Yet civilian schemes replaced some of the military projects, and the Cold War soon created new ones. Other jobs were created to service the increased population. New port projects, new civilian aircraft, new power distribution and water projects, new housing, new roads, and new freeways were all planned or under way by war's end.

The population of California increased by an again unprecedented 3.7 million people in the decade from 1940 to 1950. And the state was in good financial condition and now possessed an even stronger industrial economy than before.

# Moving and Shaking

The history of California since World War II is primarily related to growth. An explosion in population has manifested itself as a need for a host of developments, including water and power projects, road and freeway construction, and land development for residential, commercial, and industrial uses. The population of the state, under ten million at war's end, almost doubled by 1960 and had doubled again by the beginning of the twenty-first century, and California now has a population of about thirty-six million people. After taking a century to reach the ten-million mark, California has since 1945 been adding almost that number every twenty years. On average, the state adds over half a million people a year.

Only about half of this growth comes from natural increase; the rest comes from people moving in—net in-migration—and foreign net in-migration accounts for the majority of this movement. A quarter of Californians are now foreign-born, with the major groups being Hispanics and Asians. And California, always highly urbanized, has become even more so. It is the most urbanized state in America, with over 90 percent of it citizens living in towns and cities.

The result of the population growth—or is it the cause, for it is self-perpetuating—is the economic dynamo that is modern California. The state, if considered as a country, would rank in the top ten economies in the world, and it is an economy on the leading edge. A high-tech industry has emerged in the state in the last half century, growing in some cases out of the heavy military investment during World War II, particularly in aerospace. The Santa Clara Valley has become famous the world over as Silicon Valley, a name given to it by a journalist in 1971 that just stuck. Usually acknowledged as the "founders" of Silicon Valley are William Hewlett and David Packard, who graduated from Stanford in 1934 and set up Hewlett Packard after being persuaded to stay in the area (rather than migrate to Los Angeles) by Stanford professor Frederick Terman, who managed to make venture capital available to the pair. High-tech companies, spawned from advanced weapons research at the University of California Radiation Laboratory at Livermore, set up shop in the valley. Silicon was introduced by William Shockley, a pioneering semiconductor and integrated circuit inventor, in 1956, when he set up a laboratory in Mountain View. Many of his staff left to form other companies; in 1968 Robert Noyce and Gordon Moore left to found Intel.

We should probably have a map of garages in Silicon Valley, since these were the oft-quoted venues for innumerable high-tech startups. One of the first was Apple Computer, founded by Steve Jobs and Steve Wozniak in 1976. The Apple 1, the computer that really started the personal computer revolution, was first produced in Jobs's parents' garage in 1977. The success of Apple encouraged many venture capital companies to move to the valley, making money available for other high-tech ventures promising to make millions for their early investors. Despite the burst of the dot-com "bubble" in April 2000, the valley is still home to thousands of high-tech companies, including virtually all the modern computer "names" save for Washington-based Microsoft. They include Adobe; AMD; Cisco; eBay; Google; Intel; Intuit; Maxtor; Oracle; Sun Microsystems; Symantec; and Yahoo! The presence in one place of all these global leaders in their fields puts California in a near unassailable position in world trade.

Growth has not always been without cost, and prosperity was not evenly distributed, as the social upheaval that exploded as a riot in the Los Angeles suburbs of Watts and Willowbrook in the summer of 1965 demonstrated. The arrest of a black youth by the California Highway Patrol triggered six days of burning and looting; 34 died and 1,032 were wounded, and property damage was estimated at

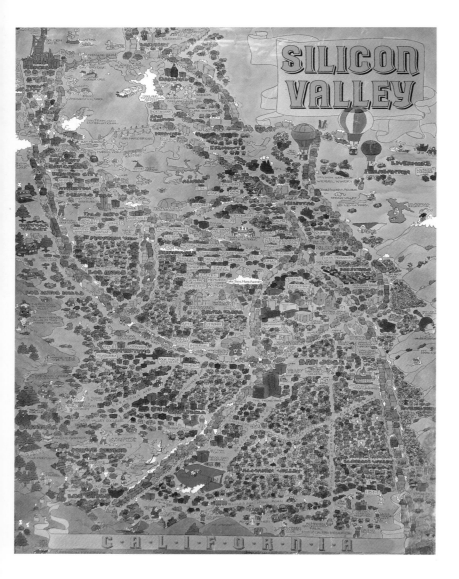

Map 451 (*left*).
A pictorial map of Silicon Valley, published in the late 1990s. The names of high-tech companies are plastered across the face of the land, and the freeways are depicted fancifully but not entirely inaccurately as lines of blue, jam-packed vehicles. Also shown are the myriad facilities available to residents including a number of universities. There is a street in San José named Disk Drive.

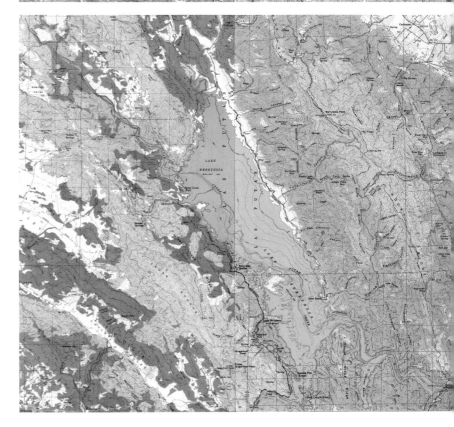

Map 452 (*above*), Map 453 (*right, top*), and Map 454 (*right, bottom*). Numerous water projects have been undertaken in the last fifty years to accommodate the explosive growth of the state. An early one was the controversial flooding of the Berryessa Valley, the next major valley east of the Napa Valley. The valley was said to possess some of the best soils in California. Nevertheless, the Monticello Dam was constructed by the federal Bureau of Reclamation between 1953 and 1957 across Putah Creek, and the reservoir, known as Lake Berryessa, was filled by 1963. At the time it was the second-largest man-made lake in the state, behind only Lake Shasta. The main town in the valley, Monticello, shown in 1895 (Map 452), was abandoned and lost. The lake now provides domestic water to half a million people and irrigation water to farms in Solano and Yolo counties. U.S.G.S. topographic maps graphically illustrate the loss of the valley. Map 453 is from surveys between 1943 and 1945. Map 454 shows the same area surveyed in 1957–60. Both of these maps are composites of two sheets.

$40 million. White Angelenos learned in a hurry of the frustrations of black people living in an urban slum that had inadequate schools and hospitals and was patrolled by insensitive white police.

Yet even this paled beside the 1992 Los Angeles riot. It was triggered this time by the acquittal of four police officers accused of beating a black man, Rodney King, the year before, an incident that had been captured on videotape. In four days, before the Army was called in to restore order, 50 or 60 died, as many as 2,000 were injured, and 3,600 arson fires destroyed 1,100 buildings; property damage may have been as high as $1 billion. Ten thousand people were arrested.

Always a factor in California, earthquakes are something every Californian must live with but that few care to think about when they are driving across San Francisco Bay on a bridge. The graphic image of a portion of the Bay Bridge collapsed after the 1989 Loma Prieta earthquake (Map 458, *overleaf*) is never far from the minds of many, yet is in fact a testament to the overall safety of this and other structures, most now built or retrofitted to address seismic concerns.

There are numerous earthquakes in California almost every day (Map 462, *page 236*) but only a few are both violent enough to cause damage or death and centered on densely populated areas. The 1868 Hayward earthquake caused major damage but few deaths because the area was lightly populated at this time. The 1906 San Francisco earthquake (see page 182) hit the major population center; more damage was caused by the resulting fires than by the shaking

itself. Other major earthquakes were in Eureka in 1922, Lompoc in 1927, Imperial Valley in 1940, Kern County in 1952, and Humboldt County in 1980. The somewhat milder San Fernando earthquake of 1971 caused far more damage, because its epicenter was in a heavily populated, freeway-crossed area with several dams that came close to total collapse, an event that would have surely caused more loss of life than any other quake (see pages 196–97). The major geological fault, that of the San Andreas, was responsible for the 1906 San Francisco quake, the San Fernando, and the Loma Prieta and creates a zone of higher risk from shaking all along the coast of Central and Southern California (Map 459, *page 235*). After the San Fernando quake California implemented measures to control building on and adjacent to fault lines. The Alquist-Priolo Fault Zoning Act, enacted

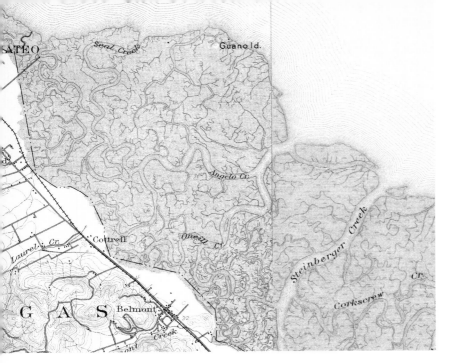

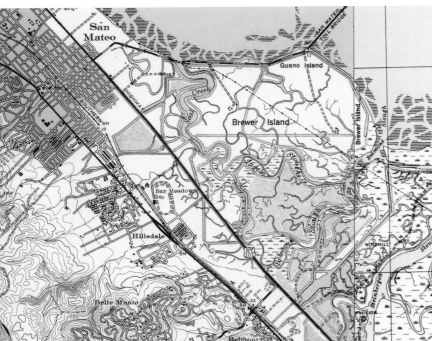

Map 455 (*left, top*), Map 456 (*left, center*), and Map 457 (*left, bottom*).
Brewer Island, just down the shoreline from San Francisco International Airport, was the site of one of the new planned towns of the 1960s and 1970s, which also include Reston, Virginia, and Lake Havasu City, Arizona. Foster City was the brainchild of T. Jack Foster, who put $4.7 million of his own money into the development project beginning in 1962. The island and its salt marsh tidelands were drained with the aid of ditches and ponds—which were termed lagoons for marketing purposes—and a detailed master plan was drawn up, which included plans for a city center, an industrial park, a shopping center, office buildings, and apartments. There were also plans for innovative schools, and a number of recreational areas and greenbelt walkways. More than 14 million cubic yards of fill were dredged from the bay and used to raise the level of Brewer Island. The operation took six years, twenty-four hours a day, seven days a week. At the same time 2.5 million cubic yards of material were excavated to create the central lagoon, an integral part of the drainage system devised for the island. A city was incorporated in 1971 and went through a period of financial strain and political upheaval; Centex, a development company that had purchased Jack Foster's interest, refused more than once to pay taxes to the city. The city hired and fired thirteen city managers between its incorporation and 1977, though matters stabilized after that date. Foster City remains a bold experiment in town planning, advertised at the time as the "first actual new town in America." The maps show Brewer Island and Foster City in (from top to bottom) 1892, 1939, and 1973.

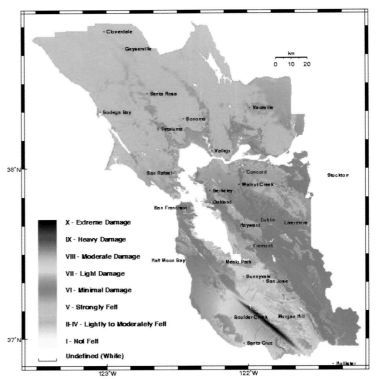

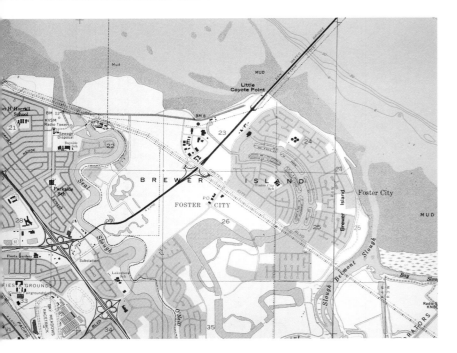

Map 458 (*above*).
The Loma Prieta earthquake, which caused widespread damage in San Francisco, had its epicenter at Loma Prieta, a peak in the Santa Cruz Mountains, on the San Andreas Fault. This U.S. Geological Survey map, created after the quake, defines areas by shaking intensity. Far more damage would have been caused if the epicenter had been in an urban area. The fifteen-second quake struck just after 5 P.M. on 17 October 1989 and killed twelve people in San Francisco and another forty-two in Oakland; the latter were trapped in their cars on the bottom level of a collapsed two-tier elevated freeway. One person died on the San Francisco–Oakland Bay Bridge; two vehicles plunged into the bay when a section of the bridge failed. The death toll from the quake is reckoned to be lower than it might have been because traffic was light due to the fact that a major league baseball game at Candlestick Park was about to begin.

# Earthquake Shaking Potential for California
## Spring, 2003

This map shows the relative intensity of ground shaking and damage in California from anticipated future earthquakes. Although the greatest hazard is in the areas of highest intensity as shown on the map, no region within the state is immune from potential for earthquake damage. Expected damages in California in the next 10 years exceed $30 billion.

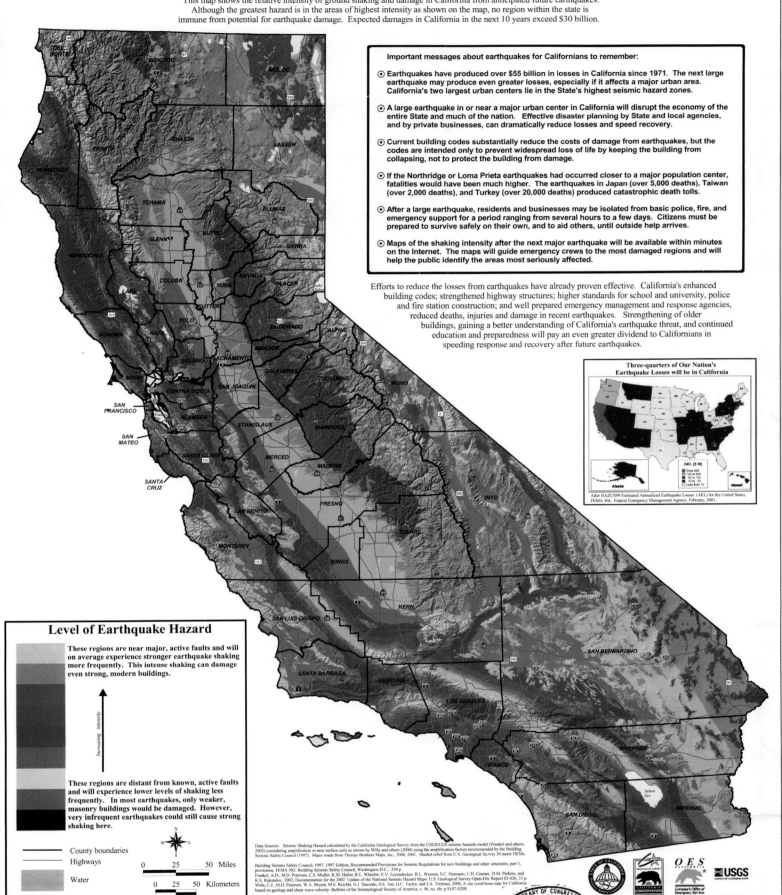

**Important messages about earthquakes for Californians to remember:**

⊙ Earthquakes have produced over $55 billion in losses in California since 1971. The next large earthquake may produce even greater losses, especially if it affects a major urban area. California's two largest urban centers lie in the State's highest seismic hazard zones.

⊙ A large earthquake in or near a major urban center in California will disrupt the economy of the entire State and much of the nation. Effective disaster planning by State and local agencies, and by private businesses, can dramatically reduce losses and speed recovery.

⊙ Current building codes substantially reduce the costs of damage from earthquakes, but the codes are intended only to prevent widespread loss of life by keeping the building from collapsing, not to protect the building from damage.

⊙ If the Northridge or Loma Prieta earthquakes had occurred closer to a major population center, fatalities would have been much higher. The earthquakes in Japan (over 5,000 deaths), Taiwan (over 2,000 deaths), and Turkey (over 20,000 deaths) produced catastrophic death tolls.

⊙ After a large earthquake, residents and businesses may be isolated from basic police, fire, and emergency support for a period ranging from several hours to a few days. Citizens must be prepared to survive safely on their own, and to aid others, until outside help arrives.

⊙ Maps of the shaking intensity after the next major earthquake will be available within minutes on the Internet. The maps will guide emergency crews to the most damaged regions and will help the public identify the areas most seriously affected.

Efforts to reduce the losses from earthquakes have already proven effective. California's enhanced building codes; strengthened highway structures; higher standards for school and university, police and fire station construction; and well prepared emergency management and response agencies, reduced deaths, injuries and damage in recent earthquakes. Strengthening of older buildings, gaining a better understanding of California's earthquake threat, and continued education and preparedness will pay an even greater dividend to Californians in speeding response and recovery after future earthquakes.

**Three-quarters of Our Nation's Earthquake Losses will be in California**

After HAZUS99 Estimated Annualized Earthquake Losses (AEL) for the United States, FEMA 366, Federal Emergency Management Agency, February, 2001.

## Level of Earthquake Hazard

These regions are near major, active faults and will on average experience stronger earthquake shaking more frequently. This intense shaking can damage even strong, modern buildings.

*Increasing intensity*

These regions are distant from known, active faults and will experience lower levels of shaking less frequently. In most earthquakes, only weaker, masonry buildings would be damaged. However, very infrequent earthquakes could still cause strong shaking here.

—— County boundaries
—— Highways
▨ Water

0   25   50 Miles
0   25   50 Kilometers

Data Sources: Seismic Shaking Hazard calculated by the California Geological Survey from the USGS/CGS seismic hazards model (Frankel and others, 2002) considering amplification in near surface soils as shown by Wills and others (2000) using the amplification factors recommended by the Building Seismic Safety Council (1997). Major roads from Thomas Brothers Maps, Inc., 2000, 2001. Shaded relief from U.S. Geological Survey 30 meter DEMs.

Building Seismic Safety Council, 1997, 1997 Edition, Recommended Provisions for Seismic Regulations for new buildings and other structures, part 1, provisions, FEMA 302: Building Seismic Safety Council, Washington D.C., 334 p.
Frankel, A.D., M.D. Petersen, C.S. Muller, K.M. Haller, R.L. Wheeler, E.V. Leyendecker, R.L. Wesson, S.C. Harmsen, C.H. Cramer, D.M. Perkins, and K.S. Rukstales, 2002, Documentation for the 2002 Update of the National Seismic Hazard Maps: U.S. Geological Survey Open-File Report 02-420, 33 p.
Wills, C.J., M.D. Petersen, W.A. Bryant, M.S. Reichle, G.J. Saucedo, S.S. Tan, G.C. Taylor, and J.A. Treiman, 2000, A site conditions map for California based on geology and shear wave velocity: Bulletin of the Seismological Society of America, v. 90, no. 6b, p S187-S208.

Additional copies can be ordered through CSSC by calling (916) 263-5506 or the map can be downloaded from http://www.seismic.ca.gov/sscgov

www.seismic.ca.gov   www.consrv.ca.gov   www.oes.ca.gov   www.usgs.gov

O E S CALIFORNIA
GEOLOGICAL SURVEY
CALIFORNIA CONSERVATION
Governor's Office of Emergency Services
USGS

MAP 459.

Potential destruction from the shaking of an earthquake is a function of more than the magnitude of the earthquake itself. Also significant are the distance from the fault that has shifted and local soil conditions. Putting these factors together, and using data from many sources, this map was published in 2003 showing the distribution of shaking potential for California. Note the information that earthquakes have cost the state $55 billion in losses since 1971.

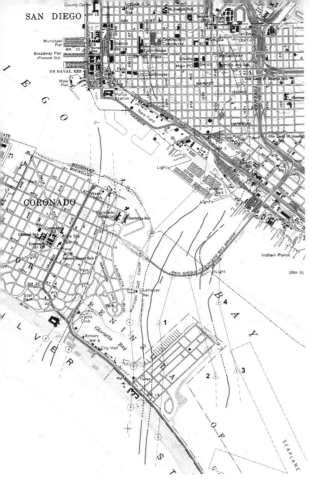

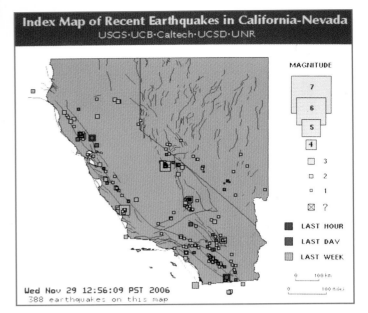

MAP 460 (*above*).
A 2003 fault zone map of part of San Diego created by the state geologist as required by law. Fault zones cross the San Diego–Coronado Bridge.

MAP 461 (*above*).
Matthew Davis of the Department of Psychology at Dominican University of California sports a tie bearing a map of the San Andreas Fault. Davis studies the way the public reacts to hazards such as earthquakes.

MAP 462 (*above*).
A U.S. Geological Survey computer-generated map of the earthquakes occurring in California in a one-week period before 29 November 2006. An astonishing 388 earthquakes were recorded in this week, and this is a typical number. Many were hardly felt, yet the fact that they took place underlines the fact that California is constantly shifting, constantly moving, as the stresses in the Earth's crust adjust.

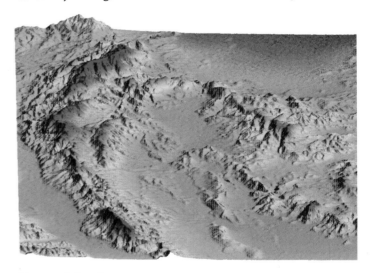

MAP 463 (*above*).
This topographic perspective–view map shows part of Ventura County, with the Simi Valley at center, looking east. It was computer-generated by NASA from satellite-borne radar in 2000.

MAP 464 (*below*).
Similar in concept to MAP 463 is this sea floor topographic map produced by multibeam bathymetry. The sonar emission and recording unit is towed, submerged, behind a ship, which makes multiple passes across the area to be mapped, in the same fashion as a tractor plowing a field. The area shown is the San Pedro Channel. Los Angeles Harbor is at top; Santa Catalina Island is at bottom left.

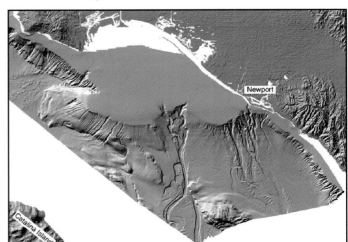

in 1971, creates zones around faults in which local authorities must regulate what may be built (MAP 460, *above*). And as of 1998, vendors of property have to disclose to potential buyers if a property is in a state-mapped hazard zone, which includes the fault zones.

In March 1964, as a result of a massive earthquake in Alaska, a tsunami swamped Crescent City, killing twelve and causing $15 million in damage. It was the only fatal tsunami ever recorded in the lower forty-eight states. Today Crescent City has a unique tsunami warning system; when a warning (which turned out to be a false alarm) was issued in June 2005 the city was evacuated in twenty minutes.

New ways of mapping are being developed all the time—new ways of looking at ourselves and our land that sometimes reveal new worlds. The development of satellite imagery has allowed mapping of just about every wavelength being emitted or reflected from the Earth, revealing much more of the dynamics of the planet than ever before. The technique of multibeam bathymetry, the simultaneous recording of multiple sonar echoes, has allowed us to view the seabed in a detail never before imagined (MAP 464, *right*, and MAPS 469 and 470, *overleaf*). It is a considerable advance on the first Pacific sonar (see MAP 429, *page 221*). In 1981 the United States declared an exclusive economic zone in the waters and seafloor 200 miles from the coast and with the stroke of a pen in effect extended California far out to sea. The zone, of course, needed to be mapped. One could argue the domination of the land still requires it to be defined on paper, just as the Spanish drew maps of California to define their new province and Americans drew maps of their conquest. These days, however, the medium is more likely to be a computer screen.

**Map 465** (*left*) and **Map 466** (*above*).

This 1992 LandSat satellite photo qualifies as a map because it has been orthorectified, adjusted to appear as if every point were being directly looked down upon from a camera vertically above it. The result is identical to that of a normal modern map. The image is a composite of six photographs and is extremely detailed; details such as the individual runways of airports are clearly visible (though are not on this whole state version). A larger-scale part of the map is shown above. This shows the islands of the San Joaquin–Sacramento deltas just northwest of Stockton. The center island is Bouldin Island, with State Highway 12 running west-east through it. South of it is Venice Island. The wide river channel is the San Joaquin. LandSat has been a succession of seven satellites; the first launched in 1972 and the seventh in 1999. Purple areas are urban, pink have much bare rock, and vegetated areas are green.

**Map 467** (*below*).

Part of the Los Angeles Basin. This is one frame from a 3,336-frame movie, an aerial ride over Los Angeles, created from a *single* two-dimensional LandSat satellite photo and existing elevation data by NASA scientists in 2006. The animation technique was developed to allow three-dimensional study of global cloud cover; this movie was but a test.

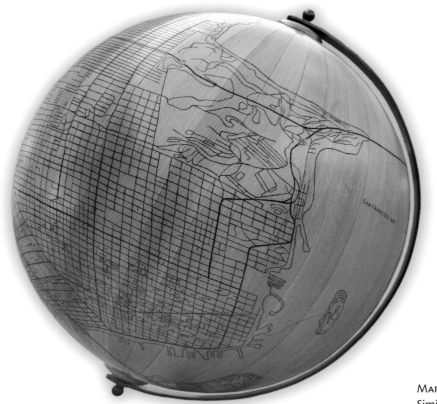

MAP 468 (*left*).
The map as art—and certainly a new way of looking at San Francisco—is well shown in artist and furniture designer Mike Farruggia's *Planet San Francisco*, a three-foot-diameter globe with a street map of San Francisco burned into it. Farruggia created the globe-map in 2001–03 from thirty-six pieces of wood. He described the process as "somewhere between instrument bending and boat building." He feels the piece sums up the way city-centric, peninsula-dwelling San Franciscans feel about their city. The globe was first exhibited in the Ferry Building and now resides in the San Francisco History Center, in the main city library.

MAP 469 (*left, center*) and MAP 470 (*left, center, inset*).
A detailed map of the Monterey Canyon, a very deep undersea chasm in Monterey Bay, the cause of early navigators' complaint that they could not find anchorage in the bay. The contour map (MAP 469) was created using multibeam bathymetry; MAP 470 is a three-dimensional representation of the canyon created from the same data. The canyon is so deep that it could not be properly mapped until the invention of the multibeam technique.

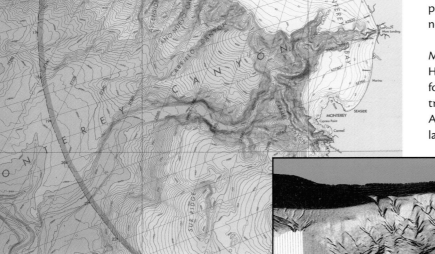

MAP 471 (*bottom, left*) and MAP 472 (*bottom, right*).
Similar maps of San Francisco Bay created by the U.S. Geological Survey also using multibeam bathymetry. Both the vertical view (MAP 471) and the perspective view (MAP 472) have their uses: the vertical is more accurate and useful for scientific purposes since the position of every feature is exactly shown, whereas the perspective view gives an excellent visualization of the scene. And that is one part of what maps are for—to give a perception of a geographic area otherwise not viewable by an observer on the ground.

MAP 473 (*right*).
Here's a simple yet useful and almost revolutionary new way of looking at California. This is the *Upside Down Map of California* from Santa Barbara map distributor and publisher Map Link. The idea was developed in the 1970s by Briton Ashley Sims after his father thought of the idea for driving south from Scotland to England. In 1996 Sims published an *Upside Down Map of Great Britain*.

The concept was brought to the map of California by Map Link the following year. The fold-out map contains this map, for driving south, as well as a conventional map for driving north. Since California is a relatively long and thin state with much long-distance traffic flowing north-south, this idea works very well here.

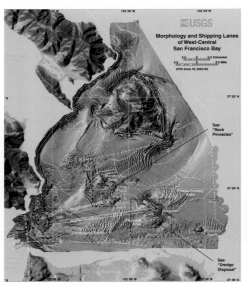

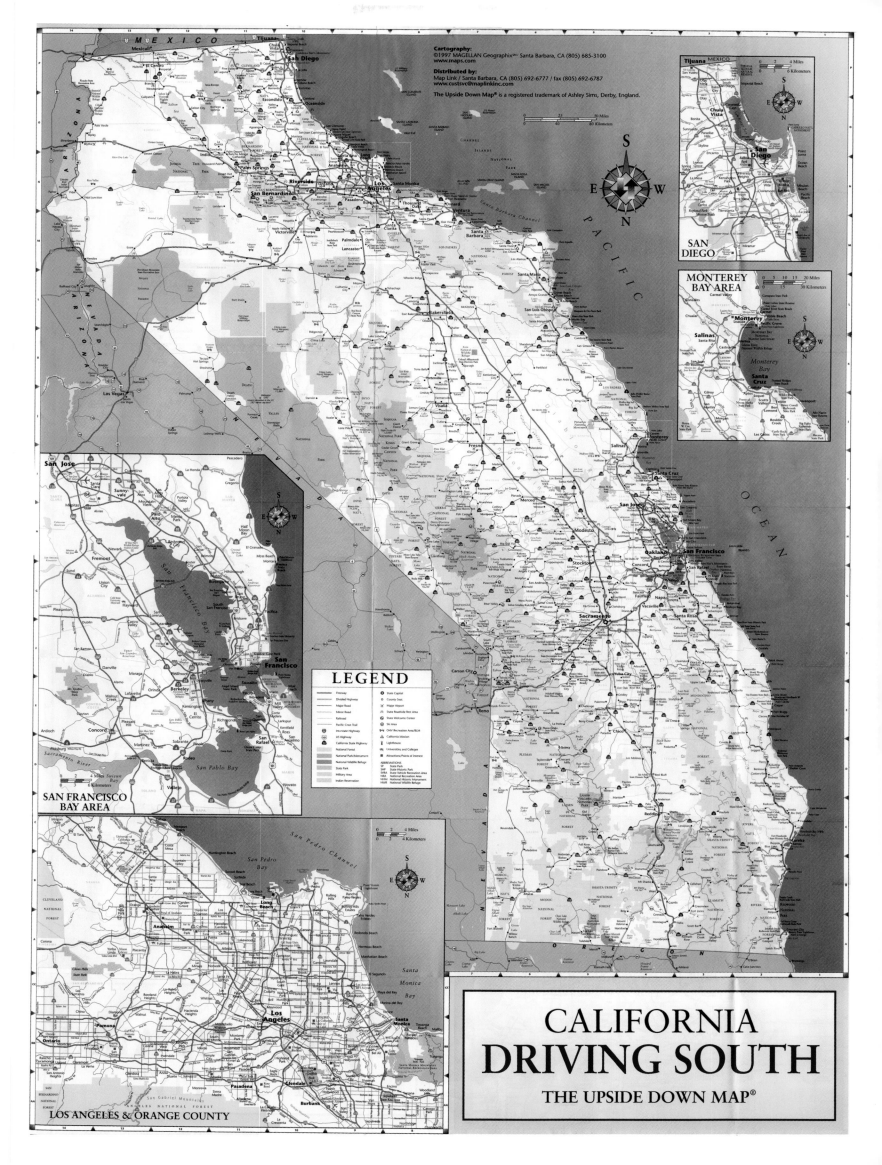

# CALIFORNIA
# DRIVING SOUTH
## THE UPSIDE DOWN MAP®

# CATALOG OF MAPS

*Maps without sources quoted are from private collections.*

**MAP 1** (*half-title page*).
*California*
Jo Mora, 1945
Carte reproduction provided by and used with permission of the Jo Mora Trust

**MAP 2** (*title pages, left*).
*Britton & Rey's Map of the State of California*
George Henry Goodard, 1857
David Rumsey Collection

**MAP 3** (*page 4*).
*Amerique septentrionale diviseé en ses principales parties*
Alexis Hubert Jaillot, 1694
Library of Congress G3300 1694 .J2 Vault

**MAP 4** (*page 6*).
*Map of the State of California*
[?] Vincent, 1860
David Rumsey Collection

**MAP 5** (*page 7*).
*The United States as viewed by California (very unofficial), Distorted and Drawn by Ernest Dudley Chase*
Ernest Dudley Chase, 1940
Los Angeles Public Library

**MAP 6** (*page 9*).
*Map of Linguistic Stocks of American Indians*
John Wesley Powell, 1890
From: *Annual Report of the Bureau of Ethnology*, vol. 7, 1890
Library of Congress G3301.E3 1890 .M3 TIL

**MAP 7** (*page 9*).
*Ancestral Homelands of the Indigenous People*
California State Indian Museum, Sacramento

**MAP 8** (*page 9*).
[Map of shipwrecks of junks in the Pacific Ocean]
Charles Brooks, 1876
From: *Early Migrations: Japanese Wrecks Stranded and Picked Up Adrift in the North Pacific Ocean*, 1876

**MAP 9** (*page 10*).
*Geographische Vorstelling eines Globi, welchen Anno 1492. Herr Martin Behaim*
Johann Doppelmayr, copy of 1492 Behaim globe, 1730

**MAP 10** (*page 10*).
*Nova, et Integra Universi Orbis Descriptio*
Oronce Finé, 1531
Library of Congress G3200 1531 .F5 Vault

**MAP 11 and MAP 12** (*page 11*).
*Universalis Cosmographia Secundum Ptholomaei Traditionem et Americi Vespucci Aliou[m]que Lustrationes*
Martin Waldseemüller, 1507
Library of Congress G3200 1507 .W3 Vault

**MAP 13** (*page 11*).
[Map of the world]
Diogo Ribiero, 1529 (Copy made in 1886 or 1887)
Library of Congress G3200 1529 .R5 MLC

**MAP 14** (*page 12*).
[Baja California and adjacent coasts]
Hernán Cortés, 1535–37
Facsimile of map in Archivo General des Indias, Seville, Spain

**MAP 15** (*page 12*).
*Nueva Espana*
From: Hernán Cortés, *Historia de Nueva Espana*, 1770
Huntington Library 10134

**MAP 16** (*page 13*).
[World map]
Sebastian Cabot, 1544
Bibliothèque nationale de France
RES Ge AA 582 Rc C 2486

**MAP 17** (*page 14*).
[Southern North America]
Portolan atlas of Battista Agnese, 1544
Library of Congress G1001.A4 1544

**MAP 18** (*page 14*).
*Tartariae Sive Magni Chami Regni*
Abraham Ortelius, 1570
From: *Theatrum Orbis Terrarum*
Library of Congress G7270 1570.O7 Vault

**MAP 19** (*page 15*).
[Baja California and adjacent coasts]
Domingo del Castillo, 1541
From: Hernán Cortés, *Historia de Nueva Espana*, 1770
Huntington Library 10134

**MAP 20** (*page 15*).
*Carte Cosmographique, ou universelle description du Monde, avex les Ventes*
Peter Apian, 1544

**MAP 21** (*page 15*).
*Universale Descittione di tutta la terra conosciuta fin qui*
Paolo Forlani, c. 1565
Library of Congress G3200 1565 .F6 Vault

**MAP 22** (*page 16*).
[Map of California, Japan, and the Pacific Ocean]
Joan Martines, 1578
British Library Harley MS 3450, Map 10 in atlas

**MAP 23** (*page 16*).
*Descripcion de las Indias Ocidentalis*
After Juan López de Velasco, 1601
From: Antonio de Herrera y Tordesillas, *Historia General de las Indias*, 1622

**MAP 24** (*page 16*).
*Americae sive Indiae Occidentalis tabula generalis*
Joannes de Laet, 1630
Bill Warren Collection

**MAP 25** (*page 17*).
*Universalis exactissima atque non recens modo*
Giacomo Gastaldi, 1555

**MAP 26** (*page 17*).
*Hemispheriv ab Aequinoctiali Linea*
Cornelius de Jode, 1593
From: Adolf Eric Nordenskiöld, *Facsimile Atlas*, 1889

**MAP 27** (*page 18*).
*Carte Universelle du Monde*
Pierre Du Val, 1684
Library of Congress GM Neg. 259

**MAP 28** (*page 18*).
*Nova et Rece Terraum et Regnorum Californiæ*
Gabriel Tatton, c. 1600.

**MAP 29** (*page 19*).
*Quiveræ Regnu cum alijs versus Borea*
Cornelius de Jode, 1593
From: *Speculum Orbis Terrae*

**MAP 30** (*page 19*).
*Limes Occidentalis Quivera et Anian 1597*
Cornelius Wytfliet, 1597
From: *Descriptionis Ptolemaicae Augmentum sive Occidentalis*

**MAP 31** (*page 19*).
*Granata Nova et California*
Cornelius Wytfliet, 1597
From: *Descriptionis Ptolemaicae Augmentum sive Occidentalis*

**MAP 32** (*page 20*).
*Carta de los reconociemientos hechos en 1602 por el Capitan Sebastian Viscayno*
From: *Relación del Viage . . . Atlas*, 1802

**MAP 33** (*page 21*).
[Cape Mendocino and vicinity]
Antonio de la Ascension, diary (facsimile), 1602

**MAP 34** (*page 21*).
[Point Reyes and vicinity]
Antonio de la Ascension, diary (facsimile), 1602

**MAP 35** (*page 21*).
[Monterey Bay and vicinity]
Antonio de la Ascension, diary (facsimile), 1602

**MAP 36** (*page 21*).
[San Diego Bay and vicinity]
Antonio de la Ascension, diary (facsimile), 1602

**MAP 37** (*page 22*).
[Portrait of Sir Francis Drake with world map]
Crispin van de Passe, 1598

**MAP 38** (*page 22*).
*Vera Totius Expeditionis Nauticae descriptio D. Franc. Draci*
Joducus Hondius, 1595
Library of Congress G3201.S12 1595 .H6 Vault

**MAP 39** (*page 23*).
*La herdike enterprinse faict par le Signeur Draeck D'Avoir cirquit toute la Terre*
Nicola van Sype, 1581
Library of Congress G3201.S12 1581 .S9

**MAP 40** (*page 23*).
[Inset: Portus Novæ Albionis] from *Vera Totius Expeditionis Nauticae descriptio D. Franc. Draci*
Joducus Hondius, 1595
Library of Congress G3201.S12 1595 .H6 Vault

**MAP 41** (*page 23*).
*Novus Orbis*
Peter Martyr, 1587
From: Richard Hakluyt, *The Principall Navigations*, 1589

**MAP 42** (*page 23*).
[Island of California]
Joan Vinckeboons, c. 1650
Library of Congress G3291.S12coll .H3
Harrisse No. 10

**MAP 43** (*page 24*).
[Map of the world]
Title page from: Samuel Purchas, *Purchas His Pilgrimes*, 1625

**MAP 44** (*page 24*).
[Map of the world]
Humfray Gylbert, 1576

**MAP 45** (*page 25*).
*Illustri Viro, Dimino Philippo Sidnaes Michael Lok Civis Londinensis Hanc Chartum*
Michael Lok, 1582
From: Richard Hakluyt, *Divers Voyages touching the Discoverie of America*, 1852

**MAP 46** (*page 25*).
[Map of the world on Mercator's projection]
Edward Wright, 1599

**MAP 47** (*page 26*).
*Carta particolare dello stretto di Iezo fra l'America è l'Isola Iezo*
Robert Dudley, 1647
From: Robert Dudley, *Dell Arcano del Mare*, 1647

**MAP 48** (*page 26*).
*A mapp of Virginia discovered to ye hills*
John Farrer, 1651
From: Edward Bland, *The Discoveries of New Britaine*, 1651

**MAP 49** (*page 27*).
*Chart of North and South America*
From: Thomas Jefferys, *A General Topography of North America and the West Indies*, 1768
Library of Congress G1105 .J4 1768

**MAP 50** (*page 27*).
*Louisiana*
Samuel Lewis, 1804
From: Aaron Arrowsmith and Samuel Lewis, *A New and Elegant Atlas*, 1804
Library of Congress G4050 1805 .L4 TIL

MAP 158 (*page 75*).
*P.S. Ogdens Camp Track 1829*
Peter Skene Ogden, 1829
Hudson's Bay Company Archives,
B202/a/8, fo. 1

MAP 159 (*page 75*).
*Map of the Territory West of the Rocky Mountains*
Benjamin Louis Eulalie de Bonneville, 1837
From: Washington Irving, *The Adventures of Captain Bonneville*, 1837

MAP 160 (*page 76*).
*Map of an Exploring Expedition to the Rocky Mountains in the Year 1842 and to Oregon & North California in the Years 1843–44*
John Charles Frémont, 1845
Library of Congress G4051.S12 1844 .F72 Vault

MAP 161 (*page 77*).
*Map of Upper California by the U.S.Ex.Ex. and Best Authorities 1844*
Charles Wilkes, 1844

MAP 162 (*page 78*).
*Map of Oregon and Upper California*
John C. Frémont and Charles Preuss, 1848
David Rumsey Collection

MAP 163 (*page 79*).
*Map of the Emigrant Road Independence Mo. to S*$^t$*. Francisco (sheet 4 of 4)*
T.H. Jefferson, 1849
Rare Books and Special Collections, Princeton University Library

MAP 164 (*pages 80–81*).
*Map of the Route to California*
From: Joseph E. Ware, *The Emigrants' Guide to California*, 1849

MAP 165 (*page 80*).
*Map of Oregon and Upper California*
John C. Frémont and Charles Preuss, 1848
David Rumsey Collection

MAP 166 (*page 80*).
*Das Fort Neu Helvetien*
John Augustus Sutter, 1848
Sutter's Fort State Historic Park

MAP 167 (*page 81*).
[*Diseño del Rancho Nueva Helvetia*]
Land case map, 1840s
Bancroft Library, Land case 319

MAP 168 (*page 82*).
*Sketch of the Actions Fought at San Pasqual in Upper California Between the Americans and the Mexicans Dec. 6*$^{th}$ *& 7*$^{th}$ *1846*
From: William Hemsley Emory, *Notes of a Military Reconnoissance*, 1848

MAP 169 (*page 82*).
*Sketch of the Passage of the Rio San Gabriel, Upper California by the Americans discomfiting the opposing Mexican Forces January 8*$^{th}$ *1847*
From: William Hemsley Emory, *Notes of a Military Reconnoissance*, 1848

MAP 170 (*page 83*).
Topographic map (Sonoma sheet)
for army use
U.S. Geological Survey, 1919

MAP 171 (*page 83*).
*Map of a Military Reconnaissance of the Arkansas Rio del Norte and Rio Gila*
William Hemsley Emory, 1847
From: William H. Emory, *Notes of a Military Reconnoissance*, 1848

MAP 172 (*page 83*).
*Sketch of the Battle of Los Angeles Upper California Fought between the Americans and the Mexicans Jan*$^y$ *9*$^{th}$ *1847*
From: William Hemsley Emory, *Notes of a Military Reconnoissance*, 1848

MAP 173 (*page 84*).
*View of San Francisco Formerly Yerba Buena, in 1846–7 before the Discovery of Gold*
Bosqui Eng. & Print Co., 1884
Library of Congress G4364.S5A35 1847 .B6

MAP 174 (*page 84*).
*Map of Upper California showing the military stations and distribution of troops*
Joseph Goldsborough Bruff, 1847
Library of Congress G4361.R2 1847 .B7 TIL Vault

MAP 175 (*page 85*).
*San Francisco September 1848*
Augustus Harrison, 1853
New York Public Library 54829

MAP 176 (*page 86*).
*Map of the City of Benicia*
Benjamin W. Barlow, 1847 (c. 1851)
Huntington Library 256751

MAP 177 (*page 87*).
*N. America*
Thomas T. Smiley, 1842
From: *Smiley's Atlas, For the Use of Schools And Families*, 1842
David Rumsey Collection

MAP 178 (*page 87*).
*Map of the United States of America*
J.H. Colton, 1848
David Rumsey Collection

MAP 179 (*page 88*).
*Topographical Sketch of the Gold & Quicksilver District of California*
Edward Otho Cresap Ord, 1848
Library of Congress G4361.H1 1848 .O7 TIL

MAP 180 (*page 89*).
*Map of the Valley of the Sacramento including the Gold Region*
John Bidwell, 1848
David Rumsey Collection

MAP 181 (*page 90*).
*Map of California New Mexico Texas &c.*
Henry S. Tanner, 1849
David Rumsey Collection

MAP 182 (*page 90*).
*Sketch of General Riley's Route through the Mining Districts*
George Horatio Derby, c. 1849
Library of Congress G4360 1849 .D4

MAP 183 (*page 91*).
*Map of the Gold Regions of California, Showing the Routes via Chagres and Panama, Cape Horn, &c.*
Ensigns and Thayer, 1849
David Rumsey Collection

MAP 184 (*page 92*).
*Map of the Gold Regions of California*
James Wyld, 1849
Library of Congress G4361.H2 1849 .W9 TIL

MAP 185 (*page 93*).
[*Voyage of the Apollo, 1849*]
From: Joseph Perkins Beach, notebook
San Francisco Maritime National Historical Park SAFR 13575

MAP 186 (*page 94*).
*Map of the United States The British Provinces Mexico &c.*
J.H. Colton, 1849
David Rumsey Collection

MAP 187 (*page 95*).
*Map of the Mining District of California*
William A. Jackson, 1850
Library of Congress G4361.H2 1850 .J3 TIL

MAP 188 (*page 96*).
*Chart of the Sacramento River from Suisun City to the American River*
Cadwalader Ringgold, 1850
From: *A Series of Charts, with Sailing Directions*, 1852
David Rumsey Collection

MAP 189 (*page 97*).
*General Chart*
Cadwalader Ringgold, 1850
From: *A Series of Charts, with Sailing Directions*, 1852
David Rumsey Collection

MAP 190 (*page 97*).
*Mapa del Valle del Sacramento*
John Bidwell, 1851
Bancroft Land case 397

MAP 191 (*page 98*).
*Sacramento City, Ca. from the foot of J Street*
Charles Parsons, c. 1850
Library of Congress PGA-Parsons-Sacramento City, Ca (C size)

MAP 192 (*page 98*).
*View of Sacramento City As it Appeared During the Great Inundation in January 1850*
Napoleon Sarony, 1850
Library of Congress PGA-Sarony (N.) -- View of Sacramento City (D size)

MAP 193 (*page 99*).
*Plan von Suttersville*
John Augustus Sutter, 1847

MAP 194 (*page 99*).
*Map of Sacramento City & West Sacramento*
William Warner, 1850
Sutter's Fort State Historical Park

MAP 195 (*page 100*).
*Official Map of San Francisco*
William M. Eddy, 1849
Library of Congress G4364.S5 1849.E3 Vault

MAP 196 (*page 100*).
*Map of San Francisco*
Britton & Rey, 1852
David Rumsey Collection

MAP 197 (*page 101*).
*Bai San Francisco und Vereinigung de Sacramento mit dem San Joaquin*
Henry Lange, 1854
David Rumsey Collection

MAP 198 (*page 101*).
[*Four square leagues; the pueblo lands of San Francisco*]
Land case map, 1854
Bancroft Library Land case 427ND

MAP 199 (*page 102*).
*Mapa de los Estados Unidas de Méjico*
John Disturnell, 1847 (revised edition)
U.S. National Archives

MAP 200 (*page 103*).
*Vereinigte Staaten von Nord America und Mexico*
From: *Meyer's Zeitungs Atlas*, 1850
Steve Boulay Collection

MAP 201 (*page 104*).
*Map of the United States of America*
J.H. Young, 1850
Steve Boulay Collection

MAP 202 (*page 104*).
*Map of the State of California, the Territories of Oregon & Utah, and the chief Part of New Mexico*
Samuel Augustus Mitchell, 1850
David Rumsey Collection

MAP 203 (*page 105*).
*The Official Map of the State of California (Approved and Declared to be the Official Map of the State of California by an Act of the Legislature Passed March 25th 1853)*
William M. Eddy, 1854
David Rumsey Collection

MAP 204 (*page 106*).
*San Pedro and vicinity*
Inset in: *Sketch J No. 2 Showing the Progress of the Survey on the Western Coast of the United States Section X & XI From 1850 to 1855*
United States Coast Survey, 1855

MAP 205 (*page 107*).
[*San Francisco Bay area, part of*] *Sketch J No. 2 Showing the Progress of the Survey on the Western Coast of the United States Section X & XI From 1850 to 1855*
United States Coast Survey, 1855

MAP 206 (*page 108*).
(*J No. 4*) *San Diego Entrance and Approaches California*
United States Coast Survey, 1853

MAP 207 (*page 108*).
*Sketch J No. [blank] showing the progress of the Survey in the Bay of San Diego, California*
Inset in: *Sketch J No. 2 Showing the Progress of the Survey on the Western Coast of the United States Section X & XI From 1850 to 1855*
United States Coast Survey, 1855

MAP 208 (*page 109*).
(*J No. 2*) *Reconnaissance of the Western Coast of the United States Middle Sheet From San Francisco to Umpquah River*
United States Coast Survey, 1854

MAP 319 (*page 169*).
*New San Diego*
A.B. Gray and T.D. Johns, 1850, with
land ownership added to c. 1870
Huntington Library 431875a

MAP 320 (*page 170*).
*Bird's Eye View of San Diego, California 1876*
E.S. Glover, 1876
Library of Congress G4364.S4A3 1876 .G6

MAP 321 (*page 170*).
*Bird's Eye View of Coronado Beach, San
Diego Bay and City of San Diego, Cal, in
distance*
E.S. Moore, c. 1886
Library of Congress G4364.C77A3 188- .M6
MLC

MAP 322 (*page 171*).
*Map of Palmdale*
Palm Valley Land Company, 1888
Huntington Library 471218

MAP 323 (*page 172*).
*Sacramento*
W.W. Elliott & Company, 1890s
Library of Congress G4364.S2A3 189- .E5

MAP 324 (*page 172*).
*Fairoaks*
U.S.G.S. topographic map, 1901–02

MAP 325 (*page 172*).
*Map of the Carmichael Colony Located in
the San Juan Grant, Sacramento County,
California*
Charles Lawrence [?] and C.L. Knight, 1909
Steve's Pizza Place, Carmichael

MAP 326 (*page 173*).
*View of the City of Stockton, the
Manufacturing City of California*
Dakin Publishing Company, 1895
Library of Congress G4364S9A3 1895 .D3

MAP 327 (*page 173*).
*Plat of the City of Fresno and Additions*
[Inset in] *Official Map of Fresno County*
Schmidt Label & Litho Company, 1886
Huntington Library 273058

MAP 328 (*page 173*).
*Fresno, California*
L.W. Klein, Britton & Rey, 1901
Library of Congress G4364.F8A3 1901 .K5

MAP 329 (*page 174*).
*Bakersfield, Kern County, California, 1901*
N.J. Stone, 1901
Library of Congress G4364.B2A3 1901 .S7

MAP 330 (*page 174*).
*La California Le Sue Risorse ed
Opportunita*
*Relief Map of California*
California Development Board, 1910
San Francisco Public Library

MAP 331 (*page 174*).
*Map of Visalia, California*
From: *Tulare County Historical Atlas*, 1892

MAP 332 (*page 174*).
*Bird's Eye View of Santa Barbara,
California, 1877*
E.S. Glover, 1877
Library of Congress G4364S68A3 1877 G6

MAP 333 (*page 174*).
*Eureka, Humboldt County, California*
A.C. Noe & G.R. Georgeson, 1902
Library of Congress G4364.E9A3 1902 N6

MAP 334 (*page 175*).
*Official Township Map of Humboldt Co.
Cal.*
[With insets] *Map of Eureka* and *Map of
Arcata*
A.J. Doolittle, 1865
Warren Heckrotte Collection

MAP 335 (*page 176*).
*Bancroft's Map of the Cable Railway
Systems and Connections of San Francisco.
1890*
F.G. Burgess, 1890
Huntington Library 353215

MAP 336 (*page 177*).
*Interurban Rapid Transit System Bay District*
Rand McNally Company, 1923

MAP 337 (*page 178*).
*The Exposition City San Francisco*
North American Press Association, 1912

MAP 338 (*page 178*).
*Map of Twin Peaks Tunnel and Rapid
Transit Suburban Route*
A.R. Hunt, 1913
San Francisco Public Library

MAP 339 (*page 178*).
*Municipal Railway Lines of San Francisco,
Cal. 1920*
San Francisco City information booklet, 1922
San Francisco Public Library

MAP 340 (*page 178*).
*Key System Map of Lines*
From a timetable booklet, 1941

MAP 341 (*page 179*).
[Map of the Sacramento Northern Railway]
Sacramento Northern Railway, 1939

MAP 342 (*page 180*).
*Birds-eye View of Mount Lowe California*
Anon., 1913

MAP 343 (*page 180*).
*Map Showing Operated Lines of Pacific
Electric Railway*
From: *Journal of Electricity, Power, and Gas*,
January–June 1911
San Francisco Public Library

MAP 344 (*page 180*).
*Security Map and Street Railway Guide
of the City of Los Angeles and Vicinity with
Map of Beaches and Nearby Points of Interest*
Security Savings Bank, 1908
David Rumsey Collection

MAP 345 (*page 181*).
*Map of Los Angeles County, Electric, Steam
Railway Lines, and Mountain Guide and
also portion of Orange County*
T. Newman, 1912
Library of Congress G4363.L6P3 1912 .N4

MAP 346 (*page 181*).
*Relief Map of Territory Served by Lines
of Pacific Electric Railway in Southern
California*
Pacific Electric Railway Company, 1920
Huntington Library 127146

MAP 347 (*page 182*).
*The Greatest Conflagration in the History
of the World: The Burning of San Francisco,
April 18, 19, 20, 1906*
Carl A. Beck, 1906
Bancroft Library BANC PIC 1963.002:0582--E

MAP 348 (*page 182*).
*Great Fire in San Francisco*
W.B. Cooke Company, 1850

MAP 349 (*page 183*).
[Map showing course of fire]
From: Frank Aitken, *A History of the
Earthquake and Fire in San Francisco*, 1906

MAP 350 (*page 183*).
[Where fires started and situation at 3 A.M.
next day]
From: Frank Aitken, *A History of the
Earthquake and Fire in San Francisco*, 1906

MAP 351 (*page 183*).
[Fire extent, water systems, and earthquake-
related failures]
Richard L. Humphreys, 1907
From: *The San Francisco Earthquake and
Fire of April 18, 1906 and their effects on
structures and structural materials*, U.S.G.S.
Bulletin 324, 1907
San Francisco Public Library

MAP 352 (*page 184*).
[Fire extent and conduit breaks]
Richard L. Humphreys, 1907
From: *The San Francisco Earthquake
and Fire of April 18, 1906 and their effects
on structures and structural materials*,
U.S.G.S. Bulletin 324, 1907
San Francisco Public Library

MAP 353 (*page 184*).
*Map of Burned District* [showing water
lines broken and repaired as of 18 July 1906]
Chief Engineer, San Francisco Water Com-
pany, 1906
San Francisco Public Library

MAP 354 (*page 185*).
[San Francisco Burned District]
From: Frank Thompson Searight, *The
Doomed City*, 1906
David Burkhart Collection

MAP 355 (*page 186*).
*Map of San Francisco Showing Burned
District* [and relief camps]
Anon., 1906
California Historical Society FN 24212

MAP 356 (*page 186*).
*Distribution of Earth Movement on April
18, 1906 and in 1868*
U.S. Geological Survey, 1907

MAP 357 (*page 186*).
*Distribution of Apparent Shaking Intensity*
Andrew C. Lawson, 1908
From: Andrew C. Lawson et al., *Atlas of
Maps and Seismograms Accompanying
the Report of the State Earthquake
Investigation Commission upon the
California Earthquake of April 18, 1906*,
1908
San Francisco Public Library

MAP 358 (*page 187*).
*Map of Part of San Francisco California
April 18, 1908 Showing Buildings Constructed
and Buildings Under Construction During
Two Years after Fire of April 18, 1906*
California Promotion Committee, 1908
Los Angeles Public Library

MAP 359 (*page 187*).
*Map of San Francisco Showing Area Burned
in Fire of 1906, Closely Built-Up Frame
Section, Fire Limits, Fire-proof Roof Section
and Water Mains of Proposed Auxiliary
Fire Protection System*
San Francisco Board of Supervisors, 1908
From: *Letter of Marsden Manson, C.E.,
City Engineer, transmitting Reports on
an auxiliary water supply system for fire
protection for San Francisco*, 1908
San Francisco Public Library

MAP 360 (*page 188*).
*Map of the City and County of
San Francisco Showing Areas
Recommended as Necessary for Public
Places, Parks, Park Connections, and
Highways*
From: Daniel H. Burnham, *Report on
a Plan for San Francisco*, September 1905
San Francisco Public Library

MAP 361 (*page 188*).
*Bird's-eye perspective from the east
showing proposed changes*
From: Daniel H. Burnham, *Report on a Plan
for San Francisco*, September 1905
David Rumsey Collection

MAP 362 (*page 188*).
[Boulevards proposed in the Burnham Plan]
*New San Francisco Magazine*, 1906

MAP 363 (*page 188*).
*Plan of San Francisco, Showing System of
Circuit and radial Arteries, and its
Communication with San Mateo County*
From: Daniel H. Burnham, *Report on a Plan
for San Francisco*, September 1905
San Francisco Public Library

MAP 364 (*page 189*).
*The Exposition City San Francisco*
North American Press Association, 1912

MAP 365 (*page 189*).
*Attendance is what makes an Exposition
a financial success*
Panama-Pacific International Exposition
promotional ad, c. 1910

MAP 366 (*page 190*).
*Topographical Map of the Yosemite Valley
and Vicinity*
George M. Wheeler, 1883
From: *Topographical Atlas Projected to
Illustrate United States Geographical
Surveys West of the 100th Meridian of
Longitude*, 1883

MAP 367 (*page 191*).
[Proposed boundaries for Yosemite
National Park]
John Muir, 1890
Sierra Club

MAP 368 (*page 191*).
[Map of Mount Lyell Glacier, Yosemite
National Park]
U.S. Geological Survey, 1889

MAP 369 (page 192).
Yosemite National Park Showing
Boundaries Established by Act of Congress
Approved June 11 1906
Federal government report, 1909

MAP 370 (page 192).
Sketch of the Sequoia and General Grant
National Parks and the Sierra Forest
Reserve
M.F. Davis, U.S. Army, 1896

MAP 371 (page 192).
[General Grant National Park]
U.S.G.S. topographic map, 1927

MAP 372 (page 193).
Yosemite
Jo Mora, 1931
Carte reproduction provided by and used
with permission of the Jo Mora Trust

MAP 373 (page 194).
[Owens Lake and Owens Valley]
From: Topographical Map of Central
California Together with a Part of Nevada
California Geological Survey, 1873
David Rumsey Collection

MAP 374 (page 195).
Topographic Map of the Los Angeles
Aqueduct and Adjacent Territory
City of Los Angeles Board of Water and
Power Commissioners, 1908
Library of Congress G4361.N44 1908 .C5

MAP 375 (page 195).
Southern part of the State of California
Showing Inset of Photograph of Los Angeles
Aqueduct Relief Map
From: Department of Public Service, City of
Los Angeles, Complete Report on Construction
of the Los Angeles Aqueduct, 1916

MAP 376 (page 196).
[Relief map of the Los Angeles Aqueduct]
William Mulholland and employees of
L.A.D.W.P., 1915
Exhibit at Los Angeles Department of Water
and Power, 2006

MAP 377 (page 196).
Los Angeles Aqueduct Fernando Reservoirs
From: Department of Public Service,
City of Los Angeles, Complete Report on
Construction of the Los Angeles Aqueduct,
1916

MAP 378 (page 196).
[Map showing location of Los Angeles Dam]
U.S. Geological Survey, 2006

MAP 379 (page 196).
Topographic Map of the Los Angeles
Aqueduct and Adjacent Territory
City of Los Angeles Board of Water and
Power Commissioners, 1908
Library of Congress G4361.N44 1908 .C5

MAP 380 (page 197).
St. Francis Reservoir and Adjacent
Developments
From: Report of the Commission on the
Causes Leading to the Failure of the
St. Francis Dam, 1928
San Francisco Public Library

MAP 381 (page 197).
Plan of Dam
From: Report of the Commission on the
Causes Leading to the Failure of the
St. Francis Dam, 1928
San Francisco Public Library

MAP 382 (page 198).
[Distribution system of] Spring Valley
Water Co. San Francisco - California
Spring Valley Water Company, 1922.

MAP 383 (page 198).
[Map showing proposed Hetch Hetchy
Aqueduct]
Anon., 1915

MAP 384 (page 199).
[Bird's-eye map of the Hetch Hetchy
Aqueduct]
From: San Francisco and its Great Water
Project, 1930
San Francisco Public Library

MAP 385 (page 199).
Map Showing Location of Hetch Hetchy
Valley and Yosemite Valley (Scenic Park)
and Lake Eleanor in the Yosemite National
Park, 1910

MAP 386 (page 199).
Map showing location of the Proposed
Municipal Water District to be served from
the Hetch Hetchy Reservoir Site, 1910
San Francisco Public Library

MAP 387 (pages 200–201).
The Metropolitan Water District of Southern
California Colorado River Aqueduct
From: Annual Report of the Metropolitan
Water District of Southern California, 1939

MAP 388 (page 200).
Alternative Preliminary Main Aqueduct
Routes
From: Annual Report of the Metropolitan
Water District of Southern California, 1939

MAP 389 (page 201).
[Plan of the Parker Dam, Colorado River]
From: Annual Report of the Metropolitan
Water District of Southern California, 1939

MAP 390 (page 202).
[Relief model/map for planning the
route of the Colorado Aqueduct]
From: Annual Report of the Metropolitan
Water District of Southern California, 1939

MAP 391 (page 202).
[Water distribution system,
Los Angeles region]
From: Annual Report of the Metropolitan
Water District of Southern California, 1953

MAP 392 (page 203).
[Southern part of the San Diego Aqueduct]
From: Annual Report of the Metropolitan
Water District of Southern California, 1953

MAP 393 (page 203).
[San Diego Aqueduct]
San Diego County Water Authority
From: Annual Report of the Metropolitan
Water District of Southern California, 1953

MAP 394 (page 204).
[Map of bike paths around Los Angeles]
From: George W. Blum, The Cyclers' Guide
and Road Book of California, 1896
David Rumsey Collection

MAP 395 (page 204).
[Map of bike paths around San Francisco
Bay]
From: George W. Blum, The Cyclers' Guide
and Road Book of California, 1896
David Rumsey Collection

MAP 396 (page 205).
Map of California Roads for Cyclers
George W. Blum, 1895
Library of Congress G4361.P2 1895 .B5 TIL

MAP 397 (pages 206–7).
[Map of Los Angeles and the San Gabriel
Mountains]
Automobile Club of Southern California,
1915
Library of Congress G4364.L8 1915 .A8

MAP 398 (page 206).
Automobile Road Map From San Diego to
Campo Part One San Diego to Descanso
Automobile Club of Southern California,
1917

MAP 399 (page 206).
Automobile Routes from Los Angeles to
Sunland, La Crescenta, and La Cañada
Automobile Club of Southern California,
1912
Library of Congress G4360 1912 .A8

MAP 400 (page 207).
Western Motor Car Route Guide
Anon., 1915
Library of Congress G4231.P2 1915 W4 TIL

MAP 401 (page 208).
California [showing automobile roads]
L.L. Poates Eng. Co., 1919

MAP 402 (page 209).
Rand McNally Road Map California
Nevada
Rand McNally and Company, 1926
David Rumsey Collection

MAP 403 (page 210).
United States Touring Map / Good Roads
Everywhere
Automobile Club of America and the Na-
tional Highways Association, 1925

MAP 404 (page 211).
Master Plan of Metropolitan Los Angeles
Freeways
Regional Planning Commission, 1947

MAP 405 (page 211).
National System of Interstate Highways
From: General Location of National System
of Interstate Highways,
Bureau of Roads, U.S. Department of Com-
merce, Washington D.C., 1955

MAP 406 (page 211).
[San Francisco Bay Area]
From: General Location of National System
of Interstate Highways,
Bureau of Roads, U.S. Department of Com-
merce, Washington D.C., 1955

MAP 407 (page 211).
[Los Angeles Area]
From: General Location of National System
of Interstate Highways,
Bureau of Roads, U.S. Department of
Commerce, Washington D.C., 1955

MAP 408 (page 212).
[Map of the Los Angeles Basin]
Edward Otho Cresap Ord, 1849

MAP 409 (page 212).
Street and Section Map of the Los Angeles
Oil Fields, California
A. Hoen & Co., 1906
Library of Congress G4364.L8H8 1906 .H6

MAP 410 (page 213).
Map of California Kern County Oil Fields
New Amsterdam Oil Company, c. 1901
Colin Wood / Huntington Library

MAP 411 (page 214).
Oil Fields of California
Barlow & Hill, 1910
San Francisco Public Library

MAP 412 (page 214).
Map of the Kern River Oil Field
Barlow & Hill, 1910
San Francisco Public Library

MAP 413 (page 215).
Transmission Systems California — Nevada
From: Journal of Electricity, Power, and Gas,
January–June 1911
San Francisco Public Library

MAP 414 (page 215).
Electric Power Production and
Transmission Systems in California, 1927
From: Report on the Kennett Reservoir
Development, 1929
San Francisco Public Library

MAP 415 (page 215).
[Plan of the proposed Boulder (Hoover)
Dam]
From: Compressed Air Magazine, 1931

MAP 416 (page 216).
First in America Aviation Meet
Poster, 1910

MAP 417 (page 216).
Plat of the Rancho Buri-Buri
Land case map, 1864
Bancroft Library Land case 101ND

MAP 418, MAP 419, and MAP 420 (page 216).
[U.S.G.S. topographic maps of eastern San
Mateo County], 1892–99; 1939–42; 1968–78

MAP 421 (page 217).
Temporary Municipal Airport Site
Contract No. 1 Grading (Filling of Depres-
sions)
San Francisco Department of Public Works,
1927
San Francisco Airport Museums
1999.046.039

MAP 422 (page 218).
San Francisco Airport and Treasure Island
Airport Vicinity Map
San Francisco Public Utilities Commission,
Airport Department, 1934
San Francisco Airport Museums
1999.046.012

MAP 423 (*page 218*).
*Oakland Municipal Airport* [with planned expansion]
Postcard, c. 1946[?]

MAP 424 (*page 219*).
[U.S.G.S. topographic map of the site of Los Angeles International Airport], 1947–50

MAP 425 (*page 219*).
[Proposal for San Diego Municipal Airport at Lindbergh Field], 1927–28

MAP 426 (*page 219*).
[Air California route map]
From: Air California timetable, 1979
Chris Cummings Collection
Reproduced with permission from American Airlines

MAP 427 (*page 220*).
*California Pacific International Exposition*
Poster, 1935
Los Angeles Public Library

MAP 428 (*page 220*).
*The California Pacific International Exposition San Diego*
Poster, 1935
Los Angeles Public Library

MAP 429 (*page 221*).
*Special Soundings Taken by USS Hull with Sonic Depth Finder Type 1378*
U.S. Navy, 1922
U.S. National Archives, RG 37, Archives section, 1908–1924, 251959-6

MAP 430 (*page 221*).
*Radio Broadcasting Stations in the United States*
Clason Map Company, 1930
David Rumsey Collection

MAP 431 (*page 221*).
[California]
*PWA Builds the Nation*
Public Works Administration, 1935
David Rumsey Collection

MAP 432 (*page 221*).
*California*
Tourist map, All-Year Club and Californians, Inc., 1936

MAP 433 (*page 222*).
*Ragsdale's Movie Guide Map*
Albert Ragsdale, 1938
Library of Congress G4364.B6 1938 .R3

MAP 434 (*page 223*).
[Bird's-eye map of the San Francisco Bay Area]
Anon., postcard, 1930s

MAP 435 (*page 223*).
[Golden Gate] *The Redwood Empire*
Tourist map, 1938

MAP 436 (*page 223*).
[West Coast Greyhound Bus routes]
Greyhound Bus Co., c. 1940

MAP 437 (*page 223*).
[Golden Gate Interntional Exposition site and Bay Bridge], 1936
Los Angeles Public Library

MAP 438 (*page 224*).
*Redwood Empire*
Tourist map, 1938

MAP 439 (*page 224*).
[Pictorial map of the San Francisco Bay Area]
Published for Bank of America, 1939

MAP 440 (*page 225*).
*A cartograph of Treasure Island in San Francisco Bay Golden Gate International Exposition*
Huntington Library 319284

MAP 441 (*page 225*).
[Bird's-eye map of the San Francisco Bay Area]
Poster, Pacific Gas & Electric, 1943

MAP 442 (*page 226*).
["Battle of Los Angeles"]
*Galveston Daily News*, 26 February 1942

MAP 443 (*page 226*).
*Battery Imperial* [Fort Emory]
U.S. Engineer's Office, December 1942
U.S. National Archives RG 77, OCE, Box 129, File 600.914

MAP 444 (*page 227*).
[Harbor defenses on Point Loma, San Diego]
U.S. Engineer's Office, 1945
U.S. National Archives RG 407, Box 118, Supplement to harbor defense project

MAP 445 (*page 227*).
*Battery Ashburn* [Fort Rosecrans]
U.S. Engineer's Office, 1941
U.S. National Archives RG 77, OCE, Box 129, File 600.914

MAP 446 (*page 228*).
*Camp Layout, Mazanar War Relocation Project*
War Relocation Authority, 1945
Japanese American National Museum NRC.1999.43.7

MAP 447 (*page 229*).
*Japanese Evacuation Program Relocation Center Destinations*
Western Defense Command and Fourth Army Wartime Civil Control Administration, 1942
From: *Final Report: Japanese Evacuation from the West Coast*, 1942
Japanese American National Museum 2001.72.4_map3

MAP 448 (*page 230*).
[Alien exclusion zones, West Coast]
U.S. Army, 1942

MAP 449 (*page 230*).
[Mare Island and Vallejo]
U.S.G.S. topographic map (composite), 1937–42

MAP 450 (*page 231*).
*Regional Aeronautical Chart*
[of Southern California]
U.S. Coast and Geodetic Survey, 1943

MAP 451 (*page 232*).
[Pictorial map of] *Silicon Valley*
c. 1990s
Los Angeles Public Library

MAP 452 (*page 233*).
*Official Map of the County of Napa, California*
O.H. Buckman, 1895
Library of Congress G4363.N3 1895 .B8

MAP 453 and MAP 454 (*page 233*).
[Lake Berryessa, site and lake]
U.S.G.S. topographic maps, 1943–45; 1957–60

MAP 455, MAP 456, and MAP 457 (*page 234*).
[Foster City]
U.S.G.S. topographic maps, 1892–99; 1939–42; 1973

MAP 458 (*page 234*).
*Productive Intensity for the Loma Prieta Earthquake*, 1989
U.S. Geological Survey, c. 2006

MAP 459 (*page 235*).
*Earthquake Shaking Potential for California*
California Geological Survey, 2003
Used with permission, California Department of Conservation, California Geological Survey

MAP 460 (*page 236*).
*State of California Earthquake Fault Zones Point Loma Quadrangle*
California Geological Survey, 2003
Used with permission, California Department of Conservation, California Geological Survey

MAP 461 (*page 236*).
[Matthew Davis wearing a tie with San Andreas Fault], 2006

MAP 462 (*page 236*).
*Index Map of Recent Earthquakes in California–Nevada*
U.S. Geological Survey, 29 November 2006

MAP 463 (*page 236*).
[Radar satellite map of the Simi Valley]
NASA, 2000

MAP 464 (*page 236*).
[Multibeam sonar map of the sea bed in San Pedro Bay]
U.S. Geological Survey, c. 2000

MAP 465 (*page 237*).
[LandSat view of California]
NASA, 1992

MAP 466 (*page 237*).
[LandSat view of California, detail of San Joaquin–Sacramento deltas]
NASA, 1992

MAP 467 (*page 237*).
[Computer-generated oblique view of Los Angeles]
NASA, 2006

MAP 468 (*page 238*).
*Planet San Francisco*
Mike Farruggia, 2001–03
San Francisco Public Library

MAP 469 (*page 238*).
*Monterey Bay National Marine Sanctuary Bathymetric Map MS-2*
National Oceanic and Atmospheric Administration, National Ocean Service, U.S. Coast and Geodetic Survey, 1992

MAP 470 (*page 238*).
Computer-derived three-dimensional view from data used in compilation of MAP 469

MAP 471 (*page 238*).
*Morphology and Shipping Lanes of West-Central San Francisco Bay*
U.S. Geological Survey, c. 2000

MAP 472 (*page 238*).
[Multibeam sonar view of Golden Gate]
Postcard, U.S. Geological Survey, 2006

MAP 473 (*page 239*).
*California Driving South*
*The Upside Down Map*
Magellan Geographix and Map Link, 1997

MAP 474 (*page 249*).
*California*
Jo Mora, 1927
Carte reproduction provided by and used with permission of the Jo Mora Trust

MAP 475 (*page 249*).
*Map of the Territory of the United States from the Mississippi to the Pacific Ocean*
Gouverneur Kemble Warren, 1858
Library of Congress G4050 1857 .W32 Vault

MAP 476 (*page 254*).
*Map of California and the Adjacent Country*
F.A. Goodwin, 1855
David Rumsey Collection

## Additional image credits (by page number)

San Francisco Public Library: 187, 190, 212, 217
California State Railroad Museum: 116, 118
Library of Congress: 8
San Francisco Maritime National Historic Park: 93 (2), 178 (bottom)
Los Angeles Department of Water and Power: 194, 197
Metropolitan Water District of Southern California: 203
Huntington Library: 224
National Park Service, Cabrillo National Monument: 226
U.S. National Archives: 228, 230
U.S. Bureau of Reclamation: 139
Paul C. Trimble Collection: 179 (top)

All other images are from private collections. Additional photographs are by the author.

MAP 474 (*right*).
The first of artist Jo Mora's well-known whimsical pictorial maps illustrating the history of California was this one, published in 1927. Mora produced a number of such maps, each updated. The 1945 edition is shown as MAP 1, on the first page of this book, and it is interesting to compare the two.

California

This whimsical Carte of Topographic and Historic intention, depicting that fabled Isle of Montalvo's dream — the El Dorado of '49 — the glorious California we know and love — is hereby presented by the Limner for what it may be worth — possibly more in smiles than cosmographic value. Yet, as the World is with you when you smile, it may be worth the perusal.

A devoted adopted son made it.

Jo Mora

# BIBLIOGRAPHY

**American Bridge Company.** *The San Francisco–Oakland Bay Bridge.* [Pittsburgh, Ohio]: United States Steel Corporation, 1936.

**Beck, Warren A., and Ynez D. Haase.** *Historical Atlas of California.* Norman: University of Oklahoma Press, 1974.

**Becker, Robert H.** *Diseños of California: Maps of Thirty-Seven Land Grants, 1822–1846, from the Records of the United States District Court, San Francisco.* San Francisco: Book Club of California, 1964.

———. *Designs on the Land: Diseños of California Ranchos and their Makers.* San Francisco: Book Club of California, 1969.

**Bolton, Herbert Eugene.** *Font's Complete Diary: A Chronicle of the Founding of San Francisco.* Berkeley: University of California Press, 1931.

**Brands, H.W.** *The Age of Gold: The California Gold Rush and the New American Dream.* New York: Doubleday, 2002.

**Brechin, Gray A.** *Imperial San Francisco: Urban Power, Earthly Ruin.* Berkeley: University of California Press, 1999.

**Burkhart, David.** *Earthquake Days: The 1906 San Francisco Earthquake & Fire in 3-D.* San Bruno: Faultline Books, 2005.

**Burns, Helen.** *Salton Sea Story.* Palm Desert: Desert Magazine Press, [1958].

**Carle, David.** *Introduction to Water in California.* Berkeley: University of California Press, 2004.

**Caughey, John, with Norris Hundley Jr.** *California: History of a Remarkable State.* Englewood Cliffs, NJ: Prentice Hall, 1982.

**Commission on Wartime Relocation and Internment of Citizens.** *Personal Justice Denied: Report of the Commission on Wartime Relocation and Internment of Citizens.* Seattle: University of Washington Press/Washington: Civil Liberties Public Education Fund, 1997 (original report 1982 and 1983.)

**Cook, Warren.** *Flood Tide of Empire: Spain and the Pacific Northwest, 1543–1819.* New Haven: Yale University Press, 1973.

**Delgado, James P.** *To California by Sea: A Maritime History of the California Gold Rush.* Columbia, SC: University of South Carolina Press, 1990.

**Department of Public Service, City of Los Angeles.** *Complete Report on Construction of the Los Angeles Aqueduct.* Los Angeles, 1916

***Dogtown Territorial Quarterly.*** Special Sutter's Fort Issue, No. 19, Paradise, California, Fall 1994.

**Eldredge, Zoeth S.** *The March of Portolá and the Discovery of the Bay of San Francisco.* With Molera, E.J. (trans.). *The Log of the San Carlos.* San Francisco: The California Promotion Committee, 1909.

**Emory, William Hemsley (U.S. Army Corps of Topographical Engineers).** *Notes of a Military Reconnoissance from Fort Leavenworth, in Missouri, to San Diego, in California.* Washington: Wendell and Van Benthuysen, 1848.

**Fagan, Brian.** *Before California: An Archaeologist Looks at Our Earliest Inhabitants.* Walnut Creek: AltaMira Press, 2003.

**Fey, Marshall, R. Joe King, and Jack Lepisto.** *Emigrant Shadows: A History and Guide to the California Trail.* Virginia City, Nevada: Western Trails Research Association, 2002.

**Fradkin, Philip L.** *The Great Earthquake and Firestorms of 1906: How San Francisco Nearly Destroyed Itself.* Berkeley: University of California Press, 2006.

**Galvin, John (ed.).** *The First Spanish Entry into San Francisco Bay 1775: The Original Narrative.* San Francisco: John Howell Books, 1971.

**Goetzmann, William H.** *Army Exploration in the American West, 1803–1863.* New Haven, CT: Yale University Press,1965.

**Gumprecht, Blake.** *The Los Angeles River: Its Life, Death, and Possible Rebirth.* Baltimore: Johns Hopkins University Press, 1999.

**Gutiérrez, Ramón A., and Richard J. Orsi (eds.).** *Contested Eden: California Before the Gold Rush.* Berkeley: University of California Press, 1998.

**Harding, S.T.** *Water in California.* Palo Alto: N-P Publications, 1960.

**Harlow, Neil.** *Maps and Surveys of the Pueblo Lands of Los Angeles.* Los Angeles: Dawson's Book Shop, 1976.

———. *Maps of the Pueblo Lands of San Diego.* Los Angeles: Dawson's Book Shop, 1987.

**Hayes, Derek.** *Historical Atlas of the Pacific Northwest.* Seattle: Sasquatch Books, 1999.

———. *America Discovered: A Historical Atlas of North American Exploration.* Vancouver: Douglas & McIntyre, 2004.

———. *Historical Atlas of the United States.* Berkeley: University of California Press, 2006.

**Hill, John H., with Dan Seaver and Jane Sullivan.** *SFO: A Pictorial History of the Airport.* San Francisco: San Francisco Airport Commission, 2000.

**Hornbeck, David.** *California Patterns: A Geographical and Historical Atlas.* Palo Alta: Mayfield Publishing, 1983.

**Howard, Thomas Frederick.** *Sierra Crossing: First Roads to California.* Berkeley: University of California Press, 1998.

**Jones, Holway R.** *John Muir and the Sierra Club: The Battle for Yosemite.* San Francisco: Sierra Club, 1965.

**Kalani, Lyn, Lynn Rudy, and John Sperry (eds.).** *Fort Ross.* Fort Ross Interpretive Association, n.d. [c. 2006].

**Karhl, William L. (ed.).** *The California Water Atlas.* Sacramento: Governor's Office of Planning and Research, 1979.

———. *Water and Power.* Berkeley: University of California Press, 1982.

**Lippincott, Joseph Barlow.** *California Hydrography.* United States Geological Survey Water Supply and Irrigation Paper No. 81. Washington: Government Printing Office, 1903.

**MacPhail, Elizabeth C.** *The Story of New San Diego and of its Founder Alonzo E. Horton.* San Diego: San Diego Historical Society, 1979.

**Mathes, W. Michael.** *Vizcaíno and Spanish Expansion in the Pacific Ocean 1580–1630.* San Francisco: California Historical Society, 1968.

———. *Conquistador in California.* Los Angeles: Dawson's Book Shop, 1973.

**McLaughlin, Glen, with Nancy Mayo.** *The Mapping of California as an Island: An Illustrated Checklist.* [Saratoga]: California Map Society, 1995.

**Metropolitan Water District of Southern California.** *Fifteenth Annual Report, 1953/Report for the Fiscal Year July 1, 1952 to June 30, 1953.* Los Angeles: Metropolitan Water District of Southern California, 1953.

**Mulholland, Catherine.** *William Mulholland and the Rise of Los Angeles.* Berkeley: University of California Press, 2000.

**Myers, Paul A.** *North to California: The Spanish Voyages of Discovery 1533–1603.* Coral Springs, Florida: Llumina Press, 2004.

**Ng, Wendy.** *Japanese American Internment During World War II: A History and Reference Guide.* Westport, CT: Greenwood Press, 2002.

**Olmsted, Nancy.** *Vanished Waters: A History of San Francisco's Mission Bay.* San Francisco: Mission Creek Conservancy, 1986.

**Orsi, Richard J.** *Sunset Limited: The Southern Pacific Railroad and the Development of the American West 1850–1930.* Berkeley: University of California Press, 2005.

**Paddison, Joshua (ed.).** *A World Transformed: Firsthand Accounts of California Before the Gold Rush.* Berkeley: Heyday Books, 1999.

**Paul, Rodman W.** *The California Gold Discovery: Sources, Documents, Accounts and Memoirs Relating to the Discovery of Gold at Sutter's Mill.* Georgetown, CA: Talisman Press, 1967.

Pierce, R.A. (ed. and trans.). *Atlas of the Northwest Coasts of America.* Compiled by M.D. Teben'kov, 1852. Kingston, ON: The Limestone Press, 1981.

Pierce, R.A., and Hohn H Winslow (eds.). *H.M.S. Sulphur on the Northwest and California Coasts, 1837 and 1839: The Accounts of Captain Edward Belcher and Midshipman Francis Guillemard Simpkinson.* Kingston, ON: The Limestone Press, 1979.

Polk, Dora Beale. *The Island of California: A History of the Myth.* Lincoln: University of Nebraska Press,1991.

Poole, Jean Bruce, and Tevvy Ball. *El Pueblo: The Historic Heart of Los Angeles.* Los Angeles: Getty Publications, 2002.

Rawls, James J., and Walton Bean. *California: An Interpretive History.* New York: McGraw-Hill, 1993.

Righter, Robert W. *The Battle Over Hetch Hetchy: America's Most Controversial Dam and the Birth of Modern Environmentalism.* New York: Oxford University Press, 2005.

Rolle, Andrew. *California: A History.* Wheeling, IL: Harlan Davidson, 1998.

Sackman, Douglas Cazaux. *Orange Empire: California and the Fruits of Eden.* Berkeley: University of California Press, 2005.

Southern California Earthquake Center. *Putting Down Roots in Earthquake Country.* [Los Angeles]: Southern California Earthquake Center, 2006.

Starr, Kevin. *Embattled Dreams: California in War and Peace, 1940–1950.* New York: Oxford University Press, 2002.

———. *California: A History.* New York: Random House, 2005.

Thiel, Charles C., Jr. (ed.). *Competing Against Time: Report to Governor George Deukmejian from the Governor's Board of Inquiry on the 1989 Loma Prieta Earthquake.* [Sacramento]: State of California, Office of Planning and Research, 1990.

Thompson, Erwin N. *The Guns of San Diego: San Diego Harbor Defenses 1796–1947.* San Diego: National Park Service, 1991. Online: http://www.cr.nps.gov/history/online_books/cabr/hrs7.htm

Tooley, R.V. *California as an Island.* London: *The Map Collectors' Circle,* [1964].

Treutlein, Theodore E. *San Francisco Bay: Discovery and Colonization, 1769–1776.* San Francisco: California Historical Society, 1968.

Trimble, Paul C. *Sacramento Northern Railway.* Charleston, SC: Arcadia Publishing, 2005.

Wagner, Henry Raup. *Spanish Voyages to the Northwest Coast of America in the Sixteenth Century.* San Francisco: California Historical Society, 1929.

———. *Cartography of the Northwest Coast of America to the Year 1800.* Mansfield Center, CT: Martino Publishing, 1965 (original publication 1937).

Walker, Dale L. *Bear Flag Rising: The Conquest of California, 1846.* New York: Tom Doherty Assoc., 1999.

———. *Eldorado: The California Gold Rush.* New York: Tom Doherty Assoc., 2003.

Ware, Joseph E. *The Emigrants' Guide to California.* With Introduction and notes by John Caughey. Princeton: Princeton University Press, 1932.

Watkins, T.H. *California: An Illustrated History.* New York: American Legacy Press, 1983.

White, Stewart Edward. *Old California In Picture and Story.* New York: Doubleday, Doran & Company, 1937.

Wyatt, David. *Five Fires: Race, Catastrophe, and the Shaping of California.* Reading, MA: Addison-Wesley, 1997.

MAP 475.
This is one version of Gouverneur K. Warren's great map of the West, produced in 1857–58 as a synthesis of all geographic knowledge at that time, and in particular incorporating all the information from the Pacific Railroad Surveys, which began in 1853 (see page 110). Warren was one of the most skilled of the Army's Topographical Engineers. The boundary shown in red is the military *Department of California* boundary, not that of the state of California.

# Index

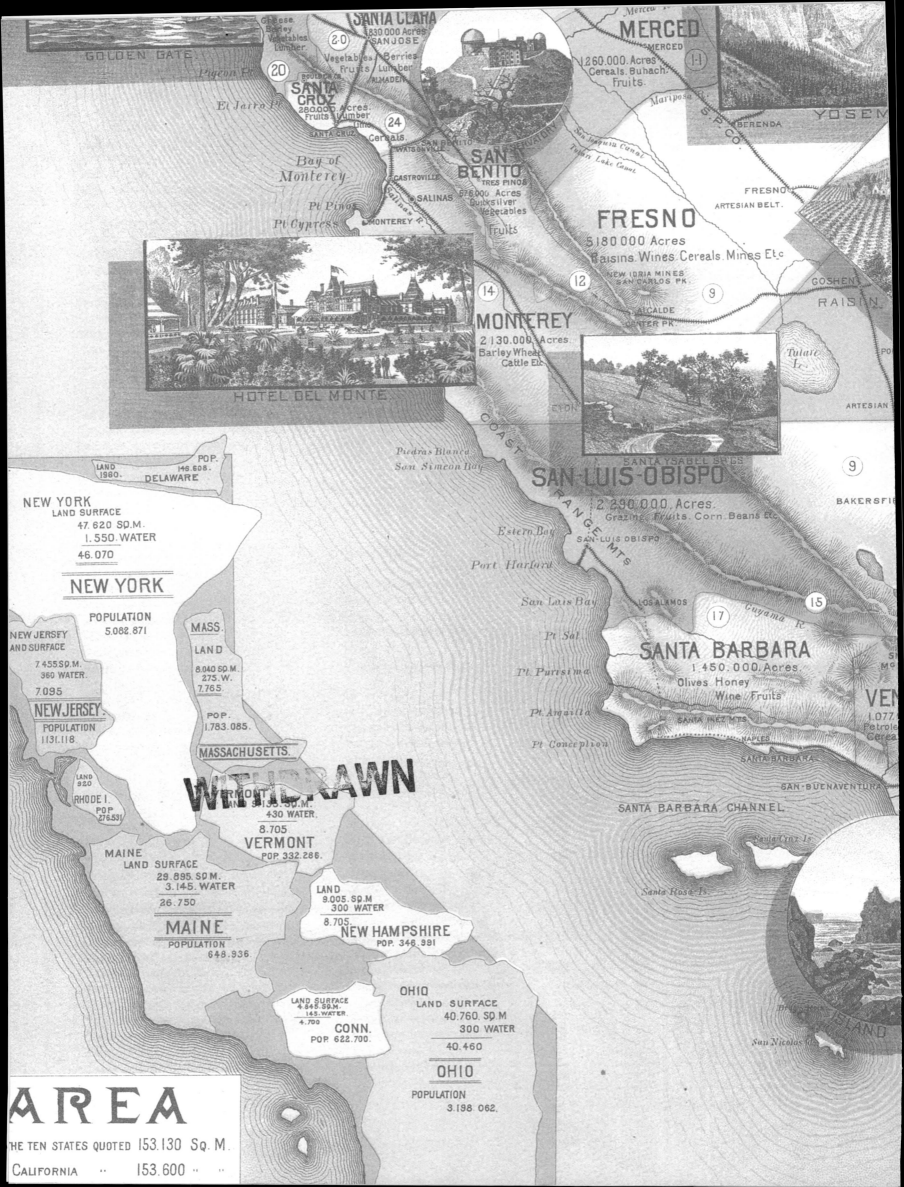